LANGUAGE LEARNING STRATEGIES AROUND THE WORLD: CROSS-CULTURAL PERSPECTIVES

TECHNICAL REPORT #13

LANGUAGE
LEARNING
STRATEGIES
AROUND
THE WORLD:
CROSS-CULTURAL
PERSPECTIVES

edited by REBECCA OXFORD

 SECOND LANGUAGE TEACHING & CURRICULUM CENTER
University of Hawai'i at Mānoa

Funds for the publication of this technical report were provided in part by a grant to the University of Hawai'i under the Language Resource Centers Program of the US Department of Education.

ISBN 0–8248–1910–1

∞™ The paper used in this publication meets the minimum requirements of the American National Standard for Information Sciences–Permanence of Paper for Printed Library Materials.

ANSI Z39.48–1984

Book design by Deborah Masterson

Distributed by
University of Hawai'i Press
Order Department
2840 Kolowalu Street
Honolulu, HI 96822

ABOUT THE NATIONAL FOREIGN LANGUAGE
RESOURCE CENTER

THE SECOND LANGUAGE TEACHING AND CURRICULUM CENTER of the University of Hawaiʻi is a unit of the College of Languages, Linguistics, and Literature. Under a grant from the US Department of Education, the Center has since 1990 served as a National Foreign Language Resource Center (NFLRC). The general direction of the Resource Center is set by a national advisory board. The Center conducts research, develops materials, and trains language professionals with the goal of improving foreign language instruction in the United States. The Center publishes research reports and teaching materials; it also sponsors a summer intensive teacher training institute. For additional information about Center programs, write:

Dr. Richard Schmidt, Director
National Foreign Language Resource Center
East-West Road, Bldg. 1, Rm. 6A
University of Hawaiʻi
Honolulu, HI 96822

or visit our Web site: http://www.lll.hawaii.edu/nflrc

NFLRC ADVISORY BOARD

Kathleen Bardovi-Harlig
Center for English Language Teaching
Indiana University

John Clark
Defense Language Institute
Monterey, California

James Pusack
Project for International Communication Studies (PICS)
University of Iowa

Ronald Walton
National Foreign Language Center
Washington, DC

Representatives of other funded NFLRCs

CONTENTS

Rebecca L. Oxford
University of Alabama, USA

PREFACE

WHY IS CULTURE IMPORTANT FOR LANGUAGE LEARNING STRATEGIES?

Culture is the social cement of all human relationships.
–Tom Scovel, 1991

This book, which focuses on cross-cultural use of language learning strategies, is useful to foreign language teachers around the world who have students from just one culture. It is also helpful for second language teachers who have more than one culture represented in their classes. Language researchers and language program administrators would also benefit from a greater and more practical understanding of cross-cultural similarities and differences in learning strategy assessment and instruction. Finally, advanced language learners are likely to gain from a greater comprehension of the cultural dynamics of strategy use.

Culture and its influence on language learning strategies are the keystones of this preface and indeed of this whole book. This preface defines culture and cross-culturalism, defines learning strategies and explains cultural influences on those strategies, and displays the organization and special features of this book.

CULTURE AND CROSS-CULTURALISM

Culture (relating to patterns of living) refers to the individual's role in the unending kaleidoscope of life situations of every kind and the rules or models for attitudes and conduct in them. By reference to these models, all human beings, from infancy onward, justify the world to themselves as best they can, associate with those around them, and relate to the social order to which they are attached... What is important in culture... is what one is expected to think, believe, say, do, eat, wear, pay, ensure, resent, honor, laugh at, fight for, and worship, in typical life situations... (Brooks, 1968, pp. 218–221)

The famous metaphor of the "cultural iceberg" (Hall & Hall, 1990; Oxford, 1995) indicates that many aspects of culture, such as certain beliefs, perceptions, and values, are below the surface of consciousness (in the submerged part of the iceberg). Other aspects of culture, like clothing and TV-watching habits, are in the conscious area (above the waterline). The less conscious cultural aspects often influence how people learn languages. Research by Yang (1992b) suggests that culture clearly includes beliefs, perceptions, and values which affect language learning, including *general learning styles* (visual, auditory, hands-on; intuitive, sensing; global, analytic; see Reid, 1995) and *specific learning strategies* (the particular behaviors and steps learners use to improve their learning such as note-taking, finding conversation partners, and analyzing words). Oxford, Hollaway, and Horton-Murillo (1992, p. 441) emphasize, "Although culture is not the single determinant, and although many other influences intervene, culture often does play a significant role in the learning styles [and strategies]... adopted by many participants in the culture."

The importance of culture is reflected in the concept of "situated cognition," which holds that the setting and the activity in which knowledge is developed are not separable from learning, nor are they neutral; they are an integral part of the learning (Brown, Collins, & Duguid, 1989; Geertz, 1983; Lave, 1988; Lave & Wenger, 1991; Rogoff & Lave, 1984; Suchman, 1987). Thus, in the foreign or second language classroom, the activities and cultural influences cannot be separated from what is learned. Language learning is fully situated within a given cultural context. The student becomes enculturated (apprenticed into a particular learning culture that in many ways reflects the general culture) through classroom activities and through the modeling and coaching of the teacher and many others (Lave, 1988; Rogoff & Lave, 1984). Rather than just the teacher/learner dyad, there exists "a richly diverse field of essential actors and, with it, other forms of relationships of participation" (Lave & Wenger, 1991, p. 56). In this view, learning is never a mere process of transmission or transfer but is instead nothing less than a process of transformation.

Cross-Culturalism (Banks & Banks, 1993; Batchelder & Warner, 1977; Gaston, 1984; Luce & Smith, 1987; Oxford, 1995; Putsch, 1986; Seelye, 1987; Weeks, Pedersen, & Brislin, 1977) deals with a dynamic system of understandings across cultures or subcultures. Comprehending cross-cultural similarities and differences involves carefully considering crucial aspects of culture, such as concepts of time, personal space, body language, worship, relationships, hatred, prejudice, love, and respect — and, as shown in this book, language learning strategies within a particular culture and across cultures.

LANGUAGE LEARNING STRATEGIES IN THE CULTURAL CONTEXT

Strategies are the tools for active, self-directed involvement that is necessary for developing communicative ability (Wenden & Rubin, 1987; O'Malley & Chamot, 1990). Strategies are not a single event, but rather a creative sequence of events that learners actively use. Hundreds of foreign and second learning strategies exist. For example, Bob seeks out conversation partners. Zoltan groups words to be learned and then labels each group. Marlen gives herself encouragement through positive self-talk before getting up to give a speech in the target language. Louelle uses gestures to communicate in the classroom when the words do not come to mind. Mariam learns words by breaking them down into their components. Sayed draws "semantic maps" with lines and arrows pictorially showing the linkages between new words according to their meaning. Deena finds an American pen pal. Darlene consciously uses guessing while reading as many books as she can in the second language. L2 learning strategies like these are very important, because research has repeatedly shown that the conscious, "tailored" use of these strategies is related to language achievement and proficiency.

Learning strategy investigations within and outside the language field have shown that effective learners actively associate new information with existing information in long-term memory, building increasingly intricate and differentiated mental structures, or *schemata*. The use of well-chosen strategies distinguishes experts from novices in many learning areas. Successful learners often use *metacognitive* (i.e., "beyond the cognitive") strategies such as organizing, evaluating, and planning their learning. These are sometimes viewed as the learner's own personal "executive control" over his or her own learning. Use of these behaviors — along with *cognitive* strategies like analyzing, reasoning, transferring information, taking notes, and summarizing — might be considered part of any definition of truly effective learning (Brown, Bransford, Ferrara, & Campione, 1983). Additionally, competent learners often use *compensation* strategies such as guessing or inferring and *memory* strategies such as grouping and structured reviewing — all of which have been included as cognitive strategies by most researchers. Research results have shown that some of the best learners use *affective* and *social* strategies to control their emotional state, to keep themselves motivated and on-task, and to get help when they need it (McCombs, 1982, 1988; Dansereau, 1985). Yet many students (and their teachers) are largely unaware of the potential of affective and social strategies.

Cultural background affects *strategy choice*. Because of Hispanics' global and field dependent style preference (Reid, 1995), many Hispanic ESL/EFL students choose particular learning strategies, such as predicting, inferring (guessing from context), avoiding details, working with others rather than alone, and basing judgments on personal relationships rather than logic. In contrast, many Japanese ESL/EFL students reflectively use analytic strategies aimed at precision and accuracy, search for small details, work alone, and base judgments more on logic than on personal interactions. Cultures that encourage concrete-sequential learning styles (such as those of Korea or some Arabic-speaking countries) often produce widespread use of rote memorization strategies, while more flexible strategies (though not always higher order thinking strategies) and a more facilitative view of teachers are often found among North Americans. Extroverted learning styles, such as those of many Hispanics and Arabic speakers, are related to the use of social strategies for learning (Harshbarger et al., 1986; Willing, 1988). In contrast, according to Harshbarger et al. (1986), many introverted Asian students display strategies for working alone. These are just a few examples of cultural influences on learning strategy selection and use. In addition, gender differences in language learning strategy use have been rampant in the research (Oxford, 1993a, 1993b), and surely culture is at least one feasible, if partial, explanation. Attitudes toward authority, beliefs about how difficult (or easy) it is to learn a language, ideas about the importance of "the text" and about memorizing it, and concepts about whether personal expression and creativity are allowed — all these are cultural issues that affect the use of language learning strategies.

Culture also influences *strategy assessment*, the measurement of strategy use. Techniques often used for assessing students' language learning strategies include informal observation, formal observational rating scales, informal or formal interviews, group discussions, think-aloud procedures, language learning diaries, dialogue journals between student and teacher, open-ended narrative-type surveys, and structured questionnaires of strategy frequency (see, e.g., Cohen, 1987a). Learners in some cultures might feel too vulnerable in a think-aloud strategy assessment situation and might prefer a strategy assessment questionnaire. Likewise, culture influences *strategy instruction*. Students in certain cultures might like large and small group discussions with teacher input, while students elsewhere might prefer to improve their strategies independently through self-directed workbooks.

The following is an authentic example of how culture influences strategy use and attitudes toward learner empowerment. It was written by English teacher Milagros Flores in Venezuela. Notice the great surprise registered by some students and the skepticism of others when faced with the concept that they themselves could *actively* do something to enhance their learning:

> Whenever a strategy is used by a student in class, I stop and alert the whole class of that strategy and its effectiveness. I also try to use activities which would encourage students to use strategies, for example information gap activities, problem solving, and guessing the meaning from context. In my case after I arrived from the [strategy course for teachers], my first day of class I told my students about this new finding [learning strategies can help students learn more effectively] and I let them know most of the theory. But I realize it is big change for Latin people, I mean, it is going to involve a lot of time for them to get used to this new finding. My students' reaction varied from surprised to skeptical or mocking. *Because our students are not used to being an active part of the learning process, we have to be persistent in the discussion of the strategies and make students aware of them every time they obtain good results.*

In this culture, passivity was the norm in the learning process. In other cultures the sense of passivity in learning might not be so pronounced, and personal action and power might be felt more strongly. Each culture has its approach to learning and thus to learning strategies, and therefore no single formula for assessing and instructing learning strategies exists.

Part I concerns strategy assessment in various cultures and with different languages, and Part II delves deeply into strategy instruction as it takes place with students of contrasting cultures and languages. Chapter 1, by Anderson and Vandergrift, focuses on verbal reports, especially the well-known think-aloud procedure, and presents a major Canadian illustration highlighting learners of French as a second language. Oxford, Lavine, Felkins, Hollaway, and Saleh in chapter 2 discuss the use of diary studies and recollective studies and give examples with a variety of languages and countries. Using a variety of assessment techniques Levine, Reves, and Leaver demonstrate in chapter 3 how ex-Soviets who have been in Israel for a short time and those who have lived in Israel for decades differ in their cultural-educational learning views and their learning strategy use. Bedell and Oxford in chapter 4 review 36 studies of language learning strategy use in many different cultures, and then they center on an intensive strategy study in the People's Republic of China. Chapter 5 by Dreyer and Oxford is a view of South Africa, focusing on personality factors and learning strategies among Afrikaans-speaking learners of ESL. Kaylani, author of chapter 6, studies motivation and gender as related to learning strategy use in Jordan. In chapter 7, Cohen and Scott give a synthesis of internationally used strategy assessment options, giving advantages and disadvantages of each, as a fitting close to Part I.

Part II, with its focus on strategy instruction, starts with chapter 8 by Nyikos, who explains the conceptual shift that is essential when the teacher wants to create a learner-centered classroom (a necessity for improving students' learning strategies). Hajer, Meestringa, Park, and Oxford show in chapter 9 the power of print materials in strategy instruction, using illustrations from the UK, the US, and the Netherlands. Baily's chapter 10 proves that the computer can be a vehicle for assessing/tracking language learning strategies and for providing certain forms of strategy instruction. In chapter 11, Rubin continues the topic of media by introducing her Language Learning Strategy Program, which provides multimedia strategy instruction regarding multiple target languages, such as Russian, Korean, Spanish, and 17 others. Chapter 12 by Dadour and Robbins is a demonstration of the effectiveness of detailed, systematic strategy instruction for EFL oral communication skills in Egypt and in Japan. Chapter 13 details the CALLA model in a discussion by Chamot and O'Malley. Many of the principles of that model are applied to Japanese, Spanish, and Russian learning in chapter 14, written by Chamot, Barnhardt, El-Dinary, and Robbins. Kidd and Marquardson propose a well-articulated ESL strategy instruction model from Canada, a model known as Foresee and based somewhat on CALLA but with very specific revisions (chapter 15). In chapter 16, Yang shows how a strategy instruction program designed with group strategy interviews and discussions can affect the frequency and variety of strategy use among Taiwanese university students. Flaitz and Feyten describe a vibrant but short strategy instruction intervention and show that it can, in optimal circumstances, raise both strategic awareness and language performance. Chapter 18 by Oxford and Leaver synthesizes what we know at this time about strategy instruction around the world and refers to several key factors, such as consciousness, resource use, and degree of integration into regular classwork. The afterword brings together the key points of Parts I and II.

SPECIAL FEATURES OF THIS BOOK

This volume has a number of special characteristics not found in many other books on language learning strategies.

- This is the first book that looks closely at the nature of cultural effects on language learning strategy use, assessment, and instruction. Areas cited in this book for their language learning strategy involvement (and often for cultural influences) are Belarus, Canada, Denmark, Egypt, France, Israel, Japan, Jordan, the Netherlands, the Philippines, Puerto Rico, the People's Republic of China, the Republic of China (Taiwan), Russia, Saudi Arabia, Thailand, the Ukraine, the US, the UK, and many more.

- Unlike many other strategy books, this book discusses a wide range of *culturally appropriate* and *practical* ways to conduct strategy assessment and instruction.

- This is the first volume that shows how language learning strategies are employed, assessed, and taught with a large variety of native and second/foreign languages. In this book, a sampling of the languages specifically affected by language learning strategies includes, among others: Danish, Dutch, English (as a second language and as a foreign language), French, German, Hebrew, Japanese, Russian, and Spanish.

- This book contains chapters by most of the well-known researchers in the field of language learning strategies and also introduces some young, highly promising strategy researchers.

- This book contains new, unpublished information about language learning strategies; for instance, the volume describes recent strategy assessment and instructional projects, explores new links between strategy use and language performance, discusses computerized strategy assessment, highlights the value of print media for self-directed strategy instruction, and shows that a small amount of strategy instruction can sometimes have a surprisingly significant effect on language achievement.

- The volume is easier to read than most edited books in the language learning/teaching field. It has been carefully edited by a single individual, who aimed at eliminating major redundancies, creating smoothness and uniform quality across chapters, avoiding jargon, providing the clearest and most powerful presentation possible, offering syntheses at the end of each part of the book, and gathering references at the end of the volume.

As you read this book, consider the questions you want to have answered about language learning strategies around the world. Search for what you personally need to know. At the same time, keep an open mind for new questions and ideas you have not even considered. Enjoy this cross-cultural exploration of language learning strategies.

PART I:

WHAT DOES STRATEGY ASSESSMENT

TELL US IN VARIOUS

CULTURES AND LANGUAGES?

Neil J. Anderson
Ohio University, USA
Laurens Vandergrift
University of Ottawa, Ontario, Canada

CHAPTER 1

INCREASING METACOGNITIVE AWARENESS IN THE L2 CLASSROOM BY USING THINK-ALOUD PROTOCOLS AND OTHER VERBAL REPORT FORMATS

Speak out: What is it thou hast heard, or seen?
–Lord Tennyson

SUMMARY

Think-aloud protocols (and other verbal report formats) constitute a main technique for assessing students' learning strategies. This technique involves asking students to express their thoughts or strategies while they do a language task or soon thereafter. This chapter offers historical and conceptual background information and helpful guidelines regarding the use of such protocols. It also provides numerous examples, including a major illustration from Canada.

INTRODUCTION

Think-aloud protocols, along with related retrospective verbal report protocols, have been used in many second language (L2) research efforts to uncover the mental processes or strategies that second language learners use while engaged in language learning tasks. Such protocols allow "insight into the dynamic and interactive nature" of the language learning process (MacLean and d'Anglejan, 1986, p. 814). These protocols have helped redirect attention from a focus on products of language use to a focus on the ongoing process, which includes attending to language input, arriving at spoken utterances, processing a text, generating a text, and learning and retrieving vocabulary. Using think-aloud protocols and other verbal report formats is a beneficial metacognitive activity and helps students become more aware of the options available to them in understanding language and being a better language learner.

Anderson, N. J., & Vandergrift, L. (1996). Increasing metacognitive awareness in the L2 classroom by using think-aloud protocols and other verbal report formats. In Rebecca L. Oxford (Ed.), *Language learning strategies around the world: Cross-cultural perspectives.* (Technical Report #13) (pp. 3–18). Honolulu: University of Hawai'i, Second Language Teaching & Curriculum Center.

EARLY DEVELOPMENT

Think-aloud protocols and other related verbal report formats were first developed by Newell and Simon (1972) in the US to examine problem solving activities that individuals go through to get answers to math problems (Dobrin, 1986). Newell and Simon wanted a model to make computers more efficient in problem solving. By asking people to explain the cognitive process they used to solve problems, Newell and Simon found out that people use heuristics. In other words, people apply strategies to improve performance through using feedback about what does and does not work in problem solving settings. These researchers learned that they could not teach a computer to use heuristics in the same way that human beings do (although recent neural net technology allows expert systems to more closely approximate human thinking process than has been previously possible). From this beginning, protocol analysis has evolved to identify the internal process that people use in problem solving activities, including L2 learning tasks.

USES AND TYPES

A verbal report protocol is produced when a language learner verbalizes his or her thought process while completing a task or immediately after having completed a task (Ericsson and Simon, 1984; Olson et al., 1984). Cohen (1983, 1987a, 1987c) suggests three basic categories of verbal report data: self-report, self-observation, and self-revelation. *Self-report* is a generalized statement about one's own typical behavior. *Self-observation* requires that the specific processes used to accomplish a particular language task be reported simultaneously or within a very short period of time (introspection) or through probing for information soon after completing the task (retrospection). *Self-revelation* is a disclosure of thought processes in a stream of consciousness while the information is in the focus of the learner's attention. Self-revelation data are basically unedited and unanalyzed; by contrast, this suggests that self-observation might be at least partially analyzed or subject to a bit of reflection. Think-aloud protocols are usually of the self-revelatory variety and are thus unanalyzed, but retrospective protocols conducted a little later than the target task might be more self-observational and thus somewhat analytic.

CRITICISMS

The use of think-aloud protocols and other related verbal report formats is not without criticism. Tomlinson (1984) advises researchers to be beware when retrospective protocols are gathered, because subjects may rely on their background knowledge and opinions of a topic to fill in void areas where they cannot remember what they were actually thinking. Tomlinson also points out that sometimes subjects forget that their task is to report on the mental process they have used to complete a task and not interpret or explain what they have done.

Dobrin (1986) poses four objections to think-aloud protocols and associated formats. First, he is concerned with possible methodological flaws, such as those mentioned immediately above. Second, inferences are made from protocol analyses about whole processes. These inferences are made from "traces" of mental processes. Dobrin contends that reports do not show that the traces are large enough to make inferences about the mental process that occur. Third, there is no mechanism to determine if a trace is relevant to the actual process being described. Finally, Dobrin concludes that the studies that have used protocols have not provided enough information that common sense does not already offer.

Afflerbach (1986) advises that think-aloud protocols may not give helpful information if the process under investigation is automatic. "Automatic processes bypass working memory, and hence are not available for verbal reports" (p.1). When the strategies or steps followed in a process have become automatic, we no longer think about what we are doing; we simply do the task.

WHICH LANGUAGE TO USE

When think-aloud protocols or related formats are used with L2 learners, one consideration which is debated is which language the learner should use, the native language or the second language. Devine (1987) recommends that think-aloud protocols to be given in the L2 learner's first language (L1). She points out that "the limited oral language proficiency of many second language readers makes the use of oral summaries or retellings of text of questionable value" (Devine, 1987, p. 77).

Likewise, Anderson (1989) found that L2 learners were able to provide much more information about their cognitive processes in reading if they were allowed to provide the protocol in their L1. In a later study (Anderson, 1992), advanced second language learners reported on their reading strategies in their L2 and exhibited difficulties verbally describing the strategies they had used during the reading task.

However, Block (1986) showed that two ESL students, after a short orientation, were able to think aloud in English. Thus, researchers disagree somewhat as to which language is the most effective for think-alouds. The most reassuring situation for the student would be to allow the protocol to occur in whatever language the student is most fluent.

A POSITIVE JUDGMENT

In spite of any weaknesses, the use of think-aloud protocols and their retrospective cousins provides valuable insight into a rich source of data that is inaccessible to observation and would otherwise be lost. Ericsson and Simon emphasize that

> for more than half a century... the verbal reports of human subjects have been thought suspect as a source of evidence about cognitive process... [Yet] verbal re-

ports, elicited with care and interpreted with full understanding of the circumstances under which they are obtained, are a valuable and thoroughly reliable source of information about cognitive process... They describe human behavior that is as readily interpreted as any other human behavior. (1980, p. 247)

FOUR STEPS TOWARD EFFECTIVE USE OF PROTCOLS

Precautionary measures can be taken to minimize any concerns about the use of think-aloud protocols and related formats. The following four steps help learners to produce useful and accurate protocols.

First, the teacher or researcher provides training for learners in thinking aloud prior to having to actually produce a think-aloud protocol. Following a demonstration by the teacher or researcher, learners should be provided with an opportunity to practice. This assures everyone that the learner understands what is to be reported in the protocol.

Second, the teacher or researcher elicits the protocol as close to the learners' completing the language task as possible (or even better, during the language task). This avoids putting the learner in a situation of having to rely on long-term memory of what he or she was doing during the task. Some researchers have carefully constructed the language task so that the learner is asked to provide the think-aloud protocols at specific places. For example, red dots may be placed in a reading passage every few paragraphs to signal to the readers that they should stop and verbalize their reading comprehension strategies. While gathering think-aloud protocols during written tasks, teachers or researchers inform the writers that if they are silent for more than five seconds, they will be reminded to think aloud and continue to verbalize their thought process. The learners providing the think-aloud protocols should clearly understand when they are to speak.

Third, if the protocol is retrospective, the teacher or researcher provides the learner with some contextual information to help him or her remember thoughts that occurred or strategies that were used during the learning task. Videotaping the learners during the learning task and then allowing them to view the video while completing the think-aloud protocol is an excellent stimulus.

Finally, the teacher or researcher allows the language learner to use either the L1 or the L2 to produce the protocol. It is important for learners to speak freely, so they should use any language that is comfortable.

USES OF THINK-ALOUD PROTOCOLS AND RELATED FORMATS IN L2 RESEARCH

Think-aloud protocols and related kinds of verbal reports have been used as part of the research methodology in L2 studies in all four language skills, i.e., listening, speaking, reading, and writing, as well as in research related to language testing and teacher training. The use of think-aloud protocols or related formats in one research project in each of the above areas will be discussed. The main purpose of the following paragraphs is not to provide a comprehensive research review but instead to examine how verbal reports have been used to strengthen our understanding of how individuals use strategies to learn a new language.

LISTENING COMPREHENSION

Murphy (1987) examined the listening strategies of ESL learners. One of Murphy's purposes "was to bring listening research into the era of process-oriented research" (p. 29). The design incorporates an interesting application of the use of think-aloud protocols. Twelve intermediate ESL learners listened to six taped selections. While engaged in these listening tasks, learners were asked to "interrupt the speakers" to discuss their own thought processes. The interruption was signaled by a hand gesture to the researcher. Learners were encouraged to interrupt at any time they had something to say and were cautioned not to wait too long before interrupting. They were instructed to report two things during their recall protocols: a summary of what they were listening to and any other thoughts "running through their minds."

Allowing the listeners the opportunity to determine when to provide the protocol left them in charge of the monitoring process. This "'stop-and-go' procedure proved to be an effective means for collecting [data]" (Murphy, 1987, p. 4). Murphy emphasizes that think-aloud protocols "provide an exploration of the listening process in action" (p. 44).

SPEAKING

Cohen and Olshtain (1993) have applied protocols to get L2 learners to report the ways in which they "assess, plan, and execute" their spoken utterances. The researchers videotaped 15 L2 learners participating in role-play situations with a native speaker of English. Six speech act situations were provided for each learner (two apologies, two complaints, and two requests). After each set of two speech acts the video was repeated for the learners, who then responded in their L1 to a set of questions about what they were thinking during the role-plays. Note the strengths of this research in regards to the use of protocols. The videotape provided the source of the recall stimulus. The learners were not asked to remember great amounts of material before providing the protocol. The tasks were structured so that after each speech act pair the strategies for the two speech acts could be reported.

READING COMPREHENSION

Anderson (1991) used retrospective protocols with a group of 28 native Spanish speakers while engaged in two reading tasks: taking a standardized reading comprehension test and reading academic texts. Students gave the protocols in the L1 or the L2 after reading each passage on the standardized reading comprehension test and after answering reading questions on each of two parts of two academic passages. By dividing the reading material into smaller chunks it was easier for the learners to recall what strategies they were using while engaged in the reading tasks.

WRITING

Cohen (1987b) employed written protocols to investigate how L2 learners accept teacher corrections on their written work. Through the use of a questionnaire, learners were asked to think back to the last paper on which they received feedback from their teachers (presumably a day or two before receiving the questionnaire). The survey was not administered at the same time as the papers were turned back so as not to interfere with how the learners read and interpreted the comments from their teachers. In this research the retrospective protocol was written rather than oral, providing an additional format for gathering introspective data from second language learners.

LANGUAGE TESTING

Anderson et al. (1991) used a special type of protocol to examine the test-taking strategies of L2 learners. To preserve the integrity of the timing of the testing condition essential to a reading comprehension test and at the same time to help the participants verbalize the strategies they were using during the exam, the testing conditions were slightly modified. The assumption was that readers might employ different strategies if allowed to take the test without time limitations. Participants were told they would have 30 minutes to complete as much of the test as possible and that after reading and answering the comprehension questions for each passage they were to say "stop." The exam time was suspended, and participants were asked to describe the reading and test-taking strategies they had used while reading the passage and answering the multiple-choice comprehension questions. Participants were to indicate when they had completed the next passage. The time was suspended a second time allowing them to describe their reading and testing strategies. The test was administered in this way until a total elapsed testing time of 30 minutes had passed. Participants were allowed to produce protocols in their L1 (Spanish) or their L2 (English) or both languages.

TEACHER TRAINING

Johnson (1992) demonstrated that retrospective protocols can be used to enable pre-service ESL teachers to examine their instructional actions and decisions. She evaluated six pre-service ESL teachers, who viewed videotapes of lessons which they had taught. Their task while viewing the tapes was to provide a report about the decisions they were making while engaged in the act of teaching. This demonstrated most that videotapes can be an effective tool for stimulating recall.

THINK-ALOUD PROTOCOLS AND
RELATED FORMATS IN THE CLASSROOM

Think-aloud protocols and other verbal report formats have been developed and used primarily for research purposes. The following nine suggestions (which are not necessarily sequential) can be applied in adapting these research tools to the classroom (Davey, 1983; Irwin, 1991). The procedures below have been applied to protocols for L2 reading activities. These same basic procedures can be easily adapted for any of the other language skills.

1. The teacher demonstrates the use of think-aloud protocols by selecting a passage which s/he has never read before in order to show in as natural a fashion as possible what is going on in the mind while reading. The teacher reads the passage aloud while the students follow silently. While reading, the teacher verbally reports what is going on in his or her mind. Teachers who are fluent, advanced readers, particularly native speakers, may need to slow down their thinking processes in order to be aware of what they actually do while reading.

2. At the conclusion of the demonstration, the teacher encourages the students to add any thoughts that occurred to them during the reading.

3. Additional demonstrations may need to be provided so that students see what is involved in producing a think-aloud protocol.

4. Students are then grouped into pairs or groups of three and work together to practice thinking aloud. One student in the group reads aloud while the other(s) follow silently. The teacher encourages students to verbalize their thoughts and the strategies that they are using during the reading.

5. Students who act as listeners during this activity then add their thoughts to what their classmate has already shared.

6. The activity can also be done in a "reading round robin" format (Irwin, 1991). The class is given a reading passage, and each student is asked to read one sentence at a time and then verbalize thoughts and strategies. This activity works best if the readers cover the passage and reveal only one line of text at a time.

7. A "hot seat" activity can also be conducted. One student reads a short passage and thinks aloud, while the others in the class follow along silently.

8. Think-aloud protocols can also be used in regular silent reading periods. Occasionally during a silent reading activity, students are stopped and asked to verbalize what they are thinking. Alternatively, the think-aloud protocol can be implemented by having students stop at certain points and turn to a partner to verbalize their thoughts.

9. Finally, students can practice this activity while reading silently, outside the classroom. Davey (1983) has suggested that students be asked to read silently and then complete a checklist to report the kinds of strategies they

were implementing during the silent reading sessions. This can very easily be conducted as a homework assignment.

A CANADIAN ILLUSTRATION OF THREE KINDS OF VERBAL REPORTS

An important study by Vandergrift (1992) in Canada used three kinds of verbal reports to assess listening comprehension of second language (French) learners. Listening involves transforming "input" into "intake," changing the buzzing whirl of spoken sound into a meaningful subset that is internalized by the learner. Listening is a complex problem-solving skill (Wipf, 1984) that is the most frequently used of all language abilities (Duker, 1971; Feyten, 1991; Oxford, 1993d). Ordinary speech contains many ungrammatical, reduced, or incomplete forms; numerous hesitations and false starts; and significant amounts of redundancy. Listening comprehension in the foreign or second language therefore requires the use of learning strategies such as comprehension monitoring, analyzing, purpose-identification, and guessing (Byrnes, 1984; Chamot et al., 1988a; 1988b; Oxford, 1990a, 1990b). Like reading, listening can be considered a skill involving both "bottom-up" and "top-down" processing (Byrnes, 1984; Richards, 1983; Rost and Ross, 1991).

OVERALL DESIGN

Three different categories of verbal report, each one closer to the actual learning event, were used to elicit data on listening comprehension strategies: (1) self-report through delayed retrospection with a structured interview about strategies, (2) self-observation through immediate retrospection after an oral proficiency interview, and (3) self-revelation through introspection with a think-aloud procedure.

SUBJECTS

After permission was obtained from the school district, teachers were consulted and participants recruited from two large public high schools. School A is one of the few city schools where any "pure" language learners (those without previous French instruction) exist in their first (French 10) or second (French 20) year of French study. Students in their first, second, and fifth (French 20S) years of language study participated from School A. Since School A does not offer a nine-year French as a second language program, students in their eighth year (French 20N) were studied at School B. Participation was strictly voluntary, but only one female in French 20 declined to participate; all other selected students agreed to participate. Different numbers of students participated in each phase.

PHASE 1: SAMPLE, INSTRUMENTS, AND PROCEDURES

Thirty-six students, drawn from the four course levels (10, 11, 11, and 4 students respectively), participated in the individual semi-structured interview to give retrospective self-reports of their strategy use (adapted from Zimmerman and Pons, 1986). Interviewees were asked to recall the strategies they used to comprehend spoken French in a number of different contexts. Interviews were audio recorded, and students were encouraged to make changes and/or additions as needed to reflect accurately their strategy use. Analysis used a strategy classification scheme based on the work of O'Malley and Chamot (1990). Interrater reliability was .88 on the codings.

Generally the categories of strategy analysis used in Phase 1 proved to be a useful coding guide, but a few additions and revisions were made to reflect listening comprehension strategy use and distinguish more clearly between strategies. For example, the category of inferencing was broken down into different types: linguistic (use of words in context to infer meaning), voice/paralinguistic (e.g., tone of voice, sighs), kinesic (e.g., facial expressions, body language), and extra-linguistic (e.g., background sounds).

Some strategies in the original list were removed because they did not pertain to listening and others were clarified for more consistent coding. A number of affective strategies not on the list were identified. Building on the work of Oxford (1990b), these strategies were identified as lowering anxiety (use of mental techniques to make one feel more competent), self-encouragement (providing personal motivation through positive self-talk, a combination of what O'Malley and Chamot called "self-talk" and "self-reinforcement"), and taking emotional temperature (getting in touch with one's feelings and voicing them). These strategies reflect some of the ways in which learners gain control over their emotions and attitudes about learning.

Another category was isolated for strategies used to deal with breakdown of comprehension while interacting with another person. Repair strategies, commonly associated with the literature on communication strategies, are important in achieving comprehension (Rost and Ross, 1991) and can be divided into direct appeals and indirect appeals for assistance (Ellis, 1986).

PHASE 2: SAMPLE, INSTRUMENTS, AND PROCEDURES

Based on the Phase 1 interviews, 21 participants were chosen for stimulated recall (Phase 2). Selection was based on reported strategy use in Phase 1 and consultation with the teacher. Those reporting the greatest frequency, variety, and sophistication of strategy use were classified as more successful listeners. Those reporting the least frequency, variety, and sophistication were classified as less successful language learners. All students invited to continue with Phase 2 did so. Participants were distributed as follows: French 10 (one female successful listener, three female and one male less successful listeners); French 20 (two male and one female successful listeners, one male and one female less successful listeners); French 20S (two female and one male successful listeners, two female and two male less successful listeners); and French 20N (three female successful listeners, one male less successful listener).

Phase 2 involved retrospective self-observation using a stimulated-recall session. Each participant was interviewed individually in French to determine the level of proficiency (using the ACTFL/ETS Oral Proficiency interview discussed below), which resulted in a designation of either novice or intermediate proficiency. The videotape was played back to the participant immediately following the interview, with the participant or investigator stopping the video at any time for the participant to comment on what s/he was thinking at that point in the interview. The audiotape recorder was left on, recording both the interview and the retrospective comments. Coding of protocols for Phase 2 paid special attention to all nonverbal, indirect strategies used by the listener to clarify meaning or solicit input, as well as repair strategies. Differences in opinion about coding were resolved through discussion. Most results were useful.

PHASE 3: SAMPLE, INSTRUMENTS, AND PROCEDURES

The sample used in Phase 2 also participated in Phase 3, which centered on introspective, self-revelation through a think-aloud procedure adapted from O'Malley, Chamot, and Küpper (1989) and Rankin (1988). Students were first taught how to think aloud rather than retrospect about their listening strategies. These training sessions took 30–40 minutes.

An independent group of students helped to designate various texts by difficulty level, I — IV with I being the easiest. Only authentic texts reflecting naturalness of form and appropriate situational context were used. Easier texts (I-III levels) were taken from A la radio! (Porter and Pellerin, 1989), and the most difficult texts (IV) were taken from Communication +3 (Boucher and Ladouceur, 1988). Tapes were administered to participants as follows: French 10, level I; French 20, level II; French 20S less successful learners, level III; and French 20S successful learners and French 20N, level IV.

Data collection was done individually, with audio recording for later transcription and coding. Sessions (30–40 minutes each) took place within a week after training. Each session included three stages: warm-up, transition, and think-aloud. In the last stage, think-aloud data were recorded for at least three different texts, with uniform stopping points occurring for participants to tell what they were thinking.

OTHER INSTRUMENTS AND PROCEDURES

The ACTFL/ETS Oral Proficiency Interview (Lowe, 1982) is a conversational yet structured procedure for eliciting speech samples, which are then rated for proficiency. Interrater reliability was .85 between the interviewer and an independent rater in the present study. This interview was used as part of Phase 2.

The Learning Style Inventory (LSI) by Kolb (1985) was also applied to all participants in Phases 2 and 3. This instrument measures how people perceive reality (sensing/feeling vs. thinking) and how they process information (doing vs. watching/reflecting). Four learning style categories result when these dimensions are superimposed: (1) innovative learner or intuitors, (2) analytic learners or intellectuals, (3) common sense learners or implementors, and (4) dynamic learners or inventors.

The observation scheme known as Communicative Orientation of Language Teaching (COLT, Allen, Fröhlich, and Spada, 1984) was used to characterize the instructional features of the classes involved. This is a descriptive tool to provide interactive data and has been validated in many different instructional settings. Instructional features were coded in real time onto an observation form and notes taken.

PROFILES AND OTHER ANALYSES

For Phase 1, the listening profiles revealed the percentage of different kinds of strategies used by each individual and the average number of strategies reported by participants at each proficiency level. For Phase 2, a profile was created to identify the use and frequency of listening comprehension strategies used during participatory listening at each level of proficiency. Each strategy identified during the stimulated recall session (covert strategies related to thought processes) was counted and a profile created for each participant. Profiles were also created for each proficiency level. For Phase 3, a profile was created for each participant by representing each strategy and strategy group as a percentage of total strategy use by that participant. Analysis of the profiles was exploratory and interpretive, with the aim of hypothesis formation. Separate analyses were made for each of the variables: (1) successful and less successful listeners, (2) level of language proficiency, (3) gender, and (4) learning style.

RESULTS

TYPICAL EXERCISES

In general, the COLT found that the type of listening exercise used in the classes from which participants came was mainly discrete-point, with little emphasis on meaning. Authentic documents were never used at the lower levels, and little global listening practice was done at a normal speed.

PHASE 1: RETROSPECTIVE INTERVIEWS

Overall, there was an increase by course level in the mean number of distinct strategies reported (11%, 10%, 14%, 16%), except for a slight drop in French 20. Except for French 10, females reported using more distinct strategies than their male classmates (6% to 8%, 11% to 10%, 16% to 12%, 17% to 13%).

Mean number (and percentage) of *metacognitive* strategies increased at each course level, and females reported using a greater variety of metacognitive strategies than males at each course level. Planning strategies were by far the most popular of the metacognitive strategies. *Cognitive* strategies were the most widely used for all course levels, but use of these strategies appeared highest in French 10 (55%) and then decreased to 42–43%. Females reported using more cognitive strategies than did males. Linguistic inferencing, kinesic inferencing, resourcing, and elaboration were widely used cognitive strategies within the whole sample. The average number of *socio-affective* strategies was small and increased at each course level, but when viewed as a percentage of total strategies reported, it rose markedly after French 10 (17%, 23%, 22%, 22%). The most popular socioaffective strategies were questioning for clarification, cooperation, and self-encouragement. *Repair* strategies, not reported by many students, were present at advanced course levels only.

PHASES 2 AND 3: ORAL INTERVIEW FOLLOWED BY STIMULATED-RECALL RETROSPECTION AND THINK-ALOUD

During the oral proficiency interview, it was observed that novice learners clearly relied on kinesic inferencing, that is, guessing from the body language of the speaker. Predictably, there was a gradual decline in the use of this strategy between novice and intermediate learners. Participants appeared to be using strategies called continuation signals (or backchanneling cues), such as nods, "mmmm," or faking (a noncommittal response in spite of obvious noncomprehension, used mostly at the novice level). As learners became more proficient, there was less need to seek clarification or to verify comprehension, and more advanced learners did these in the target language.

During the stimulated-recall session after the oral proficiency interview, the videotape was stopped for a strategy check whenever it appeared the participant was having difficulty understanding. Since strategies were elicited only when participants had difficulties, strategy use decreased with each rise in proficiency level. *Cognitive* strategies were used the most to solve comprehension problems, but the use decreased across proficiency levels (85% to 68%). Of the cognitive strategies, inferencing was used at all levels, and transfer and translation were used by novices. *Metacognitive* strategies, however, increased in use across proficiency levels (2% to 32%), with comprehension monitoring and problem identification the most popular of these strategies. *Socioaffective* strategy use was small, appearing only among novices and including only self-encouragement. These results clearly indicate that strategy use changes across proficiency levels and also show that covert listening strategies are important to assess.

In Phase 3, the language learners were directly involved in a think-aloud procedure while listening to an oral French text. *Cognitive* strategies were most used by all participants (average 88%). The most widely used cognitive strategies were summarization, elaboration, and inferencing. *Cognitive strategy* use decreased (91% to 80%) from novice to intermediate. Novice listeners relied on surface-processing cognitive strategies such as translation, transfer, and repetition far more than did intermediate listeners. Both novice and intermediate listeners used elaboration, summarization, and inferencing rather often (range of 16%–30%). Overall, elaboration and inferencing appeared to be the most important cognitive strategies for listeners, regardless of proficiency level.

Metacognitive strategies (average 12%) followed. The most popular metacognitive strategies were comprehension monitoring, planning including selective attention, and problem identification, with an overall and very important metacognitive increase from novice to intermediate (9% to 19%). Since the nature of a think-aloud interview is not conducive to eliciting the use of *socioaffective* strategies, this category occurred in less than 1% of total strategy use.

Few differences in actual use of strategies during the Phase 3 think-aloud occurred by *gender*. The same six cognitive strategies (summarization, elaboration, inferencing, translation, transfer, and repetition) continued to be used most often, followed by the metacognitive strategy of comprehension monitoring. A difference lay in the use of repetition, with males using it more than females (9% to 7%). While females did use slightly more metacognitive strategies, this difference can be attributed to the almost exclusive use of self-evaluation strategies as well as the greater use of voice/paralinguistic inferencing (attributable to female sensitivity and attention to metamessages, Tannen, 1986). On the other hand, the greater general use of inferencing by males is not as easy to explain but might relate to a greater propensity for logical, rational thinking (Oxford, 1993a, 1993b).

In terms of learning styles of the 21 learners on the LSI, 12 — all males except one — were identified as Type 2 learners (analytic, assimilating intellectuals). Of the remainder, two were identified as Type 1 (innovative, divergent intuitors); two were Type 3 (common-sense, convergent implementors); and three were Type 4 (dynamic, accommodating inventors). Two produced poor data and were not included, and three more were not used because their scores fell close to dividing lines between quadrants. Sensing and feeling learners (Types 4 and 1) exhibited the same pattern of strategy use as successful learners: monitoring, elaborating in personal ways, inferring, avoiding repetition, using less non-personal elaboration, and using less transfer. They generally used more metacognitive strategies than did others with a different learning style. Learners who actively involved themselves in language experiences (Types 3 and 4) appeared to engage in more questioning and inferencing than did their more reflective counterparts (Types 1 and 2), who used repetition, translation, and transfer.

The biggest difference between successful and less successful learners seemed to lie in the use of *metacognitive* strategies (16% and 8%), a finding further strengthened by a qualitative analysis of selected protocols. The most notable differences occurred in the use of comprehension monitoring and problem identification, both used twice as often by successful than by less successful learners. Differences between these two groups was not as marked for *cognitive* strategies. Less successful learners used more transfer, inferencing, and induction/deduction, but surprisingly, translation and repetition were used almost equally by both successful and less successful learners.

Even within a given proficiency level (novice or intermediate), there were differences in strategy use. Novice-low listeners relied heavily on elaboration, inferencing, and transfer, as shown by both Phases 2 and 3. They were limited by cognitive constraints: the cognitive strategies needed to deal with the language did not leave enough attentional energy or memory space for deeper processing strategies such as comprehension monitoring. Novice-mid listeners used the above strategies but also felt compelled to translate, while novice-high listeners used superficial summarization, inferencing, and elaboration along with repetition and translation.

DISCUSSION OF CANADIAN STUDY

For novices in this study, listening comprehension was an interactive process in which listeners drew upon both bottom-up (linguistic) processing and top-down (background or world knowledge) processing, with reliance on the latter to construct a meaningful interpretation of a text in memory. Novice listeners, because of their limited linguistic knowledge, relied heavily on cognates (transfer) and contextual, extra-linguistic clues such as text type, background noise, tone of voice, body language, and relationships between speakers to employ world knowledge (elaboration) and to understand the input (inferencing). The essential difference in strategy use between novice and intermediate listeners was the increased use of metacognitive strategies, primarily comprehension monitoring. This dramatic increase might have been partially explained by the difference in listening ability. Intermediate listeners have learned that success in listening and in second language learning requires metacognitive control. Those who have not learned this have probably withdrawn from language study. In spite of the increased use of metacognitive strategies, intermediate listeners still use predominantly cognitive strategies: elaboration, inferencing, and summarization (the last allowing processing of larger chunks of language). Yet because of their greater internalization of vocabulary and structures, they are able to allocate more resources to metacognitive comprehension monitoring. Inefficient surface-level cognitive strategies, such as repetition, transfer, and translation, have now been superseded in frequency by deeper processing strategies. At the intermediate level, listeners hardly ever rely on body language for meaning, hypothesis testing is done in the target language, and positive continuation signals increase four-fold; listeners can hold their own in a conversation. At this level, fewer differences in strategy use emerge between sublevels.

Successful listeners appeared to use world knowledge more effectively, relating it to their own experience. Meaning was accumulated by successful listeners as the new linguistic input interacted with previous knowledge sources. Greater use of comprehension monitoring, prediction, and very rich summarization occurred. Less successful listeners experienced more problems because they squandered precious time and attentional resources on efficient surface-processing strategies and because they did not use their native-language metacognitive listening strategies.

Phase 1 suggested that females reported more strategy use than males, but the findings of Phase 3 implied that gender differences in actual strategy use in a think-aloud situation were minimal. Gender differences in actual strategy use and strategy reporting should be further investigated. Of particular value might be an exploration of the gender of the investigator (in this case male) versus the gender of the respondent.

Learning style tended to relate to language learning success. Differences between feeling/sensing learners and thinking learners were similar to those characterizing successful and less successful learners. The former tended to experience language learning in more concrete and global ways and more often used monitoring, personal elaboration, and inferencing — all deep-processing strategies. Analytical learners, on the other hand, focused on detail, lost the main idea, and used surface-feature strategies such as transfer and repetition. However, because successful learners also placed at the analytic end of the continuum, it would be unjustified to conclude on the basis of this study that a particular learning style might lead to greater success in listening comprehension.

This study confirms via verbal reports that listening is an active process of constructing meaning. It is not a top-down nor a bottom-up process, but an interactive process by which a listener draws upon a number of sources simultaneously (Byrnes, 1984; Rost and Ross, 1991). Listening comprehension is also influenced by external factors such as the purpose for listening, the difficulty of the text, the context of interaction, and the level of anxiety, as well as by internal student factors (Faerch and Kasper, 1986; Richards, 1983). This study confirms what L1 studies have shown about the crucial role of metacognitive strategies for listening comprehension, with comprehension monitoring as a superordinate strategy that is vital to selective attention, appropriate elaborating, and successful inferencing.

Given that the use of metacognitive strategies, particularly comprehension monitoring, appears to be crucial for successful learners, teaching strategies should foster the growth of metacognition among students. Prelistening activities encourage listeners to plan, organize their prior knowledge, and anticipate; teachers can foster these strategies. During the listening phase, comprehension monitoring and inferencing strategies can be developed. During postlistening, evaluation strategies can be nurtured. Authentic texts are essential (Scarcella and Oxford, 1992), along with tasks that are appropriate to students' proficiency levels (Lund, 1991) and practice time that reduces students' anxiety (Oxford, 1990b; Rubin, 1987). Using different response formats for verifying successful listening comprehension adds variety and interest (Lund, 1991; Oxford, 1990b; Richards, 1990; Ur, 1984).

This study was exploratory, and suggestions arose for further research. First, a listening comprehension test should be administered to all participants at the beginning of the study, not just to those at a mid-phase in the study. Second, future research should study learner's background knowledge, linguistic knowledge, and use of planning strategies in such a way that these threads can be teased apart. Third, during the Phase 1 structured interview, the interviewer should be especially alert to self-management strategies, asking participants how they arranged conditions for successful accomplishment of listening tasks; their answers would elicit more evidence of affective strategy use. Fourth, the proficiency interview should not be used to study strategy use in interactive listening; instead, both participants should be equal partners in a communication task, in which the student is not just questioned but is required to understand the interlocutor in order to complete the task. Fifth, a larger sample at each proficiency level should be used.

Sixth, similar research at different ages should be conducted. Seventh, the effects of text difficulty on strategy use at different proficiency levels merits study. Eighth, the information processing framework used here (O'Malley and Chamot, 1990) should be reviewed. It is helpful for understanding cognitive processes but not affective processes, such as motivation, self-concept, and anxiety (Skehan, 1991). Integrated models might be even more useful. Ninth, validation of a general comprehension skill would enhance our understanding of cognitive processes in second language comprehension, for both listening and reading. Finally, strategy instruction needs to be conducted to determine its influence on strategy use.

CONCLUSIONS

The use of think-aloud protocols and other verbal report formats is expanding in L2 research. As both a research tool and as a class activity, such protocols provide a window into the often hidden processes that language learners use to accomplish their purposes in the second language. Think-aloud protocols and associated types of verbal reports have been used as a research tool in studies on all four language skills, as well as for identifying test-taking strategies and teacher decision-making processes. In each case, the individual is asked to reflect upon what he or she is thinking about or doing while engaged in a task. When used by students, think-aloud protocols and related formats allow learners to become more metacognitively aware of what they are doing, which can lead to improved performance in the development of language skills.

The use of verbal reports provides an important avenue of investigation into language learning strategies. The Canadian research of Vandergrift demonstrates how rich and illuminating verbal report data can be for second language listening comprehension. Such data can offer keen insight into the process of language learning.

Rebecca L. Oxford
University of Alabama, USA
Roberta Z. Lavine
University of Maryland, USA
Gregory Felkins
University of Alabama, USA
Mary Evelyn Hollaway
Mountain Brook High School, Alabama, USA
Amany Saleh
University of Alabama, USA

CHAPTER 2

TELLING THEIR STORIES: LANGUAGE STUDENTS USE DIARIES AND RECOLLECTION

Educating the mind without educating the heart is no education at all.
–Aristotle

SUMMARY

This chapter highlights the value of language learning diaries and recollection for heightening learners' own awareness of their strategies as used in language tasks. Depending on the nature of the instructions given to students, diaries and recollection can also uncover affective aspects of language learning, such as anxiety and motivation. Both students and teachers benefit from diaries and recollection.

INTRODUCTION

Students derive the maximum benefit from language learning strategies in developing language skills when they and their teachers are aware of and pay attention to these strategies. Strategies range from cognitive techniques such as analyzing to metacognitive techniques such as planning to social and affective strategies such as empathizing with others. Unfortunately, research tells us that teachers are often unaware of or mistaken about their students' strategy preferences (Chamot and Küpper, 1989; Cohen, Glasman, Rosenbaum-Cohen, Ferrara, and Fine, 1979; Hosenfeld, 1977; Oxford, Lavine, and Crookall, 1989). Two useful ways to assess strategies and thus enhance teacher and student awareness are language learning diaries and recollection (sometimes called recollective studies; see Cohen and Scott, chapter 7, this volume). Both of these techniques allow students to tell their own stories. Diaries give students the chance to tell the story of their current language

---

Oxford, R. L., Lavine, R. Z., Felkins, G., Hollaway, M. E., & Saleh, A. (1996). Telling their stories: Language students use diaries and recollection. In Rebecca L. Oxford (Ed.), *Language learning strategies around the world: Cross-cultural perspectives.* (Technical Report #13) (pp. 19–34). Honolulu: University of Hawai'i, Second Language Teaching & Curriculum Center.

learning, while recollection affords the opportunity for students to share the tale of their previous language learning. Rather than encountering skepticism or reticence, we met with students' eagerness to tell about their language learning. Our experience with both diaries and recollection is that students respond by expressing, orally or in writing, the idea that "No one ever asked me before to talk about my learning! Let me tell you all I can."

These techniques — diaries and recollection — can be interpreted in either an *analytical*, detailed way (which enables the researcher to do quantitative calculations of strategies cited by each learner and which does not usually say much about the emotional or social situation) or in a *global*, narrative way (which allows qualitative impressions of strategy use in the context of many other factors, such as social setting, emotions, attitudes, and motivation). In our case, we chose to use diaries for analytic, quantitative interpretation and recollection for global, qualitative interpretation in an entirely separate investigation. We could have just as well decided to analyze diaries qualitatively and recollection quantitatively. Had we structured our research differently, we might have used both diaries and recollection in a single investigation. Our particular usage, as shown in this chapter, by no means exhausts all the possibilities.

This chapter provides a research review concerning each of the two techniques, then descriptions and results of the two studies, and finally implications.

RESEARCH REVIEW ON DIARIES AND RECOLLECTION

Keeping a *language learning diary* helps learners become more aware of their strategies at any given time and across a long period. It also helps them pay attention to specific strategies they use in certain circumstances, and it heightens their attention toward the strategies their peers use. Language learning diaries are a type of self-report which allows learners to record on a regular basis numerous aspects of their learning process, including but not limited to the use of specific language learning strategies. Often the diarist is a language student, but sometimes the diarist is a specialist who writes about his or her language learning experience. In some instances, such as the accounts by Bailey (1983) or Schmidt and Frota (1986), the diarist-learner and the researcher are one and the same. Learners can write diaries in a totally free-form manner, with no direction from the teacher as to content or format, but Rubin (1981) found that directed diary reporting was a good way to obtain learning strategy data.

Sometimes diaries are kept by and for the learner alone, without being read by anyone else. However, in other cases, students share their diaries with their peers or with their teacher. When another student or the teacher actively responds to what the diarist writes, a intensely communicative dialogue occurs, creating a *dialogue journal* (Albertini, 1990; Maguire, 1989; Meath-Lang, 1990; Peyton, 1990; Peyton and Reed, 1990; Spack and Sadow, 1983; Staton, 1980, 1983, 1987; Steffenson and Lin, 1989). In addition, keeping a diary is an excellent means of expression for students who are reluctant to participate orally in class (Gaies, 1983). Teachers have said that they gain great insights into their optimal instructional roles through reading diaries and participating in dialogue journals, and instructors sometimes change their way of teaching based on what they learn from diaries and journals (Meath-Lang, 1990; Vanett and Jurich, 1990).

Language learners benefit by keeping a diary or journal because they become more aware of and attentive to their own learning processes. Long (1979) shows how students become "participant observers" in their own learning by writing a language learning diary. A study of the diary allows for self-evaluation, improvement, and growth by the writer (Brown, 1985b). If students share their diaries with classmates, they begin to compare their learning processes and strategies. Bailey and Ochsner (1983), Bailey (1983, 1991), Brown (1985b), and Matsumoto (1994) discuss diaries as research documents. While there are of course limitations to self-reporting formats, diaries are excellent sources for the exploration of affective, social, and cognitive variables (Jones, 1977; Rivers, 1979; Schumann and Schumann, 1977). For instance, Bailey (1983) explores anxiety and competition in diaries, Oxford, Ehrman, and Lavine (1991) and Oxford and Lavine (1992) investigate learning style conflicts between students and teachers, and Brown (1985a) examines requests for specific input by language learners. In addition, diaries can provide specific instructional information, converting these first-person reports into useful aids for assessing both the curriculum and the classroom for possible adjustments (Howell-Richardson, 1989).

Recollection can also be a fine source of data for heightening awareness of and attention to one's own language learning strategies (see Cohen and Scott, chapter 7, this volume; Green, Oxford, and Green, 1995). One disadvantage of recollective accounts of language learning strategies is that they are occasionally subject to memory lapses. Other potential disadvantages (which might actually be advantages in many cases) are their strong subjectivity, their personal nature, and their individuality. Despite any possible problems, recollection has powerful benefits. It can often offer a rich, multifaceted perspective. It gives the "distance of time" that can put things into perspective and allow linkages to become more apparent. Recollection allows the individual to summarize strategy use and general learning experiences over a long period of time. Unless the directions given by the researcher constrain learners to write only about certain topics in a specific and potentially quantifiable way, recollection often permits great freedom to discuss strategies, styles, emotions, attitudes, motivations, barriers, and breakthroughs. Finally, recollection is inexpensive to conduct and does not typically require the involvement of more than one person. The main requirement is a perceptive, honest, open person with clear research goals — an individual who is willing to take the time and the emotional and cognitive energy to reflect on the past.

The next part of this chapter discusses the diary study. The first two authors helped plan the study and analyzed and interpreted the data; the second author conducted the entire data collection with her students.

THE DIARY STUDY

PURPOSE

The primary purpose of this study was to use diaries to determine the learning strategies used by university foreign language students in areas of listening, grammar learning, and vocabulary learning. A secondary goal was to expand students' awareness of their own strategy use and add new strategy possibilities to their repertoire.

SAMPLE

Forty-two students of Spanish (26 women and 16 men) from the University of Maryland at College Park were involved in this study. The instructional methodology of the classes was basically communicative. The total sample was composed of three subsamples: 24 Spanish second-semester students in two sections containing 17 and 7 students each; and 18 Spanish fourth-semester students enrolled in an elective course. Most participants were native speakers of English, but other native languages were also represented: Farsi, French, and Vietnamese. All students but one, an English-dominant Hispanic without previous formal instruction in Spanish, were studying Spanish as a foreign language.

DATA GATHERING PROCEDURES

Students were asked by the teacher, the second author, to write down how they carried out a language task or approached a particular language skill. Specifically, the teacher asked students to explain in their diaries how they approached listening comprehension, how they learned grammar, and how they mastered vocabulary. Students made diary entries in either English or Spanish several times during the semester. Some students chose to deal only with one skill, others with all three skills. In total, 40 students discussed their strategies for vocabulary, 22 wrote about their grammar strategies, and 15 explained their listening comprehension strategies.

DATA ANALYSIS PROCEDURES

The first stage of analysis consisted of examining students' narrative diaries to determine the number and type of learning strategies mentioned. This involved conducting a content analysis (Krippendorf, 1980; Stempel, 1989a, 1989b) with these steps: labeling and defining strategies as described by students, who used a variety of terms; defining units of analysis; training raters to reliably identify strategies; and expanding the strategy list when necessary. In the preliminary content analyses, Oxford's (1990b) 62-item strategy system was used. Even though it is among the most comprehensive strategy systems published to date, it was still not comprehensive enough to handle the range of specific, identifiable strategies mentioned in the diaries. Oxford's system was therefore expanded by adding new strategies, such as *using sequential review*, *paraphrasing*, and *memorizing by rote*, or by breaking down compound strategies into additional discrete strategies (for example, planning for a language task became two strategies, *scheduling* and *designing a sequential plan for learning*). The expanded strategy list included 138 strategies (available from the first two authors of this chapter). Strategies shown by other research to be important for language learning were retained in this system, even if they were not all used by the students in the sample. This list was used for all subsequent content analyses of the diaries. Interrater reliability between the first two authors was virtually perfect (r=.995) using the amplified list of strategies. A further stage of analysis consisted of counting the frequencies of different strategies and frequencies of six general groups of strategies (i.e., cognitive, memory, compensation, metacognitive, affective, and social; see Oxford, 1990b) *across* all three skill areas combined (listening comprehension, grammar, and vocabulary). Then the authors calculated instances of different strategies and the six categories of strategies *within* each of the three skill areas of interest. This step proved useful, because different skills often drew upon strategies in contrasting ways. Another step involved analyzing the frequencies of different strategies and strategy types (within a given skill) by gender. The most detailed level of analysis therefore examined (1) which strategies were mentioned in the diaries (2) with reference to a specific skill area (3) by males and females.

We conducted chi-square tests to assess significance of differences between females and males in frequency of strategy use. The test-assumption was that frequencies would be the same for both genders. Anything that differed from this pattern at $p<.05$ was significant. Grades did not turn out to be useful as a reflection of language achievement and were ultimately not used in the analyses.

RESULTS

General findings

Students in this study showed a well developed repertoire of learning behaviors or strategies, totaling 75. The frequently appearing strategies were memory, cognitive, and a limited set of metacognitive strategies (focusing on evaluation and planning). All of these were familiar and required little risk-taking on the part of students. The strategies that did not appear frequently were mostly affective, social, and compensation strategies. These results are consistent with those of other research (O'Malley and Chamot, 1990; Bacon, 1992), in which learners rarely mentioned affective and social strategies.

In the present study, all students cited using a number of strategies for listening comprehension and vocabulary. However, students mentioned relatively few strategies for grammar. They seemed very confused and adrift in terms of ways to learn grammar. Males and females sometimes tended to use language learning strategies in significantly different ways.

Frequently used strategies: Cognitive, memory, and metacognitive

Learners used large numbers of cognitive and memory strategies across the three skills. Virtually all mentioned using at least one cognitive strategy and at least one memory strategy. Of the 75 total strategies mentioned, over half were either cognitive or memory strategies. The most frequently mentioned cognitive strategies include *repeating*, cited by over half the students. An example of repeating from one of the diaries is: "I study the vocabulary by looking at the word and repeating the meaning." *Formally practicing with rules* was mentioned by one-third of the learners. One diarist wrote, "I study the vocabulary by doing workbook exercises... Grammar is the same, but I do the exercises in the workbook and they are very beneficial to study and practice grammar. I have a verb wheel too that helps me go over irregular verbs and regular tenses quickly." Two other popular cognitive strategies were *seeking global comprehension* and *translating from the target language to the native language*, both used by slightly less than one-third of the diarists.

Four memory strategies were frequently mentioned in the diaries. The technique of *doing a sequential review* was cited by eight out of every ten learners, followed by these strategies: *writing down information*, mentioned by half of the learners; and *making associations or elaborations*, cited by slightly less than half. As one diarist penned, "Any word that is similar to an English word, I relate the two (tranquilo — tranquil — calm)." *Memorizing by rote* was described by almost one-third of the students. Of all the cognitive and memory strategies, only three — *making associations or elaborations*, *doing a sequential review*, and *repeating* — were uniformly used for all three skill areas (listening comprehension, grammar, and vocabulary).

All students mentioned at least one metacognitive strategy in their diaries. The 26 specific metacognitive strategies cited in the diaries were easily classified into evaluation and planning techniques. Thus, learners used a limited range of metacognitive strategies but employed them often.

Two-thirds of the learners used evaluation strategies across the three skill areas. Such use of evaluation indicates it is more common than previously thought (Chamot and Küpper, 1989). Two particular evaluation strategies were employed: one-third used *self-evaluation of overall progress in a skill*, while four-fifths *judged the relative success of a particular learning strategy* for their individual learning goals. These two diary entries give a flavor of the evaluating that students did: First, "The lessons in the textbook and the workbook help tremendously in retaining the grammar and the new vocabulary." Second, "When I'm studying vocabulary I just try and first see if the Spanish word looks or sounds like the English word. About 50% of the time this is the case."

The most popular planning strategy was *designing a sequential plan for learning*, which was used by more than two-thirds of the diarists. Diarists expressed their sequential planning in two ways: by numbering the specific steps (e.g., "To study vocabulary, (1) read carefully; (2) pronounce correctly; (3) write out the word at least five times; (4) try it in a sentence") and by narrating their steps ("First I do this, then I do that"). One student wrote: "When I study, I go through the vocabulary and all the main features. I then make flash cards to study vocabulary [and for] the main parts of the chapter, I do the exercises. If there are verbs to learn, I write the tenses over and over again. Then [there are] the review sessions."

Slightly over half of the students mentioned *having a general plan for learning*. An equal number reported *trying out specific strategies as part of a plan for learning*. Interestingly, two of these metacognitive planning strategies (developing a sequential plan for learning and trying out a strategy as part of a learning plan) have not been emphasized in the results of any previous strategy investigation, although general planning has always appeared. Almost seven out of every ten students spontaneously reported using a "sequencing cluster" composed of the metacognitive strategy of *designing a sequential plan*, followed by the memory strategy of *doing a sequential review*.

Less frequently used strategies: Compensation, affective, and social

The diaries showed very limited use of compensation, affective, or social strategies across the three skill areas. Only three compensation strategies that make up for missing knowledge were mentioned among the total 75 strategies. These were: *searching for and using clues from the target language as the basis of guessing; searching for main words as clues for guessing, or synthesizing information from main words to guess*; and *searching for and using combined clues from multiple sources to guess*. One learner wrote, "What I do to understand listening comp[rehension]: I listen for words I know and the tense [they] are in." Another said, "When I listen, I key on words that are familiar, or words that I understand, and try to interpret them in English to get the main ideas." A third explained, "When listening I just key on the important words and disregard the unimportant words." However, such compensation strategies were cited only in the skill of listening comprehension and were mentioned by fewer than two out of every ten students. Only one student of the 42 in this study mentioned using an affective strategy, which was *making a game of learning*. This student wrote, "To learn vocabulary, I usually make the word mean something to me — kind of like a game." Three students reported using a single social strategy, *asking someone for specific help*. Students only asked for help as part of a testing-oriented relationship, in which they asked a friend or relative to act as a "vocabulary quiz master." The extremely limited mention of compensation, affective, and social strategies reflects findings in other studies (see, e.g., Bacon, 1992; Horwitz, 1990; Horwitz and Young, 1991; O'Malley and Chamot, 1990).

Strategies associated with each skill

The diaries yielded interesting information about strategy use in each of the three skill areas. Vocabulary learning and listening comprehension enjoyed a wide use of strategies, though grammar learning was strategically bereft.

Half of the students who wrote about vocabulary learning used the same set of seven strategies. These included the metacognitive strategies of *designing a sequential plan for learning, trying out a strategy as part of a learning plan*, and *having a general plan for learning*; the memory strategies of *doing a sequential review, making associations or elaborations*, and *writing down information*; and the cognitive strategy of *repeating*. Expected strategies, such as *grouping words, using imagery, translating, using flashcards, memorizing by rote*, and *using cognates*, were not as often reported in the diaries.

Half of the students who wrote about listening comprehension mentioned the same five strategies: *making a conscious effort to concentrate*; *having a general plan*; *trying out a strategy*; *seeking global comprehension*; and *searching for main words as clues for guessing, or synthesizing information from main words to guess*. Of these five, the most frequently used was concentrating, used by almost all who discussed listening comprehension.

The picture for grammar strategies was entirely different. In the diaries examined here, the most important finding about grammar strategies was the general absence of them. The strategies used for grammar learning were sparse, and some students were acutely aware of their lack of grammar techniques. Common statements were: "I don't have any specific approach to [grammar], and I'm not quite sure how I study grammar." Other students were vague, stating, "I go over exercises and notes for grammar in the workbook," or "As for grammar, I just read it in the book and do the exercises assigned." These comments reflect a tendency toward passivity or reliance on the teacher or the text (Oxford and Nyikos, 1989) in the area of grammar. Some students showed a touch of anxiety or helplessness about grammar. For example, one diarist wrote, "Nothing helps me to learn grammar... I try to memorize the forms but there are too many exceptions." Another wrote, "I read the sections in the book. I watch the professor in class. *Sometimes* it sinks in." Though most students felt they had few strategies for grammar learning, some students relied on a core of five strategies: *general planning*, *designing a sequential plan for learning*, *doing a sequential review*, *writing down information*, and *formally practicing with rules*. These grammar strategies do not show a strong cognitive or creative bent.

Gender differences

Males and females tended to use somewhat different strategies. Although the percentage differences were not always large, they were sometimes significant and showed interesting trends. For instance, significantly more males than females (75% vs. 62%) used *self-evaluating* strategies across all three skill areas. In vocabulary learning, 25% of males versus 9% of females discussing that skill used *self-evaluating*, resulting in a significant difference. In vocabulary learning, 25% of males versus 13% of females reported using the technique of *judging the success of a particular strategy*, again a significant difference. Thus, males seemed to be more oriented toward self-evaluation with a focus on the outcome, a finding that rings true to previous research on male versus female "ways of knowing" (Belenky, Clinchy, Goldberger, and Tarule, 1986).

However, 44% of the women compared to 25% of the men noted *trying out a new strategy* for vocabulary learning, resulting in a significant difference. Significantly more females than males (96% vs. 80%) reported using memory strategies, with a similar pattern for cognitive strategies (88% vs. 81%). Many fewer males and females used social strategies, but again the difference significantly favored females (17% vs. 6%). Similarly, few of either gender reported using affective strategies, but the difference again significantly favored females (4% vs. 0%). Gender differences were non-significant for compensation and metacognitive strategies as a whole.

The diary study above content-analyzed the existing narrative data quantitatively. Now we turn to the recollective study, which was interpreted in a purely qualitative fashion.

THE RECOLLECTIVE STUDY

SAMPLE

The recollective study consisted of several case studies conducted by participants in an elective course in the MA-TESOL (Master of Arts in Teaching English to Speakers of Other Languages) Program at the University of Alabama. Case studies of one man and two women are excerpted here, although approximately 20 graduate students participated in the study. The three (Greg, Mary Evelyn, and Amany) reflect the general range of content and form exhibited by the whole group.

DATA COLLECTION AND ANALYSIS PROCEDURES

The participants conducted their own recollections of previous language learning strategies and experiences. That is, they freely wrote about past learning strategies, events, environments, and processes, linking these to what they knew about factors in foreign and second language development from a variety of readings. Because of the highly creative, imagistic nature of many of the narratives, we chose to interpret the data qualitatively rather than counting strategies.

RESULTS

General findings

Although not instructed to do this, the participants took the opportunity to develop their own personal metaphors for language learning (diving blindly into a pool, weaving words, strolling on the Champs Elysees with the echo of Scarlett and Rhett). *Learning strategies* were important to all participants. Greg stressed the great significance of strategies such as guessing and taking risks, Amany cited semantic mapping and a whole range of other English-learning strategies, and Mary Evelyn mentioned a paucity of strategies in an impoverished language environment and a panoply of strategies in a rich language environment. All participants exhibited signs of *language anxiety* in certain situations. Amany stopped speaking French permanently because of anxiety over her mother's criticism, Greg feared using Spanish to order dinner, and Mary Evelyn was afraid of the stern and brittle voice of the college language teacher; *self-esteem* was typically low in each of these high anxiety situations. *Low motivation* caused by lack of fulfillment of *learning style needs* was obvious when Amany lacked movement and visual simulation and when Mary Evelyn was denied the "fine, heady wines" of communicative activities while her teacher's eyes stayed "leveled at the text." *High motivation and the joy of accomplishment* shined through each of the narratives, as when Greg used strategies to help him order food, when Amany enjoyed her multidimensional learning style, and when Mary Evelyn dreamt in French.

Greg's results

Greg Felkins, who at the time was a master's degree candidate in TESOL, recollectively described his Spanish learning in lyrical terms. At the end, he summarized his experiences.

> I sat on the steps leading up to the Arco de la Estrella, the main entrance to the Ciudad Antigua of Cáceres. The sky was still light though the sun had already slipped below the horizon. The steps and the stone wall beside me radiated the day's heat, and as I looked out over the Plaza Mayor I could see a few people moving quietly and purposefully through the plaza. The plaza itself had darkened quickly and I felt the city drawing a deep breath in expectation of the night to come. The plaza was lit only by the soft light that spilled from the windows of houses and from the street-level storefronts. I had been in Spain four days...

> I was beginning to know what it is to be unable to communicate, to be unable to express one's most basic needs and desires. I had promised myself that that night I would enter a restaurant and order a meal. It seemed that the entire year ahead of me depended on this one act. I looked across the plaza to El Puchero, a restaurant-bar, waiting for it to open. At 8:15 I crossed the plaza and entered El Puchero. I asked the girl behind the counter if they were serving dinner yet and when she told me yes, I said that I'd like to eat. She asked me if I wanted to eat inside or outside. There was no way that I was going to eat outside for all the world to witness my ineptness with Spanish. She gave me a menu. I gave my order, while she smiled the entire time.

> I knew that she knew I was a foreigner who spoke horrible Spanish, but I didn't care. I actually felt as if I had crossed some sort of physical boundary. After eating I ordered a coffee with my newfound sense of self-confidence. I paid for the meal, and the girl wished me a good evening.

> About an hour had passed when I stepped back out into the plaza. It had come alive for the evening. Families strolled by, young people laughed and talked, and it seemed as if they all looked at me, but I didn't believe I needed to feel threatened. I wanted to join la movida, the liveliness of the night. I wanted to feel like a citizen of Extremadura. I walked up the street and decided to see a little of the city. I was even confident enough to stop and order an ice cream at the shop that I would come to frequent several times a week in the year to come.

> As I walked back to the residencia, I knew that I had a long way to go. I had crossed a line, leapt blindly into a pool whose depth I couldn't see. I felt the same sense of confidence and relief that I had felt after rappelling from a helicopter at night for the first time in the Army.

> What had brought me to Spain was a desire to learn the language and live in another culture. When I went to Spain I had been studying Spanish at the university

for two years. By the time that I started Spanish 202 I had decided that if I really wanted to learn the language I needed to go somewhere that I would be forced to speak it every day. I found myself the first student from my university to study at the University of Extremadura in Cáceres, Spain. After I had been there for a few months I was participating in class discussions along with everyone else. For the first four months, after the brief time in the *residencia*, I lived with a family but spoke as much English as Spanish.

In October I had started teaching English at a small language academy and had met a girl who was planning to go to England and who wanted to learn English with friends of hers. She approached me about giving her and her friends private lessons. I agreed to do so, and this turned out to be the best thing that could have happened to me. We all soon became good friends, and I spent several hours at their apartment studying every evening. Through them I met a lot of other people. I moved into the apartment when the girl and her friend went to England that next February.

I had to go shopping for groceries with my new roommates. I began to learn an incredible number of new words. I remember one day that the wife of the owner of the fish market told everyone in the store, "Can you believe it? He's American and he speaks better Spanish than I do!" I know she didn't mean it literally, but it felt great. I began to feel a sense of belonging. I knew I had been accepted as just another student who happened to be American.

In addition to the use of learning strategies, I see the main issue in language learning to be one of motivation. We are almost all capable, short of being brain-damaged, of learning a language. Do we not have an L1? If I could learn English as my L1, then surely I have the innate ability to learn an L2, or an L3, etc. My first motivation was the idea that it would be nice to be able to speak another language. My friend could do it and I was impressed by it. If he could do it, then why couldn't I? The second motivation was external: fulfilling the college language requirement. But these two motivations built upon each other.

There is literally a world of difference between language learning in the classroom and *language learning by cultural immersion*. The second of these appears to me to be the most effective. The following learning strategies are viewed with my cultural immersion experience in mind. Some of them were identified clearly in the narrative above, and others were not.

At this point Greg listed a wide variety of strategies he used for listening, guessing, encouraging his own tolerance for ambiguity, taking risks, building self-esteem, reducing anxiety, identifying progress, learning to think in Spanish, and integrating into the target culture.

Mary Evelyn's results

Mary Evelyn Hollaway, a doctoral candidate and award-winning teacher with over two decades of experience, was enrolled in the course. In her writings, she described her long-past encounters with high school and college French in two poems (1 and

---

2), then expressed in a poem (3) her more recent experience with French as a doctoral student. The first two poems embody Mary Evelyn's strategies of identifying her own emotional state and observing her learning environment carefully. Both poems reveal how the setting and the teacher's personality directly influenced Mary Evelyn's experience.

Poem 1: La Maitresse d'Ecole (The Schoolmarm)

Southern, not Parisian,
Her French, honeyed and magnoliaed,
Her fine Alsatian wines
Forever flowed to juleps on the porch.

    It wasn't that she lacked the love
    Of Paris sounds and sights and sense
    But still she drawled her way
    Along the Seine.

        I fear I'll never stroll
        The Champs Elysees
        Sans the echo of a Scarlett
        Sans the echo of a Rhett.

Poem 2: Le Professeur Peu Abordable (The Professor a Little Aloof)

He was tall and gaunt
(NOT FRENCH)
His brown suit shiny with wear
Had never seen Paree.

    His eyes I can't recall
    Perhaps a brownish-gray
    Behind the pewter rims
    Stayed leveled at the text.

        His voice I'd know
        Down any street
        Around the world.
        I hear it still.

            Stern and brittle,
            Doling the measure
            Of my meager skills:
            "Correct" or "Incorrect."

                He must have loved
                The language once,
                Strolled the Route du Vin,
                Watched the Rieslings golding in the sun.

                    Perhaps those days are there
                    Sleeping in wood-brown casks,
                    Dreaming their way
                    To fine, heady wines.

We never knew their tastes
Or heard the lusty voices hurl
"Degustation libre!"
Into dry October air.

In the third poem, Mary Evelyn retrospectively describes her experience of learning French as a mature adult in graduate school. The poem embodies many learning strategies, such as making mental images, making flashcards, playing with sounds, employing cognates, using ironical humor, and identifying emotional states and physical sensations. It also reflects a strong sense of rural French culture.

Poem 3: Dreaming in French

The room narrows and warms; the phrases blur,
Melting into strangers swaying on my flashcards.
They dip and bob like saucy dancers
(C'est curieux. C'est curieux.) in perfect time,
Flirting, slurring, riding the lazy breeze of the ceiling fan.
Blind-splintered sun lies in ribbons of light and shadow.
Après midi — I float above my bed
Or in a meadow in Bordeaux.

The ancient farmer bows and tips his hat.
His eyes, his lips — dissected by the shifting stripes —
Smile, "Que desirez-vous, mademoiselle?"
"Je ne fais que regarder, monsieur."
I speak in perfect tourist French.
(The very grass itself must be impressed.)

He smiles again, bending to begin his work,
Reeling the ribbons in, like glowing eels,
Pressing light and dark on each to one,
Their magic spilling to the ground.
Pull and push and press and smooth
and pocket — C'est fini!
All gone — the shadows and the sun.
All gone and soon he, too,
Dissolving as I look for words to make him stay.
Monsieur, je ne comprend pas.

Après midi, I float above my bed,
Still weaving words (Rapunzel spinning straw),
Searching for a charm to take me back
To dappled meadow, dappled farmer, dappled day
Where he might place a gift of shadows at my feet.

Amany's results

In her recollection, Amany Saleh, an Egyptian student, examined many psycholinguistic and sociolinguistic aspects of her own learning of English, German, and French. She learned these languages while she was a child and adolescent in Egypt. Amany's complete narrative focused on age and exposure (her most extensive exposure from an early age occurred in English); language learning and teaching strategies; motivation; anxiety, personality, and attitude; and sociocultural factors. At the end she described her learning results and gave instructional implications. Her approach was highly academic, and her recollection looked and sounded like a mini-article for publication in a professional language teaching journal. This was very different from the personal, metaphorical approach taken by Greg and Mary Evelyn. Here we excerpt Amany's ideas about language learning/teaching strategies and motivation.

Language Learning and Teaching Strategies

When I was learning English, French, and German, I was not specifically aware of learning strategies. However, in thinking back, I found that in my English learning process I used every general strategy category given by Oxford [1990b]. I used cognitive strategies such as repeating, translating, recognizing, and using formulas and patterns; memory strategies like semantic mapping, grouping, and representing sounds in memory; social strategies like cooperating with peers and developing cultural understanding; and compensation strategies such as switching to the mother tongue, adjusting the message, and combining words.

In learning French, I used mainly cognitive strategies, with the additional social strategy of asking my mother for help. While learning German, I only used non-communicative memory strategies such as grouping words and semantic mapping.

Quite clearly, the learning strategies I used had a direct effect on my performance in each language. I was much more successful in English than in French or German. This was due in part to the wide range of learning strategies I employed in English and the well-tailored way I applied them to specific language tasks.

I was exposed to many different teaching strategies and teachers over the years. Audiolingualism, with its emphasis on aural-oral drills and lack of emphasis on visual learning, was the most prevalent classroom method for English and French, but it was not the most suitable one for me as a visual learner. In English I could compensate for the lack of visual stimulation with the learning strategy of watching English language movies on TV at home, but there were no such resources available in German and French. My German teacher used the Grammar-Translation Method to achieve his goal, which was to get us to pass the required test. There was no use of truly communicative approaches in any of the three classroom language encounters.

In all three instances, the classrooms were traditional, with the teacher as the main source of information and the absolute authority. (One exception was my first year of French; the teacher used Total Physical Response and role-plays. After the first year, I was not as fortunate in French teachers.) In general, my language teachers did most of the speaking, and the students just repeated or answered questions. In most cases, humor was not permitted or at least not recommended. Perfection in performance was desired (though this was carried to an extreme in French after my first year).

Materials used were only books, but these differed significantly by language. English books were filled with pictures and colored illustrations, while French books had few pictures and they were not colored. German books had no pictures or illustrations. There was no use of audiotapes or videotapes at all. Knowing that I'm a visual learner, I can see why I liked the English books and could not study from the French and German books, in which I could not find pictures with which to associate sounds and could not make semantic maps (which I have recently discovered is my favorite learning strategy). I also discovered that I like the "hands-on" (tactile and kinesthetic) style, which was not provided at all in my classes.

Even though I do not think that the traditional, rigid classroom setting is the ideal place to learn new languages, I have to admit that the classroom has a role in teaching rules and their exceptions and in helping learners conceptualize the language.

Motivation

Motivation is an inner drive or desire to achieve a goal. Gardner [1985] differentiated two kinds of motivation: instrumental and integrative. In learning English, French, and German, my motivation was more instrumental (for completing a language requirement) than integrative (for integrating with the people who spoke the language natively). However, other motivations were also at play.

Ausubel [1968] identified six needs or desires that construct motivation: knowledge, exploration, manipulation, activity, stimulation, and ego enhancement. In my case I believe the first three needs were my motivations for learning English, because I needed the information and wanted to know the unknown and experience the excitement. The need for stimulation was my motive for learning French. I was stimulated by my mother's wish for someone to talk in French with, and I wanted to learn French because it is a sophisticated language. I wanted to learn German for ego enhancement: no one spoke this language around me, and I wanted to be different.

Crookes and Schmidt [1989] named four factors in the so-called internal structure of language learning motivation: (a) interest in the subject, (b) relevance to personal needs, (c) expectancy of success or failure, and (d) perceptions of the value of the outcomes. They also identified three so-called external aspects of motivation: (a) decision to learn the language, (b) persistence over a long period, and (c) high activity level. According to Scarcella and Oxford [1992], if any of these factors is missing or negative, motivation will weaken and success will be short-circuited.

Taking a look back at my language learning processes, I found I was interested and the material was relevant to me at the time in all three experiences. However, in each case the expectancy of success differed, as did the perceived value of the outcomes. In English, my expectancy of success was part of my expectation that I would succeed in every subject I took in school. I also perceived learning English as a very valuable outcome. Therefore, my motivation was very high for learning English. In French I was not only expected to succeed but also to excel; my mother wanted my pronunciation and performance to be perfect, and less than this was not permissible. At first I expected to succeed, but not later on. I did not see a great value in learning French, because I already knew another foreign language (English) fluently. The overbearing pressure to excel combined with the lack of need to learn French resulted in serious anxiety and a decrease in motivation. My failure in French might have made me hesitant and might have shaken my self-confidence, which made learning German difficult and lowered my motivation. No one expected me to succeed in German, not even the teacher. He thought that all students just wanted to get a good grade and would not be interested in the language, so he oversimplified the tests and exaggerated the grades. Again, I did not see the purpose in learning German, another "extra" language.

CONCLUSIONS

Keeping a language learning diary is a way of developing student awareness of strategy use and fostering active, personal attention to strategies. Diaries also help the teacher to understand what the students are doing as they try to learn. The diary study described here uncovered a wide range of important information about ordinary language learners. In particular, it showed that the university language learners used a great number of strategies but stayed within a limited, "safe" strategic range. Any language teacher can use learning diaries to great advantage for heightening both student and teacher understanding of strategy use and other aspects of the learning process. Both students and teacher can benefit from diary information, which potentially leads to greater creative flexibility in learning and teaching.

Through the recollective study described in this chapter, participants gained a significant awareness of their own language learning strategies and overall process. Recollection confirmed the importance of the affective domain in language learning. Participants' recollection allowed them to be more sensitive to their own strategies and feelings.

In this chapter, we interpreted diaries quantitatively and recollection qualitatively. Other kinds of interpretations were possible, but the existing data (emerging partly from the directions given to participants) lent themselves to these particular modes of understanding. Diaries and recollection offer rich pathways into students' minds. These techniques encourage language learners to tell their stories, often for the very first time.

Adina Levine
Bar-Ilan University, Israel
Thea Reves
Bar-Ilan University, Israel
Betty Lou Leaver
American Global Studies Institute, California, USA

CHAPTER 3

RELATIONSHIP BETWEEN LANGUAGE LEARNING STRATEGIES AND ISRAELI VERSUS RUSSIAN CULTURAL-EDUCATIONAL FACTORS

Smotret' drugimi glazami
(To look at someone or something with different eyes)
—Russian idiom

SUMMARY

This chapter indicates that language learning strategies are likely to be related to educational and cultural factors. The study described here compares the learning strategies of immigrants from the former Soviet Union to those of people who have lived in Israel for at least five years. Sharp differences, almost certainly related to education and culture, appeared between the two groups. This chapter offers an intriguing explanation based on a multimethod study.

INTRODUCTION

This chapter primarily concerns the language learning strategies of two sets of people: recent immigrants to Israel from the former Soviet Union on the one hand, and longer term Israeli residents on the other. Close comparison through a multimethod study shows many influences of cultural-educational background. Culture tends to influence the development of overall learning style, and learning style helps to determine specific choices of language learning strategies (Oxford, 1990b). Schmeck sees learning styles as a "predisposition... to adopt a particular learning strategy... used with some cross-situational consistency" (Schmeck, 1983, p. 233). The choice of strategies is also related to a number of additional variables, such as cultural background, educational experiences, attitudes, motivation, language learning goals, career orientation, age, and gender (Dörnyei, 1990; Hansen and Stansfield, 1981; McLaughlin, 1990; O'Malley et al., 1985a; Oxford, 1990a; Politzer and McGroarty,

Levine, A., Reves, T., & Leaver, B. L. (1996). Relationship between language learning strategies and Israeli versus Russian cultural-educational factors. In Rebecca L. Oxford (Ed.), *Language learning strategies around the world: Cross-cultural perspectives*. (Technical Report #13) (pp. 35–45). Honolulu: University of Hawai'i, Second Language Teaching & Curriculum Center.

1985; Rubin, 1981; Schmeck, 1980, 1983; Skehan, 1989). The recent mass immigration from the former Soviet Union to Israel offers an opportunity to compare the learning strategies of students from different educational and cultural backgrounds. The present study, conducted by the first two authors and interpreted with assistance from the last author, aims at describing the learning strategies of new immigrant learners as compared with longer term Israeli residents who have different cultural and educational backgrounds.

The question posed at the outset of the study was: To what extent are language learning strategies related to the learners' educational and cultural background? The underlying hypothesis is that students who had been brought up within a highly structured, uniform educational system developed learning strategies that differed from the strategies of those students who received a less structured, more democratic education. To respond to this question and assess the value of this hypothesis, multiple methods were employed.

METHODOLOGY

SAMPLE

The subjects of the study were 117 students in pre-academic EFL courses at Bar-Ilan University (Israel). Of these, 63 students were new immigrants from the former Soviet Union, and 54 were "old-timers" (living in Israel for over five years) whose native language (Ll) was Russian, Amharic, Spanish, Arabic, Yiddish, or Hebrew. While students at Bar-Ilan University, they studied English with teachers from different language and cultural backgrounds (Russian, American, and Israeli).

INSTRUMENTS

Several instruments were administered anonymously in the students' L1 or "main" language, as indicated in Table 3.1. The first set consisted of questionnaires. An 11-item *Personal Background Questionnaire* gathered information on subjects' L1, knowledge of other languages, educational experience, and length of stay in Israel. The five-item *English Learning Questionnaire* provided information on very general beliefs and behaviors regarding the learning of English. The 21-item *Attitude and Motivation Questionnaire* captured information on goals for learning English, attitudes toward the English language and English-speaking people, and attitudes toward the Hebrew language and Hebrew-speaking people. In the 32-item *Learning Environment Questionnaire*, subjects reported differences they perceived between the country of origin and Israel, with a special focus on the learning environment, instructional processes, teacher-student relationships, classroom atmosphere, teaching materials, and homework assignments.

Table 3.1: Instruments in the Israeli study

Instrument	Group involved	
	Immigrants	Old-timers
Personal Background Questionnaire	X	X
English Learning Questionnaire	X	X
Attitude and Motivation Questionnaire	X	X
Learning Environment Questionnaire	X	X
Self-observation strategy list	X	X
Strategy Inventory for Grammar, Vocabulary, and Reading	X	X
Semi-structured interviews	X	—
Teachers' observations of students' behavior and attitude (profiles of students)	X	X

As shown in Table 3.1, subjects were also asked to create open-ended lists (based on self-observation) of the language learning strategies they most often used in the process of learning grammatical structure and vocabulary and in reading comprehension. Later, they were given a list of 25 possible strategies related to three areas (the *Strategy Inventory for Grammar, Vocabulary, and Reading*) and were asked to check off the strategies they used. In semi-structured interviews, a randomly selected group of immigrants explained their educational experiences both in their country of origin and in Israel.

Finally, as seen in Table 3.1, classroom EFL teachers in the pre-academic courses filled out observation forms related to 15 language learning behaviors. Teachers were asked to draw the learners' profile by rating the following aspects on a four-point scale: class participation; students' requests for translation, examples, paraphrasing, and correction; and noticing fellow students' errors. Data on psychometric quality of the instruments in this study can be obtained from the first two authors.

DATA COLLECTION AND ANALYSIS PROCEDURES

Data were collected on all students in the study, with an emphasis on comparing the two groups, immigrants and old-timers. The data were analyzed with the following statistical procedures: descriptive statistics (means, standard deviations, and frequencies), correlations, t-tests, factor analysis, and regression. The standard significance level of $p<.05$ was chosen for this study. Only statistically significant findings are reported here.

To reduce the 118 variables to a manageable set, factor analysis employing Varimax rotation was performed on three groups of variables: language learning strategies, attitudes and motivation, and learning environment. Stepwise regression analysis was performed on the factors.

RESULTS

QUANTITATIVE RESULTS

Comparisons of means

Descriptive statistics, aided by t-tests to show significant differences, showed contrasts between recent immigrants and old-timers. A learning strategy favored by the immigrants was "carrying out assignments immediately" (immigrants mean=2.61, SD=0.7, old-timers mean=2.29, SD=0.5). Immigrants used more rote memorization strategies than did the old-timers, especially in the area of grammar: "learning rules and examples by heart" (immigrants mean=1.74, SD=0.4, old-timers mean=1.46, SD=0.5). The same was found regarding vocabulary learning strategies like "rote learning and learning lists of translation" (immigrants mean=1.52, SD=0.5, old-timers mean=1.19, SD=0.3).

Old-timers preferred "stimulating work" (old-timers mean=2.14, SD=0.7, immigrants mean=1.84, SD=0.8), "remembering words by their affixes" (old-timers mean=1.80, SD=0.4, immigrants mean=1.62, SD=0.5), and "paraphrasing rules" (old-timers mean=1.39, SD=0.4, immigrants mean=1.06, SD=0.2).

Correlations

Correlation analysis showed a number of interesting relationships between various strategies. Some of the word-learning strategies which required more creativity correlated with communicative types of strategies. For instance, "drawing something for association" correlated with "asking English-speaking people to use the word," r=.47. "Trying to use the word in new sentences" correlated with "listening to people and trying to find the word in their speech," r=.49. More word-bound strategies correlated with reference to the Ll in various ways. "Remembering the word by its morphological structure" correlated with "remembering a similarly sounding or similarly written word in the L1," r=.33.

Similar relationships were found between different kinds of grammar-learning strategies. "Memorizing the examples in which the grammatical form is used" correlated with "trying to compare the grammar structure to the L1," r=.43. "Trying to use the structure even at the risk of making mistakes" correlated with "asking English-speaking people to correct mistakes," r=.38.

Strategy factor analysis

Factor analysis grouped variables from the *Strategy Inventory for Grammar, Vo-cabulary, and Reading*. Loadings ranged from .86 to −.71. Factor 1 contained strategies labeled as "Association with the L1 and Other Languages": associat-ing/remembering (.72), guessing from the sentence (.68), comparing with the L1 (.56), finding similarities in sound and form with the L1 (.40), reading word by word (−.55), and copying several times (−.71). Thus, reading each word and copying were negatively related to the main theme, association.

Factor 2 included strategies collectively called "Learning Languages via Communication": asking for correction (.86), guessing from known words (.74), trying to use in a new context (.73), asking L1 speakers for frequent use (.67), and asking L1 speakers for repetition (.63).

Factor 3 included strategies related to "Using Background Knowledge to Gain New Knowledge": listening for a known word (.73), understanding something from a known structure (.72), guessing from the morphology of a previously learned word (.64), trying to use a word in similar sentences (.52), remembering according to the place in the sentence (.40), rote learning (.40), and repeating rules until they are remembered (−.53). Thus, rote learning and repetition — shallow forms of learning at best — were negatively related to the major thrust of Factor 3.

Attitudes-motivation factor analysis

The factor analysis of attitudes and motivation resulted in five factors. The first was "Atmosphere Conducive to Learning and Using English in Israel," and it contained the following items with loadings as shown: opportunities (.85), culture in Israel (.75), people's involvement (.71), speaking Hebrew (.62), freedom of behavior (.62), and English as the language of the future (.41).

Factor 2 contained items associated with "Importance of English for Success": English for communication (.83), concentrating on English lessons (.79), impor-tance of English in Israel (.74), doing English homework (.55), English as important for professional literacy (.53), English as important for career (.51), and English should be taught everywhere (.43).

"Importance of English for Everyday Life" was the central theme of Factor 3, which contained these items: English for newspapers (.80), English for general information (.77), English for reading (.62), learning English is interesting (.60), and English is beautiful (.49).

Factor 4 was "Attitude to English-Speaking People," and included these items: English as the language of the future (.84), English-speaking people are considerate (.82), English-speaking people are not sociable (.69), and authority is less respected in Israel (.45). Thus, there is a conflict here in that English-speaking people are viewed as simultaneously considerate and unsociable — both with positive weightings on this factor.

In Factor 5, known as "Attitude to the People of Israel," these items are found: people are more honest in Israel than in the home country (.64), arts are more appreciated in Israel than in the home country (.40), better manners are found in the home country (–.58), and life is crude compared to the home country (–.60). As we can see, Israel and its people look very good in terms of attitudes loading on Factor 5.

Environment factor analysis

The next factor analysis concerned perception of the learning environment. The data came from the questionnaire on which comparisons were made between learning in the home country and learning in Israel. Factor 1, labeled "Quality of Instruction," contained these items, with positive loadings referring to Israel and negative ones referring to the home country: material is presented more clearly (.73), less emphasis is given to grammar (.64), teachers know English better (.62), teachers are more creative (.56), teaching is textbook-bound (–.44), there is no difference between teachers (–.48), and there are more vocabulary exercises in books (–.78).

Factor 2, identified as "Nature of Assignments," contained these items, with the same positive and negative country linkages as above (positive toward Israel, negative toward the home country): homework is more creative (.66), homework is more useful (.64), better methods are used (.55), there is less homework (.45), English is given more importance (.44), there is less rote memorization (.43), less creative thinking is required (–.47), textbooks teach less logical thinking (–.57), and verbatim translation is frequent (–.62).

"Language Learning Ambiance," the focus of Factor 3, was loaded with the following items, associated with the two countries in the same way as above: lessons are more interesting (.84), more attention is given to the individual (.73), there is more student participation (.47), love of the language is not emphasized (–.47), content of tests is less emphasized (–.63), and tests are easier (–.66).

Factor 4, "Teacher-Student Relationship," contained these items, following the same negative/positive country contrast as mentioned earlier: distance is smaller (.64), texts discuss everyday life (.64), students who do not ask questions are also considered (.63), most of the work is done in class (.55), students freely express opinions (.52), there is less creative thinking (–.47), and teachers are not trained in English-speaking countries (–.56). Note that the last two do not fit neatly into the teacher-student theme of Factor 4.

Stepwise regression

The purpose of regression is to predict. Stepwise regression analysis used factors from the *Strategy Inventory for Grammar, Vocabulary, and Reading* as the dependent (criterion) variables and factors from the *Learning Environment Questionnaire* and the *Attitude and Motivation Questionnaire* as predictors. The set of learning strategies known as "Learning Languages via Communication" (Factor 2) was significantly predicted, with an R^2 of .36, by these factors: "Importance of English in Everyday Life" (beta=1.06, p<.0001), "Attitude to the People of Israel" (beta=.98, p<.0003), "Teacher-Student Relationships" (beta=−.21, p<.01), and "Atmosphere Conducive to Learning and Using English" (beta=−.38, p<.01). This was the only regression equation that had a meaningfully large R^2, although one other equation showed statistical significance.

QUALITATIVE RESULTS

Self-observed strategies

A random sample of students from both groups, recent immigrants and old-timers, was asked to report on self-observed strategies using an open-ended format. Results of the analysis of these two groups are shown in Table 3.2.

Table 3.2: Qualitative results of strategies for three language areas

Strategies for...	Immigrants	Old-timers
Grammar	rote learning of rules	paraphrasing
	rote learning of sentences with the grammatical structure	use structure in new (own) sentences
	grammar exercises	
Vocabulary	learning word lists by heart	mobilizing association
	requests for tests on memorized word lists	remembering words in collocations
	learning word with translation	
	repetitive writing for automaticity	
Reading	verbatim translation	prediction
		skimming
		application of background knowledge

Most of the immigrants reported learning grammar rules by heart, memorizing sentences containing certain grammatical structures, and doing exercises from a grammar book. Old-timers frequently reported as grammar-learning strategies paraphrasing sentences containing the grammatical structure to be learned and using the structure in sentences of their own.

Self-observed strategies most often reported by the immigrants for vocabulary learning were learning by heart with word lists, asking to be tested on rote-learned word lists, learning a word with its translation, and repeatedly writing words until they became automatic. Old-timers reported such strategies as using associations and trying to remember words in collocations (combinations that often occur together).

Thus, the strategies used by immigrants were more rigid, more concentrated on rote-learning and shallow processing, and less creative. The strategies of old-timers were more flexible, more centered on association and deep processing, and more creative.

Interview results

The information gained from the interviews conducted with a random sample of students from the immigrant group shed light on the students' self-perceived strategies in two different educational contexts. In addition, it complemented the findings of the quantitative data. Characteristically, the immigrants brought from their home country the feeling that they had to work harder to prove themselves. It was important for them to achieve high grades, and they all planned a university-level education. Some immigrants felt that their ambition was more justified than that of their "old-timer" counterparts, since in their new rootless situation a university degree might be the only advantage available for newcomers. They thought that while in their home country being a university student was in many cases a matter of prestige, in Israel a university degree had instrumental value.

With regard to the differences in the two educational systems (curricula, teachers, materials, testing, teacher-pupil relationship), a number of interesting interview-based observations were reported. Referring to their original country, immigrants emphasized the highly formal and impersonal character of instruction, with teachers following pre-set programs and pupils responding only when directly addressed. They reported an almost total lack of student-initiated classroom discussions. Assignments were carried out to the letter, with no interpretation either asked for or volunteered; in fact, the closer the answer was to the printed text, the higher it was valued. Mechanical recall of material was more appreciated than creative thinking, so the students were prone to memorize information verbatim. These student reports correspond highly with observed teacher behaviors of Russian teachers of EFL in Moscow (Garza, 1987), teachers of Russian as a second language in Moscow, and teachers of Russian as a foreign language in the US (Leaver and Flank, 1987).

Immigrants also reported tests as different in their country of origin, both in content and administration. Students proved their ability to reproduce the course material instead of demonstrating breadth and depth of comprehension of the issues involved. Most of the tests were formal oral tests, with open-ended questions, the answers to which could be learned by heart. This may have been the reason for their preference for open-ended questions in Israeli classrooms, since this type of question gives them a greater chance for manipulating the tester. They reported a dislike of multiple-choice questions, the reason for which may be two-fold: first, the novelty of the technique; and second, the fear of being confronted with the need to make a choice. This may be seen as another evidence of ingrained dependence on prescription.

Profiles of behavior

The teacher-created student profiles indicated passive behavior on the part of immigrants in the classroom. These students rarely requested interpretation of the material; they did, however, request translation and orally repeated or wrote down the corrected form. The old-timers, on the other hand, actively participated in discussions, often requested paraphrasing, and very seldom asked for corrections. The differences noted in class participation confirmed the information gathered in the interviews about the overall passivity which characterized the classroom in their home country.

The subjects' behavior profiles obtained from the teachers with different backgrounds emphasized differences in teacher-student relationships. Relationships were more formal and distant in the case of former-Soviet immigrant students taught by Russian teachers, a point also made by interviewed students. This kind of teacher-student relationship may have been habit carried over from teachers' and students' previous experience.

DISCUSSION

The results of the quantitative and qualitative data confirm our initial hypothesis about the relationship between learning strategies and students' cultural-educational background. Immigrant students tended to show a preference for such traditional strategies as memorizing grammar rules, rote learning, repeatedly writing down words, using lists of words in translation, doing grammar exercises from a textbook or workbook, and translating verbatim into the native language. On the other hand, old-timers tended towards more communicative approaches, using strategies such as asking native speakers for frequent use of relevant vocabulary and taking risks in the use of new structures and words.

The differences between the strategies used by the two groups may be explained by learning habits inculcated by the two different instructional systems: a strictly centralized, formal, and highly prescriptive system on the one hand, and a more autonomous, free, thought-provoking one, on the other. Immigrant students expressed their fascination with a classroom atmosphere conducive to creative language learning. They were all in favor of student-initiated discussions and of informal teacher-student relationships. Nevertheless, their actual behavior in their new learning context was characterized by the habits carried over from their previous learning environment, such as avoiding participation in classroom discussions, refraining from volunteering answers unless directly addressed, and keeping to the printed text.

In comparing the content and form of instruction between their home country and Israel, immigrants expressed their appreciation of the higher quality of instruction, the challenge of the materials, and the variety of teaching methods used in Israel. The assignments given in their country of origin required mechanical memorization of the printed word, rather than individual interpretation, initiative, and inferencing.

This explains the difficulties these immigrants confront when the assignment in their new environment asks for initiative and creative thinking. The problems these students face can be ascribed to the serious departure of the Israeli classroom from the typical classroom in the system in which they were brought up, the latter classrooms often precluding the development of learning strategies necessary for creative thinking and independent learning.

As mentioned above, the teacher-student relationship in the subjects' home country was reported as distant and formal. This ingrained "teacher equals authority" image presumably imposes an a priori constraint on the new immigrant students' classroom behavior. In spite of the formal teacher-student relationship in classes taught by teachers of Russian origin, immigrants reported feeling safer in these classes, probably because the Russian teachers' traditional teaching methods were familiar to them.

The attitudes of both groups toward English strongly motivated them in their choice of language learning strategies. In the case of immigrants, their preference for the strategy of using association with other languages can be interpreted as an ambition on the part of highly motivated students. They showed readiness to resort to any available source of knowledge; reliance on their Ll as well as their knowledge of other languages provided them with a feeling of security.

The same strategy, learning with the help of association with Ll and other languages, was also strongly predicted by their instrumental motivation for immediate and future practical use of the language. Their strong achievement orientation and their ambition for a university education was given high priority in the home country's value system.

The strategy of using background knowledge to gain new knowledge was more often used by the old-timers. This suggests that a stimulating, learning-conducive atmosphere might till the soil for activating the proper schemata.

CONCLUSIONS

The findings of this study highlight the important role of cultural-educational factors in the development of language learning strategies. They thus confirm the hypothesis that learners studying in a highly structured and uniform educational system would develop learning strategies reflecting that system. Language learners who have recently immigrated from the old Soviet regime prefer formal, structured learning and mechanical memorization of printed material. Their classroom behavior is characterized by obedience to the teacher's authority and a concomitant lack of expression of opinions, initiative, and class participation. However, they display high instrumental motivation as well as strong achievement orientation. Most of them are diligent students, seeking a university education which they no longer see as a status symbol but as a necessity for their future. The great importance they place on achieving high grades is a legacy they carried over from their inherited value system.

Yet the immigrants showed an amazing capacity to adjust to their new surroundings. When they found themselves in a stimulating atmosphere and when they were exposed to a variety of modern instructional methods, they showed the first signs of resorting to more resourceful learning strategies.

David A. Bedell
University of Bridgeport, Connecticut, USA
Rebecca L. Oxford
University of Alabama, USA

CHAPTER 4

CROSS-CULTURAL COMPARISONS OF LANGUAGE LEARNING STRATEGIES IN THE PEOPLE'S REPUBLIC OF CHINA AND OTHER COUNTRIES

A journey of a thousand li begins with a single step.
—Chinese proverb

SUMMARY

The theme of this chapter is that ethnicity or culture directly influences the choice of language learning strategies. Highlighted are 14 existing studies that use a single strategy classification system and measure (the *Strategy Inventory for Language Learning*). Parallel information is also given about 22 other studies that use different strategy systems and measures. A new study of cultural variation in strategy selection in the People's Republic of China is also explained in detail.

INTRODUCTION

Among the many factors which might influence a language learner's choice of strategies is the learner's culture or ethnicity (Hess and Azuma, 1991; Hofstede, 1986; Kachru, 1988; Oxford, 1989b, 1989c, 1990b; Oxford, Hollaway, and Horton-Murillo, 1992; Oxford and Nyikos, 1989; Reid, 1995; Rossi-Le, 1989). This chapter has two major purposes: (1) to summarize studies on cross-cultural differences in learning strategy use; and (2) to describe a new culture-related learning strategy investigation. In this chapter, the following definitions hold. As defined by Brown (1980), culture refers to the "ideas, customs, skills, arts, and tools which characterize a group of people in a given period of time" (p. 123). Culture includes how and why one thinks, learns, worships, fights, and relaxes. It pervades all human life from the cradle to the grave. Language interacts closely with culture; one's native language is both a reflection of and an influence on one's culture. Another important concept is *ethnicity*. Unlike *race*, which is supposed to refer to physical traits or biological characteristics (but which takes on many more meanings in practice), ethnicity is related to cultural characteristics. People in a given ethnic group — like the mainland Chinese, the Japanese, or the middle class in the US —

Bedell, D., & Oxford, R. L. (1996). Cross-cultural comparisons of language learning strategies in the People's Republic of China and other countries. In Rebecca L. Oxford (Ed.), *Language learning strategies around the world: Cross-cultural perspectives*. (Technical Report #13) (pp. 47–60). Honolulu: University of Hawai'i, Second Language Teaching & Curriculum Center.

are bound together by a common culture. Thus, it is often legitimate to use the term ethnicity as an equivalent of culture.

RESEARCH REVIEW ON CROSS-CULTURAL STUDIES OF LEARNING STRATEGY USE

EXAMPLES OF CULTURAL INFLUENCE ON LEARNING STRATEGIES

Empirical studies have shown additional influences of culture or ethnicity on learning strategies. Asians, compared with Hispanics, responded less positively to strategy instruction (Russo and Stewner-Manzanares, 1985a, 1985b). Sutter (1987) discovered that if strategies being taught were opposed to learners' cultural backgrounds, disaster resulted; Sutter found it necessary to "camouflage" certain new strategies under the guise of old, culturally accepted ones. Politzer (undated) and Oxford and Nyikos (1989) learned that language learning motivations, often conditioned by culture, were influential in strategy choice.

ASIAN STUDENTS' STRATEGIES AS AN ILLUSTRATION OF CULTURAL INFLUENCES

Scarcella (1990) notes that many Asian cultures view the book as containing all knowledge and wisdom. Memorization of the book word-for-word is therefore seen as the best way to gain knowledge in such cultures, according to Scarcella. Empirical studies of learning strategies show that memorization is a strongly preferred strategy among Asian students (Politzer, undated; Politzer and McGroarty, 1985; Tyacke and Mendelsohn, 1986). Memorization is popular not only in Asian cultures but also in many Arabic cultures (see Farquharson, 1989). Kachru (1988) suggests that many Chinese people dislike learning strategies that involve theoretical models and prefer dealing with strategies that handle practical questions, because the Chinese language lacks implicational statements that allow people to discuss ideas contrary to fact. (However, we believe that the preference for practical strategies might have little to do with a grammatical deficit in the Chinese language. Moreover, there is evidence that traditional Chinese culture is full of theoretical models such as the Five Elements, though these were not developed through Western-style hypotheses and experiments.) Chen (1990) asserts that Chinese students are strongly motivated to learn but not interested in taking risks or in using strategies for divergent thinking; they tend to believe that only one correct answer is possible.

REVIEW OF 36 STRATEGY STUDIES

A wide variety of cultural backgrounds have been represented in the research, involving EFL and ESL learners from many countries. *EFL learners* are learning English in their native (non-English speaking) country or region, and *ESL learners* are learning English in an English-speaking environment such as the US or the UK. Among the 36 studies described in this review, 14 used a strategy classification based on the *Strategy Inventory for Language Learning* (*SILL*, Oxford, 1990c), and 22 did not.

SILL studies of EFL/ESL strategies in different cultures

First we review the *SILL* studies. The *SILL*, most fully described in an article by Oxford and Burry-Stock (1995) and earlier described by Oxford (1986a, 1990b, 1992), has internal consistency reliability in the .90s, strong predictive validity with relation to language performance, and concurrent validity as evidenced through correlations with language performance, learning style, and setting characteristics. In addition, the *SILL* shows rather consistent differences between males and females in some settings (Oxford and Burry-Stock, 1995).

Twelve of the 14 *SILL* studies have already been reviewed in greater detail (Oxford, 1992). Two others are added by Bedell: a further study of Puerto Ricans (Green and Oxford, 1993) and a study of Chinese in the US (S-J. Chang, 1990). Most of these used the 50-item *SILL*, Version 7.0, either in the original English or in translation. In some cases the instrument was adapted to the researcher's purpose, with the original content modified to a greater (Noguchi, 1991; Wen and Johnson, 1991) or lesser (Yang, 1993a, 1993b) extent. In these cases, findings for some of the strategies can still be compared.

Following are summaries of these 14 studies. Oxford's (1990b) taxonomy is used below, where possible, to classify strategies. It consists of six major groups of strategies: memory, cognitive, compensation, metacognitive, affective, and social.

Hispanic (Puerto Rican). Green (1991) used the *SILL* 7.0 with 213 students of English at the University of Puerto Rico at Mayaguez. They showed high use of metacognitive strategies and medium use of social, cognitive, compensation, affective, and memory strategies. Higher proficient students (as measured by the *English as a Second Language Achievement Test*) used more strategies overall than lower proficient students, but mid-proficient students used more strategies than either high or low proficient students, thus creating a curvilinear pattern. Females more often than males used strategies, especially metacognitive and social.

Green and Oxford (1993) used the *SILL* 7.0 with 374 students at the same university. They found that proficiency level had a significant influence on strategy use, with higher proficient students using strategies more often than lower proficiency students in general. The curvilinear pattern of proficiency with strategy use did not continue with a larger sample. Females more frequently used strategies than males in several categories.

Arabic (Egyptian). Touba (1992) used an Arabic translation of the *SILL* 7.0 with over 500 Egyptian university students majoring in a course of preparation to become English teachers. They showed high use of metacognitive and memory strategies and low use of cognitive strategies.

Asian (mixed). Oxford, Talbott, and Halleck (1990) used the *SILL* 7.0 with 43 ESL students at Pennsylvania State University in the US. Although the sample included Asians (Japanese, Chinese, Korean, Thai, and Vietnamese) and non-Asians (Qatari, Turkish, Venezuelan, and Spanish), most were from Japan. The sample showed high use of social, metacognitive, cognitive, and compensation strategies and medium use of affective and memory strategies.

Phillips (1990, 1991) used the *SILL* 7.0 with 141 Asians (Japanese, Chinese, Korean, Indonesian, and Thai) studying ESL at seven universities in the US. Students showed high use of metacognitive, social, and compensation strategies, and medium use of cognitive, affective, and memory strategies. These results were similar to Oxford et al. (1990). Proficiency as measured by the *Test of English as a Foreign Language* (*TOEFL*) showed no correlation to the strategy categories, but it did correlate with a number of individual strategy items. As in Green (1991), mid-proficient students used more strategies overall than did either high or low proficient students. Academic major and nationality were significant influences on strategy choice, although gender was not.

Thai. Mullins (1992) used the *SILL* 7.0 with 110 English majors at Chulalongkorn University, Thailand. Students showed high or near-high use of compensation, cognitive, and metacognitive strategies, and medium use of social, affective, and memory strategies. None of the three proficiency measures correlated significantly with the overall *SILL* score, but they did correlate with certain strategy categories. For example, the university entrance examination showed a negative correlation with affective strategies, while grade point average and a placement test correlated with compensation strategies, and GPA correlated with metacognitive strategies.

Indonesian. Davis and Abas (1991) used the *SILL* 7.0 with 64 language faculty at four tertiary institutions in Indonesia. This group of language specialists showed high use of metacognitive, social, compensation, cognitive, and memory strategies and medium use of affective strategies.

Japanese. Watanabe (1990, 1991) used a Japanese translation of the *SILL* 7.0 with 315 first- and second-year English majors at a rural women's college and a prestigious coeducational urban university in Japan. Instead of examining scores for the six parts of the *SILL*, Watanabe used a factor analysis procedure to extract five strategy factors for each school. For the rural college these were communicative, compensation-guessing, socioaffective, formal learning, and memory-mental operational strategies. For the urban university the five factors were communicative, general study-cognitive (actually more akin to Oxford's metacognitive), general study-affective, memory, and compensation-guessing strategies. The rural college students showed medium use of compensation-guessing, formal learning, memory-mental operational, and socioaffective strategies and low use of communicative strategies. The urban university students showed high use of compensation and general study-affective strategies and medium use of communicative, memory, and general study-cognitive strategies. Proficiency (self-rated) among the rural college students showed positive correlations with all factors except socioaffective. First-year students used more general study-affective strategies than second-year students. Females at the university used more communicative strategies than males.

Noguchi (1991) used a SILL-based, Japanese-language *Questionnaire for Learners* with 174 junior high school students in their third year of English study in Japan. Most frequent strategies involved reading or writing new words repeatedly and using a dictionary. Least frequent were using actions, pictures, or objects to learn words and learning groups of related words. Social strategies were not popular. In practicing words, students preferred written to spoken modes in both input and output. In general, females used more strategies than males.

Korean. Oh (1992) used a Korean translation of the SILL 7.0 with 59 students at the National Fisheries University of Pusan, South Korea. They showed high use of metacognitive strategies, medium use of compensation, affective, social, and cognitive strategies, and low-to-medium use of memory strategies. Oh recommended research into the facilitative effects of strategies within a cultural context.

Chinese (mixed). S-J. Chang (1990) used a version of the SILL with mainland (PRC) and Taiwanese (ROC) students at the University of Georgia. They showed highest use of compensation strategies and lowest use of affective strategies. Three measures of proficiency showed different effects on strategy use; students who rated themselves above average in proficiency used more strategies overall than those who rated themselves below average. Neither the TOEFL scores nor the *Ilyin Oral Interview* scores significantly affected overall strategy use, but students with high scores in the oral interview used more social strategies than those with low scores. Humanities and social science majors used more strategies than science majors. Neither gender nor length of stay in the US significantly affected overall strategy use.

Chinese (Mainland). Wen and Johnson (1991) used a SILL-based questionnaire with 242 sophomore English majors at seven tertiary institutions in Nanjing and Shanghai, China. Although the questionnaire was partially based on the SILL, the selection and phrasing of items was altered to fit the Chinese context. Wen and Johnson created their own six strategy categories: management, traditional, nontraditional (communicative), mother-tongue-avoidance, vocabulary, and tolerating-ambiguity (guessing) strategies. Analysis of the published data reveals high use of tolerating-ambiguity and mother-tongue-avoidance strategies, with medium use of the other four categories. English achievement (as measured by the national *Graded Test for English Majors, GEM4*) was directly influenced by vocabulary and mother-tongue avoidance strategies and was negatively affected by tolerating-ambiguity strategies.

Chinese (Taiwanese). Yang (1993a, 1993b) used a Chinese translation of the SILL 7.0 with 505 undergraduates, mostly first-year, at six universities in Taiwan. Students showed medium use of all six SILL categories, with compensation strategies highest, followed by affective, metacognitive, social, cognitive, and memory strategies. Instead of examining these categories in detail, however, Yang used a factor analysis to extract six strategy factors: functional practice, cognitive-memory, metacognitive (akin to Oxford's metacognitive and affective categories), formal oral-practice, social, and compensation strategies. According to these factors, students showed high use of formal oral-practice strategies; medium use of compensation, social, and metacognitive strategies; and low-to-medium use of functional practice and cognitive-memory strategies. Females used more social strategies than males.

Mixed (mostly Asian and Hispanic). Rossi-Le (1989) used the *SILL* 6.0 (almost the same as 7.0) with 147 immigrant ESL students at two US community colleges. The majority were Asian or Hispanic. Most of the Asians came from three main countries (China, Laos, and Vietnam), and the Hispanics came from a variety of locations. Others in the sample were from Eritrea, Haiti, Brazil, Cambodia, Morocco, Japan, Poland, Thailand, Korea, and Czechoslovakia. Rossi-Le applied Oxford's earlier factor structure using ten factors: social, authentic language use, visualization, formal rule-related practice, self-management, memory, affective, general study, searching for and communicating meaning, and independent study strategies. Chinese speakers showed high use in eight out of the ten factors, while Hispanics scored high in seven, Vietnamese in six, and Laotians in only three. Rossi-Le also used the *Perceptual Learning Style Preference Questionnaire* (Reid, 1987) to identify sensory preferences and group versus individual study orientations. As in Hansen (1984) and Reid (1987), style preference was found to be significantly influenced by the home culture. Proficiency also influenced strategy choice: high proficient learners used more self-management and formal rule-based strategies than low proficient learners.

Non-*SILL* studies of ESL/EFL strategies in different cultures

Below are descriptions of 22 non-*SILL* studies. These, like the *SILL* studies, are grouped according to home culture or ethnicity.

Hispanic (mixed). Corrales and Call (1989) investigated communication strategies among 17 Hispanic university ESL students in the US. They found different behavior at two levels of proficiency, with communication strategies decreasing among advanced learners. In this study, communication strategies were defined as strategies to make up for missing knowledge (such as reverting back to Spanish and coining new words), so it is not surprising that these strategies would diminish with higher proficiency.

O'Malley, Chamot, and Küpper (1989) conducted think-aloud interviews to identify the learning strategies of 11 Hispanic high school students. These researchers found that effective listeners used top-down strategies (listening for phrases or sentences), while ineffective listeners used bottom-up strategies (listening for individual words). Effective listeners, compared with their less successful colleagues, were better at self-monitoring, elaborating, and inferencing strategies.

Arabic (Saudi). Al-Braik (1986) found that learning strategies were one of four attributes (along with cognitive factors, attitudes and motivation, and personality
type) associated with successful learning among 176 Saudi students.

Arabic (Egyptian). Aliweh (1989) used videotaped observation of communication
strategies of 30 Egyptian English majors. Before strategy training, the students
used a limited range of these strategies. After strategy training, the students
used a slightly wider variety of strategies.

Arabic (Sudanese). A study by Ahmed (1988) of 300 Sudanese students of many
ages used course notebooks, self-report, observations, and interviews to assess
vocabulary learning strategies. Fifty strategies were identified, the most common of which were taking notes in the book margin and asking classmates for
information. Ahmed found different stages of strategy development. Strategy
choice was also related to the extent and length of English experience and to
institutional exam procedures.

Nigerian. Adegbija (1990) used open-ended surveys, interviews, and observations to
assess the strategies of 35 senior university English majors. Most frequent strategies were reading extensively, mixing with fluent speakers, listening to English
(radio, TV, debates, symposia), and referring constantly to the dictionary.
Metacognitive strategies and strategies for writing were rarely reported; teachers, not students, were viewed as "in charge" of such areas.

Nepalese. Red (1989) used an oral questionnaire to elicit reading and studying
strategies of 55 Nepalese university students and conducted think-alouds and
interviews with 12 of these students. Frequent strategies were making notes and
summaries, recopying notes, and memorizing texts. Textbooks were seen as too
valuable to write notes in, as compared with the Sudanese practice of taking
notes in book margins.

Thai. Syananondh (1983) studied the listening comprehension strategies of 212
Thai graduate students in the US. Common strategies were watching TV, talking with native speakers, and listening to lectures.
Wangsotorn et al. (1986) examined strategy use among 97 beginning English
students in the seventh grade. There was no statistically significant relationship
between strategy use and proficiency and achievement tests at that stage. However, students who learned through visual strategies or a combination of visual
and auditory strategies had higher achievement scores than those who learned
with only auditory strategies.

Vietnamese. Tran (1988) investigated older learners (40–92 years old) who were
Vietnamese refugees in the US. For both males and females, a common strategy
was listening to TV or radio, while few sought English tutors or lived in
English-speaking neighborhoods. All strategies were more common among men
than among women.

Japanese. Pearson (1988) found that social strategies were typical of good language learners among 12 Japanese businessmen and engineers working in Singapore and Malaysia. It is difficult, however, to separate the effects of strategy use from the effects of integrative motivation in these learners. Also, the learning took place in informal settings, unlike those involved in all the other studies.

Chinese (Mainland). Huang (1984) and Huang and van Naerssen (1987) documented strategy use by 60 graduating English majors. Results showed that functional practice strategies were linked to oral proficiency. Many students often used memorizing, keeping vocabulary lists, and listening to radio in English.
Dai (1989) used a think-aloud reading task to record metacognitive strategies of 60 Chinese graduate students at three US universities. Dai found significant differences between those who had majored in English and those who had majored in engineering.
Using a word-and-concept identification task, Chen (1990) recorded communication strategies of 12 Chinese students majoring in English. Type, frequency, and effectiveness of strategies varied by proficiency level.

Chinese (Taiwanese). Shih Lo (1990) used a *Reading Strategy Survey* with 237 EFL college students in Taiwan and provided strategy training. Though strategy training had a significant effect on strategy use, it did not significantly influence reading comprehension or conceptual ability.

Chinese (Singapore). A.S.C. Chang (1989, 1990) conducted two studies using Biggs' *Learning Process Questionnaire* to investigate motives and strategies in various subjects among secondary students in Singapore. The first study involved 495 students and the second 1,165 (608 for English). Among strategies popularly used for learning English were checking answers carefully, using English often, drilling and practicing, and underlining or highlighting key words. Infrequently used strategies were writing summaries and holding group discussions. Significant differences in strategy use were found for students in different tracks.

Mixed (Asian and Hispanic). In the study by O'Malley et al. (1985a, 1985b), interviews were conducted with five Vietnamese and 65 Hispanics (from Central and South America and Puerto Rico) in US high schools. Students at the beginning level reported more strategies than those at the intermediate level. There was no attempt to explain strategy differences between the two ethnic groups, though Hispanics were reported as using transfer strategies.
Politzer and McGroarty (1985) administered a strategy survey to 19 Hispanic and 18 Asian (mostly Japanese) graduate students in the US. Of these two groups, although the Asians used fewer so-called "good learner" strategies (such as social strategies), Asians showed significantly greater language progress over the course of the study. Asians were mostly engineers, while Hispanics majored mostly in humanities and social sciences, so effects of culture and academic major were difficult to separate.

McGroarty (1989) studied 62 Chinese, 37 Japanese, and 58 Hispanic adult learners of English. She confirmed significantly greater strategy use among Hispanic subjects.

Mixed (Japanese and American). Tinkham (1989) compared 89 Japanese and 47 American high school sophomores and found that the former used more rote memorization strategies and performed better on recognition and recall tasks.

Mixed. Kim (1990) used a *Perceptual Learning Strategy Questionnaire* with 180 ESL students from many different ethnic backgrounds in a US university. Kim found that the native language (possibly reflecting the culture) was the most significant predictor of differences in strategy use.

With this background of cross-cultural studies of language learning strategies, we now turn to the first author's recent study in the People's Republic of China.

NEW CULTURAL STUDY OF STRATEGY USE

SAMPLE

In Bedell's (1993) study, the subjects were 353 students taking English classes at six secondary- and tertiary-level institutions in three cities (Guiyang, Guizhou Province; Xiangtan, Hunan Province; and Beijing) of the People's Republic of China. There were 238 university English majors (of whom 73 were first-year, 111 second-year, 54 third-year, and 1 fourth-year). These represented 67% of the total. In addition, the sample included 23 junior-college English majors, 34 short-term students, 33 engineering majors, 23 secondary school students, and one secondary school teacher. Thus, the sample was heavily loaded toward English majors but included others as well. Subjects ranged in age from 16 to 39 (mean age 20, median 19) and included 220 females and 123 males, plus 10 who did not identify their sex.

INSTRUMENTS

A Chinese translation of the 80-item *Strategy Inventory for Language Learning* (Version 5.1) was prepared for this study. This version is ordinarily used for native English speakers learning foreign languages, but it was chosen for this study because its length provided more data than the shorter Version 7.0 for learners of ESL and EFL. In this study, Cronbach's alpha for internal reliability was .94, comparing quite favorably to other studies using versions of the *SILL*. Validity of the *SILL* (predictive, concurrent, content, and construct) is detailed in Oxford and Burry-Stock (1995). Accompanying the *SILL* was a Chinese-language *Background Questionnaire* whose purpose was to identify the learners' age, gender, major, years of English study, estimated (self-rated) proficiency, degree and type of motivation, and other factors that might influence strategy use.

DATA COLLECTION AND DATA ANALYSIS PROCEDURES

Data collection occurred under conditions of anonymity. Data analysis involved descriptive statistics, factor analysis, analysis of variance, and a reliability assessment using Cronbach alpha (for internal consistency).

RESULTS AND COMPARISONS WITH OTHER STUDIES

Descriptive statistics

The overall *SILL* mean was 3.19, with a standard deviation of .47. This signifies that overall use of strategies was in the medium (2.5–3.5) range, not high (3.5+) or low (less than 2.5). Compensation strategies as a group were used in the high range (mean=3.6), but all the other five groups were used in the medium range, with means of 3.0 to 3.3.

Some individual strategies were used at a high rate (23 items, or 29% of the total number), while most (47 items, 59%) were used at a medium rate, and a few (10, 12%) were used infrequently.

Some of the high frequency items among the Chinese subjects, such as circumlocution ("talking around" a word), asking the speaker to slow down, concentrating on the speaker, and finding out how to improve language learning, are apparently common to many learners, both Asian and Hispanic, according to comparisons with other studies.

Likewise, the generally less-used items among the Chinese subjects, such as writing feelings in a learning diary, acting out new words, making summaries, writing notes and letters, using flashcards, and putting words into groups, are also generally less used in other cultures, according to previous research (Green and Oxford, 1993; Oxford, Talbott, and Halleck, 1990; Phillips, 1990; Noguchi, 1991; Wen and Johnson, 1991; Yang, 1993a).

Guessing meanings is common among Chinese learners, both mainland and Taiwanese (Yang, 1993a), but less common among Puerto Ricans (Green and Oxford, 1993), so it might be a culturally-influenced strategy. Perhaps surprisingly, mainland Chinese are more likely to discuss feelings about language learning than are Puerto Ricans. Chinese are less likely to ask an English speaker for help, but this is probably due to the relative scarcity of English speakers in China and Taiwan compared with Puerto Rico. Mainland Chinese reported frequent reviewing more than did ESL students in the mixed-culture study by Oxford, Talbott, and Halleck (1990).

Some contrasts emerge between the strategies of our Chinese subjects on the mainland and other Chinese speakers in Taiwan (Wen and Johnson, 1991; Yang, 1993a). Taiwanese were more likely to practice the sounds of English, while our mainlanders were more likely to read English for pleasure. Does this reflect an emphasis on English pronunciation in Taiwan? Is reading (in English or Chinese) a more popular pastime among mainland students than Taiwanese, perhaps because the latter have more distractions available to them? These questions deserve additional investigation.

Analysis of variance

An analysis of variance showed that the six-part *SILL* classification did not significantly account for the variance in the means of the 80 items ($F=1.69$, $df=5$, $p<.15$). The six-part classification, while useful (especially for making sense of results across many studies), was not totally sufficient. The six-part grouping was therefore supplemented by a factor analysis.

Factor analysis

The factor analysis, using Varimax rotation with only the .30 or higher loadings retained, produced nine empirically coherent factors that account for 41% of the variance in the strategy results. Several items loaded on more than one factor. One important lesson from this study is the value of factor analysis in describing the real dynamics of the data. Factor analysis sometimes provides more meaningful information than a priori groupings. Factors included:

1. *Functional Practice-Productive Strategies*. This factor consists of items related primarily to speaking, but also to writing and thinking in English. Variance explained=18.8%.

2. *Metacognitive Strategies*. This factor is similar in content and concept to the strategies in *SILL* Part D. Variance explained=3.8%.

3. *Compensation Strategies*. This factor is very similar to *SILL* Part C. Variance explained=3.5%.

4. *Functional Practice-Receptive Strategies*. This is made up mainly of strategies from *SILL* Part B (cognitive) related to listening and reading. Variance explained=3.3%.

5. *Review and Repetition Strategies*. The seven items all concern review, repetition, or routine. Variance explained=2.6%.

6. *Memory-Vocabulary Strategies*. The memory strategies in *SILL* Part A are divisible into those for learning new words and those for reviewing new material. Factor 6 is composed strictly of those strategies for learning new words. Variance explained=2.6%.

7. *Formal Practice and Affective Strategies*. This cluster is not so easily defined, but might be viewed as strategies for the learner who needs a structured schedule and affective self-support. Variance explained=2.4%.

8. *Social and Error-Correction Strategies*. This factor is composed of items from *SILL* Parts D and F. Social strategies predominate, but there are items from

both parts which relate to seeking correction from others and learning from one's errors. Variance explained=2.1%.

9. *Cognitive-Analytic Strategies.* The last factor consists of items referring to mental processes for analyzing and assimilating new information. Variance explained=2.0%.

To compare the factors with each other, a frequency "factor mean" similar to that used by Watanabe (1990, 1991) and Yang (1993a) was computed. For this calculation, the items with loadings greater than .30 in each factor were taken as equal constituents of that factor (though, in reality, items with higher loadings contribute more). The means of these items were then averaged to yield a factor mean. This value is equivalent to the factor means used by Watanabe and Yang, except that in this study items may be included in more than one factor, whereas in the earlier studies the factors were treated as mutually exclusive categories. The factor means in the current study were as follows: eight medium-frequency factors (Factor 3=3.49, Factor 4=3.48, Factor 5=3.34, Factor 2=3.31, Factor 8=3.29, Factor 1=3.14, Factor 9=3.14, Factor 6=2.86); and one low frequency factor (Factor 7=2.40). Thus, compensation strategies rank highest, while formal practice-affective strategies are at the bottom.

DISCUSSION OF COMPARISONS WITH OTHER *SILL* STUDIES

Let us now look at how these results compare against frequency ratings and rankings of strategy use in other *SILL* studies. The following comparisons and generalizations are intended to stimulate discussion but should be treated as tentative. Compensation strategies were the highest ranking category not only among the subjects in the present study but also among Chinese students studying in the US (S-J.Chang, 1990) and in Taiwan (Yang, 1993a). Furthermore, the subjects in Wen and Johnson's (1991) mainland study showed high use of tolerance for ambiguity strategies such as guessing, which are of course part of compensation strategies. Compensation or guessing strategies also ranked highest among both sets of Japanese subjects in Watanabe (1990) and among the Thai subjects in Mullins (1992); they ranked second in the Korean study (Oh, 1992). Phillips' (1990, 1991) and Oxford et al.'s (1990) mixed-Asian ESL studies showed high use of compensation strategies, though not as high as other categories. In contrast, the Puerto Rican and Egyptian studies reported only moderate use of compensation strategies. The high use of compensation strategies might be typical of Asian students.

Memory strategies were ranked lowest or second-lowest in the current study (depending on whether we are discussing a priori category scores or factor means). This was often the case in other studies, also: among Chinese students in Yang (1993a, 1993b), Koreans in Oh (1992), Indonesians in Davis and Abas (1991), mixed-Asian students in Phillips (1990, 1991) and Oxford et al. (1990), and Puerto Ricans in Green (1991). On the other hand, these strategies were ranked relatively highly by Egyptians in Touba (1992). Under somewhat different classification systems, memory strategies for vocabulary were ranked at medium use by the

Japanese in Wen and Johnson (1991), and memory-mental processing strategies were ranked at medium use by the Japanese in Watanabe (1990, 1991).

Metacognitive or management strategies were used moderately often by Chinese students in this study and other investigations (Wen and Johnson, 1991; Yang, 1993a, 1993b), but not as often among Puerto Rican, Egyptian, Indonesian, and Korean subjects. Affective strategies were generally little used, and they were ranked lowest in S-J. Chang (1990). However, they were moderately ranked by both sets of Taiwanese learners in Yang (1993a, 1993b).

Some studies have found social strategies to be generally unpopular among Chinese and Japanese subjects (Politzer and McGroarty, 1985; Noguchi, 1991). This held true in the current study. However, some other studies of Asians have shown that social strategies are widely used. Yang (1993a) found social strategies more popular in Taiwan, especially among students in an intensive program who had plenty of communicative stimulation (1992b). The Asians in Phillips (1990, 1991) and Oxford et al. (1990) also rated social strategies quite highly, likely because they were in the US and needed to use these strategies to survive.

Functional practice strategies were a category emerging from the present factor analysis as well as from Yang's (1993a, 1993b). Watanabe's (1990, 1991) communicative strategies and Wen and Johnson's (1991) nontraditional strategies also shared many of the elements of functional practice. All of these studies ranked functional practice strategies at or near the bottom in terms of frequency of use.

In the present study, however, functional practice strategies were divided between two factors: productive (writing and speaking) and receptive (reading and listening). Of these, the receptive functional strategies appeared quite popular in the current study and the productive functional strategies did not. This might be an important distinction to make, because strategies which involve listening and reading for meaning do not entail the same risk of embarrassment that accompanies functional speaking or writing.

In sum, high use of compensation and receptive functional strategies was evident in the current study, while formal practice and affective strategies were uncommon. Results were similar to patterns observed in other Chinese learners and, to a lesser extent, in other Asians. Where there were differences, they could be explained by differences in environment (Chinese in Taiwan or the US, for example) or by differences in definitions of strategy categories.

CONCLUSIONS

This chapter presents background information on culture and ethnicity as related to language learning strategies, examining 14 *SILL* studies and 22 non-*SILL* studies from different cultural backgrounds. Then a new study in the People's Republic of China is explored, with comparisons to previous research from other cultures.

Throughout this chapter the theme of cultural influences on the selection of language learning strategy is clear. Learners often — though not always — behave in certain culturally approved and socially encouraged ways as they learn. When students diverge from these norms of strategic behavior, they feel uncomfortable or strange and are sometimes (particularly in conformist or collectivist cultures) actively "corrected" and brought into line. However, culture should not be seen as a strait jacket, binding students to a particular set of learning strategies all their lives. Strategy instruction can help students see the value in "new" language learning strategies that are not necessarily within the limits of their cultural norms. Moreover, strategy instruction can encourage students to try such strategies for themselves.

Carisma Dreyer
Potchefstroom University, South Africa
Rebecca L. Oxford
University of Alabama, USA

CHAPTER 5

LEARNING STRATEGIES AND OTHER PREDICTORS OF ESL PROFICIENCY AMONG AFRIKAANS SPEAKERS IN SOUTH AFRICA

An understanding of the way of life [of other cultures] is important to survival in a world of conflicting value systems.
–Ned Seelye

SUMMARY

This South African response explains how assessment techniques can unearth important predictors of ESL proficiency. One of the most revealing results was that 45% of the variance in *TOEFL* (ESL proficiency) scores was predicted by learning strategy use on the *SILL*. Equally important, a canonical correlation between *TOEFL* sections and *SILL* categories was .73, meaning that language proficiency and strategy use are strongly related. Statistically and practically significant differences in frequency of strategy use were also found by gender, course type, and major field of study.

INTRODUCTION

For the last twenty years, research in the field of second language (L2) learning and teaching has shifted from instructional methods to learner characteristics. Chapelle and Roberts (1984, 1986) suggested that more research is needed before statements can be made about which combinations of learner variables is ultimately crucial to L2 proficiency in a particular setting. This study addresses that suggestion and is aimed in particular at first-year, Afrikaans-speaking students at the Potchefstroom University in South Africa.

RESEARCH REVIEW

Teachers and researchers have all observed that some language students are more "successful" (i.e., more language-proficient) than others. Some individuals appear to be more endowed with abilities to succeed; others seem, at least on the surface, to

Dreyer, C., & Oxford, R. L. (1996). Learning strategies and other predictors of ESL proficiency among Afrikaans speakers in South Africa. In Rebecca L. Oxford (Ed.), *Language learning strategies around the world: Cross-cultural perspectives*. (Technical Report #13) (pp. 61–74). Honolulu: University of Hawai'i, Second Language Teaching & Curriculum Center.

lack those abilities. This observation led researchers (e.g., O'Malley and Chamot, 1987, 1990; Oxford, 1990b; Oxford and Ehrman, 1993; Rubin, 1975; Stern, 1975; Vann and Abraham, 1990) to describe and investigate variables that account for some of the differences in how students learn. These variables include, among others:

- the field independence/dependence distinction as a learning style (Birckbichler & Omaggio, 1978; Chapelle & Roberts, 1986; Hansen & Stansfield, 1981, 1982; Hosenfeld, 1979, 1984; Ramírez, 1986; Reid, 1987, 1995; Witkin et al., 1977a, 1977b),

- language learning strategies (Bialystok & Fröhlich, 1978; Bialystok, 1981; O'Malley & Chamot, 1990; O'Malley et al., 1985a, 1985b; Oxford, 1990b, 1989c, 1993b; Rubin, 1987; Wenden, 1983, 1985a, 1986a, 1986b; Wenden & Rubin, 1987), and

- personality (Brodkey & Shore, 1976; Busch, 1982; Chastain, 1975; Guiora et al., 1975; Reid, 1995).

FIELD INDEPENDENCE/DEPENDENCE

Field independence refers to the ability to conduct cognitive restructuring of input in an objective way, and field dependence refers to a more subjective treatment of stimuli. Oxford and Ehrman (1993) have described field independence as the analytical aspect of learning, an aspect in which learners concentrate on details, rule-learning, and precision. Field dependence, sometimes known as "field sensitivity" to avoid pejorative attitudes toward it, reflects the global side of learning. Field dependent or sensitive students seek the big picture, are often socially conscious and caring, and do not have the need for accuracy shown by the analytic learners. A low score on field independence does not necessarily indicate a high degree of field dependence. It might be more plausible to consider that field independence/dependence is contextualized and variable within one person (Brown, 1987) who is capable of using both field independent and field dependent styles to some degree. The style he or she uses depends on the task at hand, as well as the degree to which the person is able to respond to the task appropriately.

Hansen and Stansfield (1981) found positive linear correlations ranging from r=.20 to r=.43, p<.001 between students' field independence/dependence and performance on various measures of Spanish proficiency. Likewise, a study of learners of the Czech language at the US Defense Language Institute indicated an advantage for field independent students in terms of end-of-course language proficiency (Leaver, November, 1993, personal correspondence). In addition, d'Anglejean and Renaud (1985) and Carter (1988) found that field independence was significantly related to French language achievement. Chapelle and Roberts (1984, 1986) found correlations of r=.55 and r=.75, p<.001 between field independence and the *Test of English as a Foreign Language* (TOEFL) administered at the beginning and end of the semester, respectively. Yet there is a piece missing in the research. As stated by Oxford and Ehrman (1993, p. 196), "Unfortunately the potential advantages of field dependence (the global tendency) in terms of cultural empathy, informal conversa-

---

tional ability in natural settings, and sociolinguistic skills have not yet been systematically examined by L2 researchers."

LANGUAGE LEARNING STRATEGIES

Language learning strategies are the steps taken by the learner, most often consciously, to improve his or her own language learning. Language learning strategy research, according to Oxford (1992, 1993c) and Oxford and Crookall (1989), has shown that (1) strategies are used by students at all instructional levels; (2) more proficient learners tend to use strategies in a more task-related, more learning-style-specific, and more organized way than less proficient learners; (3) strategy use is associated with motivation, ethnicity, learning style, and other variables; (4) strategies can be taught through well-designed learning strategy instruction; and (5) both students and teachers can become more aware of the potential of language learning strategies. In addition, it has been found that females generally report using language learning strategies more often than males (Oxford, 1993a, 1993b).

Oxford and Nyikos (1989) integrated their strategy findings in the form of a causal spiral, in which motivation leads to the use of strategies that increases self-rated proficiency and self-esteem, leading to better motivation, the use of more strategies, and so on throughout the process. Gardner and MacIntyre (1992) stated, "This is a reasonable proposal, one that captures the developmental nature of language study and postulates reciprocal causation between language performance and similar characteristics" (p. 218). According to researchers (e.g., Bialystok and Fröhlich, 1978; Oxford, 1993c; Oxford and Nyikos, 1989; O'Malley and Chamot, 1990), the use of language learning strategies is related to increased language achievement and proficiency. Bialystok and Fröhlich (1978, p. 334) state that "strategies are by definition trainable," with the implication that any language learner can improve language learning by improving the use of strategies through instruction.

Language learning strategy research, for all its promise, is, as Skehan (1989) pointed out, still "embryonic," with conflicting methods used in different studies (Vann and Abraham, 1990). Although "the research to date is clear in demonstrating that the effective use of strategies is associated with high levels of achievement in a second language" (Gardner and MacIntyre, 1993, p. 218), nevertheless we need to replicate studies using similar instruments and processes and discover the complex causal mechanisms of language learning strategies as related to proficiency and achievement (Oxford et al., 1987).

PERSONALITY

Jungian personality types, which are investigated in the current study, are of considerable importance to language learning. Personality types are derived from research on concepts originally generated by Carl Jung, a Swiss psychologist, and then elaborated by his followers. In this tradition, four dimensions of personality type exist (Ehrman and Oxford, 1990). These are *extroversion/introversion* (indicating where the person finds his or her source of energy, externally or internally); *intuition/sensing* (showing the orientation of the innovative person toward the future and random learning, as compared to the orientation of the traditional person toward the present and sequential rule-following); *thinking/feeling* (displaying the way decisions are made, through objective, logical analysis or through subjective, emotional values); and *judging/perceiving* (indicating whether the person needs rapid closure or prefers to keep things open). Reid's (1995) book provides additional information on these dimensions.

Ehrman and Oxford (1990) discovered that personality types were very important in understanding who would become a highly successful adult learner and who would use a wide variety of learning strategies. They found that feeling and perceiving type students tended to have an advantage in an intensive language learning program, and that there was a tendency for introverts to outperform extroverts in this particular study. Busch's (1982) hypothesis that extroverted students would be more proficient than introverted students was not supported.

A number of other personality characteristics relate to Jungian personality type, and their relationships are sometimes complex and powerful (Brodkey and Shore, 1976). In the current study, one of the instruments assesses personality traits, such as reserved/warm-hearted, less or more intelligent, phlegmatic/excitable, and zestful/circumspect. These might have some link with language learning as well as to personality type.

RESEARCH QUESTIONS

The field independence/dependence, learning strategies, and personality type of Afrikaans first-year students have not until this time been investigated. Therefore the focus of this study is on the following key questions:

1. Is there a statistically significant as well as a practically significant relationship between:
    • field independence/dependence and ESL proficiency?
    • learning strategy use and ESL proficiency?
    • personality and ESL proficiency?

2. What are the best predictors of ESL proficiency?

3. Is there a statistically significant as well as a practically significant difference in strategy use between students in two different kinds of English courses: 111, a grammar-based course containing more proficient learners, and 112, a communication-based course containing less proficient learners?

4. Is there a statistically significant as well as a practically significant difference in strategy use between males and females?

5. Does course status (elective vs. required) have a statistically significant as well as a practically significant relationship with strategy use?

---

6. Does major field have a statistically significant as well as a practically significant relationship with strategy use?

METHODOLOGY

SUBJECTS

A total of 305 Afrikaans first-year students (ages 18–21 years) at the Potchefstroom University taking ESL were included in this study. This group included 179 females and 126 males. First-year students taking ENG 111 (81 students) and ENG 112 (224 students) were included in the study. ENG 111 refers to the conventional academic English course, which involves grammatical analysis and attention to detail, while ENG 112 refers to the practical English course (taken mostly by law students), which focuses more on natural communication. The subjects did not represent a homogeneous group. ENG 111 and ENG 112 students had different patterns of course grades, which were strongly related to *TOEFL* scores ($r=.83$, $p<.0001$) and therefore indicative of different levels of proficiency. ENG 111 students were more significantly more proficient than ENG 112 students. It was therefore possible to compare the two groups.

It is possible to consider these students either as a population or as a sample. The group of students can be regarded as a population, because the entire first-year group was included in the study. It is, therefore, possible to draw accurate conclusions about this group. However, the subjects can be regarded as a sample, because the first-year students chosen for this study represent a typical first-year intake of students of English at Potchefstroom University and perhaps at other universities in South Africa.

INSTRUMENTATION

Five paper-and-pencil instruments were used in this study. Table 5.1 summarizes their characteristics. For complete information, see Dreyer (1992).

Table 5.1: Characteristics of instruments in the South African study

Abbreviation	Name	Purpose	Reliability	Validity
GFT	Gottschaldt Figures Test	Determine FI/D	KR21(corr.)=.79	Valid for FI only, not FD
SILL	Strategy Inventory for Language Learning	Assess frequency of strategy use	Cronbach alpha=.95 (avg.)	Content val.=.95; strong relationship with motivation, proficiency, psych. type
JPQ	Jung Personality Questionnaire	Define personality type (extrovert/ introvert, sensing/ intuitive, thinking/feeling, judging/ perceiving*)	KR20=.77 –.89 for S.A. children	Strong concurrent validity in relp. to behavior
HSPQ	High School Personality Questionnaire	Assesses 14 independent personality traits (e.g., reserved/ warm-hearted, less/more intelligent, phlegmatic/ excitable, zestful/ circumspect)	Test-Retest= .71 –.90	Validity coefficients derived from equivalence coefficients= .60–.81
TOEFL	Test of English as a Foreign Language	Measures listening, structures, and reading	Avg. .89, .87, .89 for 3 sections, .95 overall	Concurrent validity with CELT sections=.36–.79; with CELT total=.64; with Michigan= .45–.66

*   Note that Jung did not create the judging/perceiving dimension; this was added later by his followers.

DATA COLLECTION PROCEDURES

Data collection was conducted by the first author, with the cooperation of teaching assistants at the English Department, who helped with proctoring and monitoring. The students were given a *Biographical Questionnaire* to complete at the beginning of

April. Tests for the predictor variables (i.e., all but the *Test of English as a Foreign Language*) were group-administered during scheduled afternoon tutorial periods the following day in the following order: *Gottschaldt Figures Test, High School Personality Questionnaire, Strategy Inventory for Language Learning,* and *Jung Personality Questionnaire.* The criterion test, *TOEFL,* was group-administered toward the end of June. For all tests, subjects received uniform instructions, and all administrative requirements for each instrument were followed.

DATA ANALYSIS PROCEDURES

Correlational and multivariate research designs were used in this study, analyzed by means of the Statistical Analysis System (SAS Institute, 1988). Pearson product moment correlations were used to determine the direction and strength of the relationship between predictor (independent) variables and the criterion (dependent) variable (although, strictly speaking, simple correlation does not allow prediction). Canonical correlations were used to determine the relationship between the independent variables and the different sections of the *TOEFL* which functioned as dependent variables. For canonical correlations, there are two linear combinations of variables, weighted in such a way that the maximum possible correlation is achieved (Seliger and Shohamy, 1989).

Stepwise multiple regression analyses were also conducted to determine the most effective predictors of the criterion measure. A stepwise analysis was conducted separately using each of the predictors (independent variables) that allowed it, with the *TOEFL* as the criterion or dependent variable. In this analysis, a new variable is added at each step. The first predictor variable selected is the one having the highest correlation with the criterion. Each time a new predictor variable is "stepped in," the new relationship between the criterion and predictor variables is reevaluated (Seliger and Shohamy, 1989).

F-ratios are used to determine any statistically significant differences between means when considering more than two groups of students, while t-tests are used to compare the mean scores of two groups. A relationship can be regarded as statistically significant if the results are significant at the specified alpha (i.e., probability of chance occurrence). Alpha is established as a criterion, and results either meet the criterion or they do not. In behavioral research, alpha is frequently set at $p < .05$ or $p < .01$ (i.e., the odds that the findings are due to chance are either 5 in 100 or 1 in 100) (Thomas and Nelson, 1990). A relationship can be regarded as practically significant if the results are of practical value to the researcher, language practitioner, or teacher. Cohen (1977, 1988) has established various scales according to which a relationship or difference between means can be regarded as practically significant. For determining practical significance, three of Cohen's effect size scales were used: d for differences between means (small effect .2, medium .5, large .8); r for correlations (small effect .1, medium .3, large .5); and w for relationships between two categorical variables (small effect .1, medium .3, large .5).

For example, r=.5 indicates a large effect size which can, therefore, be regarded as practically significant. Very few studies, if any, conducted in the second language acquisition field have indicated the practical significance of the relationships that were investigated. According to Skehan (1991), researchers may be well advised to indicate the practical significance of a relationship, not just the statistical significance.

RESULTS

QUESTION 1. CORRELATIONS WITH ESL PROFICIENCY

Field independence/dependence and ESL proficiency

Neither of the groups of students was strongly field independent. Of the ENG 111 students (grammar-based class, higher proficiency students), 19.11% were relatively field independent, whereas only 7.4% of the ENG 112 students (communication-oriented class, lower proficiency students) were relatively field independent. The difference was statistically significant (p<.01) but not practically significant (w=.16). These findings, taken together, suggest that most students in both groups were overwhelmingly field dependent.

A statistically and practically significant relationship was expected between field independence and ESL proficiency on the *TOEFL*, but only statistical significance appeared. Pearson correlations between the *Gottschaldt* and the three parts of the *TOEFL* were positive, statistically significant, but low (all r=.15 or less) and thus had little practical significance.

However, when considered differently, a t-test comparing the means of two groups — students with a score of greater than 6 (indicating field independence) and students with a score of less than 5 (indicating lack of field independence) — showed a stronger effect of field independence on *TOEFL* performance (p<.05, d=.41, moving toward but not reaching a medium effect size).

Strategy use and ESL proficiency

Pearson correlations were calculated to determine the strength and direction of the relationship between students' strategy use (*SILL*) and their ESL proficiency (*TOEFL*). Correlations between strategy use and proficiency were positive and highly significant, both in statistical and practical ways. The strongest correlation (r=.64, p<.0001, large effect size) was between *SILL* Part D (organizing your learning/metacognitive strategies) and *TOEFL* Section 3 (reading/vocabulary). This was immediately followed by other strongly positive, statistically and practically significant relationships between *SILL* Part D (organizing your learning/metacognitive strategies) and the *TOEFL*, all at p<.001 with a large effect size: r=.62 with total *TOEFL* score, r=.55 with *TOEFL* Section 1 (listening), and r=.54 with *TOEFL* Section 2 (structures).

The *SILL* average for each person was statistically significant in its relationship with the *TOEFL*. Medium practical significance effects were found for the *SILL* average and these aspects of the *TOEFL*: total *TOEFL* score (r=.33, p<.0001) and *TOEFL* Section 3 (reading/vocabulary; r=.37, p<.0001). Small practical significance, but almost reaching the r=.3 criterion for medium practical significance, was found for the *SILL* average and *TOEFL* Section 1 (listening) and *TOEFL* Section 2 (structures), both r=.28, p<.0001.

Other highly statistically significant relationships, although often with smaller practical significance, were found between the *SILL* and the *TOEFL*. For example, *SILL* Part B (using your mental processes/cognitive strategies) was statistically significantly related to the total *TOEFL* score (r=.23, p<.0001, small effect size) and to various sections of the *TOEFL* (r=.20–.22, p<.001–.0001, small effect size).

SILL Part C (compensating for missing knowledge/compensation strategies) was correlated with *TOEFL* Section 3 (reading/vocabulary; r=.30, p<.0001, medium effect size) and with total *TOEFL* score (r=.20, p<.001, small effect size) and *TOEFL* Part 1 (listening; r=.16, p<.01, small effect size). Thus, compensation strategies were related somewhat more, both statistically and practically, to reading proficiency than to listening proficiency in this group of students.

Lower correlations, still statistically significant but of small practical significance, were found between *SILL* Part E (managing your emotions/affective strategies) and the *TOEFL*, with a range of correlations between r=.14 for the total *TOEFL* score to r=.15 for *TOEFL* Section 3 (reading/vocabulary) to r=.16 for *TOEFL* Section 2 (structures).

Yielding much more dramatic results, canonical correlations were also computed to assess the relationship between strategy use (all the parts of the *SILL*) and ESL proficiency (all the sections of the *TOEFL*). A highly significant correlation (r=.73, p<.0001) was found, with a large practical effect size. This means that all the *SILL* parts or categories of strategies, taken as a set of variables, were strongly related to all the sections of the *TOEFL*, also viewed as a set of variables.

Personality and ESL proficiency

In this study, two personality questionnaires were used to deal with as many types and traits as possible. Pearson correlations were computed to determine the direction and strength of the relationships between the various personality types/traits. None of the *Jung Personality Questionnaire* dimensions proved to be significantly correlated with the *TOEFL* total or section scores.

The correlations between the *High School Personality Questionnaire* scores and the *TOEFL* scores were also low, but slightly better than those for the *Jung Personality Questionnaire*. Factor B of the *High School Personality Questionnaire* (referring to intelligence) had the strongest relationships — most reflecting medium effect sizes —

with the *TOEFL*: r=.30 (p<.0001) with total *TOEFL*, r=.32 (p<.0001) with *TOEFL* Section 1 (listening), r=.31 (p<.0001) with *TOEFL* Section 3 (reading/vocabulary), and r=.21 (p<.001) with Section 2 (structures). Small effect sizes were found for other factors on the *High School Personality Questionnaire* as related to the *TOEFL*: Factor I (tough-minded vs. tender-minded), which correlated with aspects of the *TOEFL* in a range of r=.13 to .21 (p<.01–.001); and Factor J (zestful vs. circumspect), which correlated only with *TOEFL* Section 3 (reading/vocabulary), r=.15 (p<.01).

Using canonical correlation between *Jung Personality Questionnaire* dimensions and *TOEFL* sections, a non-significant correlation of r=.15 was found. However, between the *High School Personality Questionnaire* factors and the *TOEFL* sections, a canonical correlation of r=.46 (p<.0001) was located, with an effect size moving toward but not hitting the medium range.

A stepwise multiple regression determined the contribution of the *High School Personality Questionnaire* factors for predicting ESL proficiency (without including any learning strategies or other variables). In this regression, Factors B (intelligence) and I (tough-minded vs. tender-minded) played significant (p<.0001 and p<.01) roles but small ones — 8.5% and 2.3% respectively — in the prediction of the total *TOEFL* score. Three other factors of the *High School Personality Questionnaire* (Factors F, A, and J) added non-significantly to the prediction. Total variance explained by these five factors was just 13%, showing a meager amount of predictive power.

An explanation for the lack of stronger relationships between various personality factors and ESL proficiency might be as follows: Personality characteristics alone are not enough to account for much of the variance in English proficiency. Rather, a combination of different variables would be more likely to influence a person's success or failure in learning a second language. For this reason, the possibility that personality characteristics such as extroversion, assertiveness, adventuresomeness, and so on can play important roles in the second language acquisition process cannot be discounted.

Very importantly, it must be remembered that the *TOEFL* (in the version used here) does not cover speaking and writing, which might have more potential correlates with personality characteristics. In addition, according to Larsen-Freeman and Long (1991), cultures might value personality characteristics differently, and this might affect the way in which these characteristics influence second language acquisition.

QUESTION 2. BEST PREDICTORS OF ESL PROFICIENCY

To assess strategy use as a predictor of ESL proficiency in view of other possible predictive factors, such as field independence/dependence and personality, a stepwise multiple regression was done, with possible predictors included in the order in which they correlated with the criterion (*TOEFL*) and with a new equation figured when a new predictor is included.

In the regression analysis, approximately 45% of the total variance in the *TOEFL*, the ESL proficiency measure, was explained by strategy use as measured by the *SILL*. This percentage is figured by the contributions to the variance made by different parts of the *SILL*, as noted next.

The strategy category of organizing and evaluating your learning (*SILL* Part D, metacognitive strategies) accounted for 41.1% of the total ESL proficiency variance. As a result, *SILL* Part D had a significant effect on ESL proficiency, $F(1,303)=211.80$, $p<.0001$. Strategies for managing your emotions (Part E, affective strategies) added an additional 2.6% of predictive power, $F(2,302)=14.30$, $p<.001$, followed by strategies for learning with others (Part F, social strategies), which added 1.1% prediction, $F(3,302)=6.08$, $p<.01$.

The only other variable which showed any significant effect on ESL proficiency was *High School Personality Questionnaire* Factor B — intelligence, $F(4,300)=3.97$, $p<.05$. However, its effect was negligible, because it accounted for less than 1% of the total variance on the *TOEFL*. Although entered as possible predictors, the *Jung Personality Questionnaire* sensing-intuition dimension, *SILL* Part B (using all your cognitive processes/cognitive strategies) and *SILL* Part A (remembering more effectively/memory strategies) did not prove to be significant predictors in this regression, though they all added tiny amounts to the prediction. (*SILL* Part C, compensating for missing knowledge/compensation strategies, was not entered as a predictor in this analysis.) Note that the predictive power of each of the *SILL* parts or categories in the regression analysis does not fall in the same order of strength as the simple Pearson correlations of each of the *SILL* parts with the *TOEFL*, because the regression analysis considers the interrelationships of all the variables while the simple correlation analysis does not.

In sum, in this regression analysis the results suggest that strategies are by far the best predictors of ESL proficiency, especially strategies in the following group: organizing and evaluating your learning (Part D, metacognitive strategies). (We speculate that metacognitive strategies are excellent predictors of success in almost any subject area.) The predictive power of that set of strategies for ESL proficiency is followed very distantly by managing your emotions (Part E, affective strategies) and learning with others (Part F, social strategies).

QUESTION 3. STRATEGY USE AND COURSE TYPE

When comparing the *SILL* means for ENG 111 and ENG 112 students using a t-test, a highly significant difference ($p<.0001$) was found with a very large effect size of $d=.87$, favoring the ENG 111 students (grammar-based class, higher proficiency students). Thus, it seems that the more proficient language learners, the ENG 111 students (who performed better on the *TOEFL*), were more frequent users of strategies than the less proficient language learners in the communicative class, the ENG

112 students. The more proficient learners used strategies statistically significantly more often in the two high *SILL* ratings (usually and always/almost always) than the less proficient learners in the following *SILL* categories:

- using your mental processes/cognitive strategies (57% vs. 30%);

- compensating for missing knowledge/compensation strategies (30% vs. 21%); and

- organizing and evaluating your learning/metacognitive strategies (85% vs. 20%).

In short, the ENG 111 students, who were studying English in traditional analytical ways and whose proficiency was higher according to the *TOEFL*, frequently reported employing strategies likely to be useful in a traditional, structure-oriented ESL instructional environment geared toward tests and assignments (i.e., academic study requiring analytical abilities) — while the more communicatively-instructed, less proficient ENG 112 students used fewer of these strategies. With regard to social strategies (learning with others), the ENG 111 students, who were in a traditional academic class, used these strategies statistically significantly less often at a high level (26%) than did the ENG 112 students (46%), who were in a more communicative class. Thus, the environment and the instructional methodology has a relationship to strategy choice (as earlier suggested by Oxford, 1989c).

The practical significance of these high versus low proficiency results was large only for Parts B and D of the *SILL* (using all your mental processes/cognitive strategies, and organizing and evaluating your learning/metacognitive strategies), with an effect size set at d>.6.

QUESTION 4. STRATEGY USE AND GENDER

Males and females exhibited different patterns of strategy use. A t-test showed that females used strategies more often than males did (p<.0001, d=.62, medium effect size). Particularly notable is that females, compared with males, reported more frequent use (in the two high rating categories of usually and always/almost always) of *SILL* Part F (learning with others/social strategies). This can be related to women's desire for good symbols or results (Oxford and Nyikos, 1989), and it might reflect a need for social approval (Bardwick, 1971). Extensive research (Bardwick, 1971; Lakoff, 1975; Oxford, 1993a, 1993b; Oxford, Nyikos and Ehrman, 1988; Tannen, 1986) shows that women and men actually use their own native language differently, reflecting a greater (cooperative rather than competitive) social orientation in women.

Women also exhibited significantly greater use of metacognitive strategies (organizing and evaluating your learning), which involve setting goals and objectives, planning for a language task, evaluating one's progress, and so on. Research (Kramarae, 1981) has shown that women are known for more speech self-monitoring than men. However, in this study both male and female use of such strategies appeared to be suppressed by the traditional academic environment of the class-room, a setting that promotes and rewards performance on discrete tasks rather than interactive communicative efforts.

QUESTION 5. STRATEGY USE AND ELECTIVE/REQUIRED COURSE STATUS

Clear differences in strategy use were found for elective versus required course status for all the strategies used. Overall, the *SILL* mean for students taking English electively was higher (3.08) than for students taking English as a requirement (2.89), p<.0001, d=.45, not quite reaching a medium effect size. This difference is not as striking as the one found when examining high users of specific strategy categories. For example, 52% of students who chose to enroll for English used metacognitive strategies (Part D, organizing and planning your learning) at a high level (usually or always/almost always), compared with only 25% of students taking English as a graduation requirement (p<.0001). Similar findings occurred for the other *SILL* strategy categories.

QUESTION 6. STRATEGY USE AND MAJOR FIELD

Like other studies (e.g., Oxford and Nyikos, 1989), this investigation showed that career orientation, here reflected in university major, had a significant effect, F (2,250)=10.22, p<.0001, on strategy use. Students with different career interests used strategies differently. A follow-up Tukey multiple comparison test showed that all three majors (B.A., B. Juris., and B.Proc.) differed significantly from each other (p<.05) in terms of strategy use, with B.A. students having a higher mean (3.16) than B. Juris. students (2.93), who had a higher mean than B.Proc. students (2.78). Effect sizes were medium (d=.52) for the contrast between B.A. and B.Juris. students but large (d=.86) for the contrast between B.A. and B.Proc. students.

CONCLUSIONS

With regard to the questions posed earlier, the results of this study indicate the following:

1. A statistically significant, but not practically significant, relationship be-tween field independence and ESL proficiency; a statistically significant as well as practically significant relationship between language learning strategy use and ESL proficiency; a few statistically significant, but for the most part not practically significant, relationships between selected aspects of per-sonality and ESL proficiency;

2. A statistically significant and impressive predictive relationship between strategy use and ESL proficiency;

3. A statistically significant as well as practically significant relationship be-tween strategy use and class type (which was related to proficiency), with more proficient, more grammar-based (ENG 111) students using strategies

more frequently than less proficient, more communicatively-instructed (ENG 112) students;

4. A statistically significant as well as practically significant gender difference in strategy use, with females using strategies more often than males;

5. A statistically significant difference, but not quite reaching a medium practical effect size, in strategy use by course status (elective vs. required), with students taking English electively using strategies more often than those taking English as a requirement; and

6. Statistically significant as well as (in part) practically significant differences in strategy use by three major fields of study.

Perhaps the most important findings relate to learning strategies. Learning strategy use accounted for approximately 45% of the total variance on the *TOEFL*, which measured ESL proficiency in this study, whereas the contributions of the other variables were much smaller. This predictive finding is underscored by the fact that a canonical correlation showed strategy use to be associated strongly ($r=.73$) with ESL proficiency.

A combination of learning strategy, personality, and learning style (field independence/dependence) variables — perhaps with the addition of motivation factors — might ultimately help explain ESL proficiency. Certainly it would help to replicate and expand the current study in other universities in different countries to discern the intricate and intriguing relationships among these variables.

Cora Kaylani
The Ohio State University, USA

CHAPTER 6

THE INFLUENCE OF GENDER AND MOTIVATION ON EFL LEARNING STRATEGY USE IN JORDAN

Walk together, talk together, all ye peoples of the earth.
Then and only then shall ye have peace.
—Sanskrit saying

SUMMARY

This chapter discusses results of an extensive language learning assessment in the Middle East. The results showed that both gender and motivation were related in complex ways to strategy frequencies of 255 high school seniors in Jordan. Moreover, language proficiency explained 30% of the total variation in strategy frequency. Frequency of use of metacognitive, cognitive, and memory strategies differentiated students based on their proficiency ranking. The major roles played by motivation and gender in strategy use are explained in a sociocultural light in this study.

INTRODUCTION

A body of literature now exists that points to clear differences between what strategies male and female students choose and how they decide to use them when engaging in language learning tasks. Moreover, this literature contains findings from studies conducted in a number of cultures, so that a picture is beginning to emerge about differences in strategy use among male and female language students worldwide. The next logical step is to study the milieu and socialization process of different cultures to develop answers for interesting questions related to gender differences in strategy use: Why are these differences present? What do these gender differences mean to classroom instruction? What differences and similarities do successful male and female students share? If socialization is the main influence on gender differences, can anything be generalized about male and female language learners across cultures? What implications does this premise have on strategy instruction?

In addition to gender and culture, another factor associated with strategy use is motivation. Because humans are seen as being motivated by a complex set of interrelated factors, it is essential to view motivation as a largely social process. In studying

Kaylani, C. (1996). The influence of gender and motivation on EFL learning strategy use in Jordan. In Rebecca L. Oxford (Ed.), *Language learning strategies around the world: Cross-cultural perspectives*. (Technical Report #13) (pp. 75–88). Honolulu: University of Hawai'i, Second Language Teaching & Curriculum Center.

the socialization process and cultural milieu of a language learner, rich information about motivational influences and goals can be gathered that would augment traditional conceptions of motivation, as exemplified by Gardner and his associates, as well as extend newer conceptions of language learning motivation, as suggested by Crookes and Schmidt (1991), Dörnyei (1990), and Oxford and Shearin (1994) among others. Therefore, a study that sets out to investigate the influences of gender and motivation on language learning strategy use can be well served by a thorough cultural investigation, as shown here.

The Hashmite Kingdom of Jordan presents an intriguing cultural context in which to study the influence of gender and motivation on strategy use among students. For the study of gender, Jordan presents an ideal classroom situation. Similar to many Middle Eastern countries, students in Jordan are segregated by sex from grades five through twelve in all public and most private schools. In addition, all subjects are taught by teachers of the same sex as the students. Thus, one hypothesis is that if gender affects language learning strategy use, differences should be pronounced in these same-sex classrooms taught by same-sex teachers. Therefore, twelfth grade male and female students, having been exposed to an average of eight years of English language study in same-sex classrooms, should be the most interesting group to observe for gender differences.

As for the study of motivation, Jordan presents a rich cultural milieu. Strong religious and political factors shape attitudes students have toward English as a foreign language. Economic and social pressures to get a good job on both male and female students drive the intense competition for admissions to universities. The key to university admissions in Jordan is passing the high school exit exam, which is noted for its difficult English section. Therefore, English is seen as one of the barriers to success among high school students. Language learning motivation is thus influenced by many complementary as well as conflicting social factors.

In examining motivation, the first level of interest in this study was to test Gardner's model of motivation which has dominated second language acquisition research since 1959, when Gardner and Lambert first classified students as being integratively or instrumentally motivated. Questions that arose from this model in the context of this study were: Given that motivation is a largely social process and that males and females are socialized differently in Jordan, how would motivational orientations differ? Would Gardner's model of motivation, based primarily on establishing the goals of the learner studying a second language, prove to be adequate? What combination of social factors for male and female students influence motivation and, in turn, learning strategies among high school students in Jordan? What differences in motivation exist between successful male and female language learners? These questions have only been partially answered in the literature. Therefore, research pertinent to the influence of culture, gender, and motivation on language learning strategies will be discussed, but first, studies related to successful language learners' use of strategies will establish the theoretical background on which this study was based.

SUCCESS AND STRATEGIES

Investigations into the differences between successful and unsuccessful learners in both the fields of second and foreign language acquisition have yielded findings about the nature of learning strategies. The search for the strategies of "the good learner" began with the studies of Rubin (1975) and Stern (1975). From these initial investigations, research into the learning strategies of successful language learners steadily increased. Researchers such as A. D. Cohen (1977, 1984), O'Malley and Chamot (1987, 1990), Oxford (1986a, 1986b, 1989a, 1989b, 1990b, 1993a, 1993b, 1994b), Prokop (1989), Rubin (1975, 1981, 1987), and Wenden (1987a, 1987b) became the leaders in the field. As the literature grew in this field, larger and more varied groups of learners, both in the United States and abroad, were studied to learn more about the similarities and differences between successful and unsuccessful language learners in different contexts. Although a lot of this research is still quite recent, a picture is developing of the differences in the language learning strategies used in these different contexts. There are a variety of conclusions based on language learning strategy studies that need to be discussed. These conclusions address the assumptions found throughout the literature that the difference between successful and unsuccessful language learners is either a factor of the quantity, quality or combination of strategies that learners of each group use. A review of some of these conclusions will be made to show that the profile of the successful language learner is still emerging.

Very early on in strategy research, some rather basic conclusions were made as to the reasons for a particular learner's success. Politzer (1965) concludes that "the successful language learner is essentially the pupil who has devised a successful self-teaching method" (p. 18). Rubin (1975) set up hypotheses about what she considered to be attributes of the successful language learner based on her observations of classrooms in California and Hawai'i. In summary, Rubin characterized the good language learner as being "a willing and accurate guesser" (p. 45), as having a "strong drive to communicate" (p. 46), as not being inhibited, as focusing on form as well as communication and meaning, as practicing and seeking out opportunities to practice. What is most significant about Rubin's conclusions concerning successful language learner strategies is that strategy use will vary depending on the task; the stage of the learner in the learning process; the age; the context of learning — whether it is inside the classroom or not; individual styles such as auditory, visual or kinesthetic, and especially *the cultural differences* in cognitive learning style.

This last observation by Rubin (1975), that the use of language learning strategies may vary across cultures, implying that they are not universally effective for all learners and all tasks, has been repeated by several researchers, most notably A. D. Cohen (1977), Chamot and O'Malley (1984) and Genesee (1978).

In continuing with the description of successful and unsuccessful language learners' use of strategies, other researchers followed Rubin's (1975) lead in creating a profile of what successful learners do, and by implication, what unsuccessful learners fail to do. These results extended the perception that successful learners do something that unsuccessful learners do not, that there is a *quantitative* difference between them.

Using somewhat different methods, Reiss (1983) used teacher-assigned grades to divide a group of students who had previously filled out a self-report questionnaire. She compared the reported strategy use of the students who had gotten "A's" with the ones who received a "C" or "D". One of the conclusions Reiss drew was that the successful ("A") students in the study used more specific strategies which relied on originality and creativity than the "C/D" students. The unsuccessful ("C/D") students used general strategies and did not venture beyond what was offered to them in class or the textbook. Reiss' (1983) findings are important because they suggest that the difference between successful and unsuccessful language learners is not so much the quantity but the *quality* of learning strategies used. This notion had already been established in cognitive psychology almost twenty years earlier. A classic study by deGroot (1965) on the differences between novice and expert chess players found that it was the quality, not the quantity of strategies that consistently allowed the expert to win matches.

In addition to the notion of quality of strategy use, a study by Politzer and McGroarty (1985) led them to suggest that appropriate *complexes* of strategies might be associated with various levels of communicative competence. These findings suggest that successful students are not necessarily using more strategies, but different combinations of them. In addition, Politzer and McGroarty also reiterated Rubin's (1975) question of whether good strategies are universal or whether they might be culturally specific. They conclude that recommendations about a particular strategy as being absolutely helpful should not be made. Instead, they suggest that a strategy may be labeled as good or bad depending on the level of the learner and the frequency that it is used. This last suggestion has some research support from the work of Abraham and Vann (1987) and Vann and Abraham (1990). In their study of two unsuccessful language learners, they conclude that, although the learners were active and had quantitatively similar repertoires of strategies that successful learners had, the unsuccessful learners could not apply the appropriate strategy to the appropriate task. Vann and Abraham suggest that the unsuccessful learners lacked certain metacognitive skills which would have enabled them to assess the task and then apply the appropriate strategy. Chamot and Küpper (1989) also concluded that it was not so much the number of strategies a learner had in their study, but the flexibility and appropriateness with which the strategies were used. They pointed to a need to improve the decision-making capabilities of learners, a metacognitive skill.

What has been demonstrated in this discussion it that research results have more often shown that successful strategy users have the ability to choose the strategy or complex of strategies that is suitable to the task. Oxford (1989c) echoes Bates' (1972) conclusion that the successful learners employ strategies that are appropriate to their stage of learning, age, and purpose of learning the language. What needs to be addressed at this point is the question that has been raised by several researchers thus far, that of factors related to language learning strategy use.

FACTORS RELATED TO LANGUAGE LEARNING STRATEGY USE

Culture

Rubin's (1975) hypothesis that strategy use might be a factor of culture, age, level of proficiency, context, or individual style spurred further research into these influences. Oxford and Crookall (1989) list several other factors associated with strategy use including motivation, gender, cognitive style, national origin, and language being learned. For the purpose of the present study, only three factors are discussed: culture, gender, and motivation. The focus now is on culture. Culture has been mentioned in a series of studies that include Rubin (1975), A. D. Cohen (1977), Chamot and O'Malley (1984), Genesee (1978), and Oxford and Nyikos (1989) among others. Culture has been cited as an important variable in learning strategy use because the culture of a student is, in part, made up of prior formal and informal educational experiences. O'Malley and Chamot (1990) describe students who come from a culture whose educational system emphasizes rote memorization. Successful learners will have highly developed memory strategies, but most learners from that background will probably have less developed problem-solving and comprehension strategies.

Oxford has been mentioned several times thus far in relation to her contributions to strategy research, the influence of gender on strategy use, and the issue of motivation in language learning. She is also the developer of the *Strategy Inventory of Language Learning* (*SILL*, Oxford, 1990c), a survey instrument used cross-culturally to measure frequency of strategy use among students. Since 1985, when it was first designed, it has been used in studies involving approximately 10,000 language learners. The *SILL* has been extensively tested by Oxford, her associates and graduate students in both ESL and EFL contexts. The results of such research efforts show that differences in strategy use frequency have been found across cultures. The next step is to consider what influences are present in the socialization, educational and social milieu of those cultures that propagate such differences.

Gender

The second factor that was considered in this study is gender. Gender differences have been found in many areas of human social and cognitive development. A comprehensive review of social development studies showed several gender differences such as: Females show more interest in social activities than males; females tend to prefer less aggressive interaction than males; females are less competitive and more cooperative than males (Oxford, 1993a). Other studies reveal that females have a higher desire to please and gain approval through good grades and social behavior than males (Bardwick, 1971; Docking and Thornton, 1979; Mansnerus, 1989; Nyikos, 1990b; Oxford et al., 1988). Cognitively, verbal skills in the first language (L1) usually emerge earlier in females than in males (Larsen-Freeman and

Long, 1991). Females also tend to show greater ability in articulation, are more fluent and utter longer and more complexly formed sentences than males (Oxford, 1993a, 1993b, 1994a). Girls also usually score higher than boys in verbal ability and reading tests, especially from age eleven on (Slavin, 1988).

Second and foreign language researchers have generally found sex differences favoring females in most areas of language acquisition. Several explanations have been put forward to explain why these differences appear. The most pertinent to this study is *socialization*, which has been suggested as one of the main causes of gender differences in not only social behavior, but also cognitive development (Block, 1973; Nyikos, 1990b; Slavin, 1988). It is thought that social forces such as parental attitude and gender-related cultural beliefs influence students' expectations for success, and consequently their motivation, in various subject-matter courses (Eccles, 1989). Thus, if the study of foreign language is seen as a women's subject, it may affect the motivation of male students to achieve. This would be an important factor in understanding gender differences of successful and unsuccessful language learners in Jordan, where male and female social roles are quite pronounced. The fact that English is a required course in all high schools, and that obtaining a passing grade in it is necessary for entrance to the university may offset the social perception that it is a subject in which females excel. In addition, same-sex teachers in the case of male students may provide positive role models that are usually lacking in other contexts, a theme developed in a 1983 study conducted by Cross.

Cross's subjects were French language students in the US. Cross hypothesized that gender differences in foreign language achievement are related to the sex of the teacher who serves as a role model. As the majority of language teachers in US classrooms are female, Cross maintains that there is an interaction of sex-of-teacher effect with sex-of-student effect. This means that female teachers act as a positive role model for girls and a negative role model for boys, who generally have been socialized to believe that language study is a women's subject. In the case of Jordan, most students are taught by same-sex language teachers. Thus, boys as well as girls receive positive role models in language. Nonetheless, it is important to discover how these male role models are actually perceived by their male students.

A primary purpose of this study, as previously stated, was to explore the influence of gender on learning strategy use. There have been numerous studies, most of which have been led by Oxford, her research associates, or her graduate students on the influence of gender on language learning strategy use. Oxford and Nyikos (1989) conducted the largest study to date on strategy use and gender involving 1,200 foreign language students at a major midwestern university. Other variables affecting choice of language learning strategies were considered and included: self-perceptions of proficiency and motivation, years of foreign language study, and university major. Again frequencies of strategy use was found and a factor analysis was conducted with females showing significantly greater use of three factors: formal rule-related practice strategies, general study strategies, and conversational input elicitation strategies. Males showed no more frequent strategy use on any factors. These results show that males and females may use language learning strategies differently. How should these findings be evaluated in terms of what has been already discussed about strategy use? One of the main points that should be considered here is that a student is simply not just a male or female learner, but a male or female learner who is also either successful, mediocre, or unsuccessful as a language leaner. This observation makes the literature on successful and unsuccessful learners especially pertinent.

Motivation

The third factor considered in this study was motivation, which is a largely social process. Humans are seen as being motivated by a complex set of interrelated factors. These factors can change through time, thereby creating a picture of motivation that is not constant. The factors that influence an individual's motivation are partly represented by sex, age, level of learning, attitudes toward learning, expectancy, interest, and needs. Obviously, factors such as interest and expectancy ebb and flow throughout an individual's lifetime. Other factors come from the changing environment and are represented by teaching method, quality of materials, reward system, parental expectations and peer group. Therefore, a researcher in the study of motivation can best accomplish the taking of a snapshot of the learner's motivation that is richly embedded in the sociocultural environment of the learner.

Motivation is also influenced by the goals of the individual. Goals are a set of beliefs held by the learner which cause action and effort to be put forth during the learning process. The study of goals has received the majority of research attention, primarily because of the research efforts led by Robert Gardner into motivational goals. Much of the research in second language motivation has been dominated since the 1950's by the work of Gardner and his associates and depends primarily on a social-psychological explanation of motivation (Crookes and Schmidt, 1989). This theory defines motivation as being either integrative or instrumental, and characterizes it as the learner's orientation toward the language learning goal. Integrative motivation is identified as having positive attitudes toward the speakers of the target language and possibly an interest in self-identification with the target language community. Instrumental motivation refers to having a functional reason for learning the target language, such as for job promotion or for completion of a course requirement. Gardner and his associates have been primarily responsible for promoting this model of motivation in second language learning by embodying the integrative and instrumental motives in a test, the *Attitude/Motivation Test Battery* (AMTB) which has been subject to lengthily empirical testing. Criticism of this model has arisen from Gardner's early hypothesis that integrative motivation is not only positively associated with second language achievement but is also the cause of second language achievement (Oller, 1981; Au, 1988). More recently, Gardner and MacIntyre (1993) have stated that although both integrative and instrumental motivation have been shown to have positive relationships to language attainment, the "old characterization of motivation in terms of integrative versus instrumental orientations is too static and restricted" (p. 4).

Some researchers have questioned whether other views of motivation are not equally or possibly more applicable for second and foreign language learners (Au, 1988; Beebe, 1988; Crookes and Schmidt, 1989; Oller, 1981; Oxford and Shearin, 1994; Schumann, 1975; Skehan, 1991). This is of particular importance in the English as a foreign language (EFL) field which is concerned with the study and teaching of English in countries where English is not the native language. Several studies have already pointed to a lack of direct evidence for integrative motivation in the EFL context (Dörnyei, 1990; Kruidenier and Clément, 1985; Skehan, 1991). Intuitively, it seems correct to assume that the need to identify with the target language community, a community which may have very little meaning to the English language learner abroad, might not be a major motivating factor for English language study.

It can be concluded from Gardner's extensive research that motivation has a causal influence on language-learning success, but that the integrative and instrumental orientations may not have relevance outside of the English as a second language (ESL) context. We must continue surveying with Gardner's instrument in different contexts in order to present more data on the usefulness of the concept of integrative motivation in the EFL classroom. At the same time, however, other types of motivation must be explored and offered as possible alternatives to Gardner's integrative and instrumental orientations. Part of the aim of this study has been to investigate the integrative/instrumental question as well as to explore the sociocultural environment for clues of other motivating factors at work.

HYPOTHESES

1. Differences in strategy use accounted for by gender are significant and the percent of explained variation is high.

2. Differences in strategy use resulting from the influence of gender are not as great as differences resulting from proficiency.

3. There is no significant difference in the use of social strategies between male and female students as a result of segregated classes.

4. The use of metacognitive, cognitive, and memory strategies will differentiate students on the basis of rank.

5. Profiles of language learning strategy use significantly differ between successful and unsuccessful male and female students.

6. Both successful and unsuccessful high school students are instrumentally rather than integratively motivated, as measured by Gardner's instrument, the AMTB.

7. A sociocultural explanation of motivation will explain more about student motivation than Gardner and Lambert's sociopsychological explanation of motivation.

METHODOLOGY

This study investigated the influence of gender on language learning strategy use, as measured by Oxford's (1986a, 1990c) *Strategy Inventory for Language Learning* (*SILL*), of a sample of 255 high school seniors (12th grade) in Jordan. Eight intact classrooms were used ranging from 26 to 36 students of which four were from boys' high schools and four were from girls' high schools. Of the four schools in each group, two were public and two were private high schools. The main sample of 255 students were given an Arabic translation of the *SILL* to complete during the second week of their 12th grade school year. Part of the biographic information that they were asked to supply was their 11th grade final English scores. These scores were used to rank the students in each class. The top and bottom five students from each class were classified as successful or unsuccessful students for the purposes of the study. This group of 80 students formed the subsample of the study.

In the primary analysis, six language learning strategy types, as defined by Oxford in the *SILL* as memory, cognitive, compensation, metacognitive, affective, and social, were looked at in two different ways: how each type of strategy was used individually by different sets of students; and how types of strategies paired with other strategies for certain groups of students.

Second, this study looked at a subsample. Of each class that was surveyed with the *SILL*, the top five and bottom five students, as ranked by their 11th grade end-of-year average in English, were chosen. Defined as successful and unsuccessful students, these two groups were further surveyed with translated instruments for self-assessed proficiency, motivation, and motivational orientation. The self-assessed proficiency, or "Can Do" test, measures students' own evaluations of their skills in reading, writing, speaking and listening comprehension. This test was demonstrated by Clark (1981) to have a high correlation with corresponding objective assessments of proficiency. Motivation was defined in terms of a composite score based on three subscales from the *Attitude/Motivation Test Battery* designed by Gardner and Lambert. The three subscales were: (1) attitudes toward learning English, (2) motivational intensity, and (3) desire to learn English. Included in this test are sections which indicate a student to be more or less integratively or instrumentally oriented. These two factors, success and motivation, which are connected with type of strategy use in the literature, were then examined with gender and strategy use to determine the relationships among them.

Third, additional data on strategy use were gathered from the successful/unsuccessful students through interviews based on a strategy use protocol and self-perceived reasons for success or lack of it. This information was analyzed by counting frequency of responses and by categorizing them. Findings were intended to supplement the results of the *SILL* and to offer new insight in motivational factors for learning English.

This study used the survey method and relied on both questionnaires and interviews for data. The data from the *SILL* was used in a series of multivariate analyses with both single and multiple factors. The multivariate analyses created a profile of strategy use for each gender, these profiles were then re-examined in terms of successful and unsuccessful students.

The *Attitude/Motivation Test Battery* (AMTB) has four sections which produced subscale scores. These scores were used in a step-wise discriminant analysis to show the relative contributions each of the four factors made to motivation in successful and unsuccessful male and female students.

RESULTS

1. The first hypothesis, that the differences in strategy use accounted for by gender are significant, is accepted. For the main sample of 255 students, there were significant differences at the $p < .001$ level for MANOVA results with a main effect of sex on the *SILL*. Among strategy categories used on the *SILL*, female students used significantly more memory, cognitive compensation, and affective strategies than male students. There was no significant difference in the use of metacognitive and social strategies between male and female students.

    The second part of the first hypothesis, that the percent of explained variation attributable to sex is *high*, is rejected. The percent of total variation in *SILL* profiles explained by sex was 11%. While this percentage is respectable for a single factor in tests that yield a measure of explained variance, it is not high.

2. The second hypothesis, that the differences in strategy use resulting from the influence of gender are not as great as differences resulting from proficiency, is accepted. The results of a MANOVA test conducted on the subsample (n=80) showed that sex explained 15% of the total variation in the *SILL* profiles while proficiency, as measured by class rank, explained 30% of the total variation.

3. The third hypothesis, that there is no significant difference in the use of social strategies between male and female students as a result of segregated classes, is accepted. Both MANOVA tests conducted on the main and subsamples showed that there were no significant difference in the use of social strategies between male and female students.

4. The fourth hypothesis, that the use of metacognitive, cognitive, and memory strategies will differentiate students on the basis of rank, is accepted. Results of the MANOVA show that the use of memory, cognitive, and metacognitive strategies was significantly higher ($p < .01$) for successful students than unsuccessful ones. There were no significant differences in the use of strategies in the other three categories: compensation, affective, and social.

5. The fifth hypothesis, that the profiles of language learning strategy use significantly differ between successful and unsuccessful male and female students is rejected. As was demonstrated in hypotheses one and two, proficiency explains more of the differences in strategy use on the *SILL* than does sex. Therefore, successful female students' language learning strategy profiles resembled those of successful males more than they did those of unsuccessful females. It had been thought that successful female students' *SILL* profiles would be very different from those of successful males.

6. The sixth hypothesis, that both successful and unsuccessful high school students are instrumentally rather than integratively motivated, as measured by Gardner's instrument, the *AMTB*, is both accepted and rejected. A discriminant analysis conducted on the data from a modified version of the *AMTB* showed that only two factors from the *AMTB*, motivational intensity and instrumental motivation, were needed to classify 80% of successful female students from unsuccessful female students. In this case, the hypothesis is accepted. The same discriminant analysis conducted on male students showed that three factors from the *AMTB*, motivational intensity, integrative orientation, and desire to learn English, were needed to classify 78% of successful male students from unsuccessful male students. In this case the hypothesis is rejected.

7. The seventh hypothesis, that a sociocultural explanation will explain more about student motivation than Gardner and Lambert's sociopsychological explanation, is neither accepted nor rejected. This study represents a first attempt to explore the socialization process and cultural background of students in order to better explain factors related to motivation. The work of Gardner and Lambert and their associates in researching language learning motivation in a sociopsychological framework has set unparalleled standards for second language research for over forty years. It is without question that they brought scientific rigor and standardization into the study of this subject. What the present study set out to accomplish was to introduce additional considerations into established themes in language learning motivation research.

INTERPRETATION

The results of this study point to some intriguing directions for further research in both language learning strategies and motivation. Before exploring those directions however, some interpretations of the findings in terms of the sociocultural context of Jordan should be discussed. Certain themes emerged from the data in this study that have not been addressed until now. These themes help to situate the findings in the context of the sample thus offering possible explanations for what was observed. In terms of strategy use, successful females were found to use the strategies taught to them by their teachers. This finding came out of the interview data using a strategy protocol. What this finding suggests is that teachers sanction the use of certain strategies which is attended to differently by students in the sample. The question is, however, why would female students be more sensitive to the use of sanctioned strategies in Jordan given that male teachers also provide guidance in the use of certain strategies.

One explanation, as suggested by Nyikos (1990b) in citing Bardwick (1971), is that female students seek social approval more than male students and therefore follow the teacher's advice on how to study as a way of gaining approval. This explanation is well suited to the Jordanian context where social approval is of utmost importance for females. Women are socialized to be obedient to authority in the family context, whether that authority is the parents, the older brother, or the husband. Social pressure, in the form of "talk" from the neighbors or relatives, drives parents to try to raise their daughter to be tractable. Negative comments such as "She doesn't listen" or "She's a tough one" are often heard in both public and private conversations about girls as they are tracked by neighbors and relatives throughout their adolescence for signs of making a good marriage partner. Such comments can be extremely harmful to a girl's reputation and future. Mothers of potential suitors are discouraged from seeking out such girls. Thus, the socialization of girls to exhibit obedience in both private and public domains offers one explanation for female students' willingness to use strategies sanctioned by the teacher.

Another phenomenon observed in the interview data and related to the issue of authority was the effect of the teacher on students' feelings for the study of English. In the group interviews, both unsuccessful male and female students reported disliking English because of some quality attached to the personality of their teacher. Conversely, successful female students reported liking English because of their English teacher. Why does the teacher have such a powerful effect on the learning of English in Jordan? One explanation is because teachers have very high status in the Middle East in general because they are seen by society as having the fate of the next generation in their hands. Within Jordanian society, the teacher's judgment is unquestioned. As was previously mentioned, a common expression used by parents with teachers concerning the care of their sons in school is "Take the meat but leave us the bones." This expression suggests that the teacher is trusted by the parents to act in anyway necessary to educate the child.

Trust and respect of teachers in the Middle East can be related to the value Islamic society places on learning in general. The Qur'an, the Muslim holy book, is filled with sayings exhorting the pursuit of learning for both males and females. Before public education was widespread in Jordan, the kuttab, or Islamic school was popular. At a time when illiteracy was the norm, the prerequisites for being a teacher in the kuttab were the ability to read the Qur'an and write standard Arabic. Even the Arabic words for teacher, ustath or mu'allam connote respect and status. The fact that the teacher in present-day Jordan still carries this respect and status helps explain why the teacher's personality has such a positive or negative effect on students.

Another possible explanation of the effect of the teacher is examined by Nyikos (1990b) in her previously described study of sex-related differences in adult language learning. Nyikos cites studies conducted by Cross (1990) and Eccles (1989) demonstrating that teacher beliefs play a "major role in determining the level of confidence students place in their abilities to learn" (p. 274). Thus, it could be interpreted that the unsuccessful male and female students in the present study who reported disliking English because of their English teacher might have felt that their teacher showed lack of faith in them. This perception of the students, combined with the high status and respect given to teachers might result in self-fulfilling prophecies. The unsuccessful students may feel that if their teachers think they are weak in English, then they must be because teachers know everything. Further study is indicated to test this hypothesis about unsuccessful students' interpretations of their English teachers' attitudes.

The final issue is related to the two motivational orientations found in male and female students in the subsample. Why would male students be integratively oriented when they are under greater pressure than female students to pass English courses in order to gain admission to the university, establish a career for themselves, and thus assume their socialized roles as leaders of the society and caretakers of their families? These three challenges facing the typical middle class male student would seem to promote an instrumental orientation to learning English.

One possible explanation for this paradox is that the goals of the typical English language learner are long-term rather than short-term. English proficiency is demanded in many entry level jobs in Jordan. In addition, with the gradual expansion of technology in Jordanian society, the knowledge of English is seen as an essential part of using technology to participate in the international business sector. Although the average Jordanian male student does not display a "willingness to be like valued members of the language community" (Gardner and Lambert, 1959, p. 271), the hallmark of an integrative orientation, he probably does see himself as a member of an international English speaking community, disassociated from any particular country or culture. This speculation could explain why male students were found to be integratively motivated.

The other half of the findings was that female students are instrumentally oriented. This result could be best interpreted in light of the socially prescribed goal for women in Jordan: marriage. A girl in Jordanian society is raised to believe that she is on a continuum that ends in marriage. All of her actions and decisions during adolescence are encouraged to be made in reference to their effects on her marriagability. Finding a good marriage partner is based to some extent on how well she is known in society. A female university student is exposed to more potential partners than normally encountered by females not attending the university. Thus, attending the university enhances the marriage prospects of a female student in three ways: it exposes her to more people who might consider her for marriage, it gives her status as being educated which is prized in Jordanian society, and it makes her employable upon graduation. This last fact has become increasingly important in present day Jordanian society. Due to the weak economy, low salaries, and rising cost of living, most middle class families depend on a two-salary income to live. Therefore, in addition to the traditional qualifications for a bride, beauty and obedience, a new qualification has been added: employability.

These social conditions might explain why female students work hard to pass the high school exit exam, why they are the majority in every category of student who passes, and why passing English, one of the most difficult sections on the high school exit exam, is seen as the key to opportunity. These circumstances help explain why female students are instrumentally oriented in Jordan.

IMPLICATIONS

The previous section was intended to show the need of background information on the social and cultural context of the students who are being studied. Without it, little sense can be made of differences found not only within the sample, but between samples, when compared with other studies conducted in different cultural contexts. The interpretation of the findings was partly made possible by the researcher's extensive work background in the Middle East and familiarity with its language culture. In lieu of personal experience, researchers must employ ethnographic research, which could provide needed cultural information to make such interpretations possible. At the very minimum, research should incorporate in-depth interviews along with less detailed questionnaires. Clearly this author's bias rests in a sociocultural explanation of the data. Understanding the cultural factors that influence a student's motivation and use of strategies is considered one of the processes that underlie and affect successful language performance.

Andrew D. Cohen
University of Minnesota, USA
Kimberly Scott
Folwell Middle School, Minnesota, USA

CHAPTER 7

A SYNTHESIS OF APPROACHES TO ASSESSING LANGUAGE LEARNING STRATEGIES

Measure for measure.
—Shakespeare

SUMMARY

Researchers have been gathering data on language learning strategies for some time, and the approaches for doing so are numerous. In this chapter the authors analyze six general approaches to assessing language learning strategies: learning strategy interviews and written questionnaires, observation, verbal report, diaries and dialogue journals, recollective studies, and computer tracking. At the present time, no single assessment method prevails in the field. Certain research methods (e.g., questionnaires and observations) are well established but imperfect. Other methods (e.g., computer tracking) are emerging as new research tools, but their potential has not yet been fully explored by researchers. While the use of verbal report as a research tool has come under criticism, it nonetheless has provided numerous insights about the strategies used before, during, or after tasks involving language learning or language use. In any study, a number of variables may affect the appropriateness and outcome of a given assessment method. The authors discuss the strengths and weaknesses of each strategy assessment method in light of these research variables.

INTRODUCTION

Today we are visiting an intermediate Japanese foreign language class. The teacher has just set up a role-play situation between students and their professor in which the students need to request a postponement of the due date for a written assignment. The students are struggling in their minds to find the appropriate language for making this request to their professor, a person of higher status. They make a rapid scan through their knowledge base to identify vocabulary and structures that might be suitable. Then they worry about how to deliver this material. As they are delivering this, they realize that mid-course corrections in what they have said are necessary.

Cohen, A., & Scott, K. (1996). A synthesis of approaches to assessing language learning strategies. In Rebecca L. Oxford (Ed.), *Language learning strategies around the world: Cross-cultural perspectives*. (Technical Report #13) (pp. 89–106). Honolulu: University of Hawai'i, Second Language Teaching & Curriculum Center.

This activity also happens to be the subject of research. The researcher (who might or might not be their teacher) is faced with the task of describing the language use strategies that the students employed in this role-play situation. The problem is how to capture this information. How much can be obtained through interviews or written questionnaires? How much of it is revealed simply by observation? Would it be possible to reconstruct the use of strategies through retrospective verbal report? Might the learners make helpful, informative entries into their diaries or dialogue journals that evening? This chapter is about the choices the researcher makes in trying to collect data on language learning and language use strategies.

Since language learning strategies are generally internal or mentalistic processes, certain research approaches may fail to reveal adequately which strategies learners apply. Thus, designing a study that assesses strategy use with some accuracy is a challenge. In the body of research on language learning strategies, researchers have utilized numerous assessment methods to determine patterns of strategy use among learners. In this chapter, six of those methods are described: interviews and written questionnaires, observation, verbal report, diaries and dialogue journals, recollective studies, and computer tracking.

For each assessment method, there are a number of issues that the researcher must consider. First, not all assessment methods are suitable for studying every type of language learning strategy, and differences in assessment according to the language skill areas being studied (e.g., listening, speaking, reading, writing, and vocabulary learning) are an added consideration. Furthermore, each method of assessment has a certain number of options which can be manipulated by the researcher depending on the aims of the study.

In this chapter, some of the options relevant to language learning strategy research will be described for each method, and in several instances, suggestions for innovations in the use of these methods are provided. In addition, the advantages and disadvantages of each assessment method are offered.

LEARNING STRATEGY INTERVIEWS AND WRITTEN QUESTIONNAIRES

While in many ways oral interviews and written questionnaires are distinct strategy assessment methods, they are similar in that they both elicit learner responses to a set of questions or probes. In addition, they both require the researcher to make choices regarding question format and research procedures.

ADVANTAGES AND DISADVANTAGES OF STRUCTURE

A major dimension of both interviews and written questionnaires is the degree of structure in the questions or probes. Questions can range from those that ask for "yes or no" responses or indications of frequency (e.g., Likert scales) to less structured questionnaire items asking respondents to describe or discuss language learning strategy behavior in detail. In the latter case, the respondents clearly have more control over the information that is included in the answer.

In highly structured interviews and questionnaires, the researcher has a specific set of questions that are to be answered by the respondent in a set order. In this case the researcher has complete control over the questioning, and the respondent usually does not have an opportunity to elaborate on the answers. The data obtained from this type of interview or questionnaire are uniformly organized for all respondents and lend themselves to statistical analysis. A good example of a structured learning strategy questionnaire is the *Strategy Inventory for Language Learning* (Oxford, 1990c; see also Bedell and Oxford and Dreyer and Oxford, this volume).

At the other end of the spectrum are unstructured questions or probes that simply direct the respondents to discuss a certain area of interest. The duration and depth of the response and the choice of the focus are left largely to the respondent's discretion. Thus, the respondents have the freedom to pursue areas of personal interest with only minimal guidance from the interviewer.

There is also the possibility of semi-structured interviews and questionnaires. Such instruments may reflect anything from a combination of structured and unstructured tasks on the one hand to a completely semi-structured measure on the other. For example, an interview with predetermined questions could be used in conjunction with probes to seek elaboration and clarification. In contrast, the interview could just be based on a concise or even a lengthy list of topics rather than specific questions.

The responses to structured instruments may be simplistic or contain only brief information about any one learning strategy. For example, a question that merely asks students whether or not they use mnemonics does not get at some of the more interesting issues: how often they use mnemonics, in what language learning/use situations they think mnemonics are helpful, and whether or not they use mnemonics in their current studies. Furthermore, predetermined questions — especially those that are not carefully piloted — may have ambiguities in their wording which could lead to problems of interpretation on the part of respondents. In addition, if researchers are too explicit about what they mean in a given question (e.g., with the inclusion of specific examples), the question by its nature may motivate the respondents to select a certain response, thus making the instrument less objective.

Unstructured or semi-structured interviews have the advantage of allowing the researcher and learners to pursue topics of interest which may not have been foreseen when the questions were originally drawn up. Yet the reduction of structure also means that the volume of data is increased and the data themselves are likely to be more highly individualized, which could prevent the researcher from determining overall patterns.

ADVANTAGES AND DISADVANTAGES OF
LARGE NUMBERS OF RESPONDENTS

Another important dimension in interviews and questionnaires is the number of participants. As few as one subject can be interviewed, which could allow the interviewer to develop a detailed case study of that learner. Working together, the researcher and the learner could generate a description of the most important aspects of the learner's strategy use.

In addition to one-on-one interviews, a researcher could conduct a group interview or administer a questionnaire to learners. In a small group interview, the interviewer can introduce a topic such as "the use of paraphrasing and gesturing during role-plays" and ask students to comment. One problem with small group interviews is that some subjects' responses may be affected by social desirability. With their peers listening, respondents may be fearful of producing a socially unacceptable answer. In addition, some subjects may be unwilling to volunteer information in group settings, so that the information obtained could be biased in favor of students who are more outspoken in the given group. However, small group interviews may be more cost-effective and time-effective than individual interviews with multiple language learners.

In contrast to interviews, written questionnaires are usually administered to large groups of learners and/or to groups at various sites. A major benefit of large-scale questionnaires is the potential for generating and testing hypotheses because of the large number of respondents. On the other hand, a given questionnaire may not transfer well from one setting to another, either because there are significant differences in the way that the questionnaire is administered or because the respondents in the different sites differ in how they interpret the items. This could be especially true if the measure is translated and used in other cultures.

ADVANTAGES AND DISADVANTAGES OF FORMALITY

Yet another factor in the design of interviews and written questionnaires is the degree of formality. Of concern here is the manner in which questions are asked of learners and the extent to which the questions and the setting encourage learners to relax and provide more accurate, honest answers. To a degree, formality is affected by the rapport established between the interviewer and the subjects and is independent of the degree of structure. It is possible to have an interviewer conduct a highly structured interview in a friendly and informal manner. On the other hand, in an unstructured interview, the interviewer could have a highly formal manner for asking questions or following up on interesting topics. A manner that is too informal may not be desirable if the researcher wants to keep enough distance from the students to maintain objectivity and the ability to pursue crucial topics. Yet, the subjects should feel comfortable talking at length about their learning, including affective (emotional) aspects. In the interviewer is too formal, then the students may be reluctant to discuss the learning environment.

TOWARDS MORE ACCURATE STRATEGY DESCRIPTIONS

One of the main problems with interviews and questionnaires as a whole is that much of the data constitutes self-report or the learners' generalized statements about their learning strategy use (see the following section on verbal report for a more complete description of terminology). Once learners move away from instances of language learning or language using behavior, they may also tend to become less accurate about their actual learning strategy behavior (Cohen, 1987). Learners may overestimate or underestimate the frequency of use of certain strategies. They may also be unaware of when they are using a given strategy, and even more importantly, how they are using it.

To avoid this problem, the researcher may wish to have respondents focus on recent language learning strategy use. The questions would attempt to have the respondents think of specific learning events or activities as opposed to more generalized behavior patterns. For example, the researcher could interview students or give a questionnaire to students immediately following a language task and ask questions specific to that task. For instance, the learners could perform the task seated at a booth in the language laboratory, and they could record their verbal report data directly into the microphone at their console. This type of information would constitute self-observation. The next section discusses observation by the researcher.

OBSERVATION

The major challenge in attempting to apply observational techniques to language learning strategies is that much of the interesting information cannot be observed because it is mentalistic and not behavioristic. Access to it must come from interviews, written questionnaires, and verbal report (see below), wherein the learners generate the data. Observational methods must rely on participant or non-participant observers to produce the data — whether from structured observation schedules, from ethnographic field notes, or from other methods. In planning an observational study, the researcher needs to consider a variety of factors: the number of observers and observed, the frequency and duration of observations, and how the observational data are collected, tabulated, and analyzed.

With regard to the number of observers, an investigator may choose to observe a language learning activity alone or with other observers, each scrutinizing the same or different learners, at the same time or at different times. There will be tradeoffs if the observations focus on one learner as opposed to focusing on a small group or on an entire class of language learners. Especially in the observation of language learning strategies, observing the entire class may be most profitable in that waiting for one learner or a small group to reveal their use of strategies may not provide much useful data. Of course, it is possible to record nonverbal behavior (e.g., students' facial expressions, gestures, signs of alertness, and so forth), as well as to observe written behavior by sitting next to learners and taking note of what they write in their notebooks.

Another factor is the frequency and duration of the observations. First, the investigator has to determine the number of observations over time. If meaningful data are to be obtained from observation of learning strategy behavior, then it is likely that the investigator will need to visit the same class over an extended period. A more limited observational framework may work best if the objectives of the observation are limited, for example, just getting a feeling for the classroom climate in which the learning strategies took place or using the observational data simply to jog the learners' memory as to the classroom events during those specific lessons. Secondly, researchers need to make choices about their focus — whether, for example, to focus on a 15-minute role-play activity or to observe an entire class period in order to collect data on the use of speaking strategies.

Yet another factor concerns how the observation is conducted. It is likely that the investigator will be physically present in the room while the learning activity is taking place. In addition, audio and videotapes may also be taken of the class session in order to create a more permanent record of what occurred. Although sophisticated means of collecting video and audio data now exist, there are always instances of events that somehow do not get captured by the available technology, so that the presence of live observers may play a crucial role in both the collection and the interpretation of the language learning strategy data. Note that if the activity is videotaped, the investigator would also be able to replay the tapes for learners and thereby use the tapes not just for observational data but as an aid in the collection of verbal report data as well (see below).

The final factor concerns the researcher's method for recording strategy use. One option is note-taking, which can be more or less structured. The researcher can take broad, impressionistic notes of everything of relevance that occurs, or the note-taking can focus on a few types of strategies or behaviors (Oxford, 1990b). The researcher may be able to take more complete notes if the observation is recorded on audiotape or videotape. Another option is using some sort of observation scale or checklist. An example of a strategy observation scale is "The Class Observation Guide" (used in O'Malley, Chamot, Stewner-Manzanares, Küpper, and Russo, 1985a). Finally, the investigator may wish to combine the use of an observation scale with note-taking to obtain more complete data.

DISADVANTAGES OF OBSERVATION

The key drawback of the observational method is its inability to produce descriptions of internal or mentalistic strategies like reasoning or self-talk, as suggested above. Investigators can note behavior such as asking for clarification, but many strategies never result in an obvious behavior. Thus, an observational study may reflect a largely incomplete view of the learner's actual strategy use and may result in frustration. For example, Naiman, Fröhlich, Stern, and Todesco (1978) had difficulty determining when high school students of French were using circumlocutions. Fanselow (1979) noted that seemingly obvious questions asked by teachers may have implicit messages that cannot be easily interpreted, even after asking the speaker for clarification.

Another drawback is that researchers are likely to collect data only on the students who are more verbal during the class session, and this may limit the results to only the outspoken or extroverted. In fact, many students may be left out of the strategy descriptions altogether, even though these students may be among the most strategically interesting.

Yet another problem associated with observation is the bias inherent in an observer's description of strategies. The observer is always affected by prior expectations, and any observation scale or checklist limits how the observer views the students' strategy use. With student-generated data, there is much less chance that the descriptions will be affected by the researcher's expectations.

Finally, some students' behavior may change when a researcher or video camera is present in the classroom. In those instances, students may be less willing to make mistakes and consequently become less talkative. This problem, however, may be a factor in all assessment methods to differing degrees. For example, students who know they will be asked to give a verbal report following a role-play may become more deliberate in their mental planning for the role-play. With regard to observation methods, the problem of students' altering their normal behavior could be mitigated by repeated observations. After several sessions, students become accustomed to the situation and revert to their normal classroom behavior.

ADVANTAGES OF OBSERVATION

Observation has benefits when used to describe learning strategies that are clearly observable. In such instances, the data are likely to be uniform, assuming the researcher uses the same terms to describe identical phenomena. Second, external observational records may help to lend a more impartial, objective perspective to the research study, rather than relying solely on data provided by learners. Furthermore, if the observation information is collected in a structured form (such as an observation scale), the resulting data may be quantitative in nature. Thus, the data can be analyzed statistically and used to generate or test hypotheses. In spite of these potential advantages, though, observation will continue to have limited applications to learning strategy research because so much strategic behavior is unobservable.

VERBAL REPORT

Often methods such as classroom observation produce indications or clues as to the strategies learners use, rather than instances of actual strategy use. Hence, researchers have had to rely to some extent on their own intuitions in order to produce descriptions of strategy use. Verbal report measures provide a more viable — perhaps the most viable — means of obtaining empirical evidence as to strategy use. Verbal report methods are being employed as a means of obtaining strategy information in the areas of communication (e.g., Poulisse, 1989; Poulisse, Bongaerts, and Kellerman, 1986), translation (Faerch and Kasper, 1986; Krings, 1987), test taking

(Anderson, 1989; Cohen, 1980, 1984, 1994; Feldman and Stemmer, 1987; Gordon, 1987; Nevo, 1989; Stemmer, 1991), and language learning or language use (Cohen, 1990a, 1990b). A characteristic of many of the current verbal report studies across the different activity areas is their dependency on the information processing model (Ericsson and Simon, 1994, pp. 11–24), which only allows the reporting of information that is processed in a serial, controlled fashion — a notable departure from verbal report data collected in the past (see Tichener, 1912).

TYPES OF VERBAL REPORT

Verbal report measures have played a role in a significant number of research studies on language learning strategies. Many insights about these strategies have been obtained from learners as they provided verbal report data before, during, and after performing language learning or language use tasks. It is important to note that verbal report is not one measure but instead encompasses a variety of measures intended to provide mentalistic data regarding cognitive processing. Such verbal reports include data that reflect *self-report* (learners' descriptions of what they do, characterized by generalized statements), *self-observation* (inspection of specific, not generalized, language behavior introspectively or retrospectively), *self-revelation* (think-aloud, stream-of-consciousness disclosure of thought processes while the information is being attended to), or some combination of these (Cohen, 1987; Cohen and Hosenfeld, 1981; Radford, 1974).

Some examples of studies using self-report interviews and questionnaires include Naiman et al. (1978), O'Malley et al. (1985a, 1985b), Oxford, Nyikos, and Crookall (1987), Ramírez (1986), and Wenden (1985a, 1985b). In such studies, the respondents answer interview questions or complete written questionnaires about their language strategies. To mention just a few examples of studies with second or foreign language learners involving self-revelation and/or self-observation, there have been studies like those of Block (1986), Cavalcanti (1984, 1987), and Hosenfeld (1984) employing verbal report measures with respect to reading; Cohen and Aphek (1979, 1981), Cohen and Olshtain (1993), and Cohen, Weaver, and Li (1995) on speaking and vocabulary learning; Cohen and Cavalcanti (1987, 1990) concerning writing; and Neubach and Cohen (1988) regarding use of dictionaries.

Perhaps a motive for moving beyond self-report to self-observation and self-revelation is to obtain data describing an instance of language learning or language use at or near the moment it occurs. Such data might be expected to reflect more accurately what learners actually do than might the response to a questionnaire item calling for a description of generalized behavior. Questionnaire items are more likely to elicit learners' beliefs about what they do, rather than what they actually do. In effect, self-revelation and self-observation complement self-report — to produce convergent assessment of learning strategies. Let us take a look at issues of controversy regarding this method of data collection.

Critics of verbal report methods note that much of cognitive processing is inaccessible because it is unconscious (see, e.g., Seliger, 1983). Critics among second language researchers have contended that whereas verbal report methods may help to describe language use strategies, it remains to be demonstrated whether they can inform about language knowledge or skill learning, as this information is more likely to be unconscious (Seliger, 1983). Even if the processing is not unconscious, it might be either too complex to capture by verbal report (Dobrin, 1986) or might put too great a burden on learners' memories for them to report with any accuracy. Thus, researchers who use such measures either somehow have to raise the level of conscious awareness of processing or make do with insights to which respondents have conscious access. The use of such measures may also require of respondents that they unravel some of the complexity inherent in a given set of cognitive processes and/or improve their recall skills.

In addition, it is possible that if the information is not directly accessible (i.e., the tasks involved are largely automatic), probes may force the subject to produce a verbal response that is not closely related to the actual thought processes (Ericsson and Simon, 1980). Verbal reports may also be too dependent on retrospection in that it can take 20 minutes to report on one second of mental processing (Boring, 1953). What may have begun as an introspective account quickly turns into a retrospective one.

Critics likewise refer to the tendency to repress data — to supply socially acceptable data (Bakan, 1954). Thus, protocols may be systematically contaminated by an indulgence in shared assumptions (Dobrin, 1986). In fact, protocols have been depicted as an edited replay of the respondents' perception, an invention of the respondents' folk psychology (Lyons, 1986). Not only the cultural background of the respondent, but also the background knowledge or schemata that the respondent has about the performance of such verbal report tasks might play a role (Cavalcanti, 1984).

Furthermore, verbal report methods have been criticized for their potentially intrusive effect. For example, in reading research, immediate retrospection may distort the process of reading if the readers read more closely than normal, read sentence by sentence, or concentrate on the additional cognitive or metacognitive task (Mann, 1982). Not only is it possible that the verbal report task may cause reactive effects, and thus produce data no longer reflecting the processes under investigation, but it is also possible that the results will vary according to the type of instructions given, the characteristics of the participating subjects (some more informative than others), the types of material used in collecting protocols, and the nature of the data analysis.

For example, respondents may differ with respect to their verbal skills. Some may be more adept than others at providing the appropriate amount of verbal report data at the appropriate level of specificity. Also, respondents may use different terms to describe similar processes or the same terms for different processes. A way of getting around this would be to train the respondents in the terms to use in their responses. However, such a form of intervention may distort the data in cases where respondents are meant to supply their own labels for cognitive processes. In addition, differences may exist between spoken and written verbal report so that studies which combine both sources of data may ultimately find the two types of data incompatible (Afflerbach and Johnston, 1984).

Finally, there is the potential problem that could arise when respondents do a task in a target language and report on it in their first or another language. The problem is that the respondents are likely to be recoding the information, which may in itself cause information to get lost due to limits of memory capacity as well as other factors such as accuracy during the translation of thoughts. The reporting (especially in on-line self-revelation) may alter the original thought processes more than when no recoding takes place (Faerch and Kasper, 1987, p. 19).

ADVANTAGES OF VERBAL REPORT

While the critics would suggest that these numerous problems with verbal report measures seriously limit the generalizability of the findings and might even preclude their use, proponents of verbal report would argue that cognizance of these problems in planning the research design may help avoid some of them.

Perhaps the major purpose for using verbal report protocols is to reveal in detail what information is attended to while performing tasks — information that is otherwise lost to the investigator (Ericsson, 1988). Whereas the neurological origin of cognitive processes may not be available for inspection, the cognitive events themselves are often available through verbal report (Steinberg, 1986). Language learners may underestimate the extent of conscious (or potentially conscious) processing because they are not attending to it. Furthermore, the directness of introspection gives it a character not found in any other investigation of psychological phenomena (Bakan, 1954).

Whereas reliability of mentalistic measures has been questioned in comparison with behavioristic measures, research has demonstrated that verbal reports, elicited with care and interpreted with full understanding of the circumstances under which they were obtained, are, in fact, a valuable and a thoroughly reliable source of information about cognitive processes (Ericsson and Simon, 1980; Pressley and Afflerbach, 1995). In a number of settings, for example, subjects' reports of their hypotheses and strategies have proved to be highly correlated with their subsequent behavior — and are often the most accurate predictors available (Lieberman, 1979).

As noted earlier, verbal reports have been used in numerous ways as a source of data for understanding language learning and language use. With respect to second language learning, the uses of verbal report have been admittedly limited. Immediate retrospective verbal report has, for example, helped describe strategies in vocabulary learning by association, such as through mnemonic keywords (Cohen, 1990b;

Cohen and Aphek, 1981). Such strategy data provide at least partial information regarding vocabulary learning processes, regardless of whether the learner subsequently produces a correct retrieval of the vocabulary item. With respect to language using, the research literature is more extensive. For example, the think-aloud method has broadened the scope of what is described in text processing by providing insights as to the use of knowledge in text comprehension and as to the monitoring of this and other comprehension processes (Waern, 1988). Furthermore, helpful information about the writing process has been derived from protocol analysis without having to account for every mental process (Smagorinsky, 1989).

Finally, it needs to be pointed out that verbal report is not a replacement for other means of research but rather a complement to them. All research measures have their potential strengths and weaknesses.

DIARIES AND DIALOGUE JOURNALS

DIARIES

In an effort to collect data on learners' strategy use over a period of time, some researchers have turned to diaries as a research tool. Even though diaries are described as "first-person journals" (Bailey and Ochsner, 1983), they often contain longer narratives and other information that is not in the first person. Despite this, we will continue to use the term diary rather than journal for an individual written reflections on current language learning.

DIALOGUE JOURNALS

A second way to collect learners' thoughts and emotions in written form is through a dialogue journal, which adds an important element to diaries: a reader who responds (and ideally, at length) to the learners' writing. In classroom settings, the reader is generally the teacher, but other students or classroom aides may participate as readers. In theory, the dialogue journal is supposed to be an ongoing, written conversation between the student and the reader about topics that have been generated by the student (Peyton and Reed, 1990). In reality, however, respondents may make only brief — often one-sentence — comments on the writing rather than participating equally in the dialogue. Dialogue journals have been used widely in first and second language classrooms to encourage students to write frequently on topics of interest to them. It appears that dialogue journals have yet to be used as a research tool in formal studies on language learning strategies.

FORM AND CONTENT

Since diaries and dialogue journals are learner-generated and usually unstructured, the entries may cover a wide range of themes and issues. For example, the entries may include learners' written verbal reports of the cognitive, metacognitive, and social strategies they use daily in language learning. For the most part, verbal report

---

in diaries and dialogue journals constitutes retrospective self-report or self-observation since learners generally write their entries after the learning event has taken place. For example, learners could describe what they usually do when they do not understand the teacher's instructions (an example of self-report) or could describe a specific incident in that day's class session during which they requested clarification of the teacher's instructions (self-observation).

Depending on the nature of the language learning strategies being studied, the researcher may be able to elicit from learners self-revelation data in diary and dialogue journal entries. Perhaps the simplest way to obtain entries with self-revelation is to have students take notes during the language learning task and then transcribe their notes into diaries or dialogue journals later that day. (These notes could be interspersed among the regular class notes involving new vocabulary, grammar, or whatever.) If the students take good notes, they may be able to reconstruct their thoughts at the time of the learning task with some accuracy.

There is another option for using diaries to obtain self-revelation during the writing process. While performing reading or writing tasks in the target language, learners could keep a separate page or use a wide margin on the composition page to make comments about the difficulties they are encountering in strategy use or in finding strategies to use during their reading and writing tasks. For example, learners could note that they are not sure if they correctly understood or used a verb tense in a particular sentence. In addition to hearing from the students about their reading and writing problems, a teacher could review the learners' notes and respond to specific problems. The result would be a dialogue journal that provides self-revelation and self-observation data specific to the reading or writing process.

DISADVANTAGES OF DIARIES AND DIALOGUE JOURNALS

Two serious drawbacks of diaries and dialogue journals are the volume of data produced and the potentially random nature of the entries. If learners write on self-chosen topics, the data are cumbersome to read and may not suggest or support any hypotheses regarding language strategies. In fact, many learners may not even mention learning strategies at all. To avoid this problem, some researchers have directed students to write about specific language learning strategies, such as inductive and deductive inferencing (Rubin and Henze, 1981). In the diary study in this volume (Oxford, Lavine, Felkins, Hollaway, and Saleh), students were asked to focus on their strategies for listening comprehension, grammar, and vocabulary. Yet if researchers require students to write only about specific strategies, then the learners might be less cooperative than if they were simultaneously given an outlet for describing concerns about their overall language learning experience.

The dialogue journal may offer an easier way to concentrate students' writing on learning strategies. If a learner provides insufficient information regarding the use of a given strategy, the researcher could, in responding to the entry, ask for further explanation of the learner's strategy use. Even if the researcher is able to focus students' writing on a certain learning strategy, the resulting data are still difficult to work with. First, the resulting information is more qualitative than it is quantitative, and the technique for summarizing and analyzing quantitative data will not be as applicable (Bailey, 1981); thus the researcher is left without a rigorous means of testing hypotheses. However, as shown by Oxford, Lavine, Felkins, Hollaway, and Saleh (this volume), qualitative data can be transformed to quantitative data through content analysis procedures.

Second, the typically small number of subjects in diary or dialogue journal studies ordinarily restricts the ability of researchers to generalize the findings to all language learners of a given age or proficiency level (Bailey, 1991; Nunan, 1992). We should also note that diaries and dialogue journals are subject to the criticisms of verbal report since the data on learning strategies are in fact self-report and self-observation.

ADVANTAGES OF DIARIES AND DIALOGUE JOURNALS

In spite of these limitations, diaries and dialogue journals can be useful research tools. The aim of most diary studies is not to produce rigorous quantitative results which are generalizable to language learners as a whole; instead, diaries have been used to find out what is significant to the learners, a very important area of concern (Bailey, 1991). Furthermore, much of the data that are collected in a diary or dialogue journal may be inaccessible through other research techniques (Nunan, 1992). In addition, diary and journal writing may be of benefit to the students themselves because regular writing can help them become more aware of their strategies.

A final plus with regard to diaries is that they can be kept anywhere by anyone. Learners have the option of writing for even several months before giving their diaries to a researcher for analysis. Therefore, diaries may be more conducive than dialogue journals to research on learning in less structured learning environments (e.g., an overseas setting where the learner lives for three months with a family during summer vacation). One such diary was kept by Rivers (1979) during a trip to Chile.

In the case of dialogue journals, the learners and reader(s) must be able to correspond with each other easily and frequently. For this reason, most dialogue journals are kept by people who see each other regularly. On the other hand, it would be possible to set up a dialogue journal arrangement between learners in one location and readers in another, using electronic mail as the link.

RECOLLECTIVE STUDIES

Recollective studies (sometimes called "learner histories;" see Green, Oxford, and Green, 1995) involve thinking back to some prior language experience and attempting to reconstruct what it was like. While journals reflect a learner's periodic, ongoing record of strategy use while participating in the learning process, a recollective account refers to a learner's description and interpretation of a language learning experience that occurred months or even years before. Although recollective study may contain information about specific strategies or problems the learner encountered, given the time lapse the learner is more likely to recollect about the experience as a whole, possibly comparing two or more experiences. Journals, on the other hand, often focus on the specific language learning setting in which the learner is involved at the time and can be limited to a certain set of strategies that are of interest to the researcher.

Recollective studies can take a variety of forms, depending on the preferences of the subjects or the researchers. The information could be in the form of written narratives or poems (see Oxford, Lavine, Felkins, Hollaway, and Saleh, this volume) or as responses to an oral interview, where information is tape-recorded and then transcribed. The recollections often consist of a description of significant events in the learner's experience while studying the language, such as going through a silent period or dealing with different sets of emotions that emerge in various environments. If interviews are used as a means of getting the learners to recollect, the emphasis would presumably be on creating an environment in which the learner feels comfortable about describing language learning events from the sometimes distant past. A key element here would be to ensure the learners' freedom to retell the significant aspects of their personal language learning experiences in any appropriate form, most likely unstructured.

DISADVANTAGES OF RECOLLECTIVE STUDIES

The major drawback of this assessment method is the inevitable memory deterioration between language learning experience and the research study. The time lapse creates several problems: loss of detail over time, general nature of remaining information, generalizations made by learners about strategies used or problems encountered, and possible reinterpretation or distortion of events. Consequently, the results of any recollective study should be viewed as anecdotal, highly individualistic, and possibly distorted accounts of students' learning experiences.

ADVANTAGES OF RECOLLECTIVE STUDIES

In spite of these problems, recollective studies have advantages. First, this type of study may be more objective because of the learner's distance from the experience. Second, the learner can provide an overall summary of the learning experience because recollections are unlikely to be burdened with too many details. Third, this type of study allows subjects to gain important personal insights as to learning strategies that have tended to work for them (e.g., setting specific goals, such as ordering a meal in the target language) and as to settings that they have tended to prefer (e.g., chatting in a cafe versus discussing a topic with a partner in class). This self-awareness of personal learning preferences can be of significant value to students to want to take an active role in managing their own future learning experiences.

As the number of recollective studies increases, it may become possible to discern patterns in the recollections themselves. In other words, it may be found that certain types of strategies are more likely to be recollected than others. For example, a strategy dealing with an emotional upset around a language goof may come to mind more readily than a strategy for remembering certain grammar points.

COMPUTER TRACKING

Researchers are now starting to explore the potential of computer tracking in assessing language learning strategy use. This may turn out to be a promising tool for certain areas of research. Such programs can be used to collect information either with or without the learner's awareness. Such tracking could get at language learning strategies associated with the use of resource functions accompanying word processing programs, the order of processing of elements in reading text for comprehension or in producing written text, and the choice of speed for reading and writing tasks. As of the present time, the computer tracking technology has been applied in only a limited way to researching learning strategies. The strategies investigated are those supplied by computer programs in the form of resource functions.

Tracking can unobtrusively create a log of learners' uses for various resource functions contained within the computerized language program, whether in writing tasks (e.g., word processing, filling out forms), reading tasks (a summarization exercise, a close task, a multiple-choice reading comprehension task), or grammar drills. These resource functions could include a dictionary, a thesaurus, a reference grammar, a style checker, a spell checker, tutorials on how to complete given language tasks (e.g., formation of verb tenses), and background knowledge on a given topic (Chapelle and Mizuno, 1989).

With the exception of the observational method, the research methods discussed so far have relied on the learner's self-generated descriptions of strategy use, either through written or oral assessment techniques, and as noted above, results of these assessments can be problematic for various reasons. By automatically recording a learner's use of a resource function, the computer eliminates the problem of distortion through human inaccuracy or unawareness. Chapelle and Mizuno (1989), for example, studied the extent of use of resource functions by high and low proficiency ESL students doing computerized grammar lessons. Baily (this volume) reports a study using a French word-processing program to record individual adult students' use of resource functions while the students worked on essays. These resource functions included a dictionary, sets of vocabulary and phrase groups, a reference grammar, and a spell-checker. Baily looked for evidence of four compensation strategies: using synonyms, using circumlocutions, coining new words, and approximating the message.

DISADVANTAGES OF COMPUTER TRACKING

One limitation of computer tracking is its inability to describe language learning or use strategies which do not result in the use of a resource function on the computer. For example, a computer would be unable to detect a learner's use of inferencing to determine a word's meaning. In other words, the strategy must result in a concrete manipulation of the computer program; otherwise, the computer will be unable to detect the use of that strategy. Thus, computers may be better able to provide a comprehensive picture of strategy use when employed in tandem with another method, such as verbal report, which can capture mentalistic strategies.

Another limitation of computer tracking is that its very on-line nature may interfere with the collecting of data. For example, it is easier to collect such data from reading and writing tasks than from listening tasks, and next to impossible to collect such data from speaking tasks without task disruption.

Use of computer tracking as an assessment tool is also affected by other practical matters. As Baily (this volume) notes, some students are more comfortable than others with computer technology. Second, inferring strategy use by comparing computer logs to final compositions or reading comprehension tests may be difficult in certain circumstances. There is always the danger that the researcher will be mistaken in the strategy inference. Third, research might be limited by the lack of commercial availability of programs. This may limit the languages that are used for research. Finally, the resources in the computer programs themselves may be limited, causing some students to use other dictionaries or reference grammars.

ADVANTAGES OF COMPUTER TRACKING

Regardless of the above limitations, computer tracking has a potential use in certain kinds of research. In fact, such programs are quite suitable for studying strategies for producing written language while lacking adequate linguistic knowledge. To a more limited extent, computers can track strategies for forming concepts and hypotheses by keeping a log of the learner's use of resource functions to look up unknown words or phrases during the composition or reading process.

CONCLUSIONS

Every assessment method offers unique advantages as well as disadvantages. The challenge for researchers is to choose an assessment method that will provide the desired information for the given study. In a fledgling field like second language strategy use, there is as yet no fully established set of assessment procedures, so it is necessary to try out different approaches and evaluate their effectiveness.

Issues influencing choice of assessment method and selections of options within the method include the following: the purpose of the study (to generate hypotheses or to conduct a detailed case study of one learner), the number of learners and researchers, the resources available, the strategies to be studied, the types of language tasks for which the strategies are used (e.g., speaking or reading), and the context in which the language learning takes place (e.g., a university class or a three-month visit to a foreign country).

The potential of some assessment methods has yet to be extensively explored by researchers. For instance, computer technology has been used in only a limited number of studies on language learning strategies to date. As researchers become more familiar with computers and other assessment options, new assessment methods will surely be developed.

Given the problems inherent in any assessment method, researchers may want to use a combination of assessment methods. Returning to the example with which we opened the chapter, namely wanting to describe the speaking strategies used in role-playing in an intermediate-level university course in Japanese, we would ask the question, "How best might we describe the speaking strategies of these students?"

We could start by asking how much could be obtained through interviews or written questionnaires. If written questionnaires might not be appropriate in this case, it would be possible to interview the learners and to include verbal report techniques in the interview. Since the learners are usually given a few minutes to think about the role-play before starting, the researcher could request that they provide self-revelation (think-aloud) data during this time. These data are likely to include planning and rehearsing strategies such as searching for patterned (prefabricated) phrases and attempting to paraphrase in the case of unknown words.

Next we could utilize retrospective verbal report to reconstruct the use of strategies just after the generating of the utterances. For example, the researcher may wish to ask a student about the usage of a certain phrase in order to determine whether it is an instance of approximation (when learners are unable to find a particular target language word and substitute a similar, perhaps more general word instead, as in "tool" for "wrench"). The greater the time lapse between the role-play and the follow-up interview, the greater the likelihood that memory deterioration will take place.

Then we could determine whether any of the data could be collected by means of observing the learners and videotaping the conversations. As mentioned above, not many strategies are actually observable, but the researcher may see evidence of the following: keeping in the target language, translating words into the native language, miming, gesturing, appealing for assistance, and coining new words. As a backup to the observations, we could check the videotapes to see whether the use of any of these strategies was captured on video.

In addition, we could show the video of the speaking task to the learners to prompt their memory. If the learners are to view the videotape, the timing of the interview may be an issue to consider. On one hand, we may want to replay the videotape for the learners soon after the actual speaking task in order to avoid the effects of memory deterioration as much as possible. On the other hand, the researcher may wish to view the video numerous times in order to formulate questions that would be asked in a subsequent session.

Finally, the learners could be encouraged to make entries into a dialogue journal which the teacher would collect and to which he or she would respond. Special permission could be obtained to allow researchers access to these journals as well. The learner entries could provide more insights regarding strategy use, in some cases clarifying or elaborating on points made during the verbal report interviews. As an incentive to the learners, the teachers could offer extra credit for those students who keep journals. Ideally, the teachers would be knowledgeable enough about the research that their replies to the learners would help to provide more focus to future entries.

In conclusion, researchers and teachers have a variety of assessment methods at their disposal, and these methods may be combined in any number of ways to collect the most useful strategy data for a given study. The field of language learning strategies may benefit most from a wide application of assessment methods in multiple research contexts.

PART II:

HOW CAN WE

IMPROVE STRATEGY USE

AROUND THE WORLD?

Martha Nyikos
Indiana University, USA

CHAPTER 8

THE CONCEPTUAL SHIFT TO LEARNER-CENTERED CLASSROOMS: INCREASING TEACHER AND STUDENT STRATEGIC AWARENESS

It takes better teachers to focus on the learner.
–Peter Strevens

SUMMARY

This chapter focuses chiefly on teacher awareness of language learning strategies, because without such awareness, it is impossible for teachers to assist their students overtly in improving strategy use. The author shows how important it is for teachers to pay attention to their own level of understanding of learning strategies. She describes a study designed to deepen teachers' awareness, sharpen their attention, increase their intent to teach strategies, and give them metacognitive control. The analysis of this study shows that the teachers could be grouped as resisters, middle-grounders, and assimilators in the two-way process of strategic teaching and learning.

INTRODUCTION

As the field of second language education becomes more learner-centered, a simultaneous focus on learning strategies is evolving. The move from teacher-centered to learner-centered instruction has caused teachers to make a major shift in their views of instruction, away from teaching strategies to an understanding that learning strategies make up a substantial part of the teaching-learning equation. This chapter considers the success and the difficulties encountered in making this conceptual shift by examining characteristics of successful teachers' lesson planning.

The change toward increased emphasis on learning strategies was found to present major difficulties for more than one-third of a group of 47 practicing teachers in a graduate level teacher education course. Research findings based on observation and participant-generated lesson plans are reported below. Results showed that some teachers, while being aware of many language-learning strategy needs of students, found it difficult to incorporate learning strategy instruction into their lessons. In this study, insights are explored based on the concept of "teaching to learn," or how to teach learning strategies and language at the same time.

Nyikos, M. (1996). The conceptual shift to learner-centered classrooms: Increasing teacher and student strategic awareness. In Rebecca L. Oxford (Ed.), *Language learning strategies around the world: Cross-cultural perspectives*. (Technical Report #13) (pp. 109–117). Honolulu: University of Hawai'i, Second Language Teaching & Curriculum Center.

CONCEPTUAL BACKGROUND

The process that foreign language students use to understand and gain control of their learning mirrors the processes that teachers employ when they periodically reconceptualize their teaching approaches. On the conceptual level, many of the problems exhibited by teachers learning how to accommodate students' learning needs through improved teaching strategies are also the problems shown by students learning how to build strategies for their own language learning.

This section considers the similarity between learning how to use learning strategies from a student's perspective and learning how to teach in a more student-centered fashion from the teacher's perspective. In the latter case, the necessity for a conceptual shift in teacher thinking is explored by looking at the factors involve in re-thinking teaching. In a later section, a study scrutinizing the lesson plans of 47 teachers helps provide evidence of how these teachers fostered the process of helping students learn how to learn.

Making the conceptual shift has two general components. First, teachers need to understand the learning process through learners' eyes. Second, teachers need to change their teaching strategies to assist learning strategy development among students.

Teachers' conceptions about how learning occurs influence their ability to make the cognitive shift toward focusing on the needs of the learner. Teacher beliefs about the difficulty level of given tasks and the ability to enhance students' learning help determine the choice of teaching strategies, which can in turn have important implications for students' learning and achievement.

Strong focus on decision-making by teachers implies that teachers are the key agents in the teaching-learning process. The research literature often falls prey to this assumption by not fully recognizing the equally critical role of learners in the educational scheme (Nyikos, 1994). For example, seen from the goal orientation of the communicative competence perspective (e.g., Canale and Swain, 1980) in language instruction, learning is conceived to be a product to be described, with little attention given to the process by which learners attain their goals.

Commenting on two major approaches to teaching conversation in language classrooms, Richards (1990) cites an indirect and direct approach. The indirect approach occurs when "conversational competence is seen as the product of engaging learners in conversational interaction" (pp. 76–77). In this indirect approach, competence emerges given enough comprehensible input and opportunities to interact, without attention given to learning strategies. A more direct approach to teaching conversation involves teaching students to use better learning strategies. Richards asserts that "prompted by the awareness that learners may succeed despite the teacher's methods and techniques rather than because of them, researchers as well as teachers have begun to look more closely at learners themselves in an attempt to discover how successful learners achieve their results" (1990, pp. 42–43).

Second language acquisition research has begun to reaffirm the importance of the learner, not just the teacher (Larsen-Freeman, 1991). Although SLA theory has concerned itself mostly with acquisition in natural language settings, it has proven helpful in generating hypotheses about learning and teaching processes in language classroom settings as well. SLA research posits a variety of learning strategies for expediting the storage, retrieval, and use of the target language. Although these strategies are viewed differently by SLA and foreign language researchers, it is generally agreed that learners develop learning strategies gradually, in response to increasingly demanding linguistic tasks (Oxford and Nyikos, 1989). From the perspective of learner-centered research, learning strategies are deliberate steps taken by learners to make learning easier and retrieval more efficient through planful approaches. These developing strategies lead to routines that are eventually "forgotten" as awareness shifts away from consciously remembering vocabulary, phrases, and formulaic speech toward meaningful interaction through situationally and socioculturally appropriate application of language structures (as considered by pragmatics). In the latter stage of language practice and application, communication becomes paramount, and accuracy is no longer the chief concern of the learner. Naturally, these priorities vary from learner to learner and teacher to teacher. Consequently, strategies will shift from those serving immediate incremental novice needs (such as memory-based avoidance and repetition strategies) to those that support lengthier utterances, pragmatic appropriateness, cohesion, and fluency.

Recently learning models and factor analytic research have recognized that learning involves highly interdependent, parallel information processing strategies (Nyikos, 1990a) that interact with social and affective variables. This presents a complex picture. Teacher educators must help teachers deal with these strategies and variables and must help teachers incorporate learning strategy instruction into their solidly developed teaching routines. Teachers who have made the conceptual shift toward accommodating students' learning strategy needs will be able to demonstrate this shift as they construct lesson plans.

Once teachers have made this conceptual shift, their role in helping students develop strategic competence involves two steps. First, they must be aware of the types of productive and ineffective strategies certain tasks may evoke; and second, they must tailor these tasks so that students can profit from linguistic input and simultaneously receive guidance in appropriate, task-related strategy use.

The interplay of factors involved in setting learnability parameters, instructional and learner goals, and projected outcome standards influences how teacher and learner need to relate in order to achieve maximum learning effectiveness. The most crucial variable here is the extent to which the learner is involved in the teacher's instructional planning and the resulting accommodations the teacher makes to the student's needs. Many students believe that the most important determinant of teaching ability is that teachers be able to fine-tune their teaching to the level and ability of the learner (Nyikos, 1991).

Teachers who have made the strategic-conceptual shift to a learning strategy approach may enable students to override some of their educational limits and thereby help them to extend their ability to compensate for missing knowledge, increase comprehension, and develop linguistic competence. Students set their own limits to what they can cope with at any given time: "I hear it, but I ignore it" (Mangubhai, 1991). They also set the cognitive parameters of learnability (Gass, 1988). Pienemann (1989) posits a readiness factor in the learner that illustrates constraints on the effects of direct instruction, with readiness defined as an inability for or cognitive resistance to learning certain grammatical features before others. Similarly, Doughty (1991) speaks of maturational constraints causing learners to resist learning certain features. Researchers such as Ellis (1987), Gass (1988), and particularly Brindley (1991) note that intensive classroom instruction has effects on surface features only, with little evidence of transfer to naturalistic environments where attention moves from form to meaning. Much of this research fails to address how students would learn if given specific, task-appropriate strategies for transfer to social contexts. Teachers who have made the cognitive shift to teaching with learning strategies become sensitive to such student learning difficulties and thus can improve their teaching effectiveness. Whether learner readiness is a matter of confidence or competence, research should not ignore the power of strategies to compensate for or bridge gaps in learners' progress.

SLA researchers have noted that engaging students in clarification or negotiation of meaning is a key factor in communicative application of received data (Ellis, 1987; Gass, 1988; Brindley, 1991). Such clarification and negotiation demand the use of learning strategies. However, SLA researchers do not address the role of strategy instruction in overcoming learning restrictions caused by task unfamiliarity, memory limitations, or lack of awareness of available strategy choices.

A major aspect of making the conceptual shift to a learning strategy approach involves teachers' awareness that what is obvious to them might not be obvious to learners, and that constant interactive feedback is necessary for effective teaching to occur. Similar to the need for teachers to build awareness of their teaching strategies (Freeman, 1989), learning strategy research indicates that learners must gain awareness in order to exert the metacognitive control necessary to manage learning (Chamot and Küpper, 1989; Nyikos, 1991; Oxford, 1990b; O'Malley and Chamot, 1990).

Ellis (1986) discusses strategies that arise spontaneously, usually necessitated by response to a tasks or transferred from the native language. However, he makes no mention of strategy instruction. In more recent studies (Cohen, 1990b; O'Malley and Chamot, 1990; Oxford, 1990b; Wenden and Rubin, 1987), language learning strategy instruction is explicitly addressed. There is consensus that through overt strategy instruction learners can be helped in four ways: (1) to become aware of the strategies they already use; (2) to apply task-specific strategies that can make learning more efficient and allow them to compensate for nervousness, inability to remember, and lack of wait time; (3) to monitor for strategy effectiveness; and (4) to create new strategies or weed out ineffective ones via metacognitive (conscious, critical) control (Wenden, 1985a, 1985b; Chamot and Küpper, 1989; Nyikos, 1991). The teacher has an expanded role as a result of having responsibility for strategy instruction (Wenden, 1985a Ely, 1994). Nevertheless, few if any studies have examined exactly how practicing teachers or teachers-in-training incorporate into their practice the teaching of strategies suited to the learning needs of students.

THE PRESENT STUDY

SAMPLE

Participants included 47 junior high school, senior high school, and community college teachers taking part in an intensive teacher education course designed to introduce foreign language and ESL teachers to learning strategies. Of the 47 regular teachers, 3 taught two different languages, 26 taught Spanish, 14 taught French, 7 taught German, and 2 taught ESL. Five of the teachers were men. Mean age was 40 years, with a range of 23 to 57. Teaching experience ranged from 3 to 29 years with a mean of 10.9 years.

DESCRIPTION

The intensive course reviewed major findings in learning strategy research and involved participants in demonstrations, pairwork, and groupwork in which they applied strategy instruction ideas. All four language skills were involved, as well as vocabulary, communication, and grammar. Class members were assigned a term project of writing lesson plans, in which they were to show how they would incorporate learning strategy instruction through teacher modeling. Modeling was to be used so that students (1) would see learning strategies as a natural component of the information they are studying and (2) would have a greater chance for efficient data retrieval in communicative contexts. The latter point capitalized on the psycholinguistic principle that concepts stored together are retrieved together (Bransford, 1979). Participants were required to write rationales and include lists of strategies in their lesson plans. They were given the option of delivering instruction to best suit their teaching styles.

Resulting lesson plans were analyzed on the basis of (1) incorporation of several learning strategy types (cognitive, memory, social, affective, metacognitive, and compensatory; see Oxford, 1990b, 1990c) into regular class activities; (2) demonstration of how strategies were incorporated; and (3) explicitness of strategy instruction. The latter two criteria are the subject of debate in learning strategy research. The manner in which strategies are taught can be explicit (informed) or covert (blind) (Brown et al., 1983; Oxford et al., 1990). With informed training, students are given examples of strategies suited to a specific language task along with the rationale for their use; blind training does not provide this rationale, and it assumes that tasks alone are enough to cause strategy implementation. In both cases, strategies are embedded into instruction rather than being taught as a separate component.

After building content- and context-specific strategies, Perkins and Solomon (1987) advocate teaching for transfer by explicit attention to where and when to use a strategy cluster. In this way students can avoid the problems encountered when transferring training into practice (Belmont et al., 1982; Perkins and Solomon, 1987, 1988).

RESULTS

Results of the present study, based on the above three criteria, show that only one-third (16) of the 47 teachers were able to make the conceptual shift to incorporating learning strategy instruction into their classroom teaching. Another one-third (16) were middle-grounders, and the final third (15) failed to demonstrate learning strategy instruction beyond conventional strategies delivered by lecture rather than by example or teacher modeling.

The successful teachers (those who made the shift and can be called "assimilators" of the learning strategy approach) demonstrated approximately three times per lesson that they would model more than one strategy type per task. They used multiple and multisensory strategies, explicitly modeling those strategies and asking students to apply them. These strategies were most frequently cognitive strategies and social strategies. Moreover, in a post-activity phase, assimilators asked students to state in their own words the strategies they had just applied and to analyze how these helped them carry out a task. Asking students to analyze and discuss their strategies (metacognitive analysis) was key factor separating the successful teachers from those who were judged to be less successful. Assimilators treated textbooks as springboards for interactive tasks. Assimilators showed in their lesson plans that they were already teaching in a fashion that took students' interests and needs into account. To use a metaphor, these teachers often stood in their students' shoes and rarely used the teacher's desk as a dividing line. For these teachers, the conceptual shift to teaching by modeling learning strategies was natural, since the pattern in their regular routines was such that they could easily incorporate strategy instruction.

The "middle-grounders," those who almost made the conceptual shift, were found to summarize for students, thereby falling short of the opportunity to foster metacognitive strategies in their classes. These teachers were effective as managers of time and pacing, with many interactive events built into their lesson plans. Unlike the "resisters" whose lesson plans were marked by abrupt shifts in activities, middle-grounders planned smooth transitions between activities, typically providing some opportunity to engage in communication. Most strikingly, their lesson plans reflected a belief that the assignment of specific tasks would implicitly evoke the intended strategies listed in the rationale portion of the lesson plans. Many of the tasks were conventional dialogue planning and performance assignments done in pairs (rarely in small groups), with a heavy assessment component in which the teacher looks for mastery of grammar points. Many middle-grounders opted to conduct games to activate certain strategies. In some cases the games appeared time-consuming in proportion to the amount of learning. In short, middle-grounders were effective organizers, but they treated learning strategy guidance as a separate activity or else felt that tasks themselves evoked the desired strategies. Metaphorically, these teachers stepped out from behind the barrier of the desk and stood beside the desk. They moved toward understanding learning but did not yet assimilate ways to incorporate explicit learning strategy instruction.

The unsuccessful teachers or "resisters" rarely involved students in any discussion or interactive activities at all. Resisters' teaching style followed the transmission model of education, where the teacher is the knower and the primary conduit of one-way information transfer. Their lesson plans reflected a teacher-fronted classroom with little student input, except in a reactive mode. Learning strategies that were listed in the introductory rationale (asked of all teachers in their lesson plans) consisted of conventional strategies such as "cognitive" approaches, as when students memorize vocabulary and put words into thematic lists. Resisters, who were not effective teachers or strategy instructors, placed themselves squarely behind the barrier of the teacher's desk and made no attempt to understand the need of the learners. Interestingly, in their roles as students in this intensive teacher education course, these participants followed a conventional student mode of learning, taking notes and replicating in their lesson plans many of the principles in a mechanical way.

DISCUSSION

These results underscore the importance of awareness, a point highlighted in teaching research (Freeman, 1989) and in learning strategy research (Nyikos, 1991; O'Malley and Chamot, 1990). Conscious control over tasks allows for informed strategic approaches to both teaching and learning.

Novice versus expert

A relevant area of research is that of novice and expert performance. Leinhardt (1983) asserts that novice and expert teachers are equal in their abilities to judge student performance but notes that experts demonstrate a better grasp of the reasons and means for arriving at these decisions. Thus, experts not only know the facts or the "what" of teaching (declarative knowledge) but also the "how to" of accommodating these new elements into their teaching (procedural knowledge), to use Anderson's (1976, 1985) terms. Novices need explicit, clearly-modeled instruction involving overt structure and steps to lead into schema-building or reassimilation.

Yet experts are not entirely exempt from the needs faced by novices. Whenever a major shift of thinking or routinized approach is required, even practiced teachers appear to be thrust back into a seemingly novice role. The resulting cognitive dissonance in an otherwise well-orchestrated approach requires time and conscious effort to resolve. The evidence from this study points to the use of metacognitive awareness by one-third of the teachers (the assimilators). As one teacher commented at the end of the course, "I needed to realize that perhaps the reason some of my students aren't learning is not because they're not studying, but rather because they don't know *how* to study a foreign language." A 20-year veteran teacher stated, "After learning about learning strategies and seeing some concrete examples, I'm finally starting to understand what's involved in the learning process.... I'm also now able to recognize what I'm actually doing to help them learn."

Context and task

Contexts set the parameters of tasks and can facilitate solving these tasks if the elements inherent in the contexts are familiar and accessible. Yet we cannot rely on tasks or situations to allow either teaching or learning strategies to arise spontaneously. Such a reactive mode assures neither appropriate nor cogent development of teaching or learning strategies.

Teaching strategy research has much to gain from learning strategy research. It is recognized that teachers have a strong role in the learning process (Richards, 1990). Less recognized is the fact that principles such as awareness, metacognitive control, and transfer of skills are similar in learning how to teach and learning how to learn.

Practiced teachers must rethink their routines, finding appropriate moments to insert the new element of strategy instruction. In the present study, the assimilators made the shift to learning strategy modeling in a seemingly effortless manner. However, less successful teachers placed learning strategy instruction rather effortfully into a separate teaching module or simply chose to talk about strategies in a general, non-task-specific way without modeling them. They acted as though they believed that a given task would automatically conjure up a particular learning strategy in their students. This teacher belief has led many students to frustrating trial-and-error experiences, because tasks do not automatically create appropriate learning strategies.

CONCLUSIONS

When teaching must be redesigned to introduce learning strategies, the shift in a teacher's routine potentially throws the teacher temporarily into the role of novice. This causes a slow-down in teaching fluency until the new element, becomes assimilated, first on the conscious level and then in practice.

In this study, the assimilators succeeded in making the shift to teaching how to learn and needed to make smaller changes in their teaching routine than did those who viewed teaching as a the direct transfer of knowledge. In other words, those participants who made the cognitive shift most readily already demonstrated teaching styles that promoted learner-centered classrooms.

In contrast, the middle-grounders understood the rationale for learning strategy instruction but still taught with a modularized approach, relying on compartmentalized tasks and activities to carry the burden of responsibility for student learning. These teachers used their old teaching approaches and simply added on strategy instruction, or else relied on textbook activities to call up task-appropriate strategies.

The failure of the resisters to change to a learning strategy approach suggests that they themselves were once students who relied on their teachers to feed them information. As illustrated here and by Ely (1994), there is a need for teacher education courses in which participants can practice teaching strategies that are not lecture-oriented and teacher-controlled.

Procedural knowledge of how to teach learning strategies should be an integral part of teacher development programs. By making the conceptual shift toward the learner-centered classroom, teachers are better able to understand the difficulties of novice language students and can become more effective in helping students overcome their learning problems. The goal is to make learning strategies a conscious, efficient tool by which students can facilitate their own learning. One issue is that students have different learning styles, so reliance on a single learning strategy or a single set of strategies is inadequate. A solution is to teach several task-appropriate strategies with any given task, so that students can have the chance to choose the strategies associated with their particular learning styles.

The conceptual shift that allows teachers to place themselves in their learners' shoes also helps them avoid the false assumption that what is self-evident to them is also self-evident to their students. Teachers (and their students) become aware that not everyone learns the same way and with the same strategies. Teachers must make the conceptual shift to learning strategy instruction if they wish to improve the effectiveness of their teaching strategies and help students become more effective, more autonomous learners.

Maaike Hajer
Utrecht Institute for Higher and Professional Education, The Netherlands
Theun Meestringa
National Institute for Curriculum Development, The Netherlands
Young Ye Park
Korea Advanced Institute of Science and Technology, Korea
Rebecca L. Oxford
University of Alabama, USA

CHAPTER 9

HOW PRINT MATERIALS PROVIDE STRATEGY INSTRUCTION

To rede, and drive the night away.
–Geoffrey Chaucer

SUMMARY

This chapter shows how print materials provide strategy instruction. The first mode is learning strategies embedded in language textbooks. The second mode is general learner guidebooks explaining how to study any language more effectively. The third mode is self-directional strategy training materials explicitly designed to supplement a particular course of language study. An investigation concerning the first and second modes took place using materials from the US, the Netherlands, and the UK, while a different study of the third mode occurred in the US.

INTRODUCTION

Language learners are not machines; they can influence their own learning processes. We assume that strategic competence — the use of language learning strategies — is one of the main means by which learners exercise their own autonomy and self-direction (see Wenden and Rubin, 1987). Learning strategies are taught and learned via many resources, one of which is the printed word. Many books (e.g., Cohen, 1990b; O'Malley and Chamot, 1990; Oxford, 1990b; Wenden and Rubin, 1987) have mentioned some forms of print materials as part of a strategy instruction program. However, researchers have not carefully studied the following important modes. First, many current *foreign/second language textbooks* insert learning strategies into language learning material. These textbooks have the possibility, not always fully realized, of helping learners become more independent and self-directed through the use of learning strategies. Next, *foreign/second language learner guidebooks*, which do not teach a language per se but instead teach how to learn almost any language, are usually even more direct in offering strategies as a major means for improving language learning. Dozens of such guidebooks have been published in the

Hajer, M., Meestringa, T., Park, Y. Y., & Oxford, R. L. (1996). How print materials provide strategy instruction. In Rebecca L. Oxford (Ed.), *Language learning strategies around the world: Cross-cultural perspectives*. (Technical Report #13) (pp. 119–140). Honolulu: University of Hawai'i, Second Language Teaching & Curriculum Center.

US and the UK and eagerly read by at least a proportion of the language learning population. Finally, *separate, self-directed, print-based strategy instructional materials* have been designed to parallel existing courses of language study so that learners will be able, on their own, to expand their strategy repertoire while strengthening their language skills. In this chapter, we describe a US-UK-Netherlands study that deals with the first two of these modes of print materials for strategy instruction. Then we explain a US study of self-directed strategy instructional materials used with ESL students improving their reading comprehension.

In this chapter, *mother tongue* refers to the language earliest learned at home. *Foreign language* means a language learned in a setting where it is not the main language of daily use, like Hebrew learned in South Africa. *Second language* refers to a language that is learned in an environment where that language is the primary language of everyday communication, such as English learned in England. Before turning to the two studies, let us discuss relevant strategy instruction developments in Europe and the US.

SELECTIVE REVIEW OF DEVELOPMENTS IN EUROPEAN AND US STRATEGY INSTRUCTION

The movement toward learner autonomy in Europe has become a major one in the last ten to fifteen years, with the help of Henri Holec (1988) in France and Leslie Dickinson (1987) in the UK, as well as the International Association of Teachers of Foreign Language (IATEFL) special interest section on learner autonomy. "Learning to learn" is part of the New Threshold Level in Europe (van Ek and Trim, 1991). Intensive European research in the area of learning strategies has been abundant for many years, resulting in increasing numbers of prescriptions directly to language learners about how to improve their learning. Ellis and Sinclair's (1989) book, *Learning to Learn English*, included in the current study, was published in the UK for nonnative learners of English. Holec's CRAPEL group has produced numerous materials on strategies and autonomy.

The Netherlands are one of the countries taking the lead in strategy instruction. Westhoff (1981, 1989) introduced strategies for foreign language reading skills, thus closely linking strategy instruction with reading. Schouten-van Parreren (1985) studied guessing strategies for vocabulary learning. Since 1993, compensation strategies have been part of the national high school foreign language curriculum's core objectives. Within Dutch mother tongue teaching, the writing-strategy ideas of Flower and Hayes (1981) have taken hold. Sijtstra (1991), Hajer (1993), and Meestringa (1993) have argued for a more comprehensive view of strategic competence.

In the US, development of strategy instruction proceeded differently. Second and foreign language researchers built on the work on learning strategies by noted researchers in the first language reading field. The novice-to-expert research in a variety of areas such as engineering, physics, and reading had a strong effect on researchers, who quickly began to figure out what expert language learners were like in the so-called "good language learner" studies (for a summary, see Oxford, 1992/1993). The widespread thinking-skills movement in the US, symbolized by the work of Costa (1990), seeks to teach students how to use higher order thinking skills and has influenced researchers interested in language learning strategies.

Quite recently in the US, major language publishers like Heinle and Heinle, McGraw Hill, and Heath began publishing language textbooks that include language learning strategies. Heinle's *The Tapestry Program*, co-edited by one of the authors of this chapter, offers its authors instruction in how to include strategies, how to phrase them clearly, and how to make them an integral part of the text. Guidebooks for language students in the US have been popular for decades; three of these are included in the current work. These guidebooks, however, have not typically been keyed to a particular course of language study. Self-directed print materials linked with a certain course of study have been created by individuals such as Park (see Study 2 in this chapter) and have usually not been widely disseminated.

STUDY 1:
TEXTBOOKS AND GUIDEBOOKS
AS USED FOR STRATEGY INSTRUCTION

One way of understanding developments in strategy instruction in various countries is by analyzing language textbooks, as Study 1 has done. (For more details on Study 1, see the Dutch language version by Hajer, Meestringa, Oxford, and Park-Oh, 1994). One has to be very cautious in using data from textbook analyses; such analyses should be accompanied, of course, by ethnographic research about how teachers use textbooks in actual classrooms and how students use textbooks at home. Students' reactions to US-published Spanish textbooks have been explored by Young and Oxford (1993), but an in-depth view of actual use awaits investigation. Learner guidebooks, which abound in certain countries, can also be analyzed as vehicles for strategy instruction, but with the same caveats about real use of these books. As discussed by Oxford and Leaver in their chapter on strategy instruction (this volume), strategies can be included in textbooks or guidebooks either explicitly or implicitly. By *explicit* presentation we mean giving learners overt messages such as "Strategy X [for instance, breaking down words into parts to understand the meaning] is a useful technique. Here is an example of how you can use it.... Here are practice opportunities to help you learn this strategy.... Here is how you can transfer it to another exercise.... Here is how you can tell if your use of this strategy is successful." Van Parreren (1988) stresses the importance of using explicit rather than implicit strategy presentation.

RESEARCH QUESTIONS

1. Which language learning strategies have been used in mother tongue, foreign, and second language textbooks and in learner guidebooks in the US, the UK, and the Netherlands?

2. What are the frequencies and percentages of six different kinds of language learning strategies in these books?

3. Is there a difference in percentages of each kind of learning strategy across types of books (mother tongue, foreign language, second language, and guidebooks)?

4. Is strategy use linked with certain language skills in these books?

5. In what ways are strategies presented to learners: implicitly or explicitly?

6. To what extent is the use of strategies displayed to students and practiced by students?

7. Do the books encourage students' reflection on using strategies?

8. Is it possible to describe the state-of-the-art in strategy instruction in different countries based on textbooks and guidebooks?

LOCATIONS

Two countries were initially chosen as a starting point for the research: the US and the Netherlands. However, a third country, the UK, was included because of a recently published and widely used UK learner guidebook by Ellis and Sinclair (1989). We had hoped to include other countries around the world. However, at the time the research began there were few if any language textbooks in other countries that included a range of learning strategies in any implicit or explicit way.

SAMPLE

The sample consisted of selected textbooks and guidebooks. The chapter authors, all strategy specialists, chose a sample of language textbooks of foreign languages and second languages (in the US and the Netherlands). We also selected (in the US and the UK) learner guidebooks for language learning. Since learner guidebooks were not available in the Netherlands, mother tongue textbooks ("language arts" books teaching Dutch for native Dutch speakers) were used for analysis in that country in place of learner guidebooks. Because of the rather wide choice of US and UK materials, all available materials from these countries were screened for strategy use. US and UK books were included in this study only if the strategies were explicitly stated and labeled as learning strategies, tips, or techniques. Several Tapestry series titles were intentionally included for analysis because one of their main purposes is to teach language learning strategies (along with the language itself). The books from the US and the UK were to be compared with Dutch patterns of strategy use in textbooks (since learner guidebooks were not available). However, the criterion of explicitness of strategies was hardly met in the Dutch-published materials; most language textbooks in the Netherlands did not explicitly label strategies as such. Therefore, the explicitness criterion could not be applied in selecting Dutch-published books for inclusion in this study. Table 9.1 displays an overview of the book representation by country and at the same time provides definitions and examples of the three kinds of language learning (mother tongue, foreign language, and second language). Table 9.2 describes the 17 specific books analyzed in this study.

Table 9.1: Overview of book representation by country

Kinds of books	Countries		
	Netherlands	US	UK
Mother tongue textbooks	X (Dutch for native speakers of Dutch)	– – –	– – –
Foreign language textbooks	X (German and French for nonnative speakers of these languages living in the Netherlands)	X (Spanish for nonnative speakers of Spanish living in non-Spanish parts of the US)	– – –
Second language textbooks	X (Dutch for nonnative speakers of Dutch living in the Netherlands or another Dutch-speaking locale)	X (English for nonnative speakers of English living in the US or another English-speaking locale)	– – –
Learner guidebooks	– – –	X (Guidebooks for both second and foreign language learners)	X (Guidebooks for both second and foreign language learners)

Table 9.2: 17 books analyzed in this study

Key:

MT = Mother Tongue	GFL = German as a Foreign Language	LG = Learner Guidebook
FL = Foreign Language	SL = Second Language	US = United States
FFL = French as a Foreign Language	ESL = English as a Second Language	UK = United Kingdom
SFL = Spanish as a Foreign Language	DSL = Dutch as a Second Language	N = Netherlands

Country/Category	Book Title	Author(s)	Publisher/Date	Description
US ESL/EFL	Get It? Got It!	Gill & Hartmann	Heinle & Heinle/ 1993	Integrated skills, emph. on listening and speaking, low intermed., university, for non-nat. Eng. speakers
US ESL/EFL	Passages: Exploring Spoken English	James	Heinle & Heinle/ 1993	Integrated skills, emph. on listening and speaking, high intermed., university, for non-nat. Eng. speakers
US ESL/EFL	Global Views: Reading About World Issues	Sokolik	Heinle & Heinle/ 1993	Integrated skills, emph. on reading, low adv., university, for non-nat. Eng. speakers
US ESL/EFL	Power Through the Written Word	Scarcella	Heinle & Heinle/ 1993*	Integrated skills, emph. on writing, high intermed., university, for non-nat. Eng. speakers
US SFL	Esquemas	Young & Wolf	Holt, Rinehart & Winston/1990	Spanish reading comp., university, for nat. Eng. speakers
US SFL	¡A conocernos!	Long & Macian	Heinle & Heinle/ 1992	Integrated skills, basal text, beginner, university, for nat. Eng. speakers
US SFL	Visión y Voz	Galloway & Labarca	Heinle & Heinle/ 1993	Integrated skills, basal text, beginner, university, for nat. Eng. speakers
US FL LG	How to Learn a Foreign Language	Fuller	Storm King/1987	Learning ideas for nat. Eng. speakers

Country/Category	Book Title	Author(s)	Publisher/Date	Description
US FL LG	*How to Be A More Successful Language Learner*	Rubin & Thompson	Heinle & Heinle/ 1982**	Learning ideas for nat. Eng. speakers
US FL LG	*Yes! You Can Learn a Foreign Language*	Brown-Azarowicz, Stannard, & Goldin	Passport Bks./ 1987	Learning ideas for nat. Eng. speakers
UK FL/SL LG	*Learning to Learn English*	Ellis & Sinclair	Cambridge/1989	Learning ideas for non-nat. Eng. speakers
N MT	*Goed Nederlands*, Pt. 1/2	Bult et al.	Dijkstra/ 1992/1993	Integrated skills, 1st 2 yrs. sec. ed., for nat. Dutch speakers
N MT	*Nieuw Nederlands*, Pt. 1/2/3	Schlebush et al.	Noordhoff/ 1990–1992	Integrated skills, 1st 3 yrs. sec. ed., for nat. Dutch speakers
N DSL	*Lezen tot de tweede*	Olijkan	Noordhoff/1993	Reading, adv., sec. ed., for non-nat. Dutch speakers
N DSL	*Tekst en begrip*	van Loon	De Kangeroe/ 1991	Reading, adv., sec. ed., for non-nat. Dutch speakers
N GFL	*Aufzug*	Voogt & Haelen	Malmberg/ 1986/1987	Basal text, beginner, low int., sec. ed., for nat. Dutch speakers
N FFL	*Code Genial Pt 1/2/3*	Bimmel-Esteban et al.	Malmberg/ 1990–1993	Basal, beginner, low int., sec. ed., for nat. Dutch speakers

* 2 chapters were available at the time of the research
** Later version of this book is now available (1994)

DATA ANALYSIS PROCEDURES

Each of the materials was analyzed according to Oxford's (1990b) strategy typology containing six categories of strategies: memory, cognitive, compensation, metacognitive, affective, and social. Absolute frequencies were determined for each strategy category in each book. All strategy frequencies were then transformed into percentages for ease of comparison across books, and means and standard deviations of these percentages were found. By percentage we mean the proportion (relative frequency) of strategies in each strategy category relative to the total strategy use per book.

RESULTS AND INTERPRETATION

US ESL/EFL textbooks

Results indicate that each of the six strategy categories is explicitly represented in the selected books. This is not surprising, since the authors of these books were encouraged by the publisher and by the two series editors, Rebecca Oxford and Robin Scarcella, to include strategies from all of the strategy groups.

The total number of strategies in these four books is 344. Two books, Gill/Hartmann and Sokolik, use approximately the same number of strategies (104 and 107), with James using slightly fewer at 82. Scarcella's two chapters yield 51 strategies; therefore, at that rate it is likely that her whole book would contain over 300 strategies. (That analysis will occur later using all chapters.) The most commonly used strategy category is cognitive (122 strategies across the four books), followed by metacognitive (69), memory (52), social (40), affective (35), and compensation (26). The Gill/Hartmann listening and speaking book emphasizes *cognitive* strategies (54% of all strategies in that book), with *metacognitive* strategies coming in a weak second (13%). James' listening and speaking book emphasizes *cognitive* (29%) and *metacognitive* (23%) almost equally. In Sokolik's reading book, *cognitive* strategies (30%) are at almost the same proportion as James', followed by *memory* strategies (22%). The highest percentage of strategy use in Scarcella's two writing chapters is found for *metacognitive* strategies (33%), followed by *cognitive* (18%).

Overall, *cognitive* and *metacognitive* strategy use predominated in these books. *Memory, social, affective,* and *compensation* strategies had lower mean percentages of use (respectively 14%, 12%, 11%, and 8%) across these books than did the top two groups, *cognitive* (24%) and *metacognitive* (22%). Significant differences across these books were found for five out of six of the strategy categories (memory, cognitive, compensation, metacognitive, and affective strategies), but not for social strategies.

US textbooks for Spanish as a foreign language

Three US textbooks for Spanish as a foreign language were examined: Young/Wolf, Long/Macian, and Galloway/Labarca. A total of 174 strategies appeared. Clearly, the Galloway/Labarca book is the overall strategy leader, with 110 strategies compared with 37 for Long/Macian and 27 for Young/Wolf. In addition, the Galloway/Labarca book has substantial numbers of strategies in five of the six strategy categories (all but affective strategies). Interestingly, Galloway/Labarca and Long/Macian are integrated-skills basal texts from the same publisher, but they show distinctly different numbers of strategies. It might have been expectable that the Young/Wolf, which deals with just one skill (reading), might have only a small number of strategies (actual number was 27). However, the ESL reading book by Sokolik, mentioned above among the ESL/EFL books, has 107 strategies. Therefore, in actuality dealing with only one skill does not restrict the number of possible strategies.

Cognitive strategies are by far the most popular among the six strategy groups, with a total of 68 strategies across the three books, followed by compensation strategies (35), memory strategies (34), metacognitive strategies (24), social strategies (12), and affective strategies (1) . Four of the six strategy categories (affective, memory, metacognitive, and social) have only a small number of strategies for the Long/Macian and Young/Wolf books.

Percentages of strategy use in each of the six strategy categories differed for each book. Cognitive strategies lead in each book: 70% for Young/Wolf, 57% for Long/Macian, and 26% for Galloway/Labarca. However, in the Galloway/Labarca book, two other categories of strategies were almost equal in representation to cognitive: memory and compensation. Slightly over half the strategies in these books are cognitive, according to the cross-book mean of 51%. Far behind come the mean percentages for compensation strategies (17%), memory strategies (15%), metacognitive strategies (12%), social strategies (4%), and affective strategies (less than 1%).

There were significant differences found among these foreign language books for each of the six strategy categories. This means that within each strategy type, the books used widely differing numbers of strategies.

US-UK learner guidebooks

The total number of strategies found in the four US-UK learner guidebooks is 264. Metacognitive strategies are the most frequent (93 instances) in the four US-UK learner guidebooks, but cognitive strategies are not too far behind (72). These are followed by social strategies (32), memory strategies (28), compensation strategies (22), and affective strategies (17). The Rubin/Thompson book provides the greatest number of strategies (106), followed at a distance by the three other books: Brown-Azarowicz/Stannard/Goldin (60), Ellis/Sinclair (58), and Fuller (40). Clearly, Rubin and Thompson impart the greatest number of learning strategies to the reader.

Metacognitive strategies and cognitive strategies average 36% and 29%, respectively, of all strategies across the three learner guidebooks, while the lowest categories, compensation and affective, represent only 7% and 6% of all the strategies found in these books. *Memory* and *social* strategies are toward the low range, with 11% and 10%, respectively. *Cognitive* strategies are stressed by Fuller (52.5% of his total number of strategies) and less so by Rubin/Thompson (27%), but *metacognitive* strategies are favored by Brown-Azarowicz/Stannard/Goldin (45%) and Ellis/Sinclair (62%). When comparing across the three learner guidebooks, significant differences are found in terms of percentages in each of the six strategy categories. Again, the books include learning strategies in very different numbers within a given category.

Dutch as a mother tongue textbooks

In two textbooks of Dutch as the mother tongue, explicit strategies are rarely used, in contrast with the frequencies of strategies in the books found earlier. One of the two books (Schlebush et al.) included only one strategy, while the other (Bult et al.) included 17. The total for the two books was therefore 18. Schlebush et al.'s only strategy was *cognitive* (for verb conjugation). Bult et al., who were trying to integrate strategies from a strategic reading textbook (Lijmbach, Hacquebord, and Galema, 1991), included some strategies in each of these three categories: *cognitive* (in this case, skimming, scanning, using resources, note-taking, summarizing), *metacognitive* (planning and identifying the purpose), and *compensation* (guessing from context). Note that we were more tolerant about counting strategies in these books than in the US and UK books. For instance, Bult et al. failed to label the strategies, but all other aspects of explicitness were present in that book. The mean percentage for *cognitive* strategies across the two books was 77%, followed by *metacognitive* (18%) and *compensation* (6%), with absolutely no strategies in these categories: *memory*, *affective*, and *social*.

Dutch as a second language textbooks

Only 10 strategies are included in these two books, and nine of them are *cognitive* (four in Olijkan and five in Van Loon). The Olijkan and van Loon textbooks use cognitive reading strategies, and almost no other strategies are included. Interestingly, the authors of these two DSL books seem to use a computer-based instructional methodology common to Dutch mother tongue books (cf. Witte, 1992a, 1992b), in which the children by themselves have to discover how and when to use what they learn. Eighty percent of Olijkan's few strategies are *cognitive*, while the rest are *compensation*. In contrast, 100% of Van Loon's strategies are *cognitive*. The average percentages across the two books are 90% for *cognitive* and 10% for *compensation*, with no other strategy groups represented.

Netherlands-published foreign language textbooks (German and French)

We now consider the outcomes for two Netherlands-published foreign language books, one in German (Voogt/Haelen) and the other in French (Bimmel-Esteban et al.). The total number of strategies in these two books is 47, and all 47 come from Bimmel-Esteban et al.; no strategies were identifiable in Voogt/Haelen. In the

Bimmel-Esteban book, the strongest category was *cognitive* (37 strategies, dealing with recognizing and using formulas, analyzing contrastively, and other aspects), and three other categories had a sprinkling: *compensation* (5), *metacognitive* (3), and *memory* (2). Almost 80% of Bimmel-Esteban et al.'s strategies (which are called "study indicators" in that book) are *cognitive*, followed by 11% *compensation*, 6% *metacognitive*, and 4% *memory*. Because of the absence of strategies in Voogt/Haelen, the means for each category are exactly half of Bimmel-Esteban et al.'s percentages: 39%, 5%, 3%, and 2% (note rounding effects). Note that the Bimmel-Esteban textbook has been adjusted to the Netherlands' national core objectives, which include strategy use. Some strategies are recycled in the exercises found in the Bimmel-Esteban et al. textbook.

SUMMARY AND IMPLICATIONS

Before summarizing the results, we want to reemphasize that the selection of books for this study was purposive (designed for a reason, not random). Therefore, this pilot study offers only tentative answers to the research questions; more investigation must be done later on each question. In answer to Question 1, across all 17 books in general, *cognitive* strategies take the lead (except in the learner guidebooks). Metacognitive strategies are a popular second-place category. The four other strategy groups have far less representation. A total of 857 strategies are identified in the materials analyzed.

We found important differences across the types of books and across the locations, thus answering Questions 2 and 3. The inclusion of learning strategies in US and UK language textbooks and learner guidebooks is much more frequent than that in textbooks from the Netherlands. Some recent ESL textbooks in the US heavily use strategies in all six categories, but the range of strategy types is more restricted in US foreign language textbooks (with a concentration on *cognitive* strategies and a somewhat lesser emphasis on *memory*, *compensation*, and *metacognitive* strategies and little interest in *affective* and *social* strategies). Metacognitive strategies are more often used in US-UK learner guidebooks than in US language textbooks. In our sample of books from the US (and one from the UK), far less frequently found strategy groups are *memory*, *affective*, and *social*. *Compensation* strategies vary in their representation.

In the books from the Netherlands, strategy use is almost strictly confined to cognitive strategies. Other types of strategies such as memory, compensation, or metacognitive are rare, and affective and social strategies do not appear at all. Most Dutch authors have not discovered the need to include strategies in any explicit way. However, one recent book, influenced by the national core objectives, reflects a strong effort to include strategies and therefore represented more than 60% of all the strategies found in books from the Netherlands.

Languages learning strategies can be linked to all four language skills (listening, reading, speaking, and writing), as shown most clearly by the US materials, thus answering Question 4. See also Oxford (1990b) for hundreds of examples of skill-related strategies. In the Dutch materials the sporadically used strategies are often linked to receptive language skills, especially reading, and to subskills like vocabulary learning, although we perceive some recent tendencies toward greater language-skill variety in the inclusion of strategies.

Question 5 concerns the explicitness of strategy use. The strategies analyzed above are by-and-large explicit. However, we had to be merciful in our analysis: there is a variety of ways in which the book authors work with strategies. For example, some authors of the analyzed books do not encourage student reflection on or evaluation of their own strategy use: sometimes the steps or procedures to be used in the strategy are a bit unclear, even if the strategy is clearly labeled; in one book, the strategies are not labeled; and in some instances, the benefit of using the strategies is not explained fully. In response to Question 6, we can say that student self-reflection and self-evaluation about strategy use are generally weak. One purpose of metacognitive strategy use is to help students evaluate their use of other strategies, but as we have seen, many books do not emphasize metacognitive strategies (and hence self-reflection or self-evaluation). We must give only a partial answer to Question 7. Based on our non-random data, we cannot provide a full picture of strategy instruction across countries. However, we have enough data now to offer a tentative typology of strategy instruction that might be useful for further analyses. This typology is shown in Table 9.3.

Although international comparisons are difficult to make, we have tried to make them in this pilot study. We want to expand our analysis to other countries in the near future and to other books within the currently selected locations. We can see the danger of strategy-weak language textbooks and learner guidebooks in which the possibilities of strategies are not exploited in their fullest and most powerful sense. We can also envision the danger of professionals attacking the use of language learning strategies as something "new" or threatening. In the Netherlands, these trends are happening due to a lack of dissemination of research insights from abroad, compounded by the influence of conservative teachers under the Dutch educational freedom act. (Such trends are not occurring in any clear way in the US or the UK.) Possibly the typology of strategy instruction, which shows the different ways strategies can be integrated (with Type 4 being the most useful), would help allay any fears.

Table 9.3: Typology of strategy instruction

Type 0: No strategies	No strategies are included in the materials. Teachers can point out the usefulness of strategies in the language classroom, but the materials provide no guidance.
Type 1: Blind (covert) strategies	Some strategies are integrated in traditional language teaching, not explicitly or overtly. Learners might rehearse, or they might predict the theme of a reading from the title, but they would not label the strategy, reflect on their use of this strategy, or be motivated to use it again in a different activity.

Type 2: Some explicit strategies	Some strategies are integrated and explicitly labeled, e.g., "ANALYZING EXPRESSIONS: This strategy can help you look at linguistic forms" (followed by ordinary grammatical exercises).
Type 3: Explicit strategies with information on how to use them (explicit, procedured strategies)	Strategies are explicitly labeled. Instructions on how to use them is given. This allows students to know if they are using the strategies correctly and gives a small degree of self-control. Example: "LEARNING STRATEGY — FORMING CONCEPTS — Sometimes it may help to concentrate on grammar so you can understand unfamiliar constructions. [Instructions:] Examine the following questions. You may find their structures and/or vocabulary difficult. Rephrase each of the sentences into a simpler sentence. Then explain why you think the author chose the more complicated wording. Obviously, many different answers are possible. Compare your responses with a classmate's in order to see another possibility."
Type 4: Explicit strategies with information on how to use them, plus a challenge to reflect on and evaluate the success of the strategy (explicit, procedured, learner-tailored strategies)	Same as Type 3, except that reflection (self-evaluation) is also included. Example: "How did you start reading a text? Did it make a difference to look first at the title?"

To strategy researchers, we emphasize the importance of indicating the types of strategies used. We ask, if possible, for a differentiation among the six categories mentioned here or a similar set of categories. In addition, in all classroom research we must be careful to distinguish what is in the print materials from what actually happens in class. Some teachers stick closely to the materials, while others strongly diverge. Teachers can creatively supplement Type 0 materials and thus provide excellent strategy instruction (for strategy instruction without textbooks, refer to Palinscar and Brown, 1984; Helfeldt and Henk, 1990), while teachers can misuse even Type 4 materials and offer disastrous strategy instruction.

In the future, we urge more development of language textbooks and learner guidebooks as agents for strategy instruction. These materials, if developed and used well, can be a strong impetus for the creation of autonomous language learners. We also call for more research on strategy instruction that exists in current language textbooks and learner guidebooks. This study is only a beginning. Now we turn to a second investigation of print materials for strategy instruction, based on Park-Oh's (1994b, now Park) award-winning dissertation research.

STUDY 2:
PRINT MATERIALS FOR
SELF-REGULATED READING STRATEGY INSTRUCTION

Second language researchers have maintained that strategy instruction can promote language learning. Oxford et al. (1990) reported promising results of strategy instruction based on findings from six case studies in four countries. Positive attitudes as well as increased language progress were consistently noted. Chamot and Rubin (1993) listed numerous studies in which strategy use was associated with language achievement or proficiency. Similarly, research on second language reading has also claimed that effective reading strategies can be taught, thus helping learners become better readers (Loew, 1984; Phillips, 1984; Sutton, 1989). A number of studies (Barnett, 1988a, 1988b; Carrell, Pharis, and Liberto, 1989; Hamp-Lyons, 1985; Hosenfeld, 1984; Kern, 1989) have investigated the effects of reading strategy instruction on gains in reading comprehension. Based on such research, it has been suggested that strategy instruction has beneficial effects on reading performance, because this instruction enables learners to become more aware of their reading processes and strategies.

Self-regulated (self-directed) strategy instruction in the current study (Park-Oh, 1994a), conducted by the third author of this chapter, is defined as instruction which helps readers to use a variety of effective cognitive reading strategies and to raise awareness of their own reading processes through the practice of metacognitive strategies. This instruction is designed to encourage learners to take ultimate responsibility for their own learning and to become independent readers who can transfer successful reading strategies to similar reading tasks *with no direct assistance from their teachers*. The purpose of the present study is to investigate the effects of self-regulated strategy instruction on four variables in the reading performance of university ESL students: reading comprehension, strategy use, reading attitudes, and information-processing styles.

> Providing students with training in self-regulation (also referred to as self-control training) increases the likelihood of strategy maintenance and transfer — commonly acknowledged measures of the success of any kind of skill training. In the absence of this type of self-control training, learners will not become autonomous in their use of strategies and will remain dependent on their teachers, even though they may be taught to use strategies and improve their performance on specific tasks. (Wenden, 1991, p. 106)

A vast body of literature in first language acquisition has shown that learners' awareness of their own reading processes plays a significant role in improving reading comprehension (see, among many others, Baker and Brown, 1984; Bereiter and Bird, 1985). Compared to first language reading research, there has been relatively little research investigating the metacognitive strategies of second language readers, with exceptions being Barnett (1988b) and Carrell (1989).

RESEARCH QUESTIONS

1. How does self-regulated reading strategy instruction affect learners' reading comprehension, use of reading strategies, and attitudes toward ESL reading?

2. What is the relationship between learning styles and changes in reading comprehension, reading strategy use, and reading attitudes after self-regulated reading strategy instruction?

3. What are the patterns underlying the *Strategy Inventory for Reading in ESL (SIRESL)* (Park-Oh, 1992a) and the *Attitudes for Reading in ESL (AIRESL)* (Park-Oh, 1992b)?

SAMPLE

Park, the researcher, selected 64 university ESL learners enrolled in four English 120 (freshman English for nonnative speakers) sections in the spring semester of 1993 at the University of Alabama. The subjects had met the English proficiency level required by the university and had been admitted to academic programs. They represented 20 different countries, and their ages ranged from 19 to 27. The initial assignment of the students to each section of the course was random. The four sections participating in the study were randomly assigned to the experimental and control groups — two sections per group. The experimental group and the control group consisted of 29 and 25 students respectively.

STRATEGY INSTRUCTION USING PRINT MATERIALS

Self-regulated strategy instruction in second language reading was given as the treatment to the experimental group for eight weeks. The rationale for strategy instruction was explained as part of fully "informed" instruction (Oxford, 1990b), in which learners are told all about the purpose and procedures. Print materials contained a series of cognitive reading strategies: identifying key words, identifying topic sentences, skimming, scanning, making inferences, recognizing link-words, paraphrasing, and summarizing. In addition, metacognitive strategies involving monitoring, evaluating, and planning were also included. The strategies were given to the students in a printed, take-home form as weekly learning enrichment activities that the students were asked to practice independently outside the classroom.

Materials were designed to promote learner autonomy by including step-by-step practice, so the students would have little difficulty in independently completing the tasks outside the classroom. Most tasks included a trial step with instant feedback so the students could check whether they correctly understood the practice strategy. To heighten the students' metacognitive awareness of their own strategy use, each task involved activities practicing the metacognitive strategies listed earlier. Materials were reviewed by all teachers of the four sections before the strategy instruction to determine whether there would be any problems.

INSTRUMENTS

TOEFL reading comprehension subtest

The reading comprehension subtest of the *Test of English as a Foreign Language* (TOEFL), Form 3KTF12, was used by permission of the Educational Testing Service in the pretest and posttest to measure reading comprehension. The *TOEFL* reading subtest contained five reading passages on varied topics. The length of the shortest passage used in the present study was 160 words, and the longest passage was 340 words. Thirty reading items in Section 3 were adopted in the present study. Criterion-related validity of the *TOEFL* reading subtest used here was evidenced by a significantly positive relationship (r=.68, p<.01) with the reading recall protocols, detailed below. In addition, criterion-related validity was also supported by more moderate relationships with the *SIRESL* (r=.16, p<.05) and the *AIRESL* (r=.35, p<.05), both described below.

Immediate recall protocol

Reading recall protocols were employed in the pretest and the posttest to measure students' understanding of the reading passages. Bernhardt (1991), who claimed that second language assessment should provide in-depth data as well as more general data, recommended the recall protocol because it "provides a purer measure of comprehension, uncomplicated by linguistic performance and tester interference" (p. 200). Since the English 120 course emphasizes writing as well as reading, it was appropriate to ask students to recall a passage and summarize it in writing. The students' responses were assessed by two independent scorers, both reading specialists. Interrater reliabilities of the pretest and posttest were .98 and .94 respectively.

Strategy Inventory for Reading in ESL (SIRESL)

This instrument was given to students in both the pretest and the posttest to measure reading strategy use. The instrument was developed for this study based on empirical research as well as an extensive literature review (e.g., Barnett, 1988b; Block, 1986; Carrell, 1989; Cohen, 1990b; Swaffar, 1988). The inventory was constructed so that students were first required to read a short passage selected from the reading comprehension subtest of the *TOEFL*. Next, they were asked to respond to 38 items reflecting strategy use in terms of how well each statement described strategies used to comprehend the passage. Responses were determined according to a five-point Likert scale. The Cronbach alpha internal consistency of the *SIRESL* for the pretest was .87, and for the posttest it was .91 (experimental group only) and .86 (control group only). These high alphas suggest that one main trait is being assessed, thus adding to the construct validity. Test-retest reliability over the eight-week interval was .69 (p<.0001).

Content-related validity was supported by submitting the *SIRESL* to the judgment of two language instruction specialists, who agreed that the content was fully appropriate for measuring reading strategy use and that the content comprehensively reflected strategies emerging from previous research. Criterion-related validity was partially evidenced by the *SIRESL*'s positive, moderate correlations (r=.30–.59) with the *AIRESL*.

Attitudes Inventory for Reading in ESL (AIRESL)

This inventory was administered both pre- and post-test to determine students' attitudes toward reading in ESL. Since no ESL reading attitudes instrument was available, the *AIRESL* was developed for this study. Items were designed based on responses from a group of ESL students at the University of Alabama regarding their feelings and opinions about ESL reading. A number of items were also adapted from related first language research (Anderson et al., 1983; McKenna and Kear, 1990; Moore and Lemons, 1982; Pierson, 1984; Smith, 1990). A five-point Likert scale was used for responding to the *AIRESL*'s 48 items. Pretest Cronbach alpha reliability was .85, and posttest reliabilities were .83 (experimental group only) and .88 (control group only), thus suggesting a relatively unified trait and supporting construct validity. Test-retest reliability over the eight-week period was .66 (p<.0001). Content-related validity was supported by the way the items were created (representing a comprehensive and systematic blueprint based on research literature and student interviews).

Inventory of Learning Processes (ILP)

The *ILP*, developed by Schmeck et al. (1977), was used by permission of the authors to measure students' learning styles, particularly their information-processing learning styles. The *ILP* consists of 62 true-false items classified into the following four scales: deep processing, elaborative processing, fact retention, and methodical study. Deep processing indicates the extent to which students process information cognitively by evaluating, comparing, contrasting, and conceptualizing. Elaborative processing refers to the degree to which students personalize information by relating it to their own experiences. Fact retention assesses the extent to which students process details and facts. Methodological study represents the degree to which students engage in systematic study techniques (Schmeck, 1983). The *ILP* has strong reliability and validity (Curry, 1991; Schmeck, 1983). Results of pilot tests involving more than 400 undergraduates provided KR–20 reliability of .70 and alpha reliability of .63. The average test-retest reliability is .83 (N=95).

DATA COLLECTION PROCEDURES

Students were pretested during the second week of February. In the first session, the *TOEFL* reading comprehension subtest was administered for 30 minutes and the *AIRESL* for 15 minutes. The next session involved administering the *SIRESL* for 25 minutes and testing reading comprehension using recall protocols for 20 minutes. Except for the recall protocols, each test used computer-scannable NCS answer sheets. During the final week of the study, students were posttested in a similar fashion. The *ILP* was administered for 15 minutes one week before the posttest.

DATA ANALYSIS PROCEDURES

A significance level of .05 was chosen. Analysis of variance (ANOVA) was used to estimate the univariate F distribution for change scores. Multivariate analysis of variance (MANOVA) was used to determine the difference between the experimental and control groups on change scores between pretests and posttests of the following dependent variables: reading comprehension, reading recall, reading strategy use, and reading attitudes. Pearson correlations were computed to assess the relationships between the scores on four subscales of the ILP (style instrument) and change scores in reading comprehension, reading recall, reading strategy use, and reading attitudes. Factor analyses were performed on the pretests and the posttests of the SIRESL and the AIRESL to investigate their underlying patterns. Internal consistency reliability was estimated using Cronbach's alpha for both of the just-named tests. MANOVA was used to determine experimental versus control group differences on change scores between pretests and posttests of the SIRESL and the AIRESL, using scores from each factor estimated in an earlier step. In addition, a pretest was used to identify any preexisting differences. The control group outperformed the experimental group on the TOEFL reading comprehension subtest and the reading recall protocol. This ensures that there is no bias in favor of the experimental group.

RESULTS

Question 1

Results of the MANOVA indicated there was a significant difference between the experimental and control groups on change scores. Follow-up one-way ANOVAs showed that two of the variables were significant. There were significant changes from pretest to posttest in the two groups on the TOEFL reading comprehension subtest ($p<.03$) and the reading recall protocols ($p<.02$). Specifically, the experimental group gained significantly on the two reading measures (mean 1.26, SD 3.03 for the TOEFL; mean 21.42, SD 25.00 for the recall protocol) while the control group dropped significantly on both (mean −1.33, SD 2.00; mean −11.44, SD 44.83). (No significant changes occurred on the SIRESL or the AIRESL.)

Question 2

Pearson correlations were computed to estimate relationships between scores on four subscales of the ILP (deep processing, elaborative processing, fact retention, and methodical study) and change scores of the experimental group on the dependent variables noted earlier. Results showed that one learning style aspect, methodical study, was significantly correlated ($r=.47$, $p<.05$) to one of the dependent variables, the SIRESL, a measure of reading strategy use. Thus it is clear that methodical study is related to the systematic use of strategies for reading. In addition, correlations showed a significant relationship between the learning style aspects of fact retention and deep processing ($r=.48$, $p<.05$), as well as fact retention and elaborative processing ($r=.47$, $p<.05$). There was also a significant relationship on the change scores for the *SIRESL* and the *AIRESL* (r=.59, p<.01), showing that improvements in strategy use related to improvements in reading attitudes and vice versa.

Question 3

Principal components factor analysis using Varimax rotation was used to examine how the items on the *SIRESL* and the *AIRESL* clustered together and how many dimensions (factors) existed. The scree test of eigenvalues showed the possible existence of four to six factors in both measures. A four-factor solution using a loading value of .3 was selected as optimal for both instruments. Any items loading on two or more factors were included if they met the criterion of .3.

On the *SIRESL*, the variance explained by each respective factor was 25%, 12%, 8%, and 6%, totaling 51%. Sixteen items loaded on Factor 1, which included a wide range of compensation strategies and strategies for selective attention. Thirteen items loaded on Factor 2, which was centered on strategies used for understanding the organization of the text and for manipulating the passage cognitively. Factor 3 included 12 items, mostly related to strategies taught in formal classroom instruction. Not surprisingly, many strategies in Factor 3 are particularly consistent with a series of reading strategies provided as manipulation aids in the self-regulated strategy instruction. Eleven items were contained in Factor 4, including strategies associated with deep processing rather than surface processing. These deep strategies are likely to involve comprehending the text beyond word-processing by applying background knowledge (Horiba, 1990; Kern, 1989).

On the *AIRESL*, the total variance explained was 47%, comprising 20%, 12%, 8%, and 8% for the respective factors. Factor 1 contained 22 items, reflecting the extent to which students expressed pleasure/displeasure and confidence in reading in English. Factor 2 included 17 items, indicating the degree to which students expressed the importance of reading in English and the extent of benefit from such reading. Factor 3 covered 16 items, encompassing affective affects of reading such as awareness of difficulty and anxiety. Twelve items loaded on Factor 4, reflecting the extent to which students expressed their efforts to improve reading proficiency and their feelings toward reading and alternative learning modes.

The MANOVA used to determine group differences on change scores between the pretest and the posttest of the *SIRESL* (employing scores from each factor) indicated that a significant difference existed between the two groups on change scores. Follow-up one-way ANOVAs showed there were significant changes (p<.002) from pretest to posttest in the two groups on Factor 3 of the *SIRESL*: strategies associated with formal instruction. However, the MANOVA for the *AIRESL* change scores showed no significant difference between the experimental and control groups.

DISCUSSION AND INTERPRETATION

MANOVA results indicated that significant differences existed between the two groups when reading comprehension gains were measured by the *TOEFL* reading comprehension subtest and the reading recall protocols. The experimental group, which had strategy instruction, showed significant improvements on both instruments, while the control group actually lowered its scores on both measures. These results confirm the presence of positive effects of reading strategy instruction on improvement of reading comprehension.

Even though the experimental group showed significant gains in reading comprehension because of the strategy instruction, no significant differences between the two groups were found when changes in overall reading strategy use were measured before and after the strategy instruction. This result is not consistent with other studies reported earlier, in which strategy instruction resulted in significantly greater strategy use. Perhaps the reading strategies provided in the strategy instruction in the present study were a useful — but limited — set, and both groups might have reported using these with rather similar frequencies. However, apparently the experimental group was far more adept than the control group in deploying these strategies precisely when needed on the *TOEFL* reading comprehension subtest and the reading recall protocols.

No significant improvement in reading attitudes took place in the experimental group, probably because it is close to impossible to make major changes in attitudes over as brief a timespan as eight weeks. More change in attitudes might have occurred if the strategy instruction had continued for a semester or a year. Despite this nonsignificant result, this area deserves further attention; there has been almost no research on second language reading attitudes.

Factor analyses showed that the items on the *SIRESL* and the *AIRESL* were clustered around four dimensions per instrument. Each of the four factors on the *SIRESL* indicated the extent and variety of reading strategies students use in understanding structural and textual patterns and in compensating for missing knowledge. The *AIRESL* factors represented dimensions reflecting students' attitudes toward pleasure, benefits, efforts, and affective aspects of reading. The pre- and posttest factor scores for each student were used to analyze effects of strategy instruction on reading strategy use and reading attitudes. MANOVA findings indicated significant effects of the strategy instruction on one of the dimensions of the *SIRESL*, strategies linked with formal instruction. Considering that the content of the strategies in that factor was representative of strategies often included in the strategy instruction, it is not surprising that a significant improvement was made.

The experimental group's significant correlation of .59 between the change scores on the *SIRESL* and the *AIRESL* indicated that students in that group who made positive changes in strategy use also made positive changes in reading attitudes. This is a very important finding, showing that there is a marked relationship between reading strategy use and reading attitudes in the second language setting. This relationship should be more thoroughly investigated.

The correlation of .47 between one of the *ILP* subscales (methodical study) and reading strategy change scores indicates that students who were high on methodical study also made significant gains in their use of reading strategies as a result of strategy instruction. Considering that the strategy instruction was designed to promote students' autonomy and independence in second language reading, it is understandable that those scoring high on the learning style aspect of methodical study would also be very involved with improving their own reading strategies. The methodical students are apt to study "more often and more carefully than other students, and the methods that they claim to employ are the systematic techniques recommended in… 'how to study' manuals" (Schmeck, 1983, pp. 248–249).

Based on the findings of the current study, the following four implications can be drawn about L2 strategy instruction. First, self-regulated strategy instruction using print materials can improve reading comprehension. Second, learning strategies can be taught in non-teacher-dependent ways through the use of print. Third, specific kinds of print materials are needed for strategy instruction, and these materials must fit the learners' proficiency level, interests, and classroom needs. Fourth, follow-up activities are also necessary.

The effectiveness of self-regulated reading strategy instruction for improvement in reading comprehension was proven in this study. Most strategy instruction studies have focused on cognitive strategies (O'Malley, 1987), but this study included metacognitive strategies as well. Such a combination was suggested as superior by Wenden (1987b), who felt it was necessary for informed, self-regulated strategy instruction. This study effectively demonstrated that metacognitive strategies could be incorporated into self-regulated strategy instruction by encouraging students to take more responsibility for their learning.

A variety of learning strategies can be self-instructed through step-by-step print materials given to the individual. However, lack of readily available materials has been an obstacle for teachers who want to incorporate strategy instruction into the classroom (O'Malley and Chamot, 1990). Additional strategy instruction materials using the print mode need to be developed. If these materials are made available, classroom teachers with even minimal knowledge of learning strategies can assist their learners by giving them strategy practice materials to use at home.

Feedback from students suggested the need for follow-up activities using similar reading tasks in which they could transfer what they learned. This implied that objectives of strategy instruction should include evaluation of transfer and maintenance of the learned strategies in similar contexts and tasks. Moreover, individual differences should be considered in developing and implementing the strategy instruction. As noted, methodical students benefited the most from self-regulated strategy instruction in second language reading.

CONCLUSIONS

These two studies have shown that print materials exist for strategy instruction and that these materials, by themselves, can have significant effects on language skill development, at least (as shown here) in the area of reading comprehension. Teachers do not always have a great deal of understanding of language learning strategies, nor do they consistently provide adequate modeling of these strategies, as demonstrated by Nyikos (chapter 8, this volume). In strategy instruction, print materials can make up for gaps in teachers' strategic understanding. Moreover, some language students do not have a teacher, so they need print materials for self-directed strategy instruction. Therefore, use of print materials for strategy instruction deserves greater research attention and practical consideration.

Carol Ann Baily
Middle Tennessee State University, USA

CHAPTER 10
UNOBTRUSIVE COMPUTERIZED OBSERVATION OF COMPENSATION STRATEGIES FOR WRITING TO DETERMINE THE EFFECTIVENESS OF STRATEGY INSTRUCTION

True ease in writing comes from art, not chance.
–Alexander Pope

SUMMARY

There is a need for an unobtrusive way to observe language learning strategies, and computers might partially fulfill the need. This chapter describes compensation strategy assessment in the past and explains in detail how computers can provide a new way of assessing compensation strategies. This chapter also shows how computers can help in evaluating the effectiveness of a strategy instruction intervention.

INTRODUCTION

The current study builds upon preliminary observations of the potential of using computer software programs to track students' inquiries and learning strategies unobtrusively. This work documents the use of compensation strategies for writing by adult foreign language learners using a French word processing program, Système-D (Noblitt, Sola, and Pet, 1992), to write a variety of compositions. The current research also adds small-scale, formal instruction in the use of strategies. This chapter is organized as follows: (1) background, (2) goals of this study, (3) research questions, (4) methodology, (5) results and discussion, and (6) recommendations.

BACKGROUND

COMPENSATION STRATEGY RESEARCH

Certain strategy research has identified and assessed the frequency of different types of strategies, such as the six general categories noted by Oxford (1990b): memory, cognitive, compensation, metacognitive, affective, and social strategies. The focus

Baily, C. A. (1996). Unobtrusive computerized observation of compensation strategies for writing to determine the effectiveness of strategy instruction. In Rebecca L. Oxford (Ed.), *Language learning strategies around the world: Cross-cultural perspectives*. (Technical Report #13) (pp. 141–150). Honolulu: University of Hawai'i, Second Language Teaching & Curriculum Center.

here is on compensation strategies. Compensation strategies allow the language learner to communicate in the target language despite limitations in their knowledge. Compensation strategies can be used for any of the four basic language skills. In reading and listening, for example, the main compensation strategy is guessing the meaning from the context. This strategy can in turn be subdivided according to the kinds of contextual clues used to guess the meaning: linguistic, nonlinguistic, paralinguistic, and so on. Speaking and writing have a wide array of compensation strategies. Some compensation strategies, like using mime and gesture, are particular to speaking. However, others are useful for both speaking and writing. For instance, if a word needed for speech or writing is not known, students might compensate for this missing knowledge by seeking a *synonym*. They might also try to describe the concept they wish to convey by using *circumlocution*, that is, talking around the word or describing the word. (For example, if they want to talk about an *owl*, for example, they might discuss *a bird that flies at night.*) Students also alter their message by making it simpler or by changing what they say to fit the terms they know or can find easily, thus *approximating the message.* Unable to find the word they are seeking, learners might also combine words they do know to communicate the idea, thus *coining a new term*; without knowing the word for *chalk*, they might create a word such as *blackboard-pencil.* These four strategies — using a synonym, using circumlocution, approximating the message, and coining words — are the ones examined in this study of the writing process, although they can be used in speaking as well.

One of the few instruments for assessing compensation strategy use in all four skills is the *SILL* (*Strategy Inventory for Language Learning*, Oxford, 1990a). Previous *SILL*-based research among university students and adult language learners (Ehrman and Oxford, 1987, 1988; Nyikos, 1990a; Oxford and Nyikos, 1989; Oxford, 1993a, 1993b, 1994a) found that women typically use compensation strategies significantly more often than men. However, almost equal compensation strategy use was found for men and women in a Puerto Rican study (Green, 1992). Oxford (1992) notes *high* compensation strategy use among mixed-nationality university and adult ESL groups in the US (Phillips, 1990, 1991; Oxford, Talbott, and Halleck, 1990); English teachers in Indonesia (Davis and Abas, 1991); Thai university EFL majors (Mullins, 1992); hand-picked adult language learners at the US Foreign Service Institute (Ehrman and Oxford, 1989); and regular university EFL students in Japan (Watanabe, 1990), the People's Republic of China (Bedell, 1993), and Taiwan (Yang, 1992a). Dreyer (1992) found that in South Africa the more proficient university ESL students, compared with the less proficient, used compensation strategies significantly more often. Compensation strategies averaged only *medium* level use in a study of Puerto Rican students' learning strategies (Green, 1992) and in studies in Korea (Oh, 1992), the US (Douglas, 1992), and Japan (Watanabe, 1990). American university students (Oxford and Nyikos, 1989) used some compensation strategies at a *medium* level and others at a *low* level. A factor analysis by Oxford, Nyikos, Nyikos, Lezhnev, Eyring, and Rossi-Le (1989) found compensation strategies to be the second most explanatory factor (i.e., able to explain the second greatest amount of variance on the *SILL*).

USE OF COMPUTERS FOR STRATEGY RESEARCH

Chapelle and Mizuno (1989) found that they could document strategy use by ESL students using learner-controlled software. These researchers identified the strategies of resourcing (using resources such as dictionaries), practicing, self-monitoring, self-management, and self-evaluation. Designed for high intermediate and advanced ESL students, a series of grammar and paragraph development lessons were conducted by computer. Students were free to consult grammar references, dictionaries of phrases and vocabulary, and facts about the writing situation. Results "indicated only that some students did indeed use some of the strategies some of the time," and they also showed that "students are often doing something different from what instructors believe they are doing; they do not always use the optimal strategies" (Chapelle and Mizuno, 1989, p. 42). Though the findings were a bit vague and tentative, this work did point to the possibilities of tracking strategies by using computers to log the inquiries students make of the resources provided in the system.

In the field tests of Système-D, conducted among high school and traditional college students, Scott and Terry (1992) found that the Système-D Tracking Device provided evidence of students' checking synonyms in English in order to find the word in French which best expressed what they wanted to communicate. One student, for example, checked the dictionary for *to experiment, to test, to try, tested,* and *to use* before selecting the French verb *employer* to discuss a product he was promoting. Scott and Terry also indicated that certain students used circumlocution to creatively avoid certain constructions they perceived to be difficult, such as the subjunctive mood. The work reported in the current study was built upon these observations, using Système-D to document four types of compensation strategies outlined later in this chapter.

FOCUS OF THE CURRENT STUDY

This investigation looked for examples of adult language learners' use of the following four compensation strategies: adjusting or approximating the message, coining words, using circumlocution, and using synonyms. All of these compensation strategies are useful for writing (and also for speaking). The nature of this study precluded the use of other compensation strategies, such as selecting the topic, using mime or gesture, or avoiding communication. Previous Système-D observations had involved high school and traditional college students (Scott and Terry, 1992). In the current study, compensation strategy use of adults was the focus. Looking at the learning strategies of nontraditional students such as these adults broadens our understanding of how people learn foreign languages. Moreover, previous Système-D research did not include a strategy instruction intervention of any kind, while the current research offered instruction on the use of compensation strategies for writing. One limitation of the current study is that it involved highly motivated learners who might not be representative of the general adult language learning population. Yet the strategies of such learners are important, possibly representing the "best" that might be expected at a given stage. Comparisons with less motivated groups are certainly needed.

RESEARCH QUESTIONS

1. Does Système-D provide a tool to unobtrusively assess four types of compensation strategies: using circumlocution, using a synonym, adjusting the message, and coining new words?

2. Does Système-D document any difference in the use of compensation strategies following a strategy instruction intervention?

3. How do gender, age, and language learning experience relate to compensation strategy use?

METHODOLOGY

SAMPLE

Adult foreign language learners enrolled in nonacademic, conversational French classes voluntarily participated in this study. The overall sample consisted of 21 adults, ranging from age 25 through the 60s. All were highly motivated to learn French for travel (pleasure or business), for cultural appreciation, and for general intellectual development. All participants had been enrolled in intensive, three-hour-per-week conversational classes for a minimum of ten weeks prior to the study. Their level of ability in French ranged from advanced beginner to intermediate level. The sample included six males and 15 females. In the sample were 10 who had studied French for less than two years (the low experience group) and 11 who had studied it for two years or more (the high experience group).

One half (N=11) served as the control group, while the other half (N=10) acted as the experimental group and received a strategy instruction intervention. Based on data from the questionnaire described below, the two groups were matched on gender, age, and language experience.

INSTRUMENT

Each participant completed a questionnaire to determine gender, age group, amount of experience with French, and exposure to other foreign languages. The results allowed stratification of the sample and matching of the experimental and control groups.

STRATEGY INSTRUCTION FOR THE EXPERIMENTAL GROUP

The experimental group received instruction in the use of compensation strategies, and the control group did not. All participants performed two writing assignments as baseline data about compensation strategy use, and all wrote two compositions after the experimental group received the instruction. A pre-post, experimental-control group design was used to determine whether a significant increase in the frequency of compensation strategy use would occur for those who received strategy instruction as compared with those who did not receive the instruction.

The author provided four introductory sessions to familiarize participants with Système-D. These sessions offered opportunities to practice using the system to complete sample writing assignments. The four official writing assignments began once students were familiar with the system. The *first writing assignment* consisted of an informal letter of introduction to a friend of a friend in France. This letter featured present tense verbs and vocabulary about professions, family, and personal information. The *second writing task*, was to tell the story of Little Red Riding Hood in French, using vocabulary about food, clothing, animals, sickness, and the sequencing of events. This topic provided participants with a rich source of vocabulary ideas and opportunities for imaginative writing, and it produced more inquiries of Système-D, more compensation strategy use, and longer compositions than any other assignment. The *third writing topic* centered on a personal description for program notes of an international conference in the participants' professional fields. This writing assignment featured a formal letter using present tense verbs and vocabulary to describe the person's family, profession, and personal interests, similar to the first topic. The *fourth writing assignment* focused on the differences in life in the US and French-speaking countries. Each student was asked to write an essay for a European magazine describing a trip previously made to France or another French-speaking country. The writers discussed clothing, food, sports, and leisure activities, stressing the contrasts witnessed between the two cultures. This topic used the two past tenses and many of the same vocabulary terms as the second assignment.

SYSTÈME D AND ITS SPECIFIC FEATURES FOR DATA COLLECTION

Système-D functions as a normal word processing program, allowing the writer to type a composition, check spelling, move text around within the document, and make corrections, additions, and deletions. In addition, Système-D provides four very important learning tools: a dictionary, a grammar reference, sets of vocabulary, and phrase groups. If a student needs to look up a word in the dictionary, a function key produces the dictionary screen above the writing area on the computer monitor screen. The writer may ask for a word using either English or French. When found, that word is highlighted in the center of the information screen. At that point, the student may ask for examples of the word used within a sentence, or in the case of a verb, for the full conjugation in all tenses. In a similar manner, the student may inquire about particular grammar points, may select a set of vocabulary words by subject area, or may call for a phrase set on a selection of useful topics. Once again, the writer may request examples of the words in sentences or may ask for notes about the terms.

The Système-D Tracking Device, a computer log, maintains a list of each of the inquiries which a writer makes of the Système-D information functions. To unobtrusively observe compensation strategy use, the author analyzed the type of inquiries recorded on the computer log produced while the learner is writing. If the writer looked up a vocabulary word, checked examples of words in sentences, referred to verb conjugations, looked up grammar points, or called for topical groupings of words, the log revealed each of these inquiries.

Since the dictionary contained in Système-D's test version was limited, it was likely that a student would fail to find some words in the dictionary during the writing assignment. (The recently published version of Système-D nearly doubled the vocabulary contained in the dictionary.) How students handled the occurrence of missing words in the dictionary indicated which compensation strategies they used. If a student modified the message to suit the vocabulary that was easily found, it would indicate the use of the strategy for *adjusting the message*. If, on the other hand, the writer sought synonyms of the first term, the *synonym* strategy would be at work. If the writer conveyed the message by talking around the word or describing the word, the *circumlocution* strategy was used. The compensation strategy of *coining words* would be evident by both looking at the dictionary or vocabulary inquiries and the resulting composition to determine which words were not found and which were invented by the student.

DATA ANALYSIS PROCEDURES

For each of the four compositions written by each participant, the author analyzed both of the documents provided by Système-D: the composition itself and the computer log. All choices were examined, including those that students made while looking up vocabulary, grammar information, examples, notes, and other inquiries. When a choice indicated the use of one of the four target compensation strategies, the log was marked with the appropriate code: A=adjusting the message, C=using circumlocution, S=using a synonym, and W=coining a new word. Analysis of these marks on the log allowed the calculation of the frequency of the use of these strategies, discussed next.

Further statistical analysis was performed with SPSS 4.1 (SPSS Inc., 1989). This analysis included frequencies of the four different strategy types used overall and within each composition for a given student. Multivariate analysis of variance was used to determine the main (independent) effects of group (control vs. experimental), age, language experience, and gender on the frequency of use of compensation strategies (the dependent variable). The composite *absolute* frequency of strategy use on the first two writing assignments was calculated to serve as the baseline compensation-strategy score, for comparison with the frequency of use following the experimental group's instruction. In addition, for both pretest and posttest, the *relative* strategy-to-inquiry proportion (the proportion of all inquiries made while writing a composition which were counted as strategies used) was calculated and compared across the two groups for pretest and posttest situations. A significance level of $p < .05$ was chosen for all significance tests. This is the conventionally accepted level for studies of this nature.

RESULTS AND DISCUSSION

This study documented examples of all four types of compensation strategies used by adult foreign language learners. This section describes and discusses overall results, as well as results by group (experimental/control), gender, age, and language experience.

OVERALL RESULTS

Although the length of compositions and the number of inquiries varied widely for each participant and for each composition, nevertheless a consistent 10–13% of all inquiries within the total sample could be tabulated as compensation strategies. For more details on strategy frequencies, see Baily (1992, pp. 98–107).

RESULTS BY GROUP (EXPERIMENTAL/CONTROL)

Does a strategy instruction intervention make a difference in the use of compensation strategies? This study found no evidence of the effect of the instruction itself on the *absolute* frequencies of strategy use. In fact, both the control group and the experimental group demonstrated significantly less strategy use (in terms of absolute numbers of strategies) in the final two compositions than in the first two. The two groups were very similar in the decreased use of compensation strategies in the final two compositions.

However, a consideration of the *relative* number of strategies compared to the number of inquiries (the strategy-to-inquiry proportion) presents a different picture. The experimental group did show a slight increase in relative strategy use (strategy-to-inquiry proportion), from a mean of 11.9% across the two preinstruction compositions to a mean of 13.8% across the two postinstruction compositions. The control group showed a baseline mean of 11.0% across the two early compositions and had an identical mean across the two later compositions. Thus, the strategy instruction appeared to make a slight difference in terms of relative strategy use compared to the total number of inquiries.

RESULTS BY GENDER

The results did not show the same pattern of gender differences that had been found in previous studies, with females using more strategies than males. The mean for the *absolute* frequency of strategy use was significantly higher for males than females in both of the first two compositions (male mean 38.2, female mean 35.6) and in the second set of compositions (male mean 24.8, female mean 18.9). The *relative* strategy-to-inquiry proportion (i.e., the percentage of inquiries that were countable as strategies) was similar between males and females, with the females using a higher proportion of their inquiries as strategies only in the final composition.

There are several possible explanations for the gender results. One explanation might be the difference in computer experience between women and men. More of the male participants than the female participants had used computers on their jobs. Many of the women said they had never used a computer and were initially afraid of the experience. Even after the orientation period, when they were no longer afraid of the computer, women more often requested help to find the correct function keys so they could operate Système-D. Male participants were less intimidated by the equipment at first and made better use of the computer program initially, thereby displaying more inquiries and more strategies. It is interesting to note, however, that the percentage of inquiries leading to strategy use (strategy-to-inquiry proportion) was almost the same as that of the women, and by the final composition the women were even showing a significantly higher percentage of total inquiries resulting in strategy use.

It is also possible that in previous studies, females reported higher use of compensation strategies because they were more self-aware in general and more cognizant of their learning strategies in particular. Perhaps men did not as easily recall or recognize the strategies they were using. It is possible that Système-D permits a more accurate look at strategy use than some other methods, which rely on self-report.

RESULTS BY AGE

Participants younger than 45 used significantly more strategies (in terms of *absolute* frequency) than those above that age. Both groups, however, decreased their absolute frequency of strategy use in the second set of compositions, so no differential change by age group could be recorded.

Computer experience might play a role in the age difference in absolute frequencies of strategies. Most of the younger (below 45) participants had previously used computers for school and work. They asked fewer questions about the mechanics of the keyboard and its functions than did the older group. Younger students concentrated more readily on their writing tasks without concern for the operation of the computer.

The younger group demonstrated a greater percentage of use of adjusting the message and circumlocution strategies, while the older group displayed a slightly larger percentage of use of synonyms and coined words. None of these differences, however, were at a significant level.

RESULTS BY LANGUAGE LEARNING EXPERIENCE

Compensation strategy use (*absolute* values) in the first two compositions among participants with less than two years of French learning experience (the low experience group) was significantly higher than among those with more than two years of experience (the high experience group). Yet in the current study, the last two compositions showed almost equal strategy use (in *absolute* terms) for the lower experience and high experience students. Therefore, those with less experience demonstrated a differential change in strategy use, but it was a dramatic change downward in absolute numbers of strategies used. As the students with less experience in the language gained experience with Système-D, they demonstrated fewer strategies.

However, results showed that the high experience group had a significantly larger *relative* strategy-to-inquiry proportion than the low experience group in the final two compositions. Furthermore, the higher experience group gained in its strategy-to-inquiry proportion across time, while the lower experience group dropped. Low experience learners started with a strategy-to-inquiry mean percentage of 12.5% across the first two assignments and dropped slightly to 11.4% across the last two assignments; in contrast, high experience learners started at 10.7% and increased to 13.2%. Although in the current study each group used a smaller absolute number of strategies in the last two compositions, the high experience group used its inquiries more efficiently than the low experience group, resulting in a higher percentage of those inquiries which were noted to be compensation strategies. This pattern corresponds somewhat to the results of Oxford and Nyikos (1989), who found that university students with more language experience tended to use more strategies in general. It also coincides with other studies (Green, 1992; Dreyer, 1992) showing that higher proficiency students used compensation strategies significantly more often than lower proficiency students.

Système-D does provide a useful tool for unobtrusively observing four types of compensation strategies in adult foreign language learners: adjusting the message, circumlocution, synonyms, and coining new words. This computer program was successfully used, via the log and the compositions, for observing strategy use. By analyzing the series of inquiries made of the computer program and the resulting compositions, it was possible to identify specific strategies being used without stopping the writer during the writing process. Potential problems such as students' memory decay and lack of awareness are obviated.

The study found that strategy use varied significantly by gender, age, and language learning experience. Some differences in strategy use were also evident across pairs of compositions. A general survey or a concurrent think-aloud might not reveal such clear variations among the students in a class, or even within a given student across writing assignments.

RECOMMENDATIONS

The fact that Système-D functioned well as an unobtrusive strategy assessment tool will be of considerable interest and importance to researchers in the future. Such a tool could perhaps be used for assessing other kinds of strategies. A larger sample of adult language learners would be recommended in subsequent research projects. With a larger sample, an analysis of variance could reveal whether gender, age, language learning experience, and treatment (experimental/control) interact with each other in influencing strategy use, as well as having independent effects. Longitudinal designs could also provide useful information about the long-term use of Système-D for identifying strategies.

Future research is needed to determine whether computer tracking systems can replicate the results of previous studies if the orientation time were longer, if the design were longitudinal, and if composition topics were specially selected and alternated. Other investigations might study whether using a computer tracking system produces a more accurate view of strategy use, going beyond the limitations of other strategy assessment techniques. Additional study can tell us whether computer tracking can successfully document larger scale or more intensive strategy instruction interventions and to what degree computer tracking can be used for diagnosis. This means that the use of computers to *directly teach* strategies as well as to *unobtrusively assess* strategies deserves to be studied. In sum, further research could lead to better ways to employ technology for helping adult language learners utilize appropriate learning strategies.

Joan Rubin
Joan Rubin Associates, Maryland, USA

CHAPTER 11

USING MULTIMEDIA FOR LEARNER STRATEGY INSTRUCTION

We cannot teach another person directly;
we can only facilitate his [or her] learning.
–Carl Rogers

SUMMARY

This chapter provides an overview of the Language Learning Strategies Program, a multimedia instructional program designed to teach learner strategies. It starts with an introduction to the theory behind the instructional design. Then it describes the design elements. Next it describes the evaluation process. Finally it provides information about the distribution of the program.

INTRODUCTION

Learning a language involves acquiring two kinds of knowledge: *declarative knowledge* and *procedural knowledge*. Declarative knowledge is what you know about the language systems: the linguistic system, the sociolinguistic system, and the pragmatic system. Procedural knowledge is what you know about the learning process, what you know about how to learn a foreign or second language. Strategy instruction is one way to work toward enhancing your procedural knowledge. Since many adults are "language phobic" or inexperienced with language learning, they need to gain more procedural knowledge to deflect negative affective influences and to begin to experience some success.

Much of current strategy instruction is focused on first teaching teachers about learner strategies and about how to teach learners to use them more effectively. Teachers then present those strategies during a foreign or second language class.

Another productive approach to strategy instruction involves materials written specifically for learners to instruct themselves in procedural knowledge and learner strategies. The 1994 Rubin and Thompson volume, *How to Be a More Successful Language Learner*, written for the learners themselves, includes extensive information about strategies for learning vocabulary and grammar and specific strategies for the skills of listening, reading, speaking, and writing. Other student-oriented texts which include learner strategies are Brown (1989, 1991) and Marshall (1989). In addition, many language textbooks are now including explicit learner strategies.

Rubin, J. (1996). Using multimedia for learner strategy instruction. In Rebecca L. Oxford (Ed.), *Language learning strategies around the world: Cross-cultural perspectives*. (Technical Report #13) (pp. 151–156). Honolulu: University of Hawai'i, Second Language Teaching & Curriculum Center.

A second approach to teaching learners directly how to learn a second or foreign language involves semester-long courses in learner strategies. Such courses have been given at the University of Michigan, the University of Minnesota, and the University of Arizona. Similar shorter courses have been offered at the primary level in the US (Montgomery County, MD) and England.

Yet a third way to teach learners directly is the multimedia course, the Language Learning Strategies Program, developed by Joan Rubin Associates. This program includes instruction combining input from both the computer and a videodisc. The program runs on a multimedia platform consisting of an IBM PC and monitor, a Pioneer laserdisc player, and a DVA interface board (linking the computer and the player).

The LLS Program is based on 20 years of research on learner strategies (see Rubin, 1987, for an historical perspective) which identified the strategies that successful or expert learners use to solve their language learning problems. Other research has shown that strategy instruction can improve language performance (O'Malley, 1987; Rubin, 1989; Rubin et al., 1988; Thompson and Rubin, 1993; Thompson and Rubin, in press). The LLS Program has also drawn from research on developing higher order cognitive skills that demonstrates that performance improves with instruction in using cognitive and metacognitive strategies (e.g., Brown and Palincsar, 1982). Comparison of students using different kinds of strategies has shown progressive improvement of performance as learners (1) do exercises blind, that is, with no coaching; (2) do the same exercises with cognitive coaching, that is, learners are told the name of the strategy and why it is useful; and (3) do the same exercise with metacognitive coaching, that is, learners are told the name of the strategy and why it is useful and are encouraged to evaluate their strategy use.

An important component of strategy instruction is the increase in students' awareness of the background knowledge they bring to the task. Many learners fail to realize that they already know a great deal about grammar, vocabulary, and communication. They often do not know how to transfer that knowledge to learning another language. Students may not realize they can use what they know about the world and about human interaction to direct their critical thinking and problem solving. Learners need to be reminded how they filter information through that which they already know, as well as how this filter can help or hinder as they learn a new communicative system. The LLS Program provides many opportunities for learners to discover these concepts.

The objective of this program is to develop procedural knowledge (how to learn a language) and is especially geared toward novice (inexperienced) learners or "less than successful" learners. It is intended particularly for beginning language learners or for those who want to improve their language learning skills.

DESIGN

The LLS Program provides approximately eight hours of instruction on language skills (listening, reading, and speaking), on language segments (grammar, vocabulary), memory, and on sociolinguistic aspects of communication.

Characters

The four major characters in the program are: a translator at the Library of Congress who will be working on Russian texts, a plant manager in Argentina, an American military attaché assigned to Korea, and a Japanese sales manager who will promote Japanese pharmaceuticals in the US. The characters will undergo language instruction in order to perform well on their jobs. Each has a compelling reason to learn a foreign language (that is, high motivation which facilitates language learning), each has a very specific language goal to attain (which when specified makes it easier for learners to evaluate their progress), and each represents a carefully researched real-life career which requires language skills.

The characters model how real-life students may react to learning problems and the strategies they may use to resolve them. The viewer is drawn into the plot as the characters ask relevant questions and struggle through typical situations.

Multiple language exposure

The main languages of the one-hour videodisc are Russian, Korean, and Spanish, chosen to represent different levels of learning difficulty for native speakers of English. However, in the entire eight-hour instructional program, the learner is exposed to 20 languages ranging from Sesotho in South Africa to Japanese, Hebrew, Norwegian, and Persian. In this way, learners can confront an array of grammatical, lexical, sociolinguistic, and pragmatic problems and discover strategies that facilitate learning.

Language skills

In the LLS Program learners have an opportunity to work on three major language skills: listening (with visual support, i.e., television; and without visual support, i.e., radio), reading (expository, narrative, and instructional), and speaking (asking for clarification). In the reading and speaking sections, learners can opt to do exercises either in English or in a foreign language. The English section options highlight the fact that learners may use similar strategies in both their native language and in a foreign language. In reading, the strategies include: integrate text and pictures, use discourse markers to organize text and predict content, and use topic to narrow predictions. The listening comprehension strategies include: use your knowledge of the world, listen for familiar names and places, and use key words to narrow predictions. In the speaking section, the major strategy includes ways of asking for clarification or managing the conversation.

Learners practice these skill strategies using a wide range of topics: reading an instructional manual to connect a VCR, watching a spy story, reading a scuba text to recognize how a reader determines the meaning of new or unknown words, considering the meaning of some obscure English words for food, or asking for clarification in a conversation with a Korean counterpart.

Language segments

Learners have an opportunity to consider some strategies to use while learning grammar and vocabulary. In the grammar section, learners use the strategies of analogy and creating general rules based on observing, comparing, creating, and checking hypotheses. Vocabulary strategies include use of cognates; use of linguistic; visual, and auditory context to guess the meaning; use of topic and genre to guess the meaning; and social strategies to recognize false cognates.

Memory

Learners need to consider which strategies most facilitate storage and retrieval of information. In this section, learners have an opportunity to try out five strategies in addition to rote (random) memorization. The strategies include: grouping items into categories by topic; analyzing items into component parts; looking for sets of smaller, known parts; mapping words to pictures or the real thing; generating images such as sound, sight, or combinations of images; and using the whole text. After working through these strategies learners become more aware of the need to focus on memory strategies and to determine which of the above or other strategies might be most effective for them.

Cultural points

Learners work through cultural differences in expression to recognize that the way language functions are expressed is critical to meaning. The exercises on communication focus on problems in cross-cultural transfer and illustrate how values and underlying meanings are important in understanding (and communicating) what is intended. For example, in a segment on borrowing, viewers first analyze how they vary their communication strategies in English to accomplish their social purposes. They come to recognize that many factors (for example, relationship between speakers, purpose of a loan, how often a person has borrowed) can influence the expressions used. They learn strategies to recognize when their cross-cultural communication has gone astray and how to elicit clearer communication in situations where direct communication can be threatening.

Active, self-directed, interactive learning

The LLS Program requires that learners be active as they make choices about what to learn, the sequence of learning, and the pace of learning. Each section includes opportunities to select the skill, topic, language segment, or strategy learners want to work on. In some sections, learners can elect to learn about a strategy by selecting from one of several languages. Learners receive feedback enabling them to rethink their response and focus on appropriate clues to the answer. The program promotes student discovery of the strategies, associations, and modalities which best promote their own learning. It is consistent with current research, which has shown that even expert learners select and organize their strategies in different configurations.

Natural settings

The program provides natural settings in which the characters have a real-life problem. These settings offer visual, auditory, and kinesthetic clues to meaning and to errors. The program prompts the learner to recognize these contextual clues.

Screen design

The program has an interesting but clear screen design so that learners can clearly recognize the material to be worked on, the question to be answered, instructions on how to respond, and evaluation and/or feedback.

EVALUATION

An extensive evaluation of the program was conducted to determine if instructions were easy to follow and if the answer feedback was clear and useful. The LLS Program was field-tested by the expert learners at the US Defense Language Institute (San Francisco branch) with 24 student volunteers who spent two hours on the program. After that, eight of these volunteers offered to spend another six hours viewing the entire disc. Their comments indicate enthusiasm for this kind of instruction:

> "It sharpens your skills and shows you how to apply them."

> "It was fun!"

> "People can learn a language without fear."

The program was also used with both expert and novice learners at an intensive Arabic immersion survival course at the US Air Force Academy. Novice learners especially felt that the program offered considerable insights into how to begin to study a new and distinct language.

Finally the program was evaluated by Bechtel Corporation employees, who commented:

> "It helps you concentrate on what you need to know."

"I feel more comfortable about learning another language."

Not only did the program provide information and insights into metacognitive and cognitive strategies, but users were also able to report changes in affect: higher comfort level, less fear, and more motivation (fun, enjoyable, entertaining, stimulating). Thus, the program addresses the whole person.

CONCLUSIONS

The LLS Program provides opportunities for learners to experiment with a wide range of strategies. Specifically, program users can expect to derive the following benefits:

1. Gain insights into their own approach to learning.

2. Be able to decide on strategies appropriate to a specific task and to their purpose for learning.

3. Be able to use these strategies in the classroom, for self-study, or in the "real world."

4. Learn strategies specific to reading, listening, and speaking.

5. Be able to select strategies to improve memory for language learning.

6. Learn how to transfer knowledge about language and communication from one language to another.

7. Be able to deal with errors more effectively.

DISTRIBUTION

The LLS disc is distributed in the US by Joan Rubin Associates, 2011 Hermitage Ave., Wheaton, MD 20902, USA; phone 301–933–6931.

El Sayed Dadour
Mansoura University, Damietta, Egypt
Jill Robbins
Kyoto, Japan

CHAPTER 12

UNIVERSITY-LEVEL STUDIES USING STRATEGY INSTRUCTION TO IMPROVE SPEAKING ABILITY IN EGYPT AND JAPAN

I want to hear you speaking all the languages, offering your experience
as your truth, as human truth...
–Ursula Le Guin

SUMMARY

Two university-level studies of strategy instruction for speaking ability are presented in this chapter. In the first study, effects of strategy instruction are studied in oral communication classes for Egyptian EFL learners. This study shows statistically significant gains in oral ability as a result of strategy instruction, and no such gains are evident in the matched control group. The second study, which is primarily qualitative, demonstrates an application of strategy instruction in Japan and presents the case for direct (strategy-plus-control) instruction rather than blind instruction of strategies. In that study, students' reactions are explored.

INTRODUCTION

The aim of the two studies described here is to investigate the effectiveness of strategy instruction on developing the speaking ability of university-level learners of English as a foreign language in two countries: Egypt for the first study and Japan for the second. This chapter presents a review of existing research on strategy instruction for oral skills and then described the two studies, both of which highlight the benefits of strategy instruction for improving students' speaking ability. The first study is highly quantitative and the second is more qualitative.

REVIEW OF THE LITERATURE

ORAL COMMUNICATION

Communication of any type is not only complex but also dynamic, systemic, and comprised of simultaneous causes and effects (Porter, 1982). Penner (1984) explains the components of the oral or written communication process: (1) the communica-

Dadour, E. S., & Robbins, J. (1996). University-level studies using strategy instruction to improve speaking ability in Egypt and Japan. In Rebecca L. Oxford (Ed.), *Language learning strategies around the world: Cross-cultural perspectives*. (Technical Report #13) (pp. 157–166). Honolulu: University of Hawai'i, Second Language Teaching & Curriculum Center.

tion source, (2) the message, (3) the encoder (encoding is done through language expressions), (4) the channel or medium, (5) the decoder (used by the receiver to understand the message), and (6) the person who receives the communication. In oral communication, the first three relate to the speaker, the last two relate to the listener, and the fourth relates to both. Scarcella and Oxford (1992) view increasing accuracy — though not total perfection — as an eventual goal of the second or foreign language speaker. Higher level language speakers need to develop not only clarity, but some degree of accuracy.

Backlund (1990) assigns three areas of knowledge that influence oral communication effectiveness: social knowledge, self-knowledge, and content knowledge. If any one of these is weak, oral communication will be somewhat impaired. Other problems that hinder effective oral communication are: dominating the conversation, using inappropriate volume and pitch, using excessive small talk, ignoring someone, and constantly interrupting people (Newcombe, 1982). The teaching of speaking skills needs to be focused on real communication rather than on typically artificial classroom-type communication. Byrne (1986), Brown and Yule (1983), Dörnyei and Thurrell (1994), Littlewood (1981), and Scarcella and Oxford (1992) offer ideas about how to help students achieve oral communication aims and how to motivate students as they develop their speaking ability at various levels. Weir (1988) summarizes all the test formats that exist for evaluating oral communication skills of language learners.

LANGUAGE LEARNING STRATEGIES FOR ORAL COMMUNICATION

Some researchers make a distinction between learning and communication strategies (O'Malley and Chamot, 1990). These researchers say that communication strategies (such as changing the topic, using gestures, or asking for help) are used to achieve communicative goals, most notably when the person runs into a problem of missing knowledge. Learning strategies, on the other hand, are used for learning. Oxford (1990b) disagrees with this division, because so-called communication strategies result in the person's staying in the conversation and thus provide the opportunity for further learning as well as further communication — both of which would be cut off if the person did not use these strategies. Communication strategies, which thus could be considered as overlapping somewhat with learning strategies, have been studied by Selinker (1972) in his work on interlanguage and more recently by Tarone (1983) and Faerch and Kasper (1983). Oxford (1990b) has shown that the whole range of learning strategies (six categories including memory, cognitive, compensation, metacognitive, affective, and social) can influence a learner's speaking skill development. In addition, O'Malley and Chamot (1990), Strichart and Mangrum (1992) and Thompson (1987) list an array of strategies that can help in developing oral communication ability (see Dadour, 1995).

DIRECT (STRATEGY-PLUS-CONTROL) VERSUS EMBEDDED (BLIND) INSTRUCTION FOR ORAL COMMUNICATION STRATEGIES

Research in learning strategy instruction shows that the explicitness of instruction affects the degree to which students retain and transfer strategies (El-Dinary, 1993). In direct (strategy-plus-control) instruction, learners are informed of the value and purpose of strategies instruction, are given strategy names, are prompted to use certain strategies, and are told how to evaluate and transfer each strategy. In completely embedded (blind) instruction, students receive no such information. The problems with the latter approach are that (1) there is no transfer of strategy use to new tasks, (2) there is no development of independent learning strategies, and (3) there is little opportunity for students to become independent learners. Therefore, direct instruction, in which teachers explicitly present and explain the reasons for strategies use, promises to be the more effective approach and is used in the following two studies.

STUDY 1 IN EGYPT

HYPOTHESES

1. There are statistically significant differences between students in the experimental and control groups in speaking skills as measured by the COPE (see below), in favor of the former group.

2. There are statistically significant differences between students in the experimental and control groups in frequency of strategy use as measured by the SILL (see below), in favor of the former group.

3. There are statistically significant differences in the experimental group between fourth-year and first-year students on the COPE, in favor of the former.

4. There are no statistically significant differences in the experimental group between fourth-year and first-year students in frequency of strategy use as measured by the SILL.

5. There are no statistically significant differences between males and females in speaking skills as measured by the COPE.

6. There are no statistically significant differences between males and females in frequency of strategy use as measured by the SILL.

SAMPLE

In the first study, a sample of 122 first-year and fourth-year students in the Department of English studying at the Damietta Faculty of Education (Mansoura University) participated. They were assigned to four groups. The first two were randomly assigned as control groups (one included 30 first-year students, and the other included 31 fourth-year students). The other two groups were assigned as the experimental groups (one involved 30 first-year students, and the other contained 31 fourth-year students). Females outnumbered males in this study, since they typically are the ones who want to become English teachers in Egypt. In the whole group, 15 participants were male and the rest were female.

INSTRUMENTS

Four instruments were included:

1. The *EFL Teacher's Speaking Skills Inventory* was constructed by the present researcher. This instrument was constructed based on a comprehensive re-search review. The categorization of the items was checked by 35 university professors, educators, and foreign language teachers, with a Kuder-Richardson–20 reliability of .78. Categories included: linguistic/conversa-tional speaking skills, functional/instructional speaking skills, and social/affective speaking skills.

2. The *CLEAR Oral Proficiency Exam* (COPE) was developed by the Center for Applied Linguistics (Wang, Richardson, and Rhodes, 1988) to test oral communication skills. It was originally designed for primary school students but has been adapted for college students. The test offers 15-minute testing role-plays ("situations") to assess comprehension, fluency, vocabulary, and grammar. In each situation, two students conduct a dialogue while an ob-server scores their performances. The COPE has concurrent validity of r=.62 when correlated with the *IDEAL Oral Language Proficiency Test* (*IPT*) (see Bascur, 1994). (In the present research, comprehension was dropped but pronunciation was added as a skill to be observed and scored. An Arabic translation was used.)

3. Oxford's *Strategy Inventory for Language Learning* (1990c) was used in an Arabic translation. This survey contains six parts referring to different kinds of strategies: memory, cognitive, comprehension, metacognitive, af-fective, and social. This inventory uses a Likert scale for frequency and has Cronbach alpha internal consistency in the .90s. Studies have shown strong predictive and correlative relationships between strategy use on this instrument and language proficiency, gender, and learning style. See Bedell and Oxford, this volume, for additional details. See also Oxford and Burry, 1993, and Oxford and Burry-Stock, 1995.

4. The *Style Analysis Survey* (Oxford, 1993e) was used as part of the first ses-sion of strategy instruction. It was employed as a means of helping learners understand their major learning styles (visual, auditory, hands on; extro-verted, introverted; intuitive, concrete-sequential; closure-oriented, open; global, analytic), because these styles help determine choice of learning strategies. The SAS has 110 items using a Likert scale. Bascur's (1994) study showed that the SAS has a Cronbach reliability of .76 for all sections, .89 for intuitive/concrete-sequential, .82 for closure/open, .81 for intui-tive/concrete-sequential, .77 for global/analytic, and somewhat lower for

the three-part complex of visual/auditory/hands-on. Initial predictive validity studies show significant relationships among the SAS, gender, and academic major (Bascur, 1994).

DATA COLLECTION AND ANALYSIS PROCEDURES

To test the study's hypotheses, this researcher used two-way analysis of covariance (ANCOVA, four-by-two). In addition, Tukey's HSD post-hoc test was used to study significant differences among the studies subgroups. ANCOVA necessitates testing twice with the same instruments to assess and control for any initial differences in the variables in question. Thus, a pretest and a posttest were used.

STRATEGY INSTRUCTION COURSE

The aim of the course is to improve speaking skills of prospective English teachers in Egypt. The course provides the learners with instruction on using effective learning strategies. Each session has a main goal related to strategies for a specific linguistic/conversational speaking skill and subordinate goals related to developing learners' functional/instructional and social/affective speaking skills.

The course consists of 15 weekly, three-hour sessions. Except for the introductory, reviewing, and debriefing sessions, each session has five general steps, with the time allotments up to the teacher: (1) warm-up, (2) students' presentations and discussions of home assignments, (3) teacher's presentation and explanation with examples of new strategies, (4) activities for practicing the new strategies and for discussing them, and (5) home assignments for group work. In the home assignments, students work together to prepare an instructional situation that takes place with a teacher and three students of three different linguistic and/or motivational levels. In every situation the students are assigned to deal with a specific linguistic/conversational skill. The students are also required to incorporate some functional/instructional and social/affective speaking skills into the situation. Choice of these skills is left up to each group.

Although the content runs systematically, the teacher's and the learners' creativity is encouraged. In addition, the course stresses the idea of giving students more responsibility for their own learning. For example, beginning with Session 11, learners are to select the learning strategies to be included in the sessions, and beginning with Session 13, students start to prepare the warm-up activities. The course contains a teacher's guide to help the strategy instructor (teacher) understand and use the course. It includes specific recommendations for optimal use.

The course adopts both direct and indirect techniques of teaching speaking. In the direct mode, the course gives learners a clear idea about the speaking skills they need to master and the learning strategies they are required to practice to improve their skills. In the indirect mode, oral communication teaching is also conducted through role-play, drama, and problem-solving. The course makes use of charts, overhead projectors, language lab, video, and camcorder.

RESULTS

The first hypothesis, that the experimental group would outstrip the control group in speaking skills, was proven (p<.01) using ANCOVA to adjust for initial differences in speaking skills. This meant that the Strategy Instruction Course significantly affected the speaking performance of the students in the experimental group regardless of proficiency level (first- or fourth-year proficiency). Specific differences at the p<.01 level were found in fluency, vocabulary usage, and grammar, but not pronunciation.

The second hypothesis, predicting that the experimental group would show greater overall strategy use than the control group, was supported at the p<.01 level. The Strategy Instruction Course influenced the frequency of strategy use of the experimental group regardless of proficiency level. There were significant differences between the two groups (favoring the experimental group) in all six possible strategy categories: memory, cognitive, compensation, metacognitive, affective, and social.

Regarding hypothesis three, the fourth-year experimental group as expected outperformed the first-year experimental group on speaking skills as measured by the COPE. Significance appeared at the p<.01 level, thus supporting this hypothesis.

The fourth hypothesis was supported. There were no statistically significant differences in the experimental group between the fourth-year students and the first-year students in terms of frequency of strategy use (measured by the SILL).

The fifth hypothesis was not supported, because there were statistically significant differences between males and females in oral communication (COPE), in favor of males (p<.002). Males also scored significantly better on the subscales of fluency and vocabulary.

The sixth hypothesis was supported. No gender differences appeared for strategy use, despite gender differences found in previous studies. Thus, both males and females used an array of learning strategies to help them develop oral communication — even though, as seen above, females were reticent about speaking.

DISCUSSION

The Strategy Instruction Course had a significant impact on the experimental group, compared with the control group, in the areas of speaking skills and strategy frequency. This investigation showed that a well-structured strategy instruction course that allowed creativity on the part of both teacher and students could have a strongly positive affect on oral communication and the use of strategies (of all sorts). This result supports other studies on the teachability of strategies (Dörnyei, 1995; Oxford and Cohen, 1992). Course designers, curriculum developers, and classroom teachers could benefit from the Strategy Instruction Course as an aid for developing their own strategy courses.

The lack of difference between first- and fourth-year students in terms of frequency of strategy use was fully expected, because the impact of the Strategy Instruction Course was predicted to be approximately the same for both levels of students. On the other hand, it was also expected and completely confirmed that fourth-year students would have better speaking skills than first-year students.

The significant gender difference in speaking skills was likely to have occurred because of environmental factors. The research was conducted in a small Egyptian college town, where some families have raised their children on the basis that women are not, totally or partially, allowed to speak in front of men unless it is essential. This prohibition arises from many religious and cultural factors and might have resulted in lowered self-esteem as well as restricted speech for females. In instructional situations, females must speak in class, but their performance is often tempered by severe inhibition (whether men are there or not). In contrast, men are not prohibited to speak in front of women and in general might have developed a higher level of both self-esteem and motivation that allows them to speak more freely.

Even though there was a sharp gender difference in oral communication ability in favor of males, no such difference appeared in learning strategy use. This means that females and males were using strategies at approximately equivalent frequencies. Thus, the raw material of strategic knowledge was there for both males and females. Greater opportunities and encouragement should be given to females to develop their self-esteem and oral skills in settings such as this one.

Future research should focus on strategy instruction for multiple levels of students and for a variety of language skills. Strategy instruction courses should include more assistance on pronunciation strategies, and researchers should examine this aspect of speaking. Longitudinal research is essential to assess the effect of strategy instruction after the prospective teacher becomes a real teacher in classes of his or her own. A larger sample of males and females is needed to explore more fully differences in oral communication between women and men. Social aspects, such as rural versus urban, need to be regarded by researchers when conducting strategy studies; in this study, the small-town/rural setting seems to have had a cultural effect on some of the gender data. Investigators should also investigate strategy differences in second versus foreign language situations.

STUDY 2 IN JAPAN

SAMPLE

In an attempt to discover the feasibility of learning strategies instruction in Japan, the author presented this instruction to approximately 50 Japanese students of English at two universities in the Kyoto area for a period of three months.

STRATEGY INSTRUCTION PROCEDURES

Once a foundation for understanding has been laid by the acquisition of vocabulary and basic structures, the learner must have the opportunity to engage in interaction in the target language in order to expand upon that basic knowledge (Rost and Ross, 1991). Therefore, the Problem-Solving Process Model was developed by Language Research Projects to teach learning strategies to learners of foreign languages at US high schools and universities (Chamot, Robbins, and El-Dinary, 1993). The Problem-Solving Process Model presents strategies within a general framework that can overlay a strategic structure onto any classroom activity.

In the beginning of this instruction, students were first asked to brainstorm their own strategies for learning English. The purpose of this discussion was to make students more aware of the language learning process and to focus on their own active involvement with this process. During this discussion, the teacher accepted all student techniques without judging whether they are useful or not. Next the teacher modeled a language task in Japanese (answering questions about job and family) and "thought aloud" while working through it, in order to demonstrate the use of strategies. The teacher drew some pictures on the overhead to illustrate the visual images that came to her mind when thinking of particular concepts. She also asked for help from students and at one point looked up an unknown word. These were all examples of learning strategies for speaking.

The teacher presented the Problem-Solving Process Model. Every language learning task could be broken down into four basic processes: Planning, Monitoring (Regulating), Problem-Solving, and Evaluation. The teacher led the students through the model with reference to the teacher's previous think-aloud for examples of how particular strategies were applied. Following this introduction, the teacher gave the students a handout showing the four processes and a selection of strategies that were to be focused on in the coming class sessions. This model was supplemented by a set of vocabulary learning strategies, such as visualization, personalization, grouping, manipulation, cognates, using language knowledge, cooperation, and self-evaluation.

In subsequent classes, the teacher began each language task by showing how students could apply a strategy to plan for the task. For example, when the assignment involved listening, students were instructed to first *set a goal* for their listening: What information do they need to find out? Then, they *predicted* the type of language they would hear, based on information given by the teacher about the general content of the listening passage. The teacher identified several words or phrases that might appear in the passage. For example, before playing a portion of the movie "Jurassic Park," the teacher asked students to predict what words they might hear in reference to dinosaurs. Some of the predicted words were: fossil, egg, dinosaur, and meat-eating. Using this prediction strategy the class watched the video segment with these words in mind, along with several teacher-supplied words. During the task, students were encouraged to *check their comprehension*. If they found that they were not understanding, they applied strategies to solve the problem. They were encouraged to *ask questions to clarify* the listening passage, or to use *inferencing* to make an educated guess about unknown words or phrases. Once they finished with the task, students were asked to evaluate their performance. They checked to see if the goal was met and if predictions were verified. The teacher asked students to report on whether the strategies they used were helpful to them. This stage of instruction was crucial: Students had to be given the opportunity to evaluate the effectiveness of strategies used; otherwise they could not transfer strategies to other tasks.

During each lesson, the teacher modeled the use of strategies and gave students an explanation for the use of these strategies with particular tasks. Appropriate matching of strategies and tasks characterizes effective learners. The teacher also used "scaffolding," which means gradually removing teacher support so that the students became self-regulating in their use of strategies. The teacher reduced explicit prompts to use particular strategies, allowing students to choose their own most effective strategies. Throughout this process, the teacher was aware that the strategies favored by Japanese learners, who are typically more dependent on the teacher, might not be the same as those preferred by Western learners.

As a homework assignment, the teacher asked the students to keep a Language Learning Log, intended to encourage them to apply the Problem-Solving Process Model to their oral practice of English outside the classroom. Many of the students reported in their logs that they talked with native speakers of English outside of class, and they said they felt good about the fact that they had sought the opportunity. Logs revealed that some students had overly broad speaking goals such as, "Speak English" or "Speak English more naturally." Others had more specific, more useful goals: "to make a rejoinder quickly when a partner said something"; "to express body language/gestures;" "to make a conversation with many people;" "to ask your favorite food;" and "to greet the person I meet first." Asking students to keep a learning log encouraged extracurricular oral language practice and the recording of learning strategies.

STUDENT REACTIONS TO LEARNING STRATEGIES INSTRUCTION

Six weeks into the semester, the teacher gave a questionnaire to 46 students at the two universities. The questionnaire consisted of ten statements followed by a scale from one to four. Students indicated strong disagreement with the statement by circling "1" and strong agreement with the statement by circling "4." In general, the results indicated that most of the students understood the reasons for using learning strategies (statement 1), and many saw the usefulness of strategic planning (statements 2, 3, and 5). The negative response to statement 7 ("When I don't understand a word in English that I hear or read, I give up on understanding.") indicated the students were willing to try to take a more active role in their listening and reading. Most wanted to learn more strategies for speaking (73% for statement 9) and listening (78% for statement 10). However, many indicated they did not fully understand how to use learning strategies (statement 8). This was not surprising, considering the short time (three months) in which they experienced strategies instruction.

DISCUSSION

The desire of Japanese students to passively absorb information provided by teachers was the major obstacle to successful learning strategy instruction. Therefore, it was necessary to convince students of the value of active involvement. The teacher was pleased that some of her students realized that their use of strategies resulted in improved English speaking skills. Though strategy instruction was not a "magic pill" to improve anyone's speaking ability, it was an effective means of enhancing foreign language teaching and learning.

CONCLUSIONS

These two studies, conducted in very different cultural settings, nevertheless both showed that learners of English can benefit from strategies designed to improve their speaking ability. In Egypt, students who experienced strategy instruction in speaking had significantly better oral proficiency scores than did students who did not have such exposure. In Japan, students took part in a highly structured Problem-Solving Process Model of strategy instruction. They voiced the advantages of strategic planning and wanted to learn more strategies for speaking and listening.

Anna Uhl Chamot
The George Washington University, Washington, DC, USA
J. Michael O'Malley
Prince William County Public Schools, Virginia, USA

CHAPTER 13

IMPLEMENTING THE COGNITIVE ACADEMIC LANGUAGE LEARNING APPROACH (CALLA)

Let our minds be bold.
–Louis D. Brandeis

SUMMARY

This chapter provides a description of the Cognitive Academic Language Learning Approach (CALLA) and an account of recent developments and applications of this instructional model. The chapter begins with an overview of the purpose, design, and theory of CALLA. Next we discuss issues to be considered in implementing a CALLA program, including teacher education, individualizing learning strategies instruction, and assessing the components of CALLA. The chapter concludes with a discussion of future directions and applications of CALLA.

OVERVIEW OF CALLA

PURPOSE

The purpose of CALLA is to assist ESL students to succeed in school by strengthening their ability to use English, to apply content knowledge and skills, and to become independent and strategic thinkers (Chamot and O'Malley, 1986, 1987, 1989b, 1994a). CALLA is a special form of content area instruction that supports the transition from language-based programs to grade-level content classrooms, that is, classrooms with native English-speaking, age-level peers. The language-based programs may be either standard ESL approaches that focus on English language skills, or bilingual programs that include native language content area instruction with an ESL component. CALLA was originally designed particularly for students at the advanced beginning and intermediate levels of English language proficiency, although the strategic learning component of CALLA is appropriate for all students.

DESCRIPTION

CALLA has three major interrelated components: content area instruction, academic language development, and explicit instruction in learning strategies. The goals and objectives of content area instruction in CALLA represent selected

Chamot, A. U., & O'Malley, J. M. (1996). Implementing the Cognitive Academic Language Learning Approach (CALLA). In Rebecca L. Oxford (Ed.), *Language learning strategies around the world: Cross-cultural perspectives*. (Technical Report #13) (pp. 167–173). Honolulu: University of Hawai'i, Second Language Teaching & Curriculum Center.

topics from the all-English curriculum that are treated in depth. The in-depth coverage in content areas is structured to give ESL students time and opportunities to succeed at learning the concepts and skills that are important in the content areas. Students develop competence in the vocabulary, grammar, and discourse used in understanding and expressing content area information through oral and written communication. We have recommended that content subjects be introduced gradually in CALLA beginning with areas that, when taught experientially, are least language-dependent, such as science, and continuing with mathematics and eventually including social studies and language arts (Chamot and O'Malley, 1987, 1994b). Higher order concepts in the content areas can be introduced from the onset in CALLA by using extensive contextual supports and reduced language demands, such as hands-on demonstrations in science, math manipulatives, or geography maps. Teachers using an integrated curriculum will find particular advantages in introducing elements of language arts or social studies along with science or math.

The academic language development component focuses on the application of all four language skills (listening, reading, speaking, and writing) in communicating, learning, and thinking in content-area classrooms. The language of each subject area has special vocabulary and often preferred grammatical structures and discourse organization that students need to learn in addition to the concepts and skills that are essential to the discipline. Students use the language in each subject to accomplish important functions such as explaining, analyzing, evaluating, justifying, and persuading. In CALLA, academic language development is fostered by providing students with cognitively challenging experiences in the content areas assisted by contextual supports and scaffolded instruction.

The learning strategies component of CALLA introduces ESL students to effective strategies for learning in the content areas and for language learning, providing students with support for becoming independent learners. This component is grounded in cognitive theory (see below and chapter 14). The goal of strategy instruction in CALLA is to provide students with a menu of explicitly-taught strategies that they are able to deploy depending on the requirements of individual tasks or activities. Learning strategies include *cognitive strategies*, *metacognitive strategies*, and *social-affective* strategies, all described elsewhere in this book. Students also learn conditional knowledge in CALLA, which consists of knowing when and how to apply different strategies to particular problems or learning tasks encountered.

THEORY

Cognitive research and theory supporting CALLA are discussed in chapter 14. The central assertion in cognitive theory is that learning occurs through active, dynamic mental processes (Paris and Winograd, 1990; Pressley and Associates, 1990; Zimmerman, 1990). For example, learners select information from the environment, organize the information, relate it to what they already know, retain what they consider to be important, use the information in appropriate contexts, and reflect on the success of their learning efforts. What is learned? Learners retain at least two types of information in memory: *declarative knowledge*, or "what" we know (e.g., the factual information in history or science), and *procedural knowledge*, or what we know "how" to do (e.g., problem-solving procedures and reading strategies) (Anderson, 1976, 1983).

Second language acquisition has important parallels with learning complex procedural skills (O'Malley and Chamot, 1990). Language is more an example of what we know how to do rather than what we know, while the *information* gained and then expressed through language exemplify declarative knowledge. Listening, reading, speaking, and writing are all examples of complex procedures. Further, language use is goal-oriented as is procedural knowledge. In using academic language, we communicate orally or in writing to achieve a goal, such as explaining, persuading, or evaluating new information or existing knowledge. Language has important declarative components, such as the lexicon and concepts the words represent and the rules for pluralization and sentence formation. Language also has important procedural conventions, as characterized by "communicative competence," or the ability to use grammatical, sociolinguistic, discourse, and strategic skills (Canale and Swain, 1980). While these conventions can be learned like declarative knowledge, the rules are so complex that we often learn the skills by following expert models.

Learning a second language occurs most effectively when the student has an opportunity to learn meaningful language that can be applied in a context to accomplish goals important to the student. Teachers who model language sequences used in accomplishing communication goals can circumvent for students the necessity of learning the extensive rules that govern everything from the pronunciation to grammatical structures and social context in which various language conventions are appropriate. Because effective communication requires frequent opportunities to apply what is being learned, students should have varied opportunities for practice with teachers and peers in authentic interactive contexts.

Another very important aspect of the theory underlying CALLA is motivation from a social-cognitive viewpoint. For details, see chapter 14.

ISSUES IN IMPLEMENTING CALLA

Important issues to be considered in implementing CALLA include ways to develop teacher expertise, individualize learning strategies instruction, and assess student progress. In this section we discuss these issues and explain our current thinking on how to address them.

DEVELOPING TEACHER EXPERTISE

CALLA teachers should not only be effective teachers of their own specialization, whether ESL or content subject, but must also acquire additional knowledge and skills in order to meet the needs of their students. ESL teachers need to develop expertise in teaching content subjects, while content teachers need to learn how to integrate language teaching into subject matter lessons. In most cases, ESL teachers, content teachers, and bilingual teachers need to learn how to provide explicit strategies instruction designed to assist their students in learning both content subjects and academic language skills. The development of this understanding and these complex skills needs to be addressed in both preservice and inservice teacher education programs. Our experience indicates that inservice professional development activities are most successful when they are ongoing throughout each school year and when they involve both language and content teachers. Staff development for CALLA needs to be continuous, because teachers need time to develop, practice, and refine new content and teaching skills. Typically, during the first year of staff development activities, teachers gain familiarity with the model and begin experimenting with adding content to their language lessons, or in the case of content teachers, developing language activities for subject matter classes. Teachers new to learning strategies tend to provide largely implicit instruction. That is, they plan activities in which students use strategies such as brainstorming what they already know about a topic or using context clues to guess at word meanings, but fail to identify these activities to students as strategies or to explain their purpose. Teachers may find it difficult initially to model their own use of strategies by thinking aloud while performing a task. In the second year of continuing inservice workshops, ESL teachers generally begin to feel more comfortable with adding content to their language instruction, content teachers start providing some language activities, and both groups of teachers begin to develop ways to make learning strategies instruction more explicit. By the third year of staff development, teachers have generally developed skills in designing and teaching CALLA lessons and are able to share their expertise with teachers new to the program. The involvement of both content and language teachers in on-going staff development makes possible the cross-fertilization of ideas and techniques, and is helpful in developing a team approach to establishing a program that successfully integrates instruction in content subjects, academic language skills, and learning strategies.

INDIVIDUALIZING STRATEGIES INSTRUCTION

The scaffolding model we have proposed for strategies instruction is designed to provide extensive teacher support at the beginning of the instruction, followed by a fading of explanations and reminders as students learn how to use strategies autonomously (Chamot and O'Malley, 1994a, 1994b). However, the scaffolding should be sensitive to the fact that students have different needs for strategies instruction. Effective learners have already developed useful strategies for approaching learning tasks, and may profit most from instruction designed to increase metacognitive awareness of their own thinking and learning processes. Reflection, discussion, and evaluation of their use of strategies is valuable in helping students increase their ability to regulate their own learning. On the other hand, students who are encountering difficulties with language or content (or both) may need extensive strategies instruction in which the strategies are modeled by the teacher or by classmates and multiple opportunities for practice are provided. The teacher, then, must begin by finding out what strategies students are already using, judge how appropriate these strategies are for language and content tasks, and design instruction to meet differing strategic needs. When teaching strategies, teachers also need to be aware of the amount of explicit instruction needed by different students. Highly strategic students, for example, may become intolerant of extended strategies instruction because they believe that their classmates are as strategic they are, and that continuing the strategies instruction is unnecessary. What they do not realize is that while strategies are obvious approaches to them, many of their classmates are new to strategic ways of processing information and skills and do need continuing teacher support as they discover how and when to use learning strategies. Thus, the teacher needs to balance different student needs and individualize strategies instruction when necessary.

ASSESSING CONTENT, LANGUAGE, AND LEARNING STRATEGIES

The assessment component of CALLA addresses the multiple goals of the program in content areas, academic language, and learning strategies. CALLA uses assessment instruments that assist teachers in identifying the initial level of student performance, monitor student progress toward instructional goals, and determine when the goals have been attained. The multiple assessments used in evaluating these goals include teacher observations, writing samples, criterion-referenced and norm-referenced tests, self-evaluations, and performance assessments. Different examples of student progress are selected jointly by the teacher and student to keep in a work portfolio, which teachers can use to weigh each source of information for the information it provides relative to the goals and standards for student performance (Chamot and O'Malley, 1994a, 1994b; Chamot, O'Malley, and Küpper, 1992).

CALLA teachers continually observe individual students' level of performance with content activities, ability to understand and use academic language, and demonstrations of independent use of learning strategies. These observations can be recorded in anecdotal records or on rating scales which identify specific instructional objectives and levels of student achievement.

Writing samples in CALLA are assessed based on authentic instructional activities in which students read or listen to substantive input on a topic, take notes, discuss their impressions with peers, and write a draft indication their recollections and preliminary conclusions. The purpose of the writing can be narrative, expository, persuasive, or expressive. For example, the writing can be a personal reflection on progress in school, a report on a science experiment, a description of a math problem solution, a summary of a text read, a piece of creative writing, or an account of strategies used for a particular task. After writing the first draft, students should then have an opportunity to review the scoring rubric and edit and revise their paper to produce a final version to which the scoring rubric will be applied. The rubric typically contains some type of holistic or domain scoring that depends on local objectives in language arts but may include composing, style, sentence formation, usage, and mechanics. In the assessment of listening and reading, students may be asked to make schematic maps, draw and label pictures, offer explanations, and write extended prose passages to show their comprehension and ability to apply the knowledge they have acquired.

As an example of assessment in a content area, the CALLA mathematics project in Arlington, Virginia has developed a criterion-based test in computation, word problems and learning strategies, and the language of mathematics. The first section assesses students' ability to handle the basic computation skills required for entrance into grade-level math classes. In the second section students work through word problems, then indicate on a checklist which learning strategies were used. The third section assesses students' knowledge of vocabulary associated with mathematics and their ability to comprehend directions and word problems. A standardized test has also been used in mathematics as a tool for program evaluation.

Two important sources of information about students' progress toward goals and objectives in the content areas are self-evaluation and performance assessment. The self-evaluation consists of learning logs developed for each content area. These periodic assessments combine checklists with open-ended questions in which students are asked to describe what they have learned, what is easy for them, what difficulties they have encountered, which areas they need help in, and what their attitudes and feelings are about their work in the content area. In a typical performance assessment used in the Arlington CALLA science program, students are first given a problem and the materials needed to solve it. Students work collaboratively to develop a hypothesis, conduct an experiment, record their data, and find a solution. Students then write individual lab reports. These are scored using pre-established criteria or scoring rubrics for understanding the scientific concept, appropriateness of procedures, accuracy of observation and recording, reasonableness of solution, language use, and evidence of learning strategies.

CALLA PROGRAMS

CALLA programs are currently being implemented in over 25 locations in the United States and in several other countries in a variety of educational contexts. These include bilingual and ESL programs, elementary and secondary school levels, and teacher education. For example, *Project CALLA* in New York City's School District 2 is implementing CALLA bilingual and ESL programs for grades 1 through 5. These programs are operating in ten different schools and include ongoing staff development activities for teachers, curriculum development, and a strong parent education component. In Fargo, North Dakota, a middle school ESL CALLA program is focusing on science, social studies, and mathematics for a multilingual student population speaking nearly 70 different languages, including Vietnamese, Kurdish, Native American languages, Russian, Polish, Korean, Spanish, and Romanian. A CALLA program in Boston, Massachusetts began with a secondary bilingual program for Haitian students and is now expanding the program to include students from additional language backgrounds. This program has developed a series of CALLA instructional units for middle and high school classes in science, mathematics, and social studies. The University of New Mexico in Albuquerque is providing inservice professional development on the CALLA Model to secondary content teachers in Albuquerque and in neighboring school districts. A number of other universities nationwide include information about CALLA as part of their bilingual and ESL teacher preparation programs. In Canada, an instructional program derived from CALLA is being implemented in schools in Winnipeg (chapter 15, this volume). Thus, the CALLA Model and revisions of it are being used in a variety of educational settings in programs for language minority students. For specific, detailed examples of CALLA in action, contact the authors of this chapter.

FUTURE DIRECTIONS

CALLA was originally envisioned as a transitional program for intermediate level upper elementary and secondary students who had acquired initial English proficiency through ESL or bilingual programs and needed to develop content knowledge, academic language, and learning strategies prior to entering grade-level classes (Chamot and O'Malley, 1986). Ten years later, we have learned that our initial scope was too limited. The CALLA Model has been successfully implemented with beginning level ESL students and with students whose prior education has been limited.

Another promising future direction for CALLA is in the native language component of bilingual programs. In these programs, students receive content and language instruction through the medium of their native language, as well as ESL instruction. (In developmental bilingual programs, an additional goal is for students to become academically proficient in both languages.) A CALLA program could assist in meeting these goals by teaching students to use learning strategies in their native language and to transfer the strategies to similar academic contexts in English.

CALLA applications in foreign language instruction are also possible. Many foreign language educators recommend that students learn to use the target language for academic purposes in a content-based program (Curtain and Pesola, 1988; Met, 1988; Snow, Met, and Genesee, 1989). Immersion programs for elementary children are frequently cited as examples of successful content-based foreign language instruction. Adding strategies instruction to content-based foreign language programs on the CALLA Model could further enhance their effectiveness. The CALLA instructional sequence has been used in research studies conducted by researchers at Georgetown University's Language Research Projects to develop a scaffolded framework for strategies instruction in high school and college foreign language classes (Chamot, Robbins, and El-Dinary, 1993; Chamot, Barnhardt, El-Dinary, Carbonaro and Robbins, 1993). Current research in progress by the same research team is investigating learning strategies used by children enrolled in French, Japanese, and Spanish immersion programs and ways in which immersion teachers can integrate strategies instruction into their content-based language programs. Thus, this study will develop a prototype for a CALLA program for elementary foreign language immersion students.

As a final note, we would like to reiterate our belief that, inasmuch as CALLA embodies effective instruction based on research and cognitive learning theory, it is a model which can be used effectively for all students in academic settings, whether or not they are learning through the medium of a second language.

Anna Uhl Chamot
The George Washington University, Washington, DC, USA
Sarah Barnhardt
Georgetown University, Virginia, USA
Pamela El-Dinary
Georgetown University, Virginia, USA
Jill Robbins
Kyoto, Japan

CHAPTER 14

METHODS FOR TEACHING LEARNING STRATEGIES IN THE FOREIGN LANGUAGE CLASSROOM

We learn by doing.
–Aristotle

SUMMARY

This chapter reports on recent research with foreign language teachers and their students. The studies investigated learning strategies instruction in beginning and intermediate level Japanese, Russian, and Spanish classrooms. Research activities included the identification of appropriate strategies to teach for each language and level, the development and implementation of learning strategy lessons integrated with the foreign language curriculum, professional development of teachers, and evaluation of the impact of strategies instruction on students. A problem-solving process model for strategies instruction was developed, and students in classrooms using the model increased their use of learning strategies over the school year. Teachers viewed the strategies instruction positively and provided valuable information on methods of teaching language learning strategies. Major findings included increases in students' use of strategies and concomitant increases in self-confidence.

INTRODUCTION

A research program on the application of learning strategies instruction to foreign language classrooms has been conducted by Georgetown University's Language Research Projects since 1990. This research is funded through the Georgetown University/Center for Applied Linguistics National Foreign Language Resource Center and through additional grants from the International Research and Studies Program of the US Department of Education. Two of the initial studies were completed in late 1993, and three additional related studies are in progress and will be

Chamot, A. U., Barnhardt, S., El-Dinary, P., & Robbins, J. (1996). Methods for teaching learning strategies in the foreign language classroom. In Rebecca L. Oxford (Ed.), *Language learning strategies around the world: Cross-cultural perspectives*. (Technical Report #13) (pp. 175–187). Honolulu: University of Hawai'i, Second Language Teaching & Curriculum Center.

completed in 1996. This chapter describes the methodology and accomplishments of the completed learning strategies studies.

One study investigated the feasibility of teaching learning strategies to beginning level high school and college students of Japanese; the other sought to develop effective learning strategy instruction in high school beginning and intermediate level Russian and Spanish classrooms. Since both of these studies had similar designs and objectives, we will discuss them together. The major purposes were to identify appropriate learning strategies for the languages and levels studied, to develop and refine instructional materials to teach the strategies, and to describe the impact of the instruction on students and teachers. Additional objectives included identifying issues in professional development of teachers, design of materials, student affect and motivation, and teacher attitudes and teaching styles.

THEORETICAL FRAMEWORK

These studies have built on an emerging interest in a cognitive perspective in second and foreign language acquisition research. While cognitive learning theory has become a well-established model for instruction in general education, the theory's contributions to the area of second language acquisition are relatively recent. A theoretical model in second language acquisition is important as a basis for explaining how a language is learned and how second and foreign languages can best be taught. Moreover, for purposes of research on language learning processes, a theoretical model should describe the role of strategic processes in learning. A cognitive theoretical model of learning (e.g., Anderson, 1983, 1985; Gagné, Yekovich, and Yekovich, 1993; Shuell, 1986) accomplishes these objectives because the theory is general enough to explain how learning takes place in a variety of simple and complex tasks, and because cognitive theory provides important insights into second language acquisition (McLaughlin, 1987; O'Malley and Chamot, 1990).

In cognitive theory, learning is seen as an active, constructivist process in which learners select and organize informational input, relate it to prior knowledge, retain what is considered important, use the information appropriately, and reflect on the outcomes of their learning efforts (Gagné et al., 1993; Shuell, 1986). In this dynamic view of learning, second language acquisition should be most successful when learners are actively involved in directing their own learning in both classroom and non-classroom settings. Second language learners would select from target language input, analyze language functions and forms perceived as important, think about their own learning efforts, anticipate the kinds of language demands they may encounter, and activate prior knowledge and skills to apply to new language learning tasks. It is because of this intricate set of mental processes that second language acquisition has been construed as a complex cognitive skill (McLaughlin, 1987; O'Malley and Chamot, 1990).

BRIEF LITERATURE REVIEW

The intent of learner or learning strategy use is to facilitate learning (Weinstein and Mayer, 1986), in contrast to communication strategies employed to negotiate meaning in a conversational exchange (Tarone, 1983). However, many communication strategies may serve as effective learning strategies when they are used to achieve a learning goal. Cook (1991) points out that individuals use a number of these communication strategies (such as substituting an approximate word or describing the function of a word that is unknown or not immediately available) in native language communication, and that only communication strategies that reflect knowledge of another language are unique to second language interaction.

The research on strategic processes in second language acquisition has had two main approaches. Much of the original second language strategies research focused on identifying the characteristics of good language learners, and this strand of research on uninstructed learner strategies has since expanded to include descriptions of strategy use of less effective language learners. A second approach has been concerned with learning strategies instruction, in which foreign and second language students have been taught how to use learning strategies for a variety of language tasks. Learner and learning strategies may entail conceptual or affective processes (O'Malley and Chamot, 1990), or a combination, and may also involve social interaction.

THE GOOD LANGUAGE LEARNER, DIFFERENCES BETWEEN SUCCESSFUL AND LESS SUCCESSFUL LEARNERS, AND THE ROLE OF MOTIVATION

The first descriptions of the characteristics of good language learners appeared in the mid–1970s. Rubin (1975) suggested that the good language learner could be identified through special strategies used by more effective students. Stern (1975) identified a number of learner characteristics and strategic techniques associated with good language learners. These studies were followed by empirical work by Naiman, Fröhlich, Stern, and Todesco (1978) which pursued further the idea that learning strategies are an important component of second language learning ability. Hosenfeld (1976) investigated learner strategies through verbal reports or think-aloud protocols, and in a subsequent study taught high school students of French explicit reading strategies (Hosenfeld, Arnold, Kirchofer, Laciura, and Wilson, 1981). Cohen and Aphek (1981) collected anecdotal reports from students on the associations they made while learning vocabulary, and found that students who made associations remembered vocabulary words more effectively than students who did not make associations.

Research on the good language learner has led to research on strategic differences between effective and less effective language learners. This topic is explored in detail by Kaylani (this volume). In general, studies have shown that differences between more and less effective learners were found in the number and range of strategies used, in how the strategies were used, in whether they were appropriate for the task, and in individual students' metacognitive understanding of the task

(Chamot, O'Malley, Küpper, and Impink-Hernandez, 1987; Chamot, Küpper, and Impink-Hernandez, 1988a, 1988b). Explicit metacognitive knowledge about task characteristics and about appropriate strategies for task solution is a major determiner of language learning effectiveness.

Effective language learners have stronger motivation than do less effective language learners. Highly motivated students work hard, persevere in the face of difficulties, and find satisfaction in the accomplishment of a learning task. Strategies have been linked to motivation and particularly to a sense of self-efficacy leading to expectations of successful learning (Zimmerman and Pons, 1986). The development of an individual's self-efficacy, or level of confidence in successfully completing a task is closely associated with effective use of learning strategies (Zimmerman, 1990). Self-efficacy is at the root of self-esteem, motivation, and self-regulation (Bandura, 1992). Self-efficacious learners feel confident about solving a problem because they have developed an approach to problem solving that has worked in the past. They attribute their success mainly to their own efforts and strategies, they believe that their own abilities will improve as they learn more, and they recognize that errors are a part of learning. Students with low self-efficacy, on the other hand, believe themselves to have inherently low ability, they choose less demanding tasks on which they will make few errors, and they do not try hard because they believe that any effort will reveal their own lack of ability (Bandura, 1992). Having access to appropriate strategies should lead students to higher expectations of learning success, a crucial component of motivation. An important aspect in viewing oneself as a successful learner is self-control over strategy use. This type of self-control can be enhanced if strategy instruction is combined with metacognitive awareness of the relationship between strategy use and learning outcomes. Students with greater metacognitive awareness understand the similarity between a new learning task and previous tasks, know the strategies required for successful problem solving or learning, and anticipate that employing these strategies will lead to success (Paris and Winograd, 1990).

CLASSIFICATION OF LEARNER STRATEGIES

Rubin (1981) conducted interviews with second language students and suggested a classification scheme consisting of strategies that directly affect learning (e.g., monitoring, memorizing, deductive reasoning, and practice) and processes that contribute indirectly to learning (creating opportunities for practice and production tricks). More recently, others have analyzed the types of strategies used with different second language tasks based on interviews, observations, and questionnaires. Wenden (1987c) focused on describing students' metacognitive knowledge and strategies that assist them in regulating their own learning. Oxford (1990c) developed the *Strategy Inventory for Language Learning* (SILL), a Likert-type instrument which incorporates more than 60 strategies (such as cognitive, compensation, metacognitive, social, and affective strategies) culled from the literature on second language learning. In a typical study, the *SILL* was administered to 1,200 university students studying various foreign languages (Nyikos and Oxford, 1993). A factor analysis revealed that language students may not use the strategies that research indicates would be most effective, such as strategies that promote self-regulated learning and strategies that provide meaningful practice in communication. This information is of great utility in designing intervention studies to teach effective strategy use.

In research conducted by O'Malley and Chamot and their colleagues, a broad range of classroom and non-classroom tasks were analyzed in interviews on learning strategies with second language students (O'Malley and Chamot, 1990). The tasks represented typical second language classroom activities such as vocabulary and grammar exercises, following directions, listening for information, reading for comprehension, writing, and presenting oral reports, and also included language used in functional contexts outside the classroom such as interacting at a party and applying for a job (O'Malley et al., 1985a). Tasks used for think-aloud interviews included listening to and reading dialogues and stories as well as science and social studies academic content materials (Chamot and Küpper, 1989; O'Malley, Chamot, and Küpper, 1989). Participants in these interviews included students enrolled in English as a second language and foreign language classrooms at high school and university levels.

The classification system that seemed best to capture the nature of learner strategies reported by students in these studies was based on the distinction in cognitive psychology between metacognitive and cognitive strategies together with a third category for social/affective strategies (Chamot and Küpper, 1989; O'Malley et al., 1985a; O'Malley, Chamot, and Küpper, 1989). This tripartite classification scheme, developed initially with ESL students (O'Malley et al., 1985a), was later validated with foreign language learners, including students of Russian, Spanish, and Japanese in the United States (Barnhardt, 1992; Chamot and Küpper, 1989; Omori, 1992), English as a foreign language students in Brazil (Absy, 1992; Lott-Lage, 1993), and students of French in Canada (Vandergrift, 1992). Examples of strategies in each of these categories are: metacognitive strategies for planning, monitoring, and evaluating a learning task; cognitive strategies for elaboration, grouping, inferencing, and summarizing the information to be understood and learned; and social/affective strategies for questioning, cooperating, and self-talk to assist in the learning process. Additional individual strategies have been suggested (e.g., Cohen, 1990a, 1990b; Oxford, 1992; Oxford and Cohen, 1992; Rost and Ross, 1991), in particular communication strategies used in social contexts. Interactive strategies for expressing apologies (Cohen, 1990b), types of clarification questions used at different levels of proficiency (Rost and Ross, 1991), and other conversational strategies (Chamot, Küpper, Thompson, Barrueta, and Toth, 1990; Oxford, 1990b) can in general be classified in the category of social/affective strategies.

CAN STRATEGIES BE TAUGHT?

This section reviews research in both first and second language contexts that provides insights into two questions: (1) If good language learners use strategies differently than less effective language learners, can teachers help less effective language

---

learners improve through instruction in learning strategies? and (2) If so, how should strategies instruction be implemented?

While empirical verification that strategies instruction has a positive effect on second language learning is beginning to appear, considerable evidence for the positive effects of strategies intervention has already been found in first language learning instructional contexts with different kinds of learners. For example, instruction in reading strategies has significantly improved the reading comprehension of poor readers (Gagné, 1985; Gagné et al., 1992; Garner, 1987; Palincsar and Brown, 1986; Palincsar and Kienk, 1992; Pressley, El-Dinary, and Brown, 1992), and instruction in problem solving strategies has had a positive effect on student mathematics achievement (Carpenter, Fennema, Peterson, Chiang, and Loef, 1989; Pressley and Associates, 1990; Silver and Marshall, 1990). Similarly, improvements in writing performance have been reported in a series of studies in which learning disabled students were explicitly taught strategies for planning, composing, and revising their writing (Harris and Graham, 1992). This validation of learning strategy instruction has led to the development of instructional models incorporating learning strategies for content instruction (Bergman, 1992; Harris and Graham, 1992; Jones and Idol, 1990; Jones, Palincsar, Ogle, and Carr, 1987; Snyder and Pressley, 1990).

Although the cognitive instructional research in first language contexts has been concerned with a broad range of complex learning tasks, until recently much second language research on instructed learning strategies has focused mainly on vocabulary (e.g., Atkinson and Raugh, 1975; Ellis and Beaton, forthcoming; Pressley, Levin, Nakamura, Hope, Bisbo, and Toye, 1980), with relatively few studies on strategies instruction for areas such as text comprehension, interactive speaking, or written production. In strategies research in second language acquisition, two types of studies have provided empirical support for the link between strategies and learning in a second language: correlational studies (Chamot, Dale, O'Malley, and Spanos, 1992, 1993; O'Malley, 1992; Padron and Waxman, 1988; Politzer and McGroarty, 1985) and experimental interventions (Brown and Perry, 1991; O'Malley et al., 1985b; Ross and Rost, 1991; Rubin, Quinn, and Enos, 1988). Both types of studies have produced support for the influence of strategies on second language learning.

SUMMARY OF LITERATURE REVIEW

This review of research on learning strategies in second language acquisition and related studies in first language contexts indicates that appropriate strategies use is an important factor that differentiates more and less effective language learners, and that useful strategies are both teachable and learnable. The specific conditions which lead to good strategy use are not yet completely understood in second language acquisition, though advances in effective strategies instruction in first language contexts indicates that such instructional procedures have been identified.

STUDIES COMPLETED BY GEORGETOWN UNIVERSITY'S LANGUAGE RESEARCH PROJECTS

In this section we describe the objectives, subjects, instructional context, instruments, methodology, and results of the two recently completed language learning strategies studies.

OBJECTIVES

The main objective of the study *Methods for Teaching Learning Strategies in the Foreign Language Classroom* was to develop effective learning strategies instruction for beginning and intermediate level high school Russian and Spanish classrooms. Questions addressed included which strategies would be most appropriate for high school classes, how the strategies could be implemented within the curriculum, and what effects strategies instruction has on students.

The main objective of the *Japanese Learning Strategies Study* was to find out whether learning strategies instruction could be applied to beginning level Japanese study at high school and college levels. Previous research on teaching language learning strategies has focused largely on English as a foreign or second language (Brown and Perry, 1991; Chamot, Robbins, and El-Dinary, 1993; O'Malley et al., 1985b; Rost and Ross, 1991), French (Hosenfeld et al., 1981), Spanish (Rubin et al., 1988), and learning in first language contexts (e.g., Harris and Graham, 1992; Pressley and Associates, 1990); however, see the various chapters in this volume for many more languages with which strategies instruction is now being used. The study reported here was the first to use empirical research and statistical techniques to investigate learning strategies in Japanese as a foreign language (see also Dadour and Robbins, chapter 12, this volume). Questions addressed included which strategies would be most appropriate for high school and college classes, how the strategies could be implemented within the curriculum, and what effects the strategies instruction has on students.

SUBJECTS AND INSTRUCTIONAL CONTEXT

Both studies were conducted in a mid-Atlantic metropolitan area with high school Japanese, Russian, and Spanish teachers and their students, and with college Japanese instructors and their students. Three public school districts and one private school participated in the studies. High school teachers participating in the studies included two Japanese teachers, four Russian teachers, and seven Spanish teachers. Four college Japanese instructors participated. Over the three years, high school students participating included a total of 93 students of Japanese, 239 students of Russian (of whom 26 participated for two consecutive years), and 390 students of Spanish. In addition, 50 intensive beginning level college students of Japanese took part.

During the pilot-testing year (1990–1991) and the first year of instructional intervention (1991–1992), differences existed in curriculum and instructional approaches between participating high school teachers. The curriculum was textbook-based in some of the classes, whereas the other high school classes followed a proficiency-based curriculum developed by the teachers. In the third year of the project, all participating classrooms were in the same school district and followed a similar theme-based curriculum which used a variety of both teacher-developed and commercially produced instructional materials. Differences in instructional approach were evident between high school and college Japanese classes. High school students were introduced to written Japanese from the beginning of the first year course, whereas college students began with oral skills and were introduced to writing later.

INSTRUCTIONAL DESIGN AND IMPLEMENTATION

Instructional materials designed to explicitly teach learning strategies were developed and implemented for the Japanese, Russian, and Spanish classrooms participating in the learning strategies studies. These lessons were integrated with the specific curriculum each teacher was using. Thus, for the proficiency-based curricula in the Japanese and Russian high school classrooms and in the Year 3 Spanish classrooms, the learning strategies lessons provided activities related to each unit theme. Learning strategies lessons for Year 2 Spanish high school and for the college Japanese classrooms were linked to the textbook unit being studied. The lessons provided an introduction to students about the value of learning strategies, definitions and explanations of how to use the strategies, and both individual and cooperative activities for practicing and evaluating the strategies. The guidelines for teachers included additional explanations, suggestions for modeling the strategies, and directions for conducting and evaluating the strategies activities. Strategies instruction was developed for learning vocabulary, listening comprehension, reading comprehension, speaking, and self-regulated learning. In the third year of the study a problem-solving process model for comprehension was developed and implemented in participating classrooms. This model provided a metacognitive framework for explaining and practicing the strategies (see chapter 12 by Dadour and Robbins, this volume).

INSTRUMENTS

Instruments were developed to collect data from both students and teachers. Parallel forms of the student instruments reflected the language being studied and the types of language activities encountered in the class. Questionnaires administered to students included: a *Background Questionnaire* to gain information about students' age, gender, native language, and previous language study; a *Learning Strategy Questionnaire (LSQ)* designed to elicit the frequency with which students used strategies for the types of language tasks they encountered in their class; a *Self-Efficacy Questionnaire (SEQ)* which asked students to rate their degree of self-confidence for accomplishing different learning tasks in the target language; and open-ended questionnaires administered to students at the mid-year point and end of year (for Spanish in Year 3) to explore the degree to which they found the strategies instruction useful. Information about students' language proficiency and achievement was collected through criterion-referenced *Language Tests (LT)*, and a *Teacher Ranking Scale* in which teachers used criteria developed jointly by teachers and researchers to rank their students' proficiency levels.

Classroom observations were recorded on an *Observation Summary Form*, and teachers' attitudes and recommendations about the learning strategies instruction were elicited through structured interviews following a *Teacher Interview Guide*. Spanish teachers in Year 3 also completed a *Teacher Questionnaire* about the effectiveness of the strategies instruction using the scripted strategies lessons developed by project staff.

PROCEDURES

The design of the learning strategies studies called for development activities during the first year, followed by implementation of strategies instruction in high school foreign language classrooms in the second and third years. Activities in the first year focused on securing teacher and school district collaboration, observing classrooms to gain an understanding of the instructional approaches being implemented, and interviewing students to discover the strategies they used for different language tasks. Information gathered from classroom observations and student interviews was used to develop a form of the *LSQ* for each language, and these were piloted with students who would not be participating in the studies. Responses were compared to responses on the student interviews, and *LSQ* items were revised as necessary to reflect student language used to describe particular strategies. Draft versions of the other instruments were also developed. A major activity was the selection of learning strategies to teach beginning level Japanese, Russian, and Spanish students and the development of preliminary learning strategies lessons in the form of *Resource Guides* for teachers to use in subsequent years of the study. The lessons were designed to be integrated with the regular class work that each participating teacher was planning for the following year, and were correlated with the textbook or other instructional materials used by each teacher.

In the second year of the studies, the strategies lessons in the *Resource Guides* were used by participating teachers to implement strategies instruction in a quasi-experimental design in some of the participating classrooms. Three Russian and two Spanish high school classrooms implemented language learning strategies instruction, while one classroom for each language served as a control in which no strategies instruction took place. Two college beginning intensive Japanese classes team-taught by the same instructors also took part in the quasi-experimental design, with one class receiving strategies instruction and the other class as the control class. All participating students were pre- and posttested with the *LSQ*, *SEQ*, and *LT*; the *Background Questionnaire* was administered at the time of the pretest. At the time of the posttest, teachers ranked their students as High, Medium, or Low in language abilities and achievement. In early 1992, students completed a *Mid-year Questionnaire* on which they recorded their independent use of strategies and gave reasons why they used or did not use the strategies that had been taught. Correlations were conducted between the instruments and comparisons were made between the classes receiving learning strategies instruction and the control classes.

In the third year of the study, strategies instruction was developed and implemented for intermediate level Russian and Spanish, and revised *Resource Guides* were implemented in both high school and college Japanese classrooms. The instruments were revised to reflect changes in the instructional focus and administered as pretests and posttests. A quasi-experimental design was used to compare a high school strategies instruction class with a non-strategies class in Russian, and a similar design was used to compare two college level Japanese classes. Six intermediate level Spanish classrooms were randomly assigned as either control classrooms or experimental classrooms receiving strategies instruction, and two other Spanish classes also received strategies instruction. A *Teacher Interview Guide* and *Observation Summary Form* were used to gather information on teachers' perceptions of the strategies instruction and on classroom observations. A problem-solving process model for strategies instruction, which organized the strategies within a metacognitive framework, was presented in both the Russian and the Spanish experimental classrooms. Strategies lessons developed reflected the new framework and incorporated suggestions made by participating teachers.

RESULTS

In this section we discuss the results of the language learning strategies studies in terms of strategies identified by teachers, implementation of strategies instruction, and student use of strategies.

Results concerning strategies identification

Researchers worked with participating teachers to identify the learning strategies that would be most beneficial to students, considering each teacher's curriculum. Through consultations with teachers and classroom trials, a number of appropriate strategies were identified for beginning level Russian and Spanish classes. Strategies selected by teachers in Year 1 and implemented in Year 2 included: four metacognitive strategies (Directed Attention, Self-Evaluation, Selective Attention, and Metacognitive Planning); seven cognitive strategies (Transfer, Visualization, Personalization, Contextualization, Grouping, Inferencing, and Prediction); and one social strategy (Cooperation). Most of the strategies were identified with their Russian or Spanish names, such as *Ojo* (Directed Attention).

As mentioned earlier, the study of Learning Strategies in Japanese Foreign Language Instruction was the first to investigate the applications of learning strategies instruction to beginning level Japanese high school and college classes. Both high school and college Japanese teachers in Year 1 identified the learning strategies they believed would help their students and in Year 2 incorporated strategy instruction into their beginning level classes. These strategies included: metacognitive (Directed Attention, Selective Attention); Cognitive (Contextualization, Creative Repetition, Grouping, Imagery, Personalization, Prediction, Silent Repetition); and social/affective (Questioning, Cooperation). The teachers, all native speakers of Japanese, perceived the strategies as useful in helping their students to become more successful in learning Japanese.

In the third year in both studies (i.e., the Russian and Spanish study and the Japanese study), the strategies were organized within a problem-solving process model which emphasized metacognitive knowledge and strategies for Planning, Monitoring, Problem-Solving, and Evaluating (as shown in Figure 14.1). See Dadour and Robbins (chapter 12, this volume) for additional information.

Selection of strategies for instruction was closely tied to task demands. For example, when the college curriculum placed an emphasis on listening comprehension, strategies selected by teachers included Predicting the content of the listening text and Selectively Attending to key words and ideas. Beginning level Japanese teachers at both high school and college levels found that memory strategies for developing their students' knowledge of vocabulary were quite important to teach. The early introduction of writing in the high school Japanese classes also evoked an interest in teaching students strategies that would assist in recognizing and producing Japanese characters. Students found that Imagery was the most helpful strategy for learning the Japanese characters.

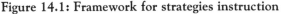

Figure 14.1: Framework for strategies instruction

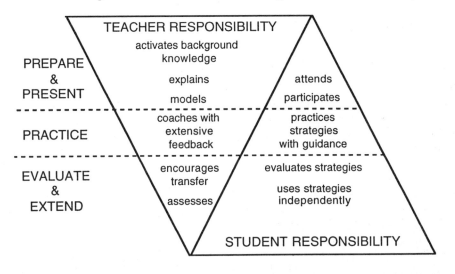

Results concerning the implementation system, problem-solving process model, and teacher workshops

A primary task underlying the success of this study was developing a system for the effective implementation of strategies instruction in the foreign language classroom. Since teachers were to be the ones implementing the instruction, an important achievement was the identification and development of a framework for teaching learning strategies (Figure 14.1). The framework described the technique of scaffolding strategies instruction so that in the early stages teachers had responsibility for explaining and modeling the strategies, but students gradually increased their responsibility until they could independently use the strategies.

In addition, a significant improvement in the delivery of strategies instruction was the development of a problem-solving process model, which not only organized the strategies by key processes (i.e., Planning, Monitoring, Problem-Solving, Evaluating), but also provided structure for developing metacognitive knowledge in both teachers and students. The model used an analogy of a mountain climber to illustrate the sequential stages of a task and types of strategies that could be selected for each stage. Teachers found the strategies model successful in communicating both a rationale and concrete examples for a strategic approach to language learning.

Professional development activities also included a workshop in which the framework and model were introduced to teachers, sample strategies lessons with guidelines to teachers for developing their own lessons, and meetings with teachers as a group or individually to provide feedback and discuss any emerging issues. The effectiveness of this approach was evident as teachers began writing their own strategies lessons that were naturally integrated into regular class activities. Teachers preferred developing lessons themselves, and students' reactions to the teachers' strategies lessons were positive. Observations also indicated that the teachers' lessons were explicit and spontaneous.

Results concerning use of strategies by students

Interviews with teachers and observation of classes revealed some patterns in the implementation and perceived effects of strategies instruction. The strategies that teachers and students identified as most effective sometimes varied across levels of language study. The tasks in the first year of language study were different than at the intermediate level. The selection of appropriate strategies depended greatly on the language learning task. For instance, teachers at the beginning level emphasized vocabulary development, which led to a greater use of memorization techniques. A main focus at the intermediate level was reading and listening, so appropriate strategies assisted in these comprehension processes. The close relationship between task and strategy was further supported through evidence provided by students' reactions, which became negative when a strategy was inappropriately chosen (i.e., using visualization for a reading passage that was not visually-oriented).

Teachers generally felt that the instruction had more of an impact on students with average learning abilities than students who were above or below average. However, they also indicated that all students could benefit from the instruction because it helped students to become more aware of their learning process and allowed teachers to show concern for how students were learning as well as what they were learning. The strategies instruction also provided students with a structured approach to language tasks, thus eliciting students' attention throughout activities.

The majority of students in both studies found the strategies instruction helpful. Many students said that the strategies helped them understand better and see new ways for learning. Some students who did not find the instruction helpful responded that they already used the strategies or had other strategies. In either case, it was clear at the conclusion of each year's strategies instruction, students were familiar with the instructed strategies and knew how to apply them. Students could also report preferences for strategies that they personally found effective, rejecting strategies that did not work for them. These expressions of strategy preferences may indicate that students had developed metacognitive awareness of their own language learning process.

In both studies, most students reported increased use of strategies after instruction and indicated familiarity with the strategies and their use. Gains in strategy use were significant for Japanese high school students in the third year of the study, and Japanese college students also reported significant gains in frequency of specific strategies. Strategy gains were also significant in intermediate level Spanish classes. Data collected from Japanese high school students through the *Self-Efficacy Questionnaire* indicated that students' levels of self-efficacy increased over an academic year. As students increased their knowledge of the target language, they became more confident in their language learning abilities. Furthermore, for Spanish and Russian students and for Japanese high school students in Year 2, the degree of confidence was correlated to students' language performance, suggesting that more effective learners are also more confident about their abilities. The information obtained in these studies indicates that further investigation into the causal relationships between and among learning strategies use, self-efficacy, and performance seems promising.

CONCLUSIONS

It was clear from these two studies that language learning strategies could be taught at high school and college levels and in various languages. It was also evident that long-term strategies instruction was beneficial, that it positively affected student strategy use and student confidence, that it enhanced students' ability to choose and evaluate their own strategies, and that it helped teachers to become effective strategies instructors. Teachers were strongly in favor of the strategies instruction program and liked the strategic structure and creativity it offered.

Richard Kidd
University of Manitoba, Canada
Brenda Marquardson
Tyndall Park Community School, Winnipeg, Manitoba, Canada

CHAPTER 15

THE FORESEE APPROACH FOR ESL STRATEGY INSTRUCTION IN AN ACADEMIC-PROFICIENCY CONTEXT

[The] soul foreseen...
–Thomas Hardy

SUMMARY

This chapter describes the Foresee Approach for ESL strategy instruction. Foresee builds upon the CALLA Model described earlier. However, Foresee differs from CALLA in theoretical ways and contrasts especially with CALLA in implementation procedures, including specific lesson techniques. This chapter clarifies the similarities and differences and shows how Foresee works in real situations.

INTRODUCTION

The Foresee Approach is a modified version, or more accurately an extension, of the Cognitive Academic Language Learning Approach (CALLA) developed by Anna Uhl Chamot and J. Michael O'Malley. Foresee has evolved gradually out of several years' experience in using CALLA as the basis for instructing elementary-level ESL pullout classes at Tyndall Park Community School in Winnipeg, Manitoba, Canada. During this period we have benefited enormously from reading the publications of Chamot and O'Malley (e.g., 1986, 1987, 1989b, 1994a), attending their workshops at the 1991 annual international meeting of Teachers of English to Speakers of Other Languages in New York, and talking with them personally when they visited Winnipeg to deliver the plenary address at the 1992 TESL Manitoba Conference. Their work has been our major inspiration, and we gratefully acknowledge our debt to their insights and achievements. Our Foresee model, like CALLA, attempts to be a "bridge to the mainstream" (Chamot and O'Malley, 1987) for post-beginner ESL students by developing their cognitive academic language proficiency through active participation in motivating and challenging content-area work. Since learning to communicate effectively in English, both in speech and writing, is an important objective of academic study, we include it in the rather lengthy title of our approach: Communication, Cognitive Academic Language Development, and

Kidd, R., & Marquardson, B. (1996). The Foresee Approach for ESL strategy instruction in an academic-proficiency context. In Rebecca L. Oxford (Ed.), *Language learning strategies around the world: Cross-cultural perspectives*. (Technical Report #13) (pp. 189–204). Honolulu: University of Hawai'i, Second Language Teaching & Curriculum Center.

Content Instruction in the Classroom. For short, we call this the "4C" or — with apologies to those who dislike puns — the "Foresee" Approach.

Foresee and CALLA share the same purpose and resemble each other in many important respects. One difference between the two is the structure of what we call the "theoretical model" underlying integrated instruction. More significant differences exist, however, on the level of practical application, as Foresee includes both a general "application process" and a repertoire of specific lesson techniques which are not a formalized part of CALLA.

Our goal in this chapter is to introduce our approach to ESL teachers and other educators who might be familiar with CALLA but wish to expand their practical expertise in planning integrated instruction. We describe both the theoretical and practical constituents of the Foresee Approach, concluding with efforts to publicize our approach, evidence of its effectiveness, and our hopes for the future.

THE FORESEE THEORETICAL MODEL

A major innovation of CALLA was to add a third instructional element, *learning strategies*, to the integration of *language* and *content*. Our Foresee theoretical model contains the same three components, but there are some differences between Foresee and CALLA regarding the interpretation, structure, and representation of "theory."

THEORETICAL DIFFERENCES BETWEEN FORESEE AND CALLA

Chamot and O'Malley (1994b), for instance, explain that the CALLA instructional model is based on a "theoretical framework" consisting of principles of cognitive psychology, especially the notions of declarative and procedural knowledge introduced by Anderson (1985). We prefer to de-emphasize these particular kinds of theoretical concerns, focusing theoretical attention instead on the three fundamental kinds of knowledge ESL students need: knowledge of the subject-matter content, language, and learning strategies. An original feature of Foresee is the diagrammatic representation of these three instructional components in triangular form in Figure 15.1. Our use of the term "theoretical" to describe this model is justified, we believe, by the fact that teachers require theoretical knowledge of other fields like linguistics, cognitive psychology, and their academic subject areas if they are to incorporate all three components into the design of effective lessons. Moreover, the specific contents of each of the main three circles and the two-way nature of the arrows, as shown in Figure 15.1, are based on theoretical principles.

Figure 15.1: The Foresee Theoretical Model

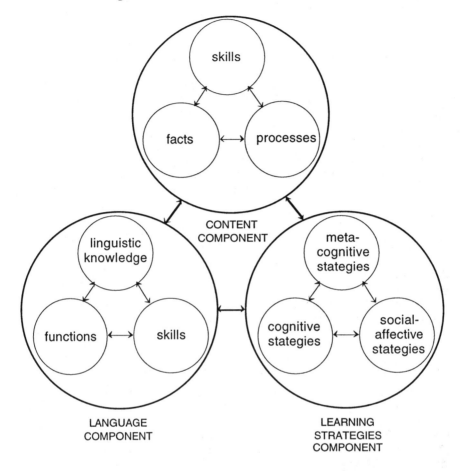

The three major instructional components of Foresee are represented by the large circles in Figure 15.1. Each contains a similarly configured triangle representing three subcomponents, as shown. We describe each of the major components and their constituents, beginning with the Content Component.

CONTENT COMPONENT

The *Content Component* refers to subject-area content. There is nothing particularly original in claiming that academic study normally involves the learning of subject-specific facts (e.g., dates and events in history), processes (e.g., the water cycle in geography), and skills (e.g., computing and solving equations in mathematics). Some skills like problem-solving, of course, are of a more generic nature and are important across the entire curriculum. Note also that many academic skills, perhaps the majority, depend heavily on language proficiency, but we prefer to include language in a separate (although connected) component.

LANGUAGE COMPONENT

The *Language Component* is organized somewhat differently from the one outlined in earlier CALLA work. Chamot and O'Malley (1987) identify four important aspects of "academic language." These are vocabulary, structures and discourse features (grouped together), academic language functions (e.g., hypothesizing, explaining, and describing), and language skills (listening, speaking, reading, and writing for academic purposes). We prefer to group vocabulary (lexical knowledge) together with structures and discourse features in a subcomponent called linguistic knowledge at the apex of the triangle shown in Figure 15.1. Academic language functions (the uses or purposes of language in academic work) and skills (the modalities through which the various functions are implemented) constitute the other two language subcomponents in Foresee.

This brief description hardly does justice to the complexity of the Language Component, which actually contains a tremendous amount of information about language forms, functions, and skills (see Kidd and Marquardson, 1993, 1994, for more details). The importance of this component cannot be overestimated. Teachers need to understand this component, that is, gain some knowledge of linguistics, in order to apply Foresee, since explicit language instruction is an important dimension in our approach. Foresee differs from CALLA in this respect, the purpose of the language component in CALLA being mainly to give students

> *sufficient practice in using* language in academic contexts so that language comprehension and production become *automatic* and students develop the ability to communicate about academic subjects. (Chamot and O'Malley, 1987, p. 234, emphasis added)

While Foresee, like CALLA, recognizes the value of academic work as an "experiential" route to language learning, we believe that explicit language instruction or "consciousness-raising" (Sharwood Smith, 1981) is often necessary to make students aware of special features and conventions of academic language: vocabulary, discourse markers and organization, grammatical structures, functions, and so on.

LEARNING STRATEGIES COMPONENT

The third part of our theoretical model is the *Learning Strategies Component*, which we adopt directly from CALLA. As shown in Figure 15.1, Foresee incorporates Chamot and O'Malley's (1987) scheme of grouping learning strategies into three categories: metacognitive, cognitive, and social-affective. We strongly agree with Chamot and O'Malley that teaching ESL students to use these strategies effectively is a crucial part of helping them develop into successful, autonomous learners. Needless to say, students become academically empowered only when they master the "how" of comprehending and assimilating academic language and content. For a complete list of the learning strategies taught via CALLA, see Chamot and O'Malley (1987, 1989b, 1994a).

AN INTEGRATED MODEL

An additional feature is that Foresee is a *highly integrated model* whose three principal components interact with each other in reciprocal and mutually supportive ways, as indicated by the two-way arrows joining the large circles in the diagram. The Content Component provides the subject matter through which academic language proficiency can be developed and the learning strategies can be learned and practiced. In fact, instructional planning usually begins with selecting suitable content, so Foresee, like CALLA, can be fairly described as "content-driven." For this reason, the Content Component appears at the apex of the triangle. Reversing the direction, the two components at the base of the triangle serve as the "base" for learning subject-area content, since students can master this material more readily if they possess good academic language proficiency and make effective use of learning strategies. As for the interaction between these two base components, appropriate learning strategies can assist students to acquire language (knowledge and skills), and conversely, language skills are often essential to the successful application of the learning strategies. As an example of this latter dependence, good listening skills are important to effective note-taking, one of the cognitive strategies identified by Chamot and O'Malley.

From the point of view of instructional planning, the Foresee theoretical model provides the teacher with a comprehensive guide to making decisions about *lesson objectives*. Every Foresee lesson, as we illustrate below, contains a comprehensive set of objectives drawn from each of the components (and subcomponents) shown in Figure 15.1. One practical advantage of our diagrammatic representation is that it makes these elements easier to remember by linking them together in a logical and visual way.

INTRODUCTION TO THE FORESEE APPLICATION PROCESS

The major innovations of Foresee lie in the area of classroom implementation. We have devised a Foresee "application process" which helps teachers to overcome the main hurdle to integrated instruction, namely the planning of motivating and effective lessons. The three elements of this process are theory, materials, and procedures. This process is certainly not "cut and dried," as it demands imagination and effort on the part of teachers using our approach. Nevertheless, it goes a long way toward providing teachers with a general but quite productive formula for lesson planning. The application of the Foresee Approach can be regarded as a dynamic interaction or synthesis of three separate elements, as shown in Figure 15.2.

Figure 15.2: The Foresee application process

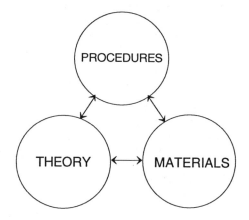

DYNAMIC INTERACTION OF THE COMPONENTS OF THE APPLICATION PROCESS

Before we explain the process in detail, a few words are in order regarding the dynamic interaction of the three components in the Foresee application process. Our symbolic representation of this interaction, the two-way arrows joining the circles in Figure 15.2, reflects a very real feature of the lesson planning process. Foresee lesson planning usually proceeds not in a linear but in a dialectic fashion, as a dynamic interplay among the three components. Teachers experienced in the application of Foresee typically move back and forth among these components, selecting or modifying materials, objectives, and procedures to suit the topic, the needs of the students, and our model itself. The following sample sequence, useful for teachers new to Foresee, is just one of many possible planning routes.

1. Select motivating and appropriate *materials* to establish the topical content of the lesson.

2. Determine the exact *content objectives* of the lesson (based on the theory component).

3. Decide upon suitable *lesson procedures* for teaching the content (perhaps, though not necessarily, by choosing one of the Foresee lesson techniques described below), and write the "basic" lesson plan (content objectives, materials required, and procedures).

4. Identify *language objectives* that suit the content (see the theory component), and adjust the lesson procedures to accommodate these.

5. Identify some *learning strategies* (from the theory component) that can be taught and/or practiced in the lesson, and adjust the procedures further to accommodate these.

The lesson planning process takes some practice to master, but we have found that most teachers have little trouble applying our approach once they understand the theoretical model and have experience with Foresee lesson techniques. Now we are ready to move on to the three parts of the Foresee application process, which makes lesson planning much easier and more straightforward for teachers.

THEORY

The *theory* component is simply the Foresee theoretical model outlined in the previous section. The purpose of this component, as we have seen, is to generate lesson objectives in a variety of categories (content, language, and learning strategies) and subcategories. Let us examine the other two components in Figure 15.2, *materials* and *procedures*.

MATERIALS

Good *materials* are an invaluable asset to the design of integrated instruction, as they give teachers something around which to build their lessons. While content-based materials are sometimes teacher-produced, they usually tend to be published resources of various types — books, stories, pictures, and so forth. — which teachers manipulate in various ways to accomplish the overall goal of teaching content, language, and learning strategies simultaneously. The best materials are those which are visually appealing to students (colorful, attractively designed, well illustrated, and so forth), motivating in content, and easily adaptable to the needs and interests of the students. Almost anything can serve as a potential resource, including textbooks, reference books, books of stories or poems, magazines, newspapers, and videos. Science, social studies, and language arts materials often provide particularly good resources on which to base appealing Foresee lessons and units.

PROCEDURES (LESSON ORGANIZATION AND LESSON TECHNIQUES)

The third indispensable element of application is *procedures*, represented by the circle at the apex of the triangle in Figure 15.2. The procedures component contains guidelines to two related but distinct levels of lesson design: lesson organization and lesson techniques. On the first level, *lesson organization*, Foresee lessons generally follow the five-stage instructional format recommended by Chamot and O'Malley (1986, 1989b) for CALLA. The five stages or phases of a CALLA lesson are: preparation, presentation, practice, evaluation, and follow-up (or expansion). We have found that this scheme provides an excellent format for including, in any Foresee lesson, target objectives of all three types: content, language, and learning strategies.

But this five-stage format, useful as it is, represents only a general scheme for lesson design; it does not assist teachers in deciding exactly what to do to teach individual topics in the classroom. Foresee partially overcomes this problem by adding a second level to the procedures component, namely *lesson techniques*. Foresee lesson techniques provide teachers with specific guidelines for using materials and devising activities in ways that will lead to motivating classroom instruction as well as to the accomplishment of all three types of objectives. At this time, our repertoire of these techniques is rather limited, as we have formalized only five of them. All, however, share three important qualities: they are systematic, easy to understand, and flexible enough to allow adaptation to multiple content-area topics. Because the techniques comprise the most original (and probably the most valuable) feature of Foresee, we describe each of them.

The five lesson techniques we describe here, one in detail (the Text Questioning Technique) and four others very briefly, all meet three important criteria mentioned earlier (systematic, easy, and flexible). They serve as "prefabricated guidelines" for designing effective classroom procedures, thus helping make Foresee lesson planning a relatively simple task for teachers. When these techniques are used, steps 4 and 5 in the planning process (shown earlier) are automatically accomplished. This is because both language and learning strategies are built into these techniques, as seen next.

Text Questioning Technique (TQT)

The TQT is particularly useful for introducing a new topic or unit. We outline the basic steps of this technique and then illustrate the technique in an actual Foresee lesson. Notice that the TQT follows the five-stage lesson format and that the learning strategies are in italics. We follow the convention of listing metacognitive strategies on the left, cognitive strategies in the middle, and social-affective strategies on the right (see Chamot and O'Malley, 1987, 1989, 1994a for the meanings of these strategies).

TQT — General Outline

PREPARATION (Brainstorming) — Speaking

Step 1   Students are given a reading passage accompanied by some of the following: title, subheadings, pictures, diagrams, captions, and so forth. (It is assumed here that the selection is in a book.) Tell students to OPEN books and predict what the passage is about, without reading it. (1 minute)

| *Advance organization* | *Prediction/inferencing* | |
| | *Imagery* | |

Step 2   Tell students to CLOSE books and write down predictions. Spelling and sentence structure are not important at this time.

Step 3   Listen to predictions (brainstorm); write the key words (vocabulary) on the board or overhead.

Step 4   Tell students to OPEN books, and conduct a discussion of the title, pictures, diagrams, and so forth. If necessary, ask pointed questions to elicit important vocabulary items not yet discussed. Try to get students to predict

---

contents as completely as possible. Students do not read the passage at this point!

Selective attention	Prediction/inferencing
Selective attention	*Prediction/inferencing*
Organizational planning	*Imagery*
	Resourcing

PRESENTATION — Listening

Step 5   Tell students to CLOSE books.
Students silently read a numbered list of questions about the passage, which the teacher now shows them on the chalkboard (previously concealed) or the overhead projector. (Note: These questions about the text are carefully prepared so they are normally answerable in one or two words. They are numbered to correspond to the order of information in the passage.)
After silent reading, read the questions aloud to the students one by one, reviewing any vocabulary they do not understand. Underline key words that students will listen for in step 7.

Selective attention

Step 6   Instruct students to number their paper (left-hand side) 1-n ("n" being the number of questions on the list) in preparation for note-taking.

Organizational planning
Self-monitoring

Step 7   Read the passage aloud fairly slowly. The students listen carefully for the answers to the questions on the board, writing these answers down in short form (one or two words, abbreviations, or numbers) beside the appropriate numbers on their papers.

Note-taking
Auditory representation

Step 8   Read the passage aloud a second (and, if necessary, third) time, to ensure that the students have answered most of the questions and to give them a chance to check their answers. Increase the speed of delivery each time.

Self-monitoring

PRACTICE — Speaking and reading

Step 9   Tell students to OPEN books. In pairs or small groups, they compare answers and check them against the open text to verify and produce correctanswers and correct spelling. Students should expand all ab

---

breviations. (10 minutes) Circulate and help students when they request assistance.

| Self-evaluation | Elaboration | Cooperation |
| | | Questioning for clarification |

EVALUATION — Speaking

Step 10 Tell students to CLOSE books, and ask individual students to contribute their answers to questions on the list. Write their correct replies (one or two words) beside the questions, using a different color chalk (or felt pen, if using the overhead). The students correct their answers at this point.

| Self-evaluation | | |

FOLLOW-UP — Writing

Step 11 Books remain CLOSED. Demonstrate how to write proper declarative sentences (answers to the questions) by using (a) most of the words in the questions and (b) answers on the board. (Phrases can be underlined and arrows drawn to show how this is done.) Then, working individually, students write answers in complete sentences.

| | Deduction/induction | |

Step 12 Working with partners, students edit their work.

| Self-evaluation | Deduction/induction | Cooperation |

Step 13 When students think their answers are correct, they present their final drafts to the teacher and read their answers aloud.

| Self-evaluation | | Cooperation |

The TQT is an invaluable tool for designing Foresee lessons, especially (though not exclusively) introductory ones. It can be used to teach virtually any topic for which a suitable reading passage can be found. As suggested in step 1 above, texts should ideally be accompanied by headings and subheadings and, most crucially, by supporting visuals of some sort (pictures, diagrams, captions). Besides being flexible, the TQT is systematic and easy to understand. As mentioned earlier, one great advantage of this technique (like all Foresee techniques) is that it relieves the teacher of the burden of worrying about how and where to include activities for teaching language and learning strategies, as they are automatically built into the procedure.

To illustrate the application of the TQT and the general structure of a typical Foresee lesson, we present an abbreviated version of Lesson 1 of our unit on the solar system (Kidd and Marquardson, 1993, 1994). This unit was originally used for the instruction of an advanced group of ESL students in grades 4–6, but it could easily be adapted for older children. Following the format of all Foresee lessons, Lesson 1 contains three sections, Objectives, Materials, and Procedures, reflecting the application process in Figure 15. 2. Notice that the categories of objectives correspond exactly to the components of the theoretical model in Figure 15.1.

Applying the TQT — Sample Lesson

OBJECTIVES

Content objective:
    To learn about the structure of the solar system (sun, planets, and so forth.)

Language objectives:

Linguistic knowledge

Vocabulary:	planet, Mercury, Venus, Earth, Mars, Jupiter, Saturn, Uranus, Neptune, Pluto, solar system, sun, star, orbit, revolve, round, circle, sphere, measure, year, rocket
Structures:	proper nouns, including capitalization; subject-verb agreement; present tense for scientific truths; declarative sentence forms (derived from questions); adverbial clauses of reason (because...), comparative and superlative forms of adjectives; prepositions (between, around, from, in)
Discourse features:	use of pronoun "it" for textual cohesion; presenting information in the order given-then-new

Functions
    Reporting factual information with declarative sentences
    Defining

Skills

Listening:	taking notes, in group discussions
Speaking:	comparing and correcting answers during group discussions
Reading:	for specific information when verifying answers
Writing:	answering questions with correct declarative sentences

Learning strategies objectives:

Metacognitive
    Advance organization, selective attention, organizational planning, self-monitoring, self-evaluation

Cognitive
    Inferencing (prediction), note-taking, deduction/induction, imagery, resourcing, auditory representation, elaboration

Social-affective
    Cooperation, questioning for clarification

MATERIALS

The teacher can use any appropriate reference book containing good visuals and an article describing the solar system. Our lesson uses a reading passage entitled "The Solar System" from the Open Sesame ESL Series, Level D: Prairie Dawn's Purple Book (Zion, 1985, pp. 74–75). This text is accompanied by an attractive diagram of the solar system (sun encircled by the nine planets, with curved lines representing their orbits) and a cartoon picture of two Open Sesame characters flying through space in a rocket ship.

PROCEDURES

Since this lesson employs the TQT, it is unnecessary to document the details of every step; refer to the general TQT outline above. The following will clarify and illustrate the application of certain key steps.

Step 1 The reading passage is described in the Materials section above.

Step 5 The numbered list of questions on this passage follows. Answers, which the students write down during the note-taking phase in step 7, are in italics.

1. How many planets are there in the solar system? *nine*
2. What are the names of the planets? *Mercury, Venus, Earth, Mars, Jupiter, Saturn, Uranus, Neptune, Pluto*
3. What is the word that means to move around the sun? *revolve*
4. Is the sun a star or a planet? *star*
5. What is the name of the path a planet takes? *orbit*
6. What do the planets get from the sun? *heat and light*
7. a. Which planet is the hottest? *Mercury*
   b. Why? *closest to the sun*
8. a. Which planet is the coldest? *Pluto*
   b. Why? *farthest from the sun*
9. Which planet is the biggest? *Jupiter*
10. Which planet is the smallest? *Mercury*
11. Which planet do we live on? *Earth*
12. Where is the planet we live on? *between Venus and Mars*
13. How many days does it take for Earth to complete one trip around the sun? *365*
14. How do we measure a year? *one orbit*

Step 11 To illustrate the process of writing correct declarative sentences (answers to questions), the teacher should underline key words in the first few questions and demonstrate visually, using arrows, how the answers can be constructed. For example:

How many <u>planets</u> <u>are</u> <u>there</u> in <u>the solar system</u>? <u>nine</u>

<u>There</u> <u>are</u> <u>nine</u> <u>planets</u> in <u>the solar system</u>.

The students can underline the key words in subsequent questions, to help them write the correct declarative-sentence answers. Note that the teacher can use items 7 and 8 to demonstrate sentence combining (specifically, writing complex sentences containing "because" clauses).

We have devoted considerable attention to the TQT because it clearly illustrates the most novel feature of the Foresee Approach, namely lesson techniques which help guide lesson design. The other four techniques share the same qualities as the TQT, but we describe them only in brief here (see full descriptions in Kidd and Marquardson, 1993, 1994).

The Research Technique

This technique gives students the opportunity to engage in individual research on aspects of the main topic. It works best when the subtopics are all of the same type; for example, in our solar system unit each student investigates a planet of his or her choice. When all subtopics are similar, the teacher prepares a common research guide or outline telling students what to look for (e.g., diameter of planets, distance from the sun, and so on) as they consult library books and other resources containing information on their individual themes. Like all Foresee lesson techniques, the Research Technique builds in language objectives and learning strategies.

The Presentations Technique

The main activity of this technique, class presentations, follows directly from the investigations done through using the Research Technique. Students have each gathered considerable information about some aspect of the main topic. In the solar system unit, for example, each has become an expert about one chosen planet. Each student now gives an oral presentation on his or her research findings to other students, who are required to take notes. To facilitate note-taking, the teacher equips every student with an outline, chart, or other guide which subcategorizes the research topic in the same fashion and order as the research format. The entire activity usually takes a number of class periods, since every student in the class has to present research findings. When the activity is completed, the entire class possesses all of the significant information about every aspect of the main topic.

The Dictated Instructions Technique (DIT)

This technique is based on Chamot and O'Malley (1986) and involves an excellent procedure for instructing or informing students about the steps of some activity they are to accomplish, for example, a science experiment. Rather than distribute a handout or have students simply copy a numbered list of instructions from the chalkboard or overhead, the teacher dictates the necessary steps to the students. They copy these individually, and then — since the notes they have taken are usually incomplete — work in small groups to pool information and try to compile a compete set of instructions. The teacher gives assistance when needed, and after the students have completed their lists they perform the activity. The dictation phase provides practice in paying selective attention to discourse markers and promotes good listening and note-taking skills.

The T-List Procedure

This idea is also based on Chamot and O'Malley (1986). Like the DIT, it improves listening comprehension and provides practice in using the strategies of selective attention and note-taking. The teacher explains to the students that they are about to hear a short lecture on a particular topic. This lecture, they are told, will contain a number of discourse markers that give clues to the sequence of ideas and that tell whether pieces of information are main ideas or supporting details. When a passage is dictated (or the tape is played), the students take notes on a T-list — a page with a vertical line down the middle, usually with certain information already on it. On the left side, the students note the main ideas of the passage. On the right, they write supporting information, details, examples, and so on beside the corresponding main ideas. The first few times the technique is used, the T-lists should already contain a good bit of information, so students only fill in short bits of missing data. As they develop more note-taking skill, students can eventually fill in their T-lists without such assistance.

FORESEE UNIT DEVELOPMENT

To this point, our discussion of Foresee application has focused exclusively on lesson design. However, each lesson forms an integral part of an extended unit centered on an overall topic or theme; thus we are using a theme-based approach (Gamberg et al., 1988; Brinton, Snow, and Wesche, 1989; Enright and McCloskey, 1988). In planning a Foresee unit, the teacher usually begins by choosing a theme or topic. Foresee units tend to be highly integrated, with many different subject areas (social studies, science, mathematics, language arts) contributing. This is especially true at the elementary level, although ESL-only classrooms allow this integration at the secondary and college level also.

We have found the following to be a very effective unit design pattern:

Lesson A: Introduction to topic. Use the TQT.
Lesson(s) B: Consolidation lesson(s). These lessons (one or more) include procedures and activities developing students' understanding of the main theme.
Lesson C: Research lesson. Use the Research Technique.
Lesson D: Presentation lessons. Use the Presentations Technique. This includes several class sessions.
Lesson E: Extension lesson(s). Science experiments, creative writing, and so forth.

Many other unit development patterns are possible. We offer this one as a good way for teachers new to Foresee to begin.

CONCLUSIONS

EVALUATING AND PUBLICIZING FORESEE

The Foresee Approach has developed gradually over several years and represents continuous experimentation in adapting CALLA-based instruction to the needs of elementary and some junior high and high school ESL students in Winnipeg. All aspects of the model have been tested in real classrooms and found effective in promoting content knowledge, language ability, and learning strategy use. The approach also increases student motivation. In other words, it works.

So convinced are we of the effectiveness of Foresee that we have begun to publicize it in our area through the TESL Manitoba Journal, Foresee workshops at local conferences, teacher education courses, and most importantly the publication of the 350-page document known as *A Sourcebook for Integrating ESL and Content Instruction Using the Foresee Approach* (Kidd and Marquardson, 1993, 1994). This manual has three introductory chapters explaining Foresee theory and application, followed by three Foresee units, complete with detailed lesson plans. Manitoba Education and Training, our provincial department of education, has made this curriculum support document available to every school in the province.

A second major success in publicizing Foresee is a teacher-training project initiated by the Winnipeg School Division and funded by Manitoba Education and Training. This project, which began in the 1992–1993 school year, involved the second author teaching the Foresee Approach to eight teachers in three elementary schools. Three of the participants were ESL teachers and five were regular classroom teachers. The project was so successful that it was renewed for 1993–1994, with a goal of teaching Foresee to 15 more teachers in seven or eight schools, including several secondary schools.

To date we have conducted no formal evaluation of Foresee's success, but we have accumulated a great deal of anecdotal evidence that the model can be applied successfully by teachers to accelerate the growth of academic proficiency among both ESL and native English-speaking students at any level. Among this evidence are comments by energized and empowered teachers who now use Foresee as the basis of their classroom instruction. Most students also responded positively to the approach, showing special enthusiasm for such standard Foresee activities as conducting library research and giving presentations. Significant improvements have been seen in writing, reading, and ability to remember content. One ESL student said,

> It's fun to write. I learned to write sentences.... I learned names of fish, experiments, animals' names, ocean, forest,... lakes, maps,... *predator – prey*,... and research – I like it. I love it. Fun to draw. Fun to read. I like to read books.

HOPES

We have high hopes of continuing to refine and publicize our approach in the years to come. We constantly monitor the ongoing application of Foresee to a variety of diverse content topics, and we are always looking for ideas to expand our current repertoire of lesson techniques. The teacher-training project will likely be renewed again, and we are particularly optimistic that Foresee will prove effective in promoting the academic proficiency of native English-speaking students who have special needs. We intend to continue delivering workshops and teacher education courses on the approach.

We are convinced that Foresee and CALLA are thoroughly compatible approaches. Chamot and O'Malley's model is far better known than ours, and their recent CALLA Handbook (1994a) contains a wealth of useful ideas for implementing integrated instruction in the ESL classroom. Since Foresee is an extension and elaboration of CALLA, sharing the same objectives and basic structure, we see no reason why our approach should not be viewed as a complementary model, enriching CALLA and offering the classroom teacher additional means to a common goal.

ACKNOWLEDGMENTS

Thanks to Manitoba Education and Training for disseminating and supporting our work and to Rebecca Oxford for editorial suggestions on this chapter. For information about ordering the *Sourcebook* mentioned in this chapter, or our more recent *Secondary Sourcebook for Integrating ESL and Content Instruction Using the Foresee Approach* (1994), write to Manitoba Textbook Bureau, P.O. Box 910, Souris, Manitoba, ROK 2C0, Canada, or call 204–945–8940.

Nae-Dong Yang
National Taiwan University

CHAPTER 16
EFFECTIVE AWARENESS-RAISING IN LANGUAGE LEARNING STRATEGY INSTRUCTION

A mighty maze! But not without a plan.
–Alexander Pope

SUMMARY

Teaching learners how to learn is crucial. The areas of discovering optimal learning strategies for language acquisition and instructing learners in strategy use have thus attracted great interest. This chapter reports a study investigating how EFL students improve their use of learning strategies through awareness-raising in group interviews and informal learner instruction. College students enrolled in freshman English classes in Taiwan were selected to participate. They answered a questionnaire at the beginning and end of the semester. During the semester they were interviewed in small groups about their strategies. Significant differences were found between students' strategy use between pre- and posttests. The interactive discussion in group interviews was especially helpful in raising strategy-related awareness and improving the use of learning strategies (both frequency and variety).

INTRODUCTION

In the past two decades, many language teachers and researchers have shifted their focus from teaching methods to what students were doing in their language learning. They found that students were not just passive subjects. Some students seemed to be successful regardless of teaching method and appeared to use a variety of learning strategies to help themselves (Brown, 1994; Hosenfeld, 1979; Tarone and Yule, 1989). These strategies are often related to beliefs and attitudes (Horwitz, 1988).

This chapter reviews related research, then reports a new Taiwanese study in which learners improved their use of language learning strategies through awareness-raising and informal learner instruction. Implications for learner instruction conclude the chapter.

Yang, N-D. (1996). Effective awareness-raising in language learning strategy instruction. In Rebecca L. Oxford (Ed.), *Language learning strategies around the world: Cross-cultural perspectives*. (Technical Report #13) (pp. 205–210). Honolulu: University of Hawai'i, Second Language Teaching & Curriculum Center.

RESEARCH REVIEW

Because most of the strategy research has already been reviewed earlier in this volume, it is important to emphasize only a few points that are new to the literature. First, Yang (1992a, 1992b) investigated the learning strategies of EFL students using a modified and translated version of the *Strategy Inventory for Language Learning* (Oxford, 1990c). She surveyed over 500 students at various levels and in various Taiwan universities. These students were found to use formal oral-practice strategies and compensation strategies more frequently and cognitive-memory strategies less frequently (Yang, 1992a, 1992b, 1993a, 1993b). The use of formal oral-practice strategies was connected with their overwhelming endorsement of the belief in the value of learning spoken English. Furthermore these students' strong self-efficacy toward their learning was closely related to the use of functional practice strategies, such as watching English-language movies and listening to English-speaking radio (Yang, 1992a, 1992b, 1993b).

Klassen (1994) adopted the same Chinese version of the SILL to survey 228 freshman English students at Feng Chia University about their strategy use. He found his students' strategy use scores lower than those of Yang's students, but they followed the same trends. Sy (1994) used a longer version of the SILL (80 items) to investigate 411 college students in Taiwan, but she focused on gender differences in the use of language learning strategies. Like Yang, Sy found students used compensation strategies most frequently and memory strategies least often. Both studies, Yang's and Sy's, showed female students generally using language learning strategies more frequently than male students.

Though strategy assessment has occurred somewhat frequently in Taiwan, strategy instruction has been generally uncommon there. This study helps fill that gap through strategy awareness-raising.

METHODS

The current research, undertaken as a continuation of Yang's (1992a, 1992b) study, intended to examine college students' use of learning strategies by using multiple methods.

SUBJECTS

The 68 subjects came from two freshman English classes at two major Taiwan universities. Among them, 38 students were English majors (19 males, 19 females), and 30 were sociology majors (7 males, 23 females). Ages ranged from 19 to 30, with an average of 20. Less than 9% of the subjects had ever traveled to English-speaking countries. By the time of the interviews, only 64 students participated, including 37 English majors (18 males, 19 females) and 27 sociology majors (4 males, 23 females).

The English Learning Questionnaire used in this study was composed by Yang (1992b). It contains a section of 49 items adapted from the *SILL* to measure strategy use. Another section of the questionnaire investigates students' beliefs and attitudes about language learning, with possible responses as (1) strongly disagree, (2) disagree, (3) neither agree nor disagree, (4) agree, and (5) strongly agree. A final item was added by the author to elicit additional beliefs: "What else do you think about English learning which is not included above?" The last section obtains students' background information, such as gender, age, major, perceived motivation and proficiency, and travel abroad.

A Group Interview Question Guide was prepared by the author to assess students' use of strategies in six specific language learning tasks for: (1) vocabulary learning, (2) listening comprehension, (3) reading comprehension, (4) writing compositions, (5) oral presentation, and (6) communicating in English.

PROCEDURES

Students took the English Learning Questionnaire at the beginning and the end of the semester. During the semester, the students were arranged in several small groups for one-hour group interviews, which were conducted in Mandarin Chinese by the author and another English teacher (the students' actual instructors). The first question, as a warm-up, asked students how they felt about their college English class so far, especially as compared with their high school English classes. The rest of the questions asked students to describe any special techniques or strategies they used in six language learning tasks noted earlier. All interviews were tape-recorded and then transcribed and summarized, followed by content analysis by the author.

Data analysis involved two major statistical procedures using $SPSS^X$ (SPSS Inc., 1989): (1) descriptive statistics such as frequencies, means, and standard deviations; and (2) paired t-tests to compare students' responses to the questionnaire at two times, pretest and posttest.

RESULTS

According to the questionnaire, commonly used strategies were compensation strategies for overcoming deficiencies in English (in the bottom of the high use range), affective strategies for managing emotions (average range), and metacognitive strategies for planning and evaluating one's learning (average range). Memory strategies were used least, but they were still in the average range of use.

Students' use of learning strategies increased in both frequency and variety by the end of the freshman English class. Among the 49 strategy items, 37 showed growth from pre- to posttest. Average scores for males and females were respectively 3.12 and 3.13 at the pretest, followed by 3.19 and 3.28 at the posttest. In general, students' scores showed average use of the strategies overall but with significant improvement over the semester from 3.13 to 3.26, a small but significant difference (t=3.25, df=65, p<.002). Increases also occurred in several of the *SILL* subscales: cognitive strategies, increasing from 3.02 to 3.23 (t=3.67, df=65, p<.0005); and memory strategies, increasing from 2.92 to 3.09 (t=3.08, df=65, p<.003).

The interviews found that different language tasks (e.g., vocabulary learning, listening comprehension, or writing) elicited different uses of strategies, although some strategies, such as advance organizers, selective attention, repetition, note-taking, and seeking assistance, were applied to a number of these tasks. In general, the strategies uncovered by the interviews can be classified into Oxford's (1990b, 1990c) categories of learning strategies and also matched their counterpart strategies on the questionnaire. However, the interviews provided more details about the individual learning strategies and in-depth information about the condition of strategy use. For example, when asked what they did to help them answer the questions on a reading comprehension test, about half of the students answered that they usually read the questions before reading the passage. When the interviewer explored the reasons, most of these students indicated that they employed this strategy because they were taught to do so and because it helped them find the answers more efficiently. Some students also explained they had developed the strategy of "jumping" between reading the passage and the questions to help them find the answer. When discussing the learning of new vocabulary, one student explained how she used sound/image associations to help her memorize a certain word. Through the use of the interviews, it was possible to explore why certain strategies were used in different situations.

DISCUSSION

Generally speaking, the questionnaire results indicated that the subjects employed a variety of learning strategies to learn English, with some groups of strategies receiving more frequent use than others. Some of the strategies most used by this group included compensation, affective, and metacognitive strategies.

The results of the paired t-tests supported the increase of strategy use during the semester for cognitive and memory strategies. Cognitive strategies which increased from pretest to posttest shared one characteristic: they all involved and required learners' actively seeking out opportunities to practice English. One possible reason for increases in strategy use might be that students' increased awareness produced greater use. The group interview was used as a vehicle for raising awareness about language learning strategies. The question-and-answer process in the interview provided learners with an important opportunity to focus not only on the language but also on the learning process itself. For instance, one student in the interview realized that though she considered herself following the "old way" of learning (learning from a Chinese translation of the English), she had started to combine that way with a new strategy (learning from the English definition). She said,

I've tried to adjust myself to the new learning environment [college], yet my methods are different from what the teacher suggested. In fact, I'm still using my old way to learn. For example, you [teacher] want us to use English-English dictionary and try to define English vocabulary in English. But I found I didn't learn much new vocabulary in the new way, while I had deeper impressions of the words if I memorized them in Chinese definition. So, I learn both English and Chinese definitions now.

In answer to the response, teachers were able to offer opportunities in the group interview to convince their students of the value of learning strategies. Once when asked about what they did in writing an essay, some students were confused. But as the interviewer asked whether they did an outline or any revisions, the students started to think about how they "finished" an essay. One answer built on the previous one. Finally students realized that people do not all write in the same way.

Interviews gave learners a chance to share their myriad learning strategies and to consider the strategies of their classmates. Some of the shared strategies, especially cognitive ones, were adopted by motivated students. Since many factors influence the effectiveness of learning strategy use, it is important to help language learners to build a repertoire of strategies. During the interviews, some instructional materials were selected to inform students about particular strategies. For example, an article about nonnative conversation partners by Tim Murphey was chosen because it introduced important affective and social strategies and challenged the native speaker myth. The interviews also encouraged learners to try out different learning strategies in their freshman English classes. Above all, the discussions during the interviews raised students' awareness about language learning strategies, and this awareness has had an effect on their subsequent use of strategies.

Though this study offered only informal strategy instruction through group interviews, it tried to adopt most of the following principles for strategy instruction recommended by Oxford (1993c):

1. Students' affective factors were accounted for in the strategy instruction (through the questionnaire and the interview).

2. Groups of strategies were chosen to fit the requirements of the language tasks and the learners' goals.

3. Strategy instruction was integrated into regular class activities over a long period of time rather than taught as a separate, short intervention unconnected with classwork. It was also taught by the students' own instructors rather than by outside researchers.

4. Strategy instruction provided plenty of practice with varied language tasks and authentic materials.

5. Students were helped to evaluate their strategy use through the questionnaire and the interviews, thus increasing learner awareness of strategies.

One limitation of the study was that it did not have a control group. Therefore, there is no way to know precisely whether factors other than the intervention described above might have affected learners' strategy use. However, since no other external factors appeared viable, we can conclude that the treatment was probably the cause of strategy use improvements. Use of a quasi-experimental design with a control group would be an alternative for future research.

RECOMMENDATIONS FOR INSTRUCTION

Here are some useful recommendations for instruction based on this study and on the literature on language learning strategies:

1. Discover students' beliefs and strategies.
2. Explain and model strategies explicitly.
3. Provide authentic context for strategy use.
4. Make strategy instruction interactive.
5. Deal with students' motivation.
6. Implement strategies-and-beliefs components in the curriculum.

CONCLUSIONS

Though this was a pilot strategy instruction study, this investigation tried to adopt most of the recommendations for strategy instruction noted in the literature. This study can provide teachers with a better understanding of students' "expectation of, commitment to, success in, and satisfaction with their language classes" (Horwitz, 1988, p. 283). Also, the author hopes that the information about students' strategy use can help language teachers in assisting their students to make learning quicker, easier, more effective, and more fun.

ACKNOWLEDGMENT
This study was funded by the National Science Council project, Taiwan (Project No. 82–0301–H–002–071–T).

Jeffra Flaitz
University of South Florida, USA
Carine Feyten
University of South Florida, USA

CHAPTER 17

A TWO-PHASE STUDY INVOLVING CONSCIOUSNESS RAISING AND STRATEGY USE FOR FOREIGN LANGUAGE LEARNERS

A little goes a long way!
–Common saying

SUMMARY

The use of language learning strategies has been observed to produce a positive effect on student achievement. This chapter describes a two-phase study that involved consciousness raising and strategy use for foreign language learners. In the first phase, an experimental group of 130 students of university-level Spanish I and II received metacognitive awareness raising (MAR) — a single 50-minute session which, by means of brainstorming and jigsaw activities, dynamically involved students in developing a general awareness of language learning strategies rather than exposing them to the selection, presentation, and practice of a set of specific strategies over a period of weeks or months. Final course grades were compared across control and experimental groups, revealing significantly higher scores for experimental group subjects. The second phase expanded the population under study to include middle school, high school, and university-level French and Spanish students. It also included a cognitive awareness raising (CAR) condition to contrast with the MAR condition. The second phase, which was more complex in design, produced more complicated and ambiguous results, explainable partly by the unit of analysis that was used.

INTRODUCTION

Joan Rubin's 1975 study of the attributes of successful language learner ushered in two decades of some of the most exciting second language acquisition research ever to affect curricula and pedagogy. The contributions of Andrew Cohen (1987a, 1990a, 1990b), Michael O'Malley and Anna Chamot (1987, 1990, 1993), Madeline Ehrman and Rebecca Oxford (1987, 1989, 1990), and Martha Nyikos (1986, 1990a, 1991) are among the best known efforts in the field of learning strategies research,

Flaitz, J., & Feyten, C. (1996). A two-phase study involving consciousness raising and strategy use for foreign language learners. In Rebecca L. Oxford (Ed.), *Language learning strategies around the world: Cross-cultural perspectives.* (Technical Report #13) (pp. 211–225). Honolulu: University of Hawai'i, Second Language Teaching & Curriculum Center.

but scores of dissertations and major and minor articles appear regularly in the profession's literature on the same intriguing topic.

One of the most interesting strands in all of this research concerns the degree of conscious awareness of language learners as they use strategies. The theme of consciousness flows through several chapters in this volume, such as Nyikos' chapter 8, Yang's chapter 16, and Oxford's and Leaver's chapter 18. The current chapter focuses on consciousness raising and language learning strategy use in a two-phase study conducted by the authors at the University of South Florida and in local area schools. The first phase involved university students of Spanish (see Flaitz, Feyten, Fox, and Mukherjee, 1995), and the second phase had a broader population base: middle school, high school, and university students of Spanish and French. Results were somewhat different in the two investigations, and we hope to explain how and why. Before that, however, we touch on the key issues in research on strategies and strategy instruction.

ISSUES IN THE LITERATURE

Much research on language learning strategies has established their role in making language learning more efficient and effective (Chamot, 1993; Cohen, 1990b; O'Malley and Chamot, 1990; Oxford, 1990b, 1992/1993; Oxford and Crookall, 1989; Rubin, 1975, 1987; Wenden and Rubin, 1987). Oxford (1990b, p. 1) defines learning strategies as "steps taken by students to enhance their own learning." According to Oxford (1990b, p. 1), students in the process of language learning can make particular use of strategies as "tools for active, self-directed involvement." The natural outcome of such discussions has been a proliferation of studies examining the effect of strategy instruction on student performance (Brown, Bransford, Ferrara, and Campione, 1983; Chamot and Küpper, 1989; Hosenfeld, Arnold, Kirchofer, Laciura, and Wilson, 1981; O'Malley, Chamot, Stewner-Manzanares, Russo, and Küpper, 1985b; Oxford, 1990b; Oxford, Crookall, Cohen, Lavine, Nyikos, and Sutter, 1990; Pressley and Associates, 1990; Pressley and Harris, 1990; Russo and Stewner-Manzanares, 1985a, 1985b; Weinstein, Goetz, and Alexander, 1988; Weinstein and Mayer, 1986).

Many teachers are uncomfortable because they themselves have never been taught the use of language learning strategies. Nevertheless, learning strategies are central to language learning, and there is a possibility that awareness raising does lead to increased performance. Researchers must investigate the effect of heightening learners' general awareness of language learning strategies in manageable, time- and cost-effective ways.

While there are indications that strategy instruction in the language learning classroom can lead to greater achievement, the research community has not as yet proven that there is a consistently positive effect *every* time. For example, in a study by O'Malley et al. (1985b), learners benefited from strategy instruction in the areas of speaking and, to some extent, in listening, but only the Hispanic students in the sample gained in the area of vocabulary enhancement. Often research design flaws are cited as critical factors in producing contradictory or inconsistent results (see Oxford, 1992/1993 for details), and little attention has been paid to the development of the affective and social domains of strategy instruction. Despite such issues, there remains a strong sense among teachers and researchers alike that strategy instruction has the potential to play a critical role in language teaching and learning.

To develop that potential, however, researchers must arrive at an effective means by which to deliver strategy instruction. Should it be short- or long-term? Most strategy instruction projects have focused on short-term delivery since long-term projects are often plagued by practical impediments. Yet brief studies can produce tenuous or marginal results, leading researchers to suggest that the duration of the instruction is at fault, and recommending sessions that continue up to and even more than a year.

How much awareness should learners have as a result of strategy instruction? In other words, should instruction be explicit or informed (producing more cognitive awareness on the part of the learner)? Or should strategy instruction be implicit or blind (producing less awareness)? Wenden (1986a) pointed out the superiority of "informed" rather than "blind" strategy instruction. In informed instruction, the need, usefulness, and anticipated benefits of a given strategy are emphasized. In blind instruction, on the other hand, strategies are embedded into tasks and materials without informing students how to use, apply, or transfer them. While blind instruction can promote success on individual tasks with which the strategy is associated, research (Brown et al., 1983) reveals that most learners are not able to generalize beyond the set task, and they eventually abandon the strategy. It appears, then, that learners benefit from developing an appreciation of the need for and effects of strategy instruction.

Should strategy instruction be comprehensive with a full range of strategies presented, or should it be limited to raising general awareness using a limited but illustrative set of strategies? One problem with detailed, comprehensive strategy instruction in which learners are exposed to the full range of strategies, is that it takes so long — months or years. Moreover, not all learners will benefit from each and every strategy, and some learners become overwhelmed and frustrated by too many options (Chamot, 1993). Finally, individual learners tend to prefer certain strategies over others, thus making the effort of accommodating an entire classroom of students unwieldy for the teacher. Given the lack of opportunity to provide comprehensive strategy instruction in our less than ideal classrooms, it might be useful to raise students' general awareness of language learning strategies, thus improving their attitudes, motivation, and beliefs about language learning, all of which fall within the socioaffective domain of learning strategies so often neglected by researchers (Oxford, 1990b, 1992/1993).

Rees-Miller (1993) raises a number of questions about research on strategy instruction. She suggests that greater empirical evidence is needed to show that conscious awareness of strategy use correlates with greater language proficiency and that students actually profit from strategy use. She also questions the ages and levels at which strategy instruction is most successful: whether it is equally useful for children and adults and equally appropriate for beginning students as for advanced students. LoCastro (1994) and Nyikos and Oxford (1993) note that the values and beliefs upheld in a given learning environment might influence the degree of success of strategy instruction. The two studies described here address many of these issues.

PHASE 1: UNIVERSITY STUDENTS

The purpose of this phase was to investigate the effect of heightening learners' general awareness of language learning strategies on student achievement in beginning and intermediate university-level Spanish courses (Flaitz, Feyten, Fox, and Mukherjee, 1995). The process of raising general awareness is distinguished from that of highly detailed strategy instruction, which involves a greater commitment of time and focused attention on specific strategies.

DESIGN AND RESEARCH QUESTIONS

In Phase 1, the authors centered their efforts on examining the effect of metacognitive awareness raising (MAR) of language learning strategies on student achievement in first and second semester university-level Spanish courses (Spanish I and II). MAR is defined as the process of heightening learners' general awareness of language learning strategies. This is accomplished through the administration of a one-time, 50-minute session which includes interaction with the material, active involvement of students, use of higher-order thinking skills, and accommodation of students' social and affective needs. The following research questions were addressed in Phase 1:

1. What effect does metacognitive awareness raising have upon achievement in Spanish I and II university-level courses as measured by final grades of students enrolled in those courses?

2. How does metacognitive awareness raising differ in its effect on the achievement of students enrolled in Spanish I versus Spanish II university-level courses?

3. Which of the strategies discussed during the MAR sessions were reported to have been used by students participating in the study?

METHODS

Sample

The sample for Phase 1 was chosen from a population of students enrolled in Spanish classes at the University of South Florida. Twelve sections of Spanish were randomly selected out of a total of 24 sections, with roughly equal sections of Spanish I and Spanish II being represented in the sample of 229 students. These twelve sections were subsequently randomly divided into 6 experimental and 6 control groups, containing totals of 130 and 99, respectively. The experimental and control groups were very similar. Based on the data culled from the demographic questionnaire regarding previous language study and results of a departmentally mandated placement test, there is strong indication of the initial equality of groups. Due to the high demand for admission into beginning language classes, the program cannot accommodate all students and therefore gives priority to seniors and juniors, hence the predominance of upperclassmen in the study. There were 109 females and 120 males in the sample. Almost all were native speakers of English.

In the sample, 62.7% (N=83) of the students (N=229) had previously studied Spanish. This reflects the distribution of subjects into Spanish I and Spanish II courses. An examination of the achievement of students in each of these levels was expected to provide insight into the possibility of differential performance between the two. In other words, would the metacognitive awareness raising sessions prove inconsequential to students with previous successful (in the sense that they had advanced to Spanish II) language learning experience?

Materials

A wide variety of materials was used during the different stages of the Phase 1 study. All subjects received a demographic questionnaire, and their final course grades were tabulated at the end of the semester. Only the control groups received a placebo questionnaire relating to myths about language learning. (Examples of myths: *A person cannot understand a foreign language without knowing its grammar. People who learn foreign languages easily are more intelligent than those who have difficulty learning them. English is one of the most difficult languages to learn. Childhood exposure is the best way to learn a foreign language. The most important factor in foreign language learning is aptitude.*) This questionnaire was a Likert-scaled instrument attempting to ascertain students' beliefs about and attitudes toward language learning. Items were based on myths and misconceptions which have been identified in the literature of the field. It was administered under the assumption that students in different Spanish classes share information about unusual class activities with each other. As the experimental groups were scheduled to receive some special attention in the form of metacognitive awareness raising in the following weeks, an effort was made through the placebo to give the control groups an impression of equal, if not identical, attention.

Materials for the experimental groups included a handout called "How To Survive Spanish I or II" outlining 26 language learning strategies (Table 17.1), a midterm checklist of strategy use, an activity involving the categorization of those strategies, and a feedback questionnaire for teachers.

Table 17.1: How to survive Spanish I or II
(strategies handout for MAR session)

Avoid heavy reliance on a dictionary.

Be assertive. Make and take opportunities to use the language in natural communication both inside and outside of class.

Compensate for your lack of linguistic ability by occasionally using your mother tongue, asking for help (repeat, clarify, slow down, give examples), using mime and gesture, describing the concept for which you lack a word, using hesitation fillers when you need time to think.

Don't be afraid to make mistakes.

Evaluate your own progress.

Forget about your age or aptitude when learning a foreign language.

Guess when in doubt.

Hypothesize. Before you read a grammar rule, try to formulate it yourself by analyzing the examples.

If you don't understand, say so.

Just be persistent.

Keep a language diary.

Limit your expectations to those that are reasonable and attainable. Be patient.

Memorize creatively using images, rhymes, sounds, and so forth.

Negotiate with your teacher when you want errors corrected.

Open your mind and develop a better attitude toward the native speakers and their culture.

Praise yourself in writing.

Quit making excuses. If you are not making improvements in the foreign language, before you blame your teacher or textbook, ask yourself if you are using the strategies of a good language learner.

Relax before you go to class and before doing homework assignments.

Study with a partner.

Try not to translate in your head. Instead, try to speak spontaneously.

Use this checklist, and refer to it periodically.

Vocabulary: Record new vocabulary and grammar rules in a notebook, but do it systematically.

Wear your successes and reward them.

eXamine your own language learning strategies, problems, successes, and preferences, and talk about them with other students. Also, learn from the successes of your classmates.

Yesterday's and before-yesterday's material should be reviewed systematically.

Zzzzz...Wake up! Don't "sleep" in class. Perform every class activity.

Adapted from *How to Be a Better Language Learner* by Joan Rubin and Irene Thompson (1982).

Procedures for strategy instruction and data collection

The research team which conducted the Phase 1 MAR sessions consisted of four faculty from the areas of Education and Applied Linguistics, whereas all the language instructors involved in the research study were graduate teaching assistants teaching in the university's Spanish program. The MAR session began with a brief statement concerning its purpose, namely that the ensuing activity would provide students with useful tips which could make the learning of Spanish more enjoyable and effective. The research team also emphasized the benefits of strategy use, pointing out that all students do use some kind of strategies to promote better learning, and that the most successful students use them consciously, purposefully, appropriately, and frequently (Oxford et al., 1990). To underscore the claim that all students use language learning strategies of some kind, students were then charged with the task of brainstorming in small groups about their own language study habits. As groups exhausted their ideas, they posted their newsprint lists on the walls of the classroom for all to read and comment upon.

Following the brainstorming activity, the handout entitled "How To Survive Spanish I or II" (see above) was distributed to each member of the class. This handout contained an easily digestible interpretation of findings and recommendations from the research community on strategy use among successful language learners and was arranged in A (Avoid heavy reliance on a dictionary) to Z (Zzzzz... Don't "sleep" in class) fashion and accompanied by visual stimuli to catch the students' attention and provide usable mnemonic tools for future reference. A jigsaw activity was then conducted to facilitate the dissemination of this information. The purpose of this activity was (1) to expose students to effective language learning strategies, thus raising their awareness of the variety of techniques that may be employed in language learning; (2) to give students ownership of the task and its product; and (3) to encourage students to refer to the strategies they had generated in their small brainstorming sessions as they discussed the strategies on the handout.

Upon completion of the MAR session for each treatment group, a compilation of all the strategies elicited from the students during the brainstorming work was made. These strategies, in combination with those from the "How To Survive Spanish I or II" handout, were converted into a simple checklist addressing students' perceived use and helpfulness of the strategies. This checklist was distributed to the students in the experimental groups at midterm. The objective of this activity was primarily to refresh and reinforce students' awareness of the strategies, but it also served to determine whether the students were using the strategies and were finding them useful.

The researchers also designed another group activity to be implemented by the teacher of each class. The activity involved organizing the by-now-familiar recommended strategies into assigned categories. While this activity was not designed to present any new information, it served to reinforce beliefs and practices concerning the kinds of effective language learning strategies discussed during the initial instruction.

Each of the teachers in the experimental group was also given a questionnaire. Teachers were asked about their general impressions of the MAR instruction sessions, whether they discerned any effect on their students, whether they personally had been affected by the sessions, what they perceived to be the constraints preventing them from incorporating MAR instruction in their lessons, and whether they would be interested in receiving MAR instruction themselves.

After all forms of the treatment had been administered and efforts made to solicit feedback from the project's participants, the only information remaining to be collected was the final course grades for both experimental and control groups. Course instructors meet on a weekly basis to plan and discuss instruction throughout the semester. Thus, identical departmentally generated exams, a uniform grading policy, and common planning ensured — as much as possible — consistency across groups. These final course grades were used to determine the effect of the MAR session on the achievement of students in the experimental group. These data, then, in addition to those culled from the strategies checklist, were subjected to statistical analyses, and the data elicited through feedback sheets added a qualitative dimension to the study.

Data analysis procedures

Levene's test was performed to ensure homogeneity of variance for treatment and control groups; this was confirmed. To determine whether the treatment administered via metacognitive awareness raising activities produced positive results in the form of higher final course grades, a t-test was used to compare the mean scores of the experimental group on one hand and those of the control group on the other. A nested analysis of variance (ANOVA) was implemented to determine whether there was any significant difference in the influence of MAR instruction between the students in Spanish I and those in Spanish II. A chi-square analysis for goodness of fit was used to determine whether certain strategies were preferred over others and perceived by the students to have been used. The phi coefficient was used to assess the degree of relationship among strategy frequencies.

KEY RESULTS

Since experimental and control groups consisted of two different levels of Spanish (Spanish I and Spanish II), the nested ANOVA looked at differences between these levels. The nested design revealed that there was no differential effect of level of Spanish, and therefore no need to keep the two groups separate. Spanish I and II students for both experimental and control groups were pooled and an N of 229 was obtained. This finding provides an answer to Research Question 2, namely that there was no significant difference in the effect of the MAR treatment between the students enrolled in Spanish I and Spanish II.

After pooling Spanish I and Spanish II groups, a t-test was performed to determine whether a difference existed between the two groups' mean Spanish achievement scores after the treatment group participated in the MAR instruction. The results of the t-test procedure revealed a significant difference: t(df=225)=4.3, p<.0005. Spanish achievement, then, as measured by final grades, was significantly higher for students who participated in the MAR sessions. This indicated, in response to Research Question 1, that metacognitive awareness raising has a positive effect upon the achievement of students in university-level Spanish I and II courses.

Finally, in response to Research Question 3, a chi-square analysis for goodness of fit examined whether students preferred certain strategies over others and whether students reported to have used them at all. Results revealed significant differences: chi-square (df=51) p<.0005. The phi coefficient revealed moderate associations: phi (df=51)=.371 in frequency of use of strategies of various kinds. The strategies identified as having been most used by the students were: guessing when in doubt (75.5%), repeating aloud (68.9%), reviewing notes (59.4%), naming objects in Spanish (58.5%), coming to class (58.5%), not being afraid of making mistakes (56.6%), speaking to others in Spanish (55.7%), eavesdropping on people talking in Spanish (54.7%), writing down unknown words (53.8%), and recording vocabulary and grammar in a notebook (51.9%).

An examination of the Teachers' Survey described in the procedures section indicated that teachers perceived the sessions very favorably. They claimed the sessions had a discernibly positive effect on the students and on themselves, specifically on the level of "bonding." Whereas several teachers observed that their students appeared to be taking better notes, more risks, and available opportunities to practice and form study groups following the MAR session, they also claimed that their classes felt more comfortable following the MAR session. In other words, they believed that the students enjoyed interacting on a task that they deemed not only relaxing but practical, and that, in turn, promoted a greater openness to language learning. Teachers unanimously expressed their desire to take MAR instruction themselves, so they could incorporate learning strategies more effectively into their classes.

DISCUSSION AND IMPLICATIONS

There are a number of possible interpretations of these findings, the most compelling of which is that brief metacognitive awareness instruction positively affects students' success in language learning. Moreover, it is clear that not only students in the first semester of university Spanish but also students in the second semester as well profited from the sessions. Indeed, second semester students gained from MAR instruction regardless of previous language learning experience. These findings are most probably related to the fact that metacognitive awareness raising involved dynamic interaction with the material, active involvement of students, use of higher order thinking skills, and accommodation of students' social and affective needs, all over an abbreviated period of time.

Teacher attitude and enthusiasm might constitute a variable which merits further investigation. However, its significance would not necessarily weaken the findings of the present study. Although the Teachers' Survey indicated that numerous experimental group teachers perceived the MAR sessions favorably (and indeed all wanted MAR instruction for teachers), it is not likely that all six teachers of classes in the experimental group were equally enthusiastic or followed through in their individual classrooms in the same way or to the same degree.

Another issue is whether the strong effect of the MAR instruction was actually a product of students' raised awareness of language learning strategies, or whether the social bonding that occurred as a result of having addressed their socioaffective needs was powerful enough to make the difference between the outcomes of the control and experimental groups. This cannot be completely decided on the basis of the data.

In any case, the Phase 1 findings suggest that the potential benefits of heightening learners' general awareness of language learning strategies through manageable, short-term activities would provide teachers with an attractive alternative to in-depth strategy instruction. Indeed, if teachers knew that a 50-minute investment of class time could significantly affect student achievement, chances are they might change their overall attitude toward the curricular viability of strategy instruction. Moreover, the regular classroom teacher can easily conduct the MAR sessions. Indeed, it is actually recommended that classroom teachers themselves provide the instruction. Teachers rather than outside consultants would be better able to offer the instruction in a timely, less disruptive manner and could incorporate and reinforce some of the concepts throughout their course, as Phase 2 (below) indicates. In the absence of an opportunity for the presentation and practice of well-defined language learning strategies, the achievement of students may still be enhanced by the development of a more general strategic awareness. These findings, then, suggest that the notion of awareness raising is important and deserves further attention. A little bit may indeed go a long way.

PHASE 2: UNIVERSITY, HIGH SCHOOL, AND MIDDLE SCHOOL STUDENTS

As mentioned earlier, Phase 2 expanded the sample to include university, high school, and middle school students. Though Spanish was the sole language involved in Phase 2 at the middle school and high school levels, French was added to Spanish at the university level in Phase 2.

DESIGN AND RESEARCH QUESTIONS

Phase 2 was designed to determine whether the significant results found in Phase 1 were attributable to the content of MAR instruction, to the process used to deliver the instruction, or to the level of the students involved. Two treatment or experimental groups and one control group were used for each level of education (university, high school, and middle school). Experimental group 1 received a 50-minute MAR session on language learning strategies. Experimental group 2 received a 50-minute cognitive awareness raising (CAR) session on the benefits of studying a foreign language. The control group received a placebo consisting of a survey on myths and beliefs about foreign language learning. Specific research questions were:

1. Within university Spanish classes, is metacognitive awareness raising (MAR) instruction superior to cognitive awareness raising (CAR) instruction and to control group treatment (a placebo on language learning myths)?

2. Within university French classes, is MAR instruction superior to CAR instruction and to control group treatment?

3. Within high school Spanish classes, is MAR instruction superior to CAR instruction and to control group treatment?

4. Within middle school Spanish classes, is MAR instruction superior to CAR instruction and to control group treatment?

METHODS

Sample

The final Phase 2 sample consisted of 33 foreign language course sections of approximately 25 students per section: 27 Spanish and 6 French sections. At the university level, 12 Spanish sections (6 of Spanish I and 6 of Spanish II) as well as 6 French I sections were randomly selected from all possible language classes, and the sections were assigned to either experimental group 1 or 2 or to the control group. At the high school level, participants included 9 sections of Spanish I from a single high school. At the middle school level, 6 sections of Spanish I from a single school were included.

Procedures for strategy instruction and data collection

All subjects completed a 10-item demographic questionnaire. The control group received the same 50-item Likert-scaled questionnaire used in Phase 1 dealing with myths about language learning. Experimental group 1 received the MAR-instruction handout "How to Survive Your Foreign Language Class" (the same as the handout "How to Survive Spanish I or II" in Table 17.1). Experimental group 2 received the handout "Why Study a Foreign Language" for CAR instruction (handout available from the authors). The two experimental-group handouts were formatted similarly with the letters of the alphabet serving as the framework for each handout. At midterm, students in experimental group 1 completed a learning strategies checklist to mark the strategies they had been using and which they found useful since the initial MAR instruction. At the end of the term, final grades were gathered for all three groups: experimental groups 1 and 2 and the control group.

At the university level, Phase 2 MAR instruction on language learning strategies (see the Phase 1 description of brainstorming followed by a jigsaw activity) was provided by a team of hired, trained facilitators, one of whom had conducted the Phase

---

1 MAR sessions as well. CAR instruction, which existed only in Phase 2, was presented by regular classroom teachers (graduate teaching assistants or adjuncts) who had earlier been trained by the researchers. CAR sessions were formatted similarly to MAR sessions with brainstorming followed by a jigsaw activity, but the focus was not on learning strategies as in MAR but rather on benefits of foreign language education.

At the middle school and high school levels, both MAR and CAR sessions were conducted by participants' regular classroom teachers, who had been selected from a larger group attending an inservice workshop on MAR and who were also given further instruction on how to conduct training sessions in their classrooms.

Data analysis

The unit of analysis in Phase 2 was the class section rather than individual students. Each type of school was handled separately using one-way ANOVA, with the ANOVA's independent variable being type of treatment (MAR, CAR, or control-placebo). Because the sample size for statistical analyses was very small due to the unit of analysis, a significance level of .10 was chosen for main effects and interactions. In addition, post hoc effect sizes were calculated using Stevens' F (Stevens, 1990). Cohen (1988) identified effect size criteria whereby .10 represents a small effect size, .25 a medium effect size, and .40 a large effect size. A large effect size indicates that, regardless of whether or not statistical significance occurs, there is good reason to believe that the difference in treatment effects is *not* meaningless. Effect sizes therefore suggest that meaningfulness of treatment can be found even in situations in which statistical significance is absent. (See Dreyer and Oxford, chapter 5, this volume, for another instance of effect size usage.)

KEY RESULTS

In answer to Research Question 1, the ANOVA on the pooled university Spanish data (Spanish I and II) did not reveal statistically significant differences between the control group and the experimental groups. However, the calculated effect sizes contradicted the statistical significance finding somewhat. The MAR (strategies) group appears to have achieved more in Spanish than the CAR (benefits of language learning) group, as indicated by the effect size of +.13 (small but worth investigating). In contrast, the differences between the CAR group and the control group were large (−1.07 and −1.20), but in favor of the control group, which received no special instruction but was exposed to the questionnaire on myths of language learning.

In response to Research Question 2 for French I university students, the ANOVA showed no statistically significant differences by treatment. However, effect sizes revealed some surprising differences according to treatment. A large difference between the MAR group and the control group (−1.90) occurred, favoring the control group. A similarly large effect size appeared between the CAR group and the control group (−1.60), again favoring the control group. These results mean that the control treatment, a placebo questionnaire on myths of language learning, was more effective in terms of French achievement than either MAR or CAR instruction. The effect size difference between the MAR group and the CAR group was +.30, or medium, favoring the MAR group. This means that strategy instruction had more of an impact on French achievement than did instruction on the benefits of foreign language learning.

At the high school level for Spanish I (in answer to Research Question 3), the ANOVA failed to show statistically significant differences by treatment, but the effect size calculations presented a different picture. Effect size differences were medium (+.26) between the MAR group and the control group, meaning that instruction on language learning strategies had a more positive effect on Spanish achievement than did the control group's placebo questionnaire on myths of language learning. Effect sizes were large between the MAR group and the CAR group (–1.00), favoring the CAR group. Thus, strategies instruction was not as effective as instruction on the benefits of foreign language learning in terms of Spanish achievement. The difference in effect size between the CAR group and the control group was also large (+1.26), this time in favor of the CAR group. This means that instruction on the benefits of foreign language learning affected high school Spanish achievement more than did the placebo questionnaire on myths of language learning.

With regard to Research Question 4 in the middle school Spanish classes, the ANOVA, followed by a post hoc Holm procedure (Holm, 1979), revealed a statistically significant difference between the MAR sections and the control sections, with MAR sections showing higher Spanish achievement. Furthermore, the CAR or benefits sections also significantly outperformed the control sections. No statistically significant differences were found between the MAR and the CAR sections. Effect sizes were very large: +5.80 between MAR and control (favoring MAR), +1.80 between MAR and CAR (favoring MAR), and +4.00 between CAR and control (favoring CAR). In the middle school, all effect sizes favored the strategies (MAR) or benefits (CAR) condition.

DISCUSSION AND IMPLICATIONS

The results of the middle school level in Phase 2 were completely consistent with the expected effect of MAR instruction and with the results of Phase 1. ANOVA results showed that the strategies (MAR) groups in the middle school outperformed the control group in Spanish achievement. This supports the claim that raising students' general awareness of language learning strategies significantly affects their performance in language class. Moreover, the benefits (CAR) group also significantly surpassed the control group in Spanish achievement. Effect size results dramatically underscored these middle school findings, with the largest effect size found in the contrast between the MAR group and the control group and the next largest effect size found between the CAR group and the control group.

The middle school represented the "cleanest" research environment in Phase 2. The middle school sample consisted of an equal number of sections assigned to the strategies (MAR), benefits (CAR), and control groups. The middle school students were also studying a foreign language for the first time and were perhaps more open to language learning and to exploring and using language learning strategies than were older students in Phase 2. An anecdotal account from a middle school teacher whose Spanish sections received MAR instruction described subjects as being clearly enthusiastic about the instruction and active in reminding classmates of various strategies to try for months after the instruction. The message delivered in the MAR sessions about empowerment through strategy use obviously impressed the middle school students.

However, the picture was more ambiguous at the university level. Using pooled Spanish I and II achievement data (which showed no significant difference) and using French I data, the university results showed that Spanish and French classes behaved very similarly. Though no significant differences in language achievement were found for either language, the data revealed large effect sizes favoring the control condition. These results do not support the expectation that MAR or CAR instruction would help students have better language achievement than a placebo, so these findings conflict with Phase 1 results which revealed a strongly positive effect of MAR treatment on students' language achievement.

What might have caused the great contrast between Phase 1 and Phase 2 at the university level? While the content and most procedures of the MAR sessions were the same in both phases, a critical difference is that the researchers themselves delivered the MAR treatment in Phase 1 but hired facilitators for the university MAR condition in Phase 2. The Phase 2 MAR treatment facilitators appeared to be less comfortable with each other, less secure with the subject matter (MAR instruction), and somewhat skeptical about the possible effectiveness of MAR instruction. In some cases, since the same facilitators delivered MAR instruction for both Spanish and French, this factor might have caused the unexpected similarity of results for both Spanish and French and might serve to explain why the control group achieved more than the MAR groups. The lesson here is that effective instruction depends heavily on effective communication and on understanding of the instructional principles, without which the delivery might well be tainted.

The high school results were at first puzzling but then seemed explainable on the basis of institutional factors, such as the foreign language requirement. While there was no significant difference in Spanish achievement across the three treatments (MAR, CAR, and control), a large effect size occurred between MAR and CAR groups favoring the CAR group. In other words, high school students appeared to profit more from learning *why* they should study foreign languages than *how* they should proceed with strategy use. The high school students faced a foreign language requirement and were frequently described as unmotivated, so the motivational CAR treatment might have been more important to them than the strategic MAR treatment. The benefits (CAR) session might have provided necessary pragmatic/instrumental incentives as well as social incentives for the students to try harder in their language study, resulting in higher achievement. (Anecdotal reports from the CAR instructors at the university level also indicated that participants demonstrated strong interest in the reasons for language learning.)

The socioaffective appeal of the instruction also deserves comment. It was suspected that sometimes the socioaffective bonding in Phase 1 among students and between students and teachers might be as important as the content of the MAR instruction in improving attitudes and ultimately inspiring better language achievement. Researchers introduced the motivation-related benefits (CAR) sessions in Phase 2 to find out if the motivational help or socioaffective bonding offered by CAR would be as valuable as MAR sessions' combination of empowerment-through-strategies content and socioaffective boost. At the middle school level, the MAR sessions were clearly more effective because of their strategy content, but this did not occur at the high school or university levels for reasons discussed above.

Phase 2 results imply that the socioaffective aspects of the instructional sessions is highly important in the MAR and CAR treatments. The CAR treatment, which involved discussing the benefits of learning a foreign language, had stronger effects than expected. This leads us to underline the importance of the motivational and affective needs of language learners. Students are pragmatists. They benefit from knowing why they are asked to engage in language learning.

Nevertheless, we cannot ignore that the soundest component of Phase 2, the middle school aspect, reinforced the findings from Phase 1 as to the significant effect of MAR instruction on language achievement. Moreover, Phase 2 effect-size data at the middle school level indicate that strategy instruction might be more powerful than benefits instruction depending on the attitudes of learners and on institutional factors.

Another implication of Phase 2 is that a design involving the student as the unit of analysis is necessary, because using the class section as the unit of analysis in an ANOVA might mask important and meaningful effects. If the student is not used as the unit of analysis, it is imperative that the study employ post hoc effect size calculations.

Phase 2 also implies that instruction must be more carefully supervised and delivered across the board. Hired facilitators cannot always be expected to deliver the message in the most effective way, since they might lack a deep understanding of or commitment to that message.

The findings and implications of Phase 2, especially when compared with those of Phase 1, help us understand the complex but potentially valuable links between learner instruction (MAR or CAR) and language performance. Simply presenting metacognitive or cognitive awareness raising instruction is not enough. Researchers must recognize a host of institutional and individual factors that can stand in the way of — or enhance — instructional effects.

Rebecca L. Oxford
University of Alabama, USA
Betty Lou Leaver
American Global Studies Institute, California, USA

CHAPTER 18

A SYNTHESIS OF STRATEGY INSTRUCTION
FOR LANGUAGE LEARNERS

Example is better than precept.
—Latin proverb

SUMMARY

Following a conceptual discussion of strategy instruction, the chapter presents a range of factors in strategy instruction as it occurs in many locations throughout the world. Important factors include: consciousness, level of education, direction, integration into regular instruction, location, and resource use.

INTRODUCTION

The goal of strategy instruction is to help students become more self-directed, autonomous, and effective learners through the improved use of language learning strategies. Strategy instruction teaches students how to be better learners in several specific ways, including: (1) identifying and improving strategies that are currently used by the individual; (2) identifying strategies that the individual might not be using but that might be helpful for the task at hand, and then teaching those strategies; (3) helping students learn to transfer strategies across language tasks and even across subject fields; (4) aiding students in evaluating the success of their use of particular strategies with specific tasks; and (5) assisting subjects in gaining learning style flexibility by teaching them strategies that are instinctively used by students with *other* learning styles.

Moreover, any variables that relate directly to the choice, use, or evaluation of language learning strategies — such as general organizational ability, personality types, beliefs, motivations, attitudes, and age — can be discussion points in strategy instruction (Oxford, 1990b, 1992/1993, 1993b; Yang, 1992a, 1992b). Some of these variables (organizational ability, beliefs, motivations, attitudes) can be altered through instruction, while others (personality types) are less instructionally malleable, and still others are given (age). Nevertheless, all these factors are important for learners to understand, particularly as they relate to students' choice of language learning strategies.

Oxford, R. L., & Leaver, B. L. (1996). A synthesis of strategy instruction for language learners. In Rebecca L. Oxford (Ed.), *Language learning strategies around the world: Cross-cultural perspectives*. (Technical Report #13) (pp. 227–246). Honolulu: University of Hawai'i, Second Language Teaching & Curriculum Center.

This chapter is organized as follows. First, we focus on the conceptual background of strategy instruction. Second, we explain how contrasts in consciousness, ranging from no consciousness to full control, relate to strategy instruction. Third, we discuss additional factors occurring in strategy instruction. Finally, we provide a critique of strategy instruction. Cultures mentioned in regard to strategy instruction in this chapter include Belarus, Canada, Denmark, France, Hungary, Israel, the Netherlands, the Philippines, Russia, Taiwan, the Ukraine, and the US.

CONCEPTUAL BACKGROUND

Strategy instruction involves active learning and growth on the part of each individual student. It does not involve helping all students to use the very same strategies. In fact, that would defeat the purpose, which is to help learners become more active, more autonomous, more self-directed, and more discerning of what strategies are best for them as individuals. Strategy instruction involves helping students know more about themselves, so they can try out, test, and become expert in using the strategies that help them the most. Nyikos (1991) observes that "less successful students often are already using several strategies well-suited to their own learning style, but may apply them haphazardly" (p. 32). Students need to experiment before finding the most appropriate learning strategies that meet their own individual needs, so there is no single set of effective learning strategies that fits every language learner. One size just doesn't fit all.

Therefore, we must reject Rees-Miller's (1993, p. 680) statement that a fundamental tenet of strategy instruction is "that learning strategies of successful learners can be codified and taught to poor language learners with a resulting increase in their learning efficiency." Less successful learners will not automatically become more successful simply by copying the full range of strategies that more successful learners are using. Weak learners do not automatically become strong learners just by imitating someone else. Strategy instruction is a highly creative, multilevel process for teaching students to optimize their learning strategies for themselves as individuals.

For a long time most teachers and administrators have been unaware of the possibility of directly teaching language learning strategies. Those who have thought about the concept have sometimes dismissed language learning strategies as "unteachable." Most efforts from the 1950s through the 1980s were spent on defining what were then frequently considered in-born attributes of the good language learner, rather than teaching all students to be good learners, hence the proliferation of studies of good language learners at that time (Rubin, 1975; Rubin and Thompson, 1982, 1994; Stern, 1975; Naiman et al., 1978). The concept was that some students were endowed with the wonderful combination of language learning aptitude and "good" strategies; others had neither benefit.

However, administrators discovered that some students had high scores on language aptitude tests but failed to develop language proficiency. One reason for this discrepancy is that language aptitude tests did not take into account the effectiveness or ineffectiveness of an individual's learning strategies. Subsequent research has shown that effective language learners tend to use more strategies and to apply them in a more appropriate fashion than less successful learners (Nyikos, 1991). Given the possibility of teaching students to be better language learners, researchers made a case for strategy instruction (Crookall, 1983; Nyikos, 1991; Oxford, 1990b, 1993b; Rodgers, 1978; Wenden and Rubin, 1987; Wenden, 1991). They cited benefits of strategy instruction such as increased motivation, improved language performance, greater autonomy and self-reliance, and ability to continue learning after the language class is over.

Here are nine examples of students for whom strategy instruction is useful. Note that these illustrations include some language learners who would be considered "good" or "excellent" in their own settings for various reasons. Nevertheless, all nine of these learners can gain from strategy instruction.

Example 1: Lorene is a learner of three languages (German, Russian, and French). She enjoys contrasting these languages with each other and likes analysis. A strong user of metacognitive strategies, she is a good planner and organizer of her language learning, and she keeps track of her progress. Lorene is also flexible enough to guess from the context and to use other strategies to compensate for missing knowledge. She wants to increase her vocabulary. Strategy instruction would help her learn to use certain memory strategies and cognitive strategies that would be useful for vocabulary growth.

Example 2: Brad uses a wide range of strategies, but he does not know which ones are best for him personally while he is learning French. He does not know when to apply which strategies, so he is rather random and haphazard in his strategy choices. This is reflected in his occasionally erratic language performance. Strategy instruction can help him identify the strategies he is using and figure out which ones most closely fit his language tasks and his needs.

Example 3: Louise has found a number of strategies that match her reflective, analytic learning style and that work well with some of the more structural, accuracy-oriented language tasks she faces in her German class. Now she wants to try some other strategies to improve her fluency. Strategy instruction can help her expand her strategy repertoire (especially social and compensation strategies) into the fluency area, where she has not dared go before.

Example 4: Tanya is linguistically talented, as her Spanish teacher has observed. At the same time, Tanya is extremely disorganized and distractible, although not clinically diagnosed as "attention deficit disordered" (ADD) or "hyperactive." Strategy instruction can teach her metacognitive strategies for organizing her time and environment and for paying attention, and it can give her affective strategies for managing her motivation and emotions. Other kinds of learning strategies, such as cognitive techniques, cannot assist Tanya very much unless she works to solve her problems of disorganization and distractibility by metacognitive and affective means.

Example 5: Mohammad's low motivation, reduced self-efficacy, and minimal self-confidence caused by previous language learning failure must be battled in order for him to become willing to try new learning strategies for learning English. Strategy instruction can include a discussion of Mohammad's current state, which directly affects his ability to learn effective strategies. Strategy instruction can also provide step-by-step successes in language learning, which Mohammad needs in order to renew his confidence.

Example 6: A visual learner like Susan, who has been trying to memorize a list of Russian vocabulary words by marching around the room and shouting them aloud (like her auditory-kinesthetic roommate does), needs to understand why this strategy does not work for her. Strategy instruction can explain that her learning style does not fit with this kind of strategy, and it can show how she can develop other strategies like using imagery and semantic mapping that would help her more.

Example 7: Sayed's personality type is extroverted and feeling-oriented, but he keeps trying to use "solo" strategies for improving his learning of English. Therefore, he feels lonely and unsuccessful. Strategy instruction can guide him to the use of appropriate social learning strategies involving cooperation, frequent interactions, and cultural understanding.

Example 8: Zhizheng's powerful but dangerous belief that English language learning consists only of rote memorization can be explicitly discussed in strategy instruction. Otherwise, she will never become adept at appropriately using a larger range of strategies. She needs to develop an in-depth set of cognitive and metacognitive strategies that go beyond rote memorization.

Example 9: Fifty-year-old George feels he is too old to learn any new language. Strategy instruction can show him the vast array of learning strategies already available to him as a mature adult learner with extensive life experience. Strategy instruction can give George a "wake-up call" to recognize his true abilities and existing strategies, as well as teaching him new strategies.

Keeping these examples in mind, we now turn to the main contrast in strategy instruction: consciousness.

CONSCIOUSNESS: CRUCIAL CONTRASTS IN STRATEGY INSTRUCTION

As Figure 18.1 shows, consciousness can be divided into four aspects: awareness, attention, intentionality, and control (Schmidt, 1994). Lack of any consciousness of strategies can be considered yet another aspect. Strategy instruction encompasses all of these.

Thus, a certain level of strategy instruction involves *no learner consciousness* of strategies at all. Another level of strategy instruction, waking students up to the idea of language learning strategies is paramount; this means raising their *awareness*. A third level of strategy instruction focuses on helping students pay *attention* to their own strategies and the strategies of other people. A fourth level of strategy instruction aids students to become *intentional* in improving their own strategies — making the commitment and taking steps. A final level of strategy instruction provides learners a greater degree of *control* over their strategy use.

Figure 18.1: Consciousness contrasts

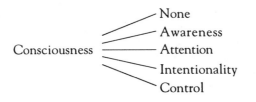

However, in any given situation, one student might be working far ahead of others; he or she might be operating with strategic intentionality or even strategic control while others are back at the awareness or attention stage. Conversely, even if the goal of a given session of strategy instruction is to provide strategic control, a few learners might be only raising their strategic awareness while other students move far ahead into control. Students operate with different time frames. They reach different strategic consciousness stages at different times, depending on difficulty of the material, learning style, interest level, prior experience, and many other factors (Oxford, 1989b). We will now explore each consciousness aspect in more detail.

NO CONSCIOUSNESS

"Blind" strategy instruction (described in Brown et al., 1983; Oxford, 1990b, 1992/1993; Wenden and Rubin, 1987) requires no learner consciousness of strategies, nor does it create any particularly strategic consciousness. In this form of strategy instruction, the tasks or materials cause the student "subconsciously" or "unconsciously" to use particular learning strategies. For instance, the textbook might say, "Look at the picture now." The picture might or might not help the learner understand what the reading passage is about. However, the learner probably won't be aware of this hidden strategy that is text-embedded but not really stated: "Look at the picture carefully to get clues about the meaning of the story." Thus, an embedded learning strategy is not expressed as a strategy, so the majority of students might not be aware of it, pay attention to it, decide to use it regularly, or want to gain control of it. In "blind" strategy instruction, the language tasks or materials do not provide any explicit information to the student about the nature or importance of learning strategies, nor about how to transfer them to new situations. In this form of strategy instruction, learners are like puppets on a string, being moved around without a sense of purpose and without real awareness of what is happening.

"Blind" strategy instruction can be found in many recent textbooks. Particularly in those textbooks associated with the Natural Approach, for example, *Dos Mundos* (Terrell et al., 1990) and task-based instruction, for example, *¿Sabías que...?* (Van Patten et al., 1992), strategy instruction is apt to be embedded into the language activities by the textbook authors. These activities often require students to plan, to paraphrase, and to make inferences, among a myriad of other language learning strategies. "Blind" strategy instruction in language textbooks can be unbalanced in terms of the types of strategies embedded in the textbook activities. This is especially true if the embedding has occurred unconsciously, not deliberately, on the part of the author. In a selected group of 17 language textbooks and learner guidebooks from the Netherlands, the US, and the UK, some of the strategy instruction was blind, and cognitive strategies were included at nearly double the frequency of any other kind of strategy (Hajer et al., 1994; also chapter 9, this volume).

Even if the learner successfully uses in the immediate task the embedded learning strategies, research shows that learners do not tend to transfer to other tasks the strategies practiced through "blind" strategy instruction (Brown et al., 1983; Oxford, 1990b). This is not surprising, because Schmidt (1994) asserts that consciousness is essential in developing a second or foreign language, implying that the lack of any consciousness is not very helpful at the pre-expert stages.

A minority opinion about "blind" strategy instruction is expressed by Sutter (in Oxford et al., 1990). He found that what he called "camouflaged" or "covert" strategy instruction (the same as "blind" instruction) was necessary for some of his adult refugee learners in Denmark. It was used with students who felt they should spend their time only on learning Danish (not learning how to learn the language) or who were threatened by the concept of taking additional responsibility for their own learning. Many of these students were older, came from Asia or Eastern Europe as refugees, and continued to adhere rigidly to the old learning strategies of their homeland. Such students were asked to undertake social and academic experiences outside school that would implicitly guide them to use new strategies, especially cooperating with peers. For instance, devout and solitary word list makers were encouraged to form groups whose job was to make and publish a glossary, dictionary, or cookbook; and analytic grammar enthusiasts were invited to work together to make a video. The aim of this strategy instruction was to help these students enlarge their strategy repertoire without actually knowing it or feeling threatened. There is no research evidence about whether these students were able to transfer these new strategies to other language tasks, but at least they were able to accomplish the immediate tasks.

AWARENESS
Awareness of language learning strategies often comes merely by taking part in a strategy assessment, as indicated earlier in this book. Some strategy assessments, such as surveys, think-alouds, and diaries, help students reflect on their strategy use and therefore spark strategic awareness. Discussions held after these strategy assessments frequently heighten awareness of strategies. (Other strategy assessments, such

as teacher observations or computer tracking, are far less awareness-producing for students.) Awareness also develops through strategy awareness games, such as the "Embedded Strategies Game" and the "Strategy Search Game" (both in Oxford, 1990b). The former game asks students to name a strategy related to a learning or communication situation. The latter requires students (often in small groups) to list useful learning strategies for a variety of role-play contexts, like being lost without a dictionary in a large foreign city. "The Best and the Worst Game" (Oxford, 1989a) is an immediate strategy-awareness tool. It causes individual participants to consider their best and worst language learning experiences and to determine what kinds of strategies they used in each. Discussion of real or fictitious "student cases" aids learners in developing their own awareness of learning strategies. Students, often in groups, read a description of a language learner who has problems. Students then analyze the problems and make recommendations for strategies the language learner could fruitfully use to improve his or her performance. The Foreign Service Institute often uses case study discussions to heighten learner awareness of strategies. The US Defense Language Institute has created a computerized learner awareness course to increase awareness of strategies.

Lectures, particularly those that are interactive, can sometimes help learners increase their awareness of strategies. The purpose of lectures is to introduce students to the concept of language learning strategies in a compact time frame. Noninteractive lectures involve the use of handouts or transparencies and a one-way presentation by the leader; such lectures are usually less effective than interactive lectures. Interactive lectures typically consist of whole-group brainstorming about learning strategies. The US Defense Language Institute often conducts interactive strategy lectures for newly arriving students in Polish, German, Turkish, Greek, and Hebrew, with the result that proficiency has increased (Granoien, 1992). Similarly, an interactive workshop on strategies has become a potent awareness-raising tool for university foreign language students (see Flaitz and Feyten, chapter 17, this volume.).

ATTENTION

Attention can occur at two levels: *peripheral* (impressionistic, nontargeted, general) or *focal* (sharp, targeted, directed). Strategy instruction typically promotes focal attention. Some students might arrive with a lack of attention to learning strategies (their own or those of other people) or might have a merely peripheral attention to strategies. One aim of strategy instruction is often to take a student's lack of attention or fuzzy attention in regard to language learning strategies and transform it into keen, targeted attention.

In an interactive lecture, the lecturer sometimes asks students to give each other advice about learning strategies that can be used at home or in school. Such a move calls students' focal attention to specific strategies, and this attention is heightened even more because peers (not authority figures) offer the information. In strategy diary discussions, students compare their own strategy use and tell each other which strategies have helped them under what circumstances. Again, the use of peer sharing is a powerful attention-getter. Focal attention can skyrocket in small group or individual activities, such as:

- planning which strategies to use in language learning tasks;
- identifying learning strategies that relate best to certain learning styles (visual, auditory, hands-on; extrovert, introvert; intuitive, concrete-sequential);
- examining personal "strategy databases" to take a look at specific strategies and considering why various people use different strategies;
- viewing language textbooks to determine which strategies found there.

Focal attention toward language learning strategies can also be raised in counseling sessions. Individual counseling focuses attention on the strengths and weaknesses of strategy use of the particular person. Films or multimedia (as described by Rubin, chapter 11, this volume) can stimulate attention to specific strategies that would be useful to try. Workshops (see Flaitz and Feyten, chapter 17, this volume) can also help students pay greater focal attention to their strategy use.

INTENTIONALITY

Intentionality (commitment or decision to do something; a key part of motivation) occurs when students have particular attitudes and beliefs that is, when they:

- view a certain strategy as helpful to them in this particular language task,
- think the strategy might be useful in other tasks as well,
- perceive the payoff as greater than or equal to the effort expended,
- perceive a real possibility of success if they use the strategy,
- think they have some self-efficacy and are not mere pawns of the situation or the teacher,
- are interested in the materials and activities involving the strategy,
- value the language they are studying in the first place, and
- believe they can get the support and input of others (Oxford and Shearin, 1994).

Note that all the above intentionality descriptors reflect attitudes and beliefs. This is why strategy instruction, particularly at the intentionality level, cannot avoid dealing with attitudes and beliefs (Wenden and Rubin, 1987, for the US perspective; Yang, 1992a, 1992b, for the Taiwanese perspective). Students who wish to improve their strategies must learn to combat any negative attitudes and beliefs they have, and strategy instruction must address these factors when they arise. This can be done through dialogue journals (written messages between students and teachers), counseling, and group discussions of helpful and dysfunctional beliefs and attitudes. It is very important for teachers not to satirize a student's attitudes and beliefs, no matter how strange or unhelpful those might seem. Respect for the student's current mental set is crucial, even while we are trying to inculcate more positive beliefs and attitudes.

Interactive lectures and strategy diary discussions can sometimes stimulate intentionality regarding language learning strategies. This is particularly true if these lectures and discussions are immediately followed up with relevant, interesting language tasks that require strategy use. Even without directed practice in applying strategies, well-structured workshops (see Flaitz and Feyten, chapter 17, this volume) have been shown to stimulate learners' intention to improve their strategy use.

Individual counseling, as used at the US Foreign Service Institute and at some universities, is effective in helping students not only direct their attention but build their intention to improve their strategies. At the University of Alabama, individual counseling revealed that one student had a serious reading disability that interfered with her Russian learning, and this counseling successfully stimulated the student's intention to develop reading strategies (especially analytic ones) that would counteract her disability. At the US Defense Language Institute, individual counseling revealed that a Russian student's slow progress in acquiring oral proficiency resulted from a missing nerve in his tongue. By developing coping strategies, this DLI student was able to catch up with his class and graduate on schedule with the required level of oral proficiency. At the American Global Studies Institute, a mother referred to individual counseling her son, who was failing first-year high school Spanish but needed to pass a Spanish entrance exam to enter a prestigious private school. The counselor-tutor worked for four weeks with the boy to improve learning strategy use, and the boy passed the Spanish entrance exam with no problem.

Group counseling sessions with students (Griggs, 1991) can be helpful for promoting intentionality. In one example students together in their class or small group, where they can safely share their feelings about their language learning, their progress, and their strategies. In the circle, students can help each other assess the effectiveness and appropriateness of their strategy use. Individuals can re-enact unsuccessful attempts at learning, and others students in the group can interpret the situation, suggest more appropriate strategies, and encourage a commitment to try these strategies.

"Informed" strategy instruction (Brown et al., 1983; Oxford, 1990b) can cause an increase in strategic intentionality. This form of strategy instruction tells the learner what a particular strategy does and why it is useful. This kind of strategy instruction results in improved performance on the given language task and maintenance of the strategy across time. However, in most instances it does not give the student enough control to evaluate the success of the strategy or to know when or how to transfer the strategy to another task.

CONTROL

Awareness, attention, and intentionality are not enough to create a proficient, skillful user of a learning strategy. Control is also necessary. With regard to learning strategy use, control involves being able to evaluate the success of using a certain strategy and also having the ability to transfer that strategy to other relevant situations and tasks. "Strategy-plus-control" instruction teaches students these two aspects of strategy use (evaluation and transfer), as well as helping them identify the strategy, know when to use it, and practice using it. Research by Brown et al. (1983) and Leaver (1988) suggests that "strategy-plus-control" instruction is significantly more valuable than "blind" instruction, "informed" instruction, or no instruction in strategies. "Strategy-plus-control" instruction is the most powerful of the strategy instruction modes, because it engenders the greatest form of consciousness: control. Moreover, it empowers learners in a greater number of increasingly responsible aspects of strategy implementation and evaluation. Oxford's (1990b) eight-step strategy development model features "strategy-plus-control" instruction. Numerous examples of "strategy-plus-control" instruction are found in the present volume. See in particular the Cognitive Academic Language Learning or CALLA Model (Dadour and Robbins, chapter 12; Chamot and O'Malley, chapter 13; Chamot, Barnhardt, El-Dinary, and Robbins, chapter 14) and Canada's Foresee Model (Kidd and Marquardson, chapter 15).

Characteristics common to most of these "strategy-plus-control" models include:

1. Identification of strategies to be taught.

2. Assessment of current strategy use as a precursor to strategy instruction.

3. Strategy instruction of students over a long period of time.

4. Explicit demonstration, discussion, use, evaluation, and transfer of specific strategies.

5. Preparation and use of specific materials tailored to the regular language learning tasks.

6. On-going evaluation by teacher and participants of the effectiveness of the strategy instruction.

7. Flexibility in individualizing or adapting strategy assistance to the needs of each student.

The Tapestry Program, edited by Rebecca Oxford and Robin Scarcella, includes "strategy-plus-control" instruction for university adult students of ESL/EFL (see, e.g., Oxford, 1995). The program, containing 45 books in an integrated-skill format for five proficiency levels, explicitly increases students' control of language learning strategies while it teaches English. These strategies are clearly labeled, for example, "Remembering New Material: Making a mental image of a word helps you remember the word." An example of this strategy follows in the text, along with a language task that provides a way to use the strategy immediately. Frequently, the strategies are explicitly "recycled" next to new language tasks, and learners are reminded to transfer the strategies to the new tasks. Strategy checklists provide self-evaluation throughout most of these books.

OTHER FACTORS IN STRATEGY INSTRUCTION

Table 18.1: Additional contrasts

Level of education	Elementary and secondary ⇔ University ⇔ Adult education
Direction	Teacher-directed ⇔ Student-directed
Integration into regular instruction	Integrated ⇔ Detached
Location	Classroom ⇔ Home ⇔ In-country
Resource use	High resource use ⇔ Low resource use

We have seen how contrasts in consciousness relate to strategy instruction. Strategy instruction can be described in at least five additional ways. Table 18.1 shows these factors.

LEVEL OF EDUCATION

Strategy instruction has expanded in the last few years to include all levels of education and all ages of students. These include elementary and secondary, university, and adult education.

Elementary and secondary education

At the elementary and secondary level, the CALLA Model of strategy instruction, described in this book, has proven popular in Canada, the US, and other parts of the world. The model, designed for ESL students but also used with foreign language students, has three components, only one of which is direct strategy instruction. The other two components are content (i.e., school subjects, such as math and history) and English language study. The three components are integrated, so that strategy instruction is implemented through language and content study. This model usually assumes that different teachers will be teaching content and language. The teachers must work together to make this model feasible.

The Foresee Model (see Kidd and Marquardson, chapter 15, this volume) is a Canadian instructional design that builds on the CALLA Model. Like the CALLA Model, the Foresee Model is targeted to ESL students. However, the Foresee Model has a slightly different theoretical underpinning. Furthermore, Foresee differs from CALLA in its general process of implementation and in its repertoire of specific lesson techniques that are not part of CALLA. Of special importance are the Foresee lesson objectives and the specific ways these objectives are applied in the classroom.

The Flower Model of Leni Dam (Dickinson, 1987; Oxford, 1990b) is applied to primary (young elementary) school English language learning in Denmark. Even at an extremely early age, students learn to analyze their own motivations and to identify, evaluate, and improve their language learning strategies in the Flower Model. Matheidesz (Oxford, 1990b) has used forms of strategy instruction in language games with high school students of English in Budapest, Hungary. The game materials are exceptionally appealing, especially to visual students, and they invoke a wide range of language learning strategies in students. This chapter's second author has conducted language learning strategy instruction at the P. K. Yonge Laboratory School in Gainesville, Florida and Columbia High School in Troutdale, Oregon. The American Global Studies Institute has set up a computerized network for teachers who are conducting strategy instruction, as well as working with learning styles, called LEARNLINK, where teachers can call in for assistance (tel. 408–455–0403). Flaitz and Feyten (chapter 17, this volume) show how strategy instruction can be implemented at middle school and high school levels. They also explain how age and institutional factors differentially affect the success of strategy instruction.

University education

University-level strategy instruction programs have taken place at the University of Maryland, the University of Alabama, Purdue University, Indiana University, Georgetown University, the University of Texas, the University of South Florida, the University of Minnesota, and the University of Manitoba, to name a few locations. An entire program of strategy instruction, supplemented by intensive research, is now being conducted at the University of Minnesota by Cohen and his staff at the National Foreign Language Resource Center. This program aims to put control for learning in the learner's hands through a variety of strategic activities, materials, and processes. The Centre de Récherches et d'Applications Pedagogiques en Langues (CRAPEL) of the University of Nancy II in France requires learners to make their own decisions on the type and amount of strategy assistance they need. Learners determine their priorities, materials, learning experiences, and evaluations, all with the aid of an experienced "helper." Flaitz and Feyten (chapter 17, this volume) conducted a two-phase study involving raising metacognitive and cognitive awareness among university foreign language students. Their intriguing results show that strategy instruction is not always simple and straightforward.

Lavine (in Oxford et al., 1990) developed a program of strategy instruction for her Spanish students at the University of Maryland. Diaries, diary discussions, modeling, and practice played a prominent role. As a result of strategy instruction, students' attitude and control over a range of strategies greatly improved. Modeling and demonstration by the teacher were primary aspects of university-level strategy instruction described by Nyikos, and many positive attitudinal and performance changes occurred as a result of strategy instruction (in Oxford et al., 1990). At Columbia University, Wenden (1986) employed strategy instruction with ESL students. She was disappointed at first because the instruction seemed to have little effect, but in retrospect she determined that the problem was related to lack of integration of strategy instruction with regular language learning. This problematic attempt helped her build a stronger model of strategy instruction later.

Adult education

France's CRAPEL provides programs for senior citizens in which these people spend a week in groups learning to design and organize their own learning strategically. Helpers take no part in the groups unless called upon, but they are available when needed (Holec, 1980; Oxford, 1990b). Cohen (in Oxford et al., 1990) served as a "language therapist" for adult learners of Hebrew at Ulpan Akiva in Israel. He provided two lectures and two rap sessions for adults each month and answered questions about their language learning progress, problems, and strategies. Though this effort, many learners reported trying out new strategies and taking more responsibility for their own learning. Sutter (in Oxford, 1990b) described his highly creative and diversified strategy instruction for adult learners of Danish.

The US Defense Language Institute designed a Learning Skills Center focused on language learning strategies and provided strategy instruction to Center directors, language teachers, deans, and coordinators. After this, although budget cuts hampered the full establishment of the Center, instructors have actively provided strategy instruction to their own students. In one program, DLI students discussed *A Practical Guide to Language Learning* (Brown, 1989) and practiced language learning strategies through exercises and small group classroom activities. Similarly, the US Foreign Service Institute has offered strategy instruction, including one-to-one counseling for troubled students, personalized strategy discussions for students who are doing well, and awareness-raising sessions about learning strategies (Ehrman and Oxford, 1988, 1989). The US Peace Corps has often used strategy instruction to enhance adult language learners' performance. With learning strategy guidebooks written for the Peace Corps (Grala, Oxford, and Schleppegrell, 1987; Schleppegrell and Oxford, 1988), leaders conducted sessions on learning strategies for teachers in the Philippines. The teachers then taught their adult students to improve learning strategy use (Oxford, 1990b). Currently the four US government language schools are working to develop a computer-mediated learner awareness course that would be useful to each school.

DIRECTION

This dimension refers to the person who directs the strategy instruction: the student or the teacher.

Student-directed

In 1990 the School of Slavic Languages at the US Defense Language Institute published a student-directed, self-instructional language learning strategy manual for students of Russian, *Navigating the DSL Russian Course: A Guide for Students* (Leaver, 1990). This manual became the model for other such strategy self-instruction manuals in German, Czech, Korean, Polish, Hebrew, and Turkish. Teachers at other government institutions, at universities, and in high school programs have also used these manuals to assist with student-directed strategy self-instruction. Guidebooks for language students are now relatively abundant (e.g., Brown, 1989; Ellis and Sinclair, 1989; Fuller, 1987; Grala, Oxford, and Schleppegrell, 1987; Leaver, 1990; Park, 1994a; Rubin and Thompson, 1982, 1994; Schleppegrell and Oxford, 1988; for a list of many more, see the notes in Oxford, 1990b). These self-instructional manuals discuss the characteristics of language learning and of successful language learners and explain to readers how they, too, could be good language learners. These books powerfully promote the use of language learning strategies in a self-instructional format. Dickinson's (1987) book on self-instructional language learning emphasizes the strategic needs of learners.

Student-directed strategy instruction can also occur during class time. If teachers allow students to have a few minutes periodically to share their favorite (or least favorite) strategies in an informal, small group discussion, students help each other become better language learners. The teacher does not have to direct these discussions. In fact, too much intervention by the teacher in these discussions would be deleterious to the student-directed flavor of the conversations.

Even though the CRAPEL programs in France are organized and administered by a university, nevertheless many of them are almost entirely student-directed. In many programs at CRAPEL, students of English determine their own objectives, materials and books, learning experiences, strategies, evaluation plans, assistance needs, and schedules. Thus, full responsibility is placed in the learners' hands, even though "helpers" are available to assist. Similarly, at the DLI, student-directed strategy instruction in Central European, Slavic, Arabic, and Korean languages includes the availability of academic coordinators, who provide language learning assistance whenever a student requests it.

Teacher-directed

Much of the strategy instruction we read about in professional journals and books (see Chamot and Rubin, 1993; Flaitz, Feyten, Fox, and Mukherjee, 1995; O'Malley and Chamot, 1990; Oxford, 1992/1993; Rees-Miller, 1993; Wenden and Rubin, 1987) is teacher-directed. This means that students do not work from beginning to end with strategy instruction manuals and without the guidance of a flesh-and-blood teacher. The teacher is very much in charge of mentioning strategies (and, in cases of in-depth strategy instruction, often modeling strategies and helping students practice, evaluate, and transfer strategies). Teacher-directed strategy instruction can take the form of in-class activities and homework assignments. Here the teacher decides which activities students need to do, which materials students need to study, and which strategies students need to work on in order to improve language performance. Thus, the direction and control of acquisition of learning strategies depends chiefly on the teacher. While this approach may reduce learner autonomy, it may be appropriate especially for less successful language learners who have been unable to develop appropriate language strategy use on their own.

In teacher-directed strategy instruction in the classroom, the instruction is typically somewhat formal, planned, and organized, and it follows a model. However, less formal teacher-directed strategy instruction also exists in language classrooms. Informal, teacher-directed strategy instruction tends to occur serendipitously. Such strategy instruction occurs "off the cuff," whenever students need it. In any language task, teachers can make informal suggestions of strategies that might be used (based often on a student displaying some hesitation or difficulty) or can elicit strategy suggestions from students throughout the class.

Oxford et al. (1990) describe a panoply of successful teacher-directed strategy instruction approaches with language students of many different ages and backgrounds. All these teacher-directed efforts are geared to enhance learners' own self-direction in the long run. As Scarcella and Oxford (1992) show, teachers can provide a great deal of assistance in the beginning and gradually lift away such scaffolding as students become increasingly self-directed and autonomous. This concept fits with the work of Vygotsky in social learning, which demonstrates the large need for teacher direction at the start and the decreased need as the student develops more learning skills (Scarcella and Oxford, 1992).

INTEGRATION INTO REGULAR CLASSROOM INSTRUCTION

Strategy instruction can either be integrated into the classroom or detached from it. Integrated strategy instruction refers to the inclusion of strategy instruction exercises woven into the regular classroom curriculum. Detached strategy instruction refers to strategy instruction that is conducted with students separate from the classroom activities.

Integrated strategy instruction

Integrated language learning strategy instruction can include classroom activities, discussions, and games. Examples of integrated instruction models include the "strategy-plus-control" instruction conducted in the CALLA and Foresee Models and in the Oxford principles of strategy instruction (1990b). Another example of integrated strategy instruction is "The Flower Model" used in the elementary schools in Denmark. The entire learning process is pictured as a flower; the learning strategy instruction component of the program is one of the petals. All components (petals) fan out around the center of the flower, in which appears the word, *negotiation*, the activity around which the entire course is built (described in Oxford, 1990b). Nyikos and Lavine depict highly integrated forms of strategy instruction in their language classes (see Oxford et al., 1990). Research has shown that strategy instruction is more often effective when the strategy instruction is integrated into classroom activities, rather than presented separately (O'Malley and Chamot, 1990; Oxford, 1990b), but at least two notable exceptions exist, those of Cohen in Israel and Flaitz and Feyten in the US.

Detached strategy instruction

One successful model of detached strategy instruction is the system of lectures conducted by Andrew Cohen at Ulpan Akiva in Israel (see Oxford, 1990b). As mentioned earlier, Cohen presented strategy instruction to students via lectures and discussions. Students took information from the detached strategy instruction provided by Cohen and on their own applied it to their own language learning situations. Likewise, in Phase 1 of the Flaitz and Feyten study and in the middle school aspect of Phase 2 of the same study (see chapter 17, this volume), students benefited from short-term, detached strategy instruction and managed to transfer it to their own learning, thus raising their language achievement. However, Wenden (1986) showed that detached strategy instruction can fail when students do not see its relevance to their everyday language learning efforts.

LOCATION

Strategy instruction can be conducted in the classroom, at home, or in-country. Classroom strategy instruction can take any of the forms of in-class activities already mentioned (strategy discussions, demonstrations, interactive lectures, and so on). Home strategy instruction consists of working with a textbook and/or supplemental materials or equipment (such as readings, learner manuals, guidebooks, workbooks, diaries, computers, and videodiscs). In-country instruction is usually preceded by classroom instruction, with or without individual counseling, followed by real-life application.

Classroom strategy instruction

A number of classroom activities have already been described in detail. The purpose of the classroom activities is to allow teachers to guide the acquisition of additional strategies, assist in the identification of needed strategies or make the identification, and provide an arena for students to learn from each other. Classroom activities usually work best in programs where students need direction, where teachers understand language learning strategies, and where students can benefit from more or less uniform instruction.

Home strategy instruction

Home activities can be teacher-directed. Teachers can make homework assignments in which students use activities from textbooks with either embedded ("blind") or "strategy-plus-control" instruction exercises. Alternatively, teachers can choose to selectively assign specific strategy exercises to specific students, depending on the nature of the students' learning strategy needs. In addition to the textbook or in lieu of it, teachers can prepare their own materials specifically designed for individual students. These types of home assignments are usually turned in for correction or discussed in class. Teachers can assign supplemental readings of articles and books on learning strategies. These can be individualized in accordance with which students most need them. While most articles and books on learning strategies have been written for teachers, not for students, some educated adult students or mature college students can use these fairly readily. Teachers can provide students with learner manuals, guidebooks, or workbooks. A number of these manuals already exist. Among them are the US Defense Language Institute language-specific manuals mentioned earlier, a workbook on learning strategies and styles (Brown, 1989), two US Peace Corps manuals (Grala, Oxford, and Schleppegrell, 1987; Schleppegrell and Oxford, 1988), a skill-specific strategy manual for speaking (Shekhtmann, 1991), a home study package aiding students in using metacognitive strategies for reading (Park-Oh, 1994a), and books directly written for self-directed language learners (e.g., Rubin and Thompson, 1982, 1994).

However, home strategy instruction can be student-directed instead of teacher-directed. Students can use any of the manuals listed above totally on their own with good success. Mature students are especially likely to benefit from student-directed use of such materials, particularly if they employ these materials at the same time as they are doing their regular homework for the language class, and if they are able to tie in the student-directed strategy instruction with their teacher-directed homework.

Another aspect of student self-direction in home strategy instruction is keeping a strategy diary or a "strategy database," with or without a computer. Computers as a source of student-directed strategy instruction are now being explored. A study currently going on at the US Army Research Institute is investigating ways to include learning strategies as aids for intelligence-career personnel practicing Spanish by personal computer (Lavine and Oxford, 1994). A well-known, computer-based videodisc program exists (Rubin, 1989; also chapter 11, this volume). Baily (chapter 10, this volume) shows that personal computers can be used to track and itemize the use of language learning strategies, so it is probably only a matter of time until actual strategy instruction by personal computers will become more commonplace.

In-country instruction

In-country instruction typically combines teacher-directed and student-directed activities. Prior to students' travel to the country in which they will study or while they are there, teachers conduct any variety of learning strategy instruction, as described earlier in this chapter. Students apply what they learn from the strategy instruction in their daily communicative interactions: home visits, hanging out with peers, watching movies or TV, casual encounters, and business transactions. They might report back on their strategy use to a teacher or mentor-counselor, keep a journal, or simply take note of their successes. The American Council of Teachers of Russian (ACTR) includes in-country strategy instruction in the support services provided to exchange students sent to Moscow and Leningrad. Using materials and lectures prior to departure, students gain information on how to choose learning strategies that are appropriate to in-country use. Counseling and feedback are currently given to students by a doctoral candidate conducting on-site research in Russia. ACTR plans to continue and expand in-country strategy instruction for future groups of students and will involve teachers at Russian universities in the effort.

RESOURCE USE

Strategy instruction has resource implications. Strategy instruction can be a high resource item, or it can involve a lower level of resources.

High resource use

Some strategy instruction efforts involve a high commitment of time, money, and energy. For example, the development and testing of the CALLA Model took many years, hundreds of thousands of dollars, and the effort of dozens of researchers and teachers as well as hundreds of students. However, at this stage, given the increasing amounts of materials being created to support this model and the relative accessibility of these materials, the resource demands are going down rapidly. Likewise, the development of the Rubin videodisc was very labor- and capital-intensive for a number of years, but now this strategy instruction tool is available to groups and individuals for far less of an investment in resources.

Teachers need strategy instruction, sometimes as much as their students do (see Nyikos, chapter 8, this volume). Though strategy instruction for teachers need not always absorb large amounts of resources, nevertheless some of it is costly. For instance, the Soros Foundation has commissioned numerous week-long strategy-and-style instruction sessions for teachers to be held in Russia, Belarus, and the Ukraine. Many other locations need the same kind of intensive assistance. The vast majority of language teachers throughout the world need instruction about language learning strategies if resources become available.

Another resource demand of strategy instruction is time. Time is needed to conduct the instruction, to practice strategies, and to find or develop materials. Finding strategy instruction time in the first place may be a significant resource issue in some instructional environments, particularly those that are tied to a particular syllabus for multisection introductory language courses. While many language programs may be pressed for time, making room for strategy instruction will likely improve the rapidity of learning.

Low resource use

Some inexpensive materials for the classroom do exist. A number of years ago Omaggio (1981) prepared a strategy instruction guide for teachers, as did the staff at InterAmerica Research Associates (Stewner-Manzanares et al., 1985). These guidebooks also provide a guide to teachers in developing materials specific to each teacher's own classroom. *Learner Strategies for Learner Autonomy* (Wenden, 1991) and *Language Learning Strategies: What Every Teacher Should Know* (Oxford, 1990b) are two books specifically designed to develop strategic understanding in teachers, so that they can provide strategy instruction activities for their students. Wenden's format can also serve as an example for teachers wanting to develop their own strategy instruction materials for students.

Even very detailed programs that took great amounts of resources to create and evaluate, such as the CALLA Model and the Rubin videodisc, are now much more accessible since the development phase is over. The resource demands of these processes and products have shrunk significantly, although users must be aware of the major time commitment that is involved in learning to apply these useful contributions.

The Tapestry Program described earlier explicitly weaves strategy instruction into ESL/EFL instruction. For the cost of a single language book, the student and the instructor receive powerful strategic assistance for learning and teaching. Increasingly, language textbooks like these are beginning to include language learning strategies as a highlighted feature in a variety of languages — English, French, and Spanish in particular. These strategies are geared to the specific linguistic requirements of a given language.

Workshops and strategy instruction sessions for learners and teachers need not vacuum up all existing resources. Flaitz and Feyten (chapter 17, this volume) and Dadour and Robbins (chapter 12, this volume), as well as other researchers represented in this book, present ways that learning strategies can be taught to students without exhausting one's time, energy, and funds. Some inexpensive teacher development sessions are available concerning language learning strategies (see, e.g., Nyikos, chapter 8, this volume). Every language conference highlights strategy instruction for teachers in the form of workshops or research sessions. If teachers have the resources to attend a local, regional, or national language teaching conference, they are likely to have the opportunity to attend a number of strategy instruction sessions. Some graduate programs in foreign language education, especially at major universities, now include information on learning strategies. Summer programs, notably the NEH-CORLAC Summer Institute in Russian Language and Culture at Bryn Mawr College, include an introduction to language learning strategies as part of their faculty development programs. The American Council on Teaching Foreign Languages offers periodic workshops on language learning strategies as part of its site-to-site teacher development program. Inexpensive, language-specific strategy instruction manuals need to be developed to go with such workshops. Teachers who have been newly introduced to the field of language learning strategies need low cost, easy-to-use instruction kits, handouts, and other kinds of supplementary materials.

CONCLUSIONS

Published research on strategies (and strategy instruction) as related to language performance shows somewhat mixed results. On the negative side, Politzer and McGroarty (1985) found that of a total of 51 supposedly "good" strategies, 80% did not correlate with higher gains in grammatical proficiency or communicative competence. In a strategy instruction experiment, O'Malley et al. (1985a, 1985b) provided eight days of instruction in listening and speaking strategies for Spanish-speaking ESL students at the high school level. Results were not significantly positive for teaching students to listen for details, take notes, and ask each other for help, but strategy instruction tied to a speaking assignment (rehearsing a two-minute taped speech) was significantly beneficial. Similarly, O'Malley (1987) reported in a study with ESL high school students that strategy instruction was not significantly helpful in areas other than making a short speech, and that strategy instruction for vocabulary learning actually proved detrimental for at least some learners for cultural reasons.

However, as Oxford and Burry-Stock (1995), Cohen (1990b), and O'Malley and Chamot (1990) demonstrate, numerous studies link language proficiency and achievement to the frequency of strategy use and to the effective use of strategies. Many investigators (Chamot, 1993; Chamot, Barnhardt, El-Dinary, Carbonaro, and Robbins, 1993; Chamot, Robbins, and El-Dinary, 1993; Cohen, 1990b; Cohen and Aphek, 1981; Hosenfeld, Arnold, Kirchofer, Laciura, and Wilson, 1981; O'Malley, Chamot, Stewner-Manzanares, Russo, and Küpper, 1985b; Rost and Ross, 1991; Rubin, 1990; Rubin, Quinn, and Enos, 1988; Thompson and Rubin, 1993) have provided empirical evidence that the use of a particular strategy causes more efficient learning than not using that strategy. To summarize this synthesis of language learning strategy instruction, we cite the hopeful words of Chamot and Rubin (1993, p. 774):

> We stress that learning strategies instruction is not a magical formula to improve learner performance and that strategy researchers have made no such claim. Researchers in this area recognize that many learner, context, task, teacher, and text variables that affect the extent to which strategies instruction can facilitate learning. Still, the evidence describing usage and intervention in both L1 contexts and L2 learning leads us to feel confident that such instruction, properly carried out, can positively assist language learners to become engaged in their own learning processes, thus taking on greater responsibility for learning. Teachers can introduce learning strategies instruction into their language class in the knowledge that it will help many, if not most, students.

Rebecca L. Oxford
University of Alabama, USA

AFTERWORD
WHAT HAVE WE LEARNED ABOUT LANGUAGE LEARNING STRATEGIES AROUND THE WORLD?

The afterword is a brief summary of what we have learned about language learning strategies around the world. Many previously discovered principles were confirmed about strategy assessment and strategy instruction, but new principles were also demonstrated and new ideas raised for future testing.

- Advantages and disadvantages exist for each kind of assessment technique. Not all assessment techniques will be useful in every culture. Think-alouds and certain other verbal report modes might be difficult to use in cultures that do not allow much oral expression of learning difficulties or confusion, or that do not encourage creative use of independent strategies "on the spot" during a language task. Group interviews can be conducted even in high face-saving cultures, but in such cultures the interviews need to be as objective and nonembarrassing as possible. Western cultures, with their greater allowance of personal expression, might warm to group interviews readily. Strategy questionnaires might be neutral and nonthreatening to most cultures, and they have been shown not to have social desirability response bias. Strategy questionnaires do not typically provide detailed, task-related information. Observations are useful and noninvasive in most cultural settings, but this technique only gives us data on strategies that are visible, leaving out the mentalistic strategies such as analysis or reasoning. Diaries and recollective studies can be designed to be cross-culturally helpful, but whether this occurs appropriately depends largely on the degree to which these techniques are guided/structured, the degree to which the culture demands structure or allows openness, and the freedom learners feel or do not feel to express themselves. Computer tracking, since it is unobtrusive, is potentially valuable in many cultures that have access to high technology machinery. Remember that most assessment techniques can become usable in a variety of cultures with the proper explanations, rationale, and warm-ups, though the quality of the data might vary across cultures somewhat because of factors noted above.

- In many cultures around the world, strategy use often differs by gender — but not always. Females typically seem to report more strategy use than do males in many different cultures and with many different target languages.

Oxford, R. L. (1996). What have we learned about language learning strategies around the world? In Rebecca L. Oxford (Ed.), *Language learning strategies around the world: Cross-cultural perspectives*. (Technical Report #13) (pp. 247–249). Honolulu: University of Hawai'i, Second Language Teaching & Curriculum Center.

However, in certain types of strategy assessments, such as Vandergrift's think-alouds, the actual strategy use sometimes fails to approximate the retrospectively reported strategy use. It might be that the language tasks used with think-alouds are somewhat limited and call forth only a small range of strategies, so the gender-related results found with retrospective interviews and questionnaires do not show up on think-aloud language tasks. Or it might be that males and females are different in how they report their strategies retrospectively but are not in reality all that different when they actually use strategies. This is an area that needs to be further studied across and within cultures.

- More possible timeframes exist for teaching learners to improve their language learning strategies than we have known in the past. Some researchers, like Chamot and colleagues, prefer long-term strategy instruction with gradually increasing awareness and control. Others such as Robbins, Park, Dadour, and Yang carry out shorter strategy instruction projects with very good effect. The Foresee model of Kidd and Marquardson can be done over a long term but might be adaptable to shorter term use. Perhaps the shortest intervention is the 50-minute strategy instruction program of Flaitz and Feyten, which has been shown to result in long-term gains in language performance for many students.

- Lesson plans used in strategy instruction appear to contrast widely with each other. Park's lesson plan is designed for students to work on at home, and it gives highly detailed, class-tailored tasks directed at the student. CALLA lesson plans and their derivatives provide very specific steps for the teacher, including a problem-solving model in some instances. Yang's lesson plan provides leading questions for group interviews and discussions. Dadour's and Robbins' lesson plans focus on one skill in a highly organized yet creative mode. Some lesson plans are teacher-led, and some are student-led. Lesson plans for strategy instruction (except perhaps for the 50-minute intervention) need to be geared to ordinary language learning tasks and must contain explicit discussion, modeling, practice, evaluation, and transfer of learning strategies. Even handbooks for self-regulated language learning must have these characteristics.

- Language learning textbooks and learner guidebooks are a hidden source of strategy instruction in many parts of the world. Only one study to our knowledge (the one in this book by Hajer and colleagues) has been conducted to determine the frequency with which strategies of various types are included in such books in different cultures. No study has sought to determine the effects of these included strategies on language learners in various cultures, though a lot of anecdotal information around the world tells us these strategies are very helpful. More study is definitely required on strategies in language books and learner guidebooks.

- Culturally-based beliefs and attitudes, as we have seen in a number of chapters, affect students' motivation and therefore their use of language learning strategies and their ultimate language performance. (Contrariwise, better language performance can also have a positive rebound effect on strategy use, which can then "wash back" to influence motivation and beliefs!) We need to look more closely at the beliefs and attitudes held by learners in cultures around the globe and determine more precisely the effects they have. It is likely that these beliefs and attitudes will differ rather widely and that their effects in many cultures will be strong. Knowledge of this array of variables can help teachers plan more effective strategy instruction.

- Different target languages and different native languages might have major influences on language learning strategy selection and on the best means for strategy instruction. Researchers have considered this issue to a small degree, but more thought and investigation is merited on this topic.

- Levels of consciousness are directly related to strategy instruction. Awareness, attention, intention, and control are all interwoven with strategy instruction stages. Nevertheless, these consciousness levels have not been treated cross-culturally in any systematic fashion. A study assessing students' consciousness at different strategy instruction stages in different cultures (with aptitude controlled) would be a highly useful investigation. One question might be: Does consciousness work the same way in different cultures, or (more likely) does the student's sense of authority, of group solidarity, of the individual, or of the role of personal learning responsibility cause cultural differences in the operation of consciousness — especially during strategy instruction?

- Many studies, particularly that of Nyikos but also others in this volume, show that before strategy instruction for students can occur, strategy instruction for teachers is often necessary. Teachers must make a conceptual shift toward a learner-centered classroom, and for some instructors this involves a real alteration of their belief systems. Moreover, teachers need to learn the specific techniques that have so far proven useful in strategy instruction with students of various cultures. They must learn that no method or technique fits every student, and a certain amount of tailoring and personalization is essential in helping students improve their language learning strategies. Teachers must be given the proper supports that enable them to try something new, because strategy instruction — no matter how basic and common-sensical it might seem to experts — is indeed novel to many teachers.

These are just some of the many threads in this cross-cultural, multilingual view of language learning strategies. These can lead to better practice, improved and extended research, and more strategic and skillful student performance. Furthermore, these ideas can lead to more efficient and effective instruction by language teachers, resulting in a more successful experience for teachers as well as students. The focus on students' language learning strategies can empower teachers just as it empowers learners.

REFERENCES

Abraham, R. G., & Vann, R. J. (1987). Strategies of two learners: A case study. In A. L. Wenden & J. Rubin (Eds.), *Learner strategies in language learning* (pp. 85–102). New York: Prentice Hall.

Absy, C. A. (1992). *Variations in approaches to EFL: A performance-based analysis of the learning strategies used by Brazilian students.* Unpublished doctoral dissertation, Georgetown University.

Adegbija, E. (1990). Learner's strategies for improving English: A case of Nigerian undergraduates. *Glottodidactica: An International Journal of Applied Linguistics, 20,* 103–111.

Afflerbach, P. (1986). *Outstanding dissertation monograph 1986: The influence of prior knowledge on expert readers' main idea construction processes.* Newark, Delaware: International Reading Association.

Afflerbach, P., & Johnston, P. (1984). On the use of verbal reports in reading research. *Journal of Reading Behavior, 16,* 307–322.

Ahmed, M. O. (1988). *Vocabulary learning strategies: A case study of Sudanese learners of English.* Unpublished doctoral dissertation, University College of North Wales, Bangor, UK.

Albertini, J. (1990). Coherence in deaf students' writing. In J. K. Peyton (Ed.), *Students and teachers writing together: Perspectives on journal writing* (pp. 127–136). Alexandria, VA: Teachers of English to Speakers of Other Languages.

Al-Braik, M. S. (1986). *Investigation of the successful attributes of English as a second language of Saudi Arabian students studying in the United States of America.* Unpublished doctoral dissertation, Pennsylvania State University, University Park, PA.

Aliweh, A. M. (1989). *The short- and long-term effect of communication strategy instruction on the speaking proficiency of Egyptian college students.* Unpublished doctoral dissertation, State University of New York at Buffalo.

Allen, P., Fröhlich, M., & Spada, N. (1984). *The communicative orientation of language teaching: An observation scheme.* In J. Handscombe, R. A. Orem, & B. P. Taylor (Eds.), *On TESOL '83* (pp. 231–252). Washington, DC: TESOL.

Anderson, J. R. (1976). *Language, memory, and thought.* Hillsdale, NJ: Erlbaum.

Anderson, J. R. (1983). *The architecture of cognition.* Cambridge: Harvard University Press.

Anderson, J. R. (1985). *Cognitive psychology and its implications.* 2nd ed. New York: Freeman.

Anderson, M. J., Hawes, K., Heerman, C. E., Johns, K. M., Seeber, S., Seltzer, K., Shaffer, J., & Silliman, B. (1983). Reading attitudes of college students: Progress toward adequate assessment. *Reading Improvement, 20,* 120–124.

Anderson, N. J. (1989). *Reading comprehension tests versus academic reading: What are second language readers doing?* Unpublished doctoral dissertation, University of Texas at Austin.

Anderson, N. J. (1991). Individual differences in strategy use in second language reading and testing. *Modern Language Journal, 75*, 460–472.

Anderson, N. J. (1992). *A preliminary investigation into the relationships between reading comprehension and language learning strategies, personality type and language aptitude.* Paper presented at the annual Second Language Reading Colloquium, Teachers of English to Speakers of Other Languages, Vancouver, British Columbia, Canada.

Anderson, N. J., Bachman, L. F., Perkins, K., & Cohen, A. D. (1991). An exploratory study into the construct validity of a reading comprehension test: Triangulation of data sources. *Language Testing, 8*, 41–66.

Atkinson, R. C., & Raugh, M. R. (1975). An application of the mnemonic keyword method to the acquisition of a Russian vocabulary. *Journal of Experimental Psychology: Human Learning and Memory, 104*, 126–133.

Au, S. Y. (1988). A critical appraisal of Gardner's social-psychological theory of second-language (L2) learning. *Language Learning, 38*, 75–100.

Ausubel, D. (1968). *Educational psychology: A cognitive approach.* New York: Holt, Rinehart & Winston.

Backlund, P. (1990). Oral activities in the English classroom. In S. Hynds & D. L. Rubin (Eds.), *Perspectives on talk and learning* (pp. 227–244). Urbana, IL: National Council of Teachers of English.

Bacon, S. (1992). Authentic listening in Spanish: How learners adjust their strategies to the difficulty of the input. *Hispania, 75*, 398–412.

Bailey, K. M. (1983). Competitiveness and anxiety in adult second language learning: Looking at and through the diary studies. In H. W. Seliger & M. H. Long (Eds.), *Classroom oriented research in second language acquisition* (pp. 67–103). Rowley, MA: Newbury House.

Bailey, K. M. (1991). Diary studies of classroom language learning: The doubting game and the believing game. In E. Sadtono (Ed.), *Language acquisition and the second/foreign language classroom* (pp. 60–102). Singapore: SEAMEO Regional Language Center.

Bailey, K. M., & Ochsner, R. (1983). A methodological review of the diary studies: Windmill tilting or social science? In K. M. Bailey, M. H. Long, & S. Peck (Eds.), *Second language acquisition studies* (pp. 188–198). Rowley, MA: Newbury House. Now Boston: Heinle & Heinle.

Baily, C. A. (1992). *Getting the message across: A study of compensation strategy use in writing by adult foreign language learners using Système-D as an unobtrusive observation tool.* Unpublished doctoral dissertation, Vanderbilt University, Nashville, TN.

Bakan, D. (1954). A reconsideration of the problem of introspection. *Psychological Bulletin, 51*, 105–118.

Baker, L., & Brown, A. L. (1984). Metacognitive skills and reading. In D. P. Pearson (Ed.), *Handbook of reading research* (pp. 353–394). New York: Longman.

Bandura, A. (1992). *Social foundations of thought and action: A social-cognitive theory.* Englewood Cliffs, NJ: Prentice Hall.

Banks, J. A., & Banks, C. A. M. (1993). *Multicultural education: Issues and perspectives* (2nd ed.). Boston: Allyn & Bacon.

Bardwick, J. (1971). *Psychology of women: A study of bicultural conflicts.* New York: Harper & Row.

Barnett, M. A. (1988a). Teaching reading strategies: How methodology affects language course articulation. *Foreign Language Annals, 21,* 109–116.

Barnett, M. A. (1988b). Reading through context: How real and perceived strategy use affects L2 comprehension. *Modern Language Journal, 72*(2), 150–162.

Barnhardt, S. (1992). *Language learning strategies in a high school Russian classroom.* Unpublished master's thesis, Georgetown University.

Bascur, S. (1994). *The relationship among language learning strategies, sex, language learning, learning styles, career choice, and Spanish language achievement.* Unpublished doctoral dissertation, University of Alabama.

Batchelder, D & Warner, E. G., (1977). *Beyond experience: The experiential approach to cross-cultural education.* Brattleboro, VT: Experiment in International Living.

Bates, E. (1972), *Language and context.* New York: Academic.

Bedell, D. (1993). *Cross-cultural variation in choice of language learning strategies: A mainland Chinese investigation with comparison to previous studies.* Unpublished master's thesis, University of Alabama, Tuscaloosa, AL.

Beebe, L. M. (1988). Five sociolinguistic approaches to second language acquisition. In L. M. Beebe (Ed.), *Issues in second language acquisition: Multiple perspectives* (pp. 43–77). Rowley, MA: Newbury House.

Belenky, M. F., Clinchy, B. M., Goldberger, N. R., & Tarule, J. M. (1986). *Women's ways of knowing: The development of self, voice, and mind.* New York: Basic Books.

Belmont, J. M., Butterfield, E. C., & Ferretti, R. P. (1982). To secure transfer of training instruct self-management skills. In D. K. Detterman & R. J. Sternberg (Eds.), *How much can intelligence be increased?* Norwood, NJ: Ablex.

Bereiter, C., & Bird, M. (1985). Use of thinking aloud in identification and teaching of reading comprehension strategies. *Cognition and Instruction, 2,* 131–156.

Bergman, J. (1992). SAIL: A way to success and independence for low achieving readers. *The Reading Teacher, 45,* 598–602.

Bernhardt, E. B. (1991). *Reading development in a second language: Theoretical, empirical, and classroom perspectives.* Norwood, NJ: Ablex Publishing Corporation.

Bialystok, E. (1981). The role of conscious strategies in second language proficiency. *Modern Language Journal, 65*(1), 24–35.

Bialystok, E., & Fröhlich, M. (1978). Variables of classroom achievement in second language learning. *Modern Language Journal, 62* (7), 327–336.

Bimmel-Esteban, A., Janssens, E., Mulder, W., Sodoyer, A., & Stok, B. (1991–1993). *Code genial.* Den Bosch: Malmberg.

Birckbichler, D., & Omaggio, A. (1978). Diagnosing and responding to individual learner needs. *Modern Language Journal, 62*(7), 336–344.

Block, E. (1986). The comprehension strategies of second language readers. *TESOL Quarterly, 20,* 463–494.

Block, J. H. (1973). Conception of sex roles: Some cross-cultural and longitudinal perspectives. *American Psychologist, 28,* 512–526.

Boring, E. G., (1953). A history of introspection. *Psychological Bulletin, 50*(3), 169–189.

Boucher, A-M., & Ladouceur, M. (1988). *Communication plus 3.* Montreal, QC: Centre Educatif et Culturel.

Bransford, J. D. (1979). *Human cognition: Learning, understanding, remembering.* Belmont, CA: Wadsworth.

Brindley, G. (1991). *Learnability in the ESL classroom.* Paper presented at SEAMEO RELC 26th Regional Seminar.

Brinton, D. M., Snow, M. A., & Wesche, M. B. (1989). *Content-based second language instruction.* New York: Newbury House.

Brodkey, D., & Shore, H. (1976). Student personality and success in an English language program. *Language Learning, 26*(1), 153–162.

Brooks, L. W., Simutis, Z. M., & O'Neil, H. F., Jr. (1983). The role of individual differences in learning strategies research. In R. Dillon & R. Schmeck (Eds.), *Individual differences in cognition* (Vol. 2, pp. 219–251). New York: Academic Press.

Brooks, N. (1968). Teaching culture in the foreign language classroom. *Foreign Language Annals,* 204–217.

Brown, A. L., Bransford, J. D., Ferrara, R. A., & Campione, J. C. (1983). Learning, remembering, and understanding. In J. H. Flavell & E. M. Markham (Eds.) *Carmichael's Manual of Child Psychology,* (Vol. 1, pp. 14–21). New York: John Wiley.

Brown, A. L., & Palincsar, A. S. (1982). Inducing strategic learning from texts by means of informed self-control training. *Topics in Learning and Learning Disabilities, 2,* 1–17.

Brown, C. (1985a). Requests for specific language input: Differences between older and younger language learners. In S. Gass & C. G. Madden (Eds.), *Input in second language acquisition* (pp. 272–281). Rowley, MA: Newbury House. Now Boston: Heinle & Heinle.

Brown, C. (1985b). Two windows on the classroom world: Diary studies and participant observation differences. In P. Larson, E. L. Judd, & D. S. Messerschmitt (Eds.), *On TESOL '94: A brave new world for TESOL* (pp. 121–134). Washington, DC: Teachers of English to Speakers of Other Languages.

Brown, G., & Yule, G. (1983). *Teaching the spoken language: An approach based on the analysis of conversational English.* Cambridge: Cambridge University Press.

Brown, H. D. (1980). Principles of language learning and teaching. Englewood Cliffs, NJ: Prentice Hall.

Brown, H. D. (1987). *Principles of language learning and teaching: A 15-week program of strategies for success*. 2nd edition. Englewood Cliffs, NJ: Prentice-Hall.

Brown. H. D. (1989). *A practical guide to language learning: Creating your own pathway to success*. New York: McGraw-Hill.

Brown, H. D. (1991). *Breaking the language barrier*. Yarmouth, ME: Intercultural Press.

Brown, H. D. (1994). *Principles of language learning and teaching*. (3rd ed.). Englewood Cliffs, NJ: Prentice-Hall Regents.

Brown, J. S., Collins, A., & Duguid, P. (1989). Situated cognition and the culture of learning. *Educational Researcher, 18*(1), 32–42.

Brown, T. S., & Perry, F. L. (1991). A comparison of three learning strategies for ESL vocabulary acquisition. *TESOL Quarterly, 25*(4), 655–670.

Brown-Azarowicz, M., Stannard, C., & Goldin, M. (1987). *Yes! You can learn a foreign language*. Lincolnwood, IL: Passport Books.

Bult, E. H., Carolus, C. G., Harmsma, G., Huijssoon, B., Peppelenbos, C., Vorenkamp, J. B., & Wieland, P. C. (1992/1993). *Goed Nederlands*. Groningen: Jacob Dijkstra.

Busch, D. (1982). Introversion-extraversion and the ESL proficiency of Japanese students. *Language Learning, 32*(1), 109–132.

Byrne, D. (1986). *Teaching oral English*. Harlow: Longman.

Byrnes, H. (1984). The role of listening comprehension: A theoretical base. *Foreign Language Annals, 17*, 317–329.

Canale, M., & Swain, M. (1980). Theoretical bases of communicative approaches to second language teaching and testing. *Applied Linguistics, 1*, 1–47.

Carpenter, T., Fennema, E., Peterson, P. L., Chiang, C., & Loef, M. (1989). Using knowledge of children's mathematics thinking in classroom teaching: An experimental study. *American Educational Research Journal, 26*, 499–532.

Carrell, P. L. (1989). Metacognitive awareness and second language reading. *Modern Language Journal, 73*(2), 121–134.

Carrell, P. L., Pharis, B. G., & Liberto, J. C. (1989). Metacognitive strategy training for ESL reading. *TESOL Quarterly, 23*(4), 647–677.

Carter, E. (1988). The relationship of field dependent/independent cognitive style to Spanish language achievement and proficiency. *Modern Language Journal, 72*, 21–30.

Cavalcanti, M. C. (1984). Frames and schemes in FL reading. *Anais VENPULI* Vol. 2. Sao Paulo, Brazil: Pontificia Universidade Catolica de Saõ Paulo, 486–506.

Cavalcanti, M. C. (1987). Investigating Fl reading performance through pause protocols. In C. Faerch & G. Kasper (Eds.), *Introspection in second language research* (pp. 230–250). Clevedon, England: Multilingual Matters.

Chamot, A. U. (1987). The learning strategies of ESL students. In A. L. Wenden & J. Rubin (Eds.), *Learner strategies in language learning* (pp. 71–83). New York: Prentice Hall.

Chamot, A. U. (1993). Student responses to learning strategy instruction in the foreign language classroom. *Foreign Language Annals, 26,* 308–321.

Chamot, A. U., Barnhardt, S., El-Dinary, P. B., Carbonaro, G., & Robbins, J. (1993). *Methods for teaching learning strategies in the foreign language classroom and assessment of language skills for instruction: Final report.* Washington, DC: Clearinghouse on Languages and Linguistics.

Chamot, A. U., Dale, M., O'Malley, J. M., & Spanos, G. A. (1992). *Learning and problem solving strategies of ESL students.* Paper presented at the annual meeting of the American Educational Research Association, San Francisco, CA.

Chamot, A. U., Dale, T., O'Malley, J. M., & Spanos, G. (1993). Learning and problem solving strategies of ESL students. *Bilingual Research Journal, 16*(3&4), 1–38.

Chamot, A. U., & Küpper, L. (1989). Learning strategies in foreign language instruction. *Foreign Language Annals, 22,* 13–24.

Chamot, A. U., Küpper, L., & Impink-Hernandez, M. V. (1988a). *A study of learning strategies in foreign language instruction: Findings of the longitudinal study.* McLean, VA: Interstate Research Associates.

Chamot, A. U., Küpper, L., & Impink-Hernandez, M. V. (1988b). *A study of learning strategies in foreign language instruction: The third year and final report.* McLean, VA: Interstate Research Associates.

Chamot, A. U. Küpper, L. Thompson, I., Barrueta, M., & Toth, S. (1990). *Learning strategies in the foreign language classroom: Resource guides for listening comprehension, reading comprehension, speaking, and writing.* McLean, VA: Interstate Research Associates.

Chamot, A. U., & O'Malley, J. M. (1984). *Using learning strategies to develop bilingual education* (National Clearinghouse for Bilingual Education). No. 16.

Chamot, A. U., & O'Malley, J. M. (1986). *A cognitive academic language learning approach: An ESL content-based curriculum.* Wheaton, MD: National Clearinghouse for Bilingual Education.

Chamot, A. U., & O'Malley, J. M. (1987). The Cognitive Academic Language Learning Approach: A bridge to the mainstream. *TESOL Quarterly, 21*(2), 227–249.

Chamot, A. U., & O'Malley, J. M. (1989b). The cognitive academic language learning approach. In P. Rigg & V. G. Allen (Eds.), *When they don't all speak English: Integrating the ESL student into the regular classroom* (pp. 108–125). Urbana, IL: National Council of Teachers of English.

Chamot, A. U., & O'Malley, J. M. (1994a). *The CALLA handbook: Implementing the Cognitive Academic Language Learning Approach.* Reading, MA: Addison-Wesley.

Chamot, A. U., & O'Malley, J. M. (1994b). Language learner and learning strategies. In N. C. Ellis (Ed.), *Implicit and explicit learning of languages* (pp. 371–392). London: Academic.

Chamot, A. U., O'Malley, J. M., & Küpper, L. (1992). *Building bridges: Content and learning strategies for ESL*. Boston: Heinle & Heinle.

Chamot, A. U., O'Malley, J. M. Küpper, L., & Impink-Hernandez, M. V. (1987). *A study of learning strategies in foreign language instruction: First year report*. Rosslyn, VA: InterAmerica Research Associates.

Chamot, A. U., Robbins, J., & El-Dinary, P. (1993). *Learning strategies in Japanese foreign language instruction: Final report*. ERIC Document Reproduction Service No. EJ385531.

Chamot, A. U., & Rubin, J. (1993). Critical comments on Janie Rees-Miller's A critical appraisal of learner training: Theoretical bases and teaching implications. *TESOL Quarterly, 27*(4), 771–781.

Chang, A. S. C. (1989). *Do students' motives in learning a subject affect their choice of learning strategies?* Paper presented at the annual meeting of the Australian Association for Research in Education, Adelaide, South Australia. ERIC Document Reproduction Service No. ED317572.

Chang, A. S. C. (1990). *Streaming and language behavior*. Paper presented at the annual convention of the International Council of Psychologists, Tokyo, Japan.

Chang, S-J. (1990). *A study of language learning behaviors of Chinese students at the University of Georgia and the relation of those behaviors to oral proficiency and other factors*. Unpublished doctoral dissertation, University of Georgia, Athens, GA.

Chapelle, C., & Mizuno, S. (1989). Students' strategies with learner-controlled CALL. *CALICO Journal, 7*, 25–47.

Chapelle, C., & Roberts, C. (1984). *Field independence and ambiguity tolerance as predictors of proficiency in English as a second language*. Paper presented at the 18th Annual Convention of Teachers of English to Speakers of Other Languages.

Chapelle, C., & Roberts, C. (1986). Field independence and ambiguity tolerance as predictors of proficiency in English as a second language. *Language Learning, 36*(1), 27–46.

Chastain, K. (1975). Affective and ability factors in second language acquisition. *Language Learning, 25*(1), 153–161.

Chen, S-Q. (1990). A study of communication strategies in interlanguage production by Chinese EFL learners. *Language Learning, 40*, 155–187.

Clark, J. L. D. (1981). *"Can do" scales*. Washington: Center for Applied Linguistics.

Cohen, A. D. (1977). Successful second-language speakers: A review of research literature. *Balshanut Shimoshit: The Journal of the Israel Association of Applied Linguists, 1*, 3–21.

Cohen, A. D. (1980). *Testing language ability in the classroom*. Rowley, MA: Newbury House.

Cohen, A. D. (1983). Studying second-language learning strategies: How do we get the information? *Applied Linguistics, 5*(2), 101–111.

Cohen, A. D. (1984). On taking language tests: What the students report. *Language Testing, 1*, 70–81.

Cohen, A. D. (1987a). Studying language learning strategies: How we get the information. In A. L. Wenden & J. Rubin (Eds.), *Learner strategies in language learning* (pp. 31–40). Englewood Cliffs, NJ: Prentice Hall.

Cohen, A. D. (1987b). Student processing of feedback on their compositions. In A. L. Wenden & J. Rubin (Eds.), *Learner strategies in language learning* (pp. 57–69). Englewood Cliffs, NJ: Prentice-Hall.

Cohen, A. D. (1987c). Using verbal reports in research. In C. Faerch & G. Kasper (Eds.) *Introspection in second language research* (pp. 82–95). Clevedon, England: Multilingual Matters.

Cohen, A. D. (1990a). *Strategies in target-language learning: Insights from research.* Paper presented at the World Congress of Applied Linguistics, sponsored by the International Association of Applied Linguistics.

Cohen, A. D. (1990b). *Language learning: Insights for learners, teachers and researchers.* NY: Newbury House/Harper & Row.

Cohen, A. D. (1994). English for academic purposes in Brazil: The use of summary tasks. In C. Hill & K. Parry (Eds.), *From testing to assessment: English as an international language* (pp. 174–204). London: Longman.

Cohen, A. D., & Aphek, E. (1979). *Easifying second language learning.* Report submitted to the Jacob Hiatt Institute. Jerusalem: Hebrew University of Jerusalem, School of Education. ERIC Document Reproduction Service No. ED163753.

Cohen, A. D., & Aphek, E. (1981). Easifying second language learning. *Studies in Second Language Acquisition, 3*, 221–235.

Cohen, A. D., & Cavalcanti, M. C. (1987). Giving and getting feedback on compositions: A comparison of teacher and student verbal report. *Evaluation and Research in Education, 1*(2), 63–73.

Cohen, A. D., & Cavalcanti, M. C. (1990). Feedback on compositions: Teacher and student verbal reports. In B. Kroll (Ed.), *Second language writing: Research insights for the classroom* (pp. 155–177). Cambridge: Cambridge University Press.

Cohen, A. D., Glasman, H., Rosenbaum-Cohen, P. R., Ferrara, J., & Fine, J. (1979). Reading English for specialized purposes: Discourse analysis and the use of student informants. *TESOL Quarterly, 13*(4), 551–564.

Cohen, A. D., & Hosenfeld, C. (1981). Some uses of mentalistic data in second-language research. *Language Learning, 31*, 285–313.

Cohen, A. D., & Olshtain, E. (1993). The production of speech acts by EFL learners. *TESOL Quarterly, 27*, 33–56.

Cohen, A. D., Weaver, S. J., & Li, T. Y. (1995). *The impact of strategies-based instruction on speaking a foreign language* (Research Report). Minneapolis: University of Minnesota, Center for Advanced Research on Language Acquisition (CARLA).

Cohen, J. (1977). *Statistical power analysis for the behavioral sciences.* (Rev. ed.) New York: Academic Press.

Cohen, J. (1988). *Statistical power analysis for the behavioral sciences* (Rev. ed.). Hillsdale, NJ: Erlbaum.

Cook, V. (1991). *Second language learning and language teaching.* New York: Edward Arnold.

Corrales, O., & Call, M. E. (1989). At a loss for words: The use of communication strategies to convey lexical meaning. *Foreign Language Annals 22,* 227–240.

Costa, A. (Ed.). (1990). *Developing minds: The teaching of thinking skills.* Alexandria, VA: Association for Supervision and Curriculum Development.

Crookall, D. (1983). Learner instruction: A neglected strategy — Parts 1 and 2. *Modern English Teacher, 11*(1), 31–33; *11*(2), 41–42.

Crookes, G., & Schmidt, R. (1989). Motivation: Reopening the research agenda. *University of Hawai'i Working Papers in ESL,* 8, 217–256.

Crookes, G., & Schmidt, R. (1991). Motivation: Reopening the research agenda. *Language Learning, 41,* 469–512.

Cross, D. (1983). Sex differences in achievement. *System, 11,* 159–162.

Curry, L. (1991). *Integrating concepts of cognitive or learning style: A review with attention to psychometric standards.* Unpublished manuscript.

Curtain, H. A., & Pesola, C. A. (1988). *Languages and children: Making the match.* Reading, MA: Addison-Wesley.

Dadour, S. (1995). *The effectiveness of selected learning strategies in developing oral communication of English Department students in faculties of education.* Unpublished doctoral dissertation, Mansoura University, Damietta, Egypt.

Dai, J. (1989). *Metacognitive strategy use: A comparative study of Chinese graduate students reading English as a second language at universities in the United States.* Unpublished doctoral dissertation, Oklahoma State University, Stillwater, OK.

d'Anglejean, A., & Renaud, C. (1985). Learner characteristics and second language acquisition: A multivariate study of adult immigrants and some thoughts on methodology. *Language Learning, 35,* 1–19.

Dansereau, D. (1985). Learning strategy research. In J. W. Segal, S. F. Chipman, & R. C. Glaser (Eds.). *Thinking and learning skills: Relating learning to basic research* (pp. 209–240). Hillsdale, NJ: Erlbaum.

Davey, E. (1983). Think-aloud — modeling the cognitive processes of reading comprehension. *Journal of Reading, 27,* 44–47.

Davis, E., & Abas, H. (1991). Second language learning strategies utilized by some members of language departments at four institutions — Sulawesi, Indonesia. Sulawesi, Indonesia: Summer Institute of Linguistics.

deGroot, A. (1965). *Thought and choice in chess.* The Hague, The Netherlands: Mouton.

Devine, J. (1987). General language competence and adult second language reading. In J. Devine, P. L. Carroll, and D. E. Eskey (Eds.), *Research in reading English as a second language* (pp. 73–86). Washington DC: Teachers of English to Speakers of Other Languages.

Dickinson, L. (1987). *Self-instruction in language learning.* Cambridge: Cambridge University Press.

Dobrin, D. N. (1986). Protocols once more. *College English, 48,* 713–725.

Docking, R. A., & Thornton, J. A. (1979). *Anxiety and the school experience.* (Research Rep.). Canberra: Australian Education Research and Development Committee.

Dörnyei, Z. (1990). Conceptualizing motivation in foreign language learning. *Language Learning, 40,* 45–78.

Dörnyei, Z. (1995). On the teachability of communication strategies. *TESOL Quarterly, 29,* 55–85.

Dörnyei, Z., & Thurrell, S. (1994). Teaching conversational skills intensively: Course, content, and rationale. *ELT Journal, 48,* 39–49.

Doughty, C. (1991). *Resilient and fragile features in SLA.* Paper presented at the SEAMEO RELC 26th Annual Seminar.

Douglas, M. (1992). *Kanji learning strategies of learners of Japanese as a foreign language.* Unpublished doctoral dissertation, University of Southern California at Los Angeles.

Dreyer, C. (1992). *Learner variables as predictors of ESL proficiency.* Unpublished doctoral dissertation, University of Potchefstroom, South Africa.

Duker, S. (1971). *Listening readings.* New York: Scarecrow.

Eccles, J. S. (1989). Bringing young women to math and science. In M. Crawford & M. Gentry (Eds.), *Gender and thought: Psychological perspectives* (pp. 36–58). New York: Springer.

Ehrman, M. E., & Oxford, R. L. (1987). *Adult language learning: Personality type, strategy, and style.* Paper presented at the Symposium on Second Language Learning Styles and Strategies, Center for Applied Linguistics, Washington, DC.

Ehrman, M. E., & Oxford, R. L. (1988). Psychological type and adult language learning strategies: A pilot study. *Journal of Psychological Type, 16,* 22–32.

Ehrman, M. E., & Oxford, R. L. (1989). Effects of sex differences, career choice and psychological type on adults' language learning strategies. *Modern Language Journal, 73*(1), 1–13.

Ehrman, M. E., & Oxford, R. L. (1990). Adult learning styles and strategies in an intensive training setting. *Modern Language Journal 74,* 311–326.

El-Dinary, P. (1993). *Teachers learning, adapting and implementing strategies based instruction in reading.* Doctoral dissertation submitted to the Faculty of the Graduate School of The University of Maryland, College Park, MD.

Ellis, G., & Sinclair, B. (1989). *Learning to learn English: A course in learner training.* Cambridge: Cambridge University Press.

Ellis, R. (1986). *Understanding second language acquisition.* New York: Oxford University Press.

Ellis, R. (1987). *Second language acquisition in context.* London: Prentice Hall.

Ely, C. (1994). Preparing second language teachers for strategy instruction: An integrated approach. *Foreign Language Annals, 27*(3), 335–342.

Enright, D. S., & McCloskey, M. L. (1988). *Integrating English.* Reading, MA: Addison-Wesley.

Ericsson, K. A. (1988). Concurrent verbal reports on text comprehension: A review. *Text, 8,* 295–325.

Ericsson, K. A., & Simon, H. A. (1980). Verbal reports as data. *Psychological Review, 87,* 215–251.

Ericsson, K. A., & Simon, H. A. (1984). *Protocol analysis: Verbal reports as data.* Cambridge: MIT Press.

Faerch, C., & Kasper, G. (Eds.). (1983). *Strategies in interlanguage communication.* London: Longman.

Faerch, C., & Kasper, G. (1986). One learner — two languages: Investigating types of interlanguage knowledge. In J. House & S. Blum-Kulka, *Interlingual and intercultural communication* (pp. 211–227). Tubingen: Gunter Narr.

Faerch, C., & Kasper, G. (1987). From product to process — introspective methods in second language research. In C. Faerch & G. Kasper (Eds.), *Introspection in second language research* (pp. 5–23). Clevedon, England: Multilingual Matters.

Fanselow, J. F. (1979). *First, I'd like to ask you a couple of questions!* Unpublished manuscript, Teachers College, Columbia University, NY.

Farquharson, M. (1989). *Learning styles of Arab students in EFL classrooms.* Paper presented at the annual meeting of International Teachers of English to Speakers of Other Languages, San Antonio, TX.

Feldman, U., & Stemmer, B. (1987). Thin_ aloud a__ a retrospective da__ in C-te___ taking: diffe____ languages — diff_____ learners — sa__ approaches? In C. Faerch & G. Kasper (Eds.), *Introspection in second language research* (pp. 251–267). Clevedon, England: Multilingual Matters.

Feyten, C. (1991). The power of listening ability: An overlooked dimension in language acquisition. *Modern Language Journal, 75,* 173–80.

Flaitz, J., Feyten, C., Fox, S., & Mukherjee, K. (1995). Raising general awareness of language learning strategies: A little goes a long way. *Hispania, 78*(2), 337–348.

Flower, L., & Hayes, J. R. (1981). Plans that guide the composing process. In C. H. Frederiksen & J. F. Dominic (Eds.), *Writing: The nature, development, and teaching of written communication.* Hillsdale, NJ: Erlbaum.

Freeman, D. (1989). Teacher training, development, and decision-making. *TESOL Quarterly, 23*(1), 27–45.

Fuller, G. E. (1987). *How to learn a foreign language.* Washington, DC: Storm King Press.

Gagné, E. D. (1985). *The cognitive psychology of school learning.* Boston: Little, Brown.

Gaies, S. J. (1983). Investigation of language classroom process. *TESOL Quarterly, 17,* 205–217.

Gagné, E. D., Yekovich, C. W., & Yekovich, F. R. (1993). *The cognitive psychology of school learning*. 2nd Ed. New York: HarperCollins.

Galloway, V., & Labarca, A. (1993). *Visión y voz*. Boston: Heinle & Heinle.

Gamberg, R., Kwak, W., Hutchings, M., & Altheim, J. (1988). *Learning and loving it: Theme studies in the classroom*. Portsmouth, NH: Heinemann.

Gardner, R. C. (1979). *Sociopsychological aspects of second language acquisition*. In H. Giles & R. St. Clair (Eds.), *Language and social psychology* (pp. 193–220). Oxford: Blackwell.

Gardner, R. C. (1985). *Social psychology and second language learning: The role of attitudes and motivation*. London: Edward Arnold.

Gardner, R. C. (1988). The socioeducational model of second language learning: Assumptions, findings, and issues. *Language Learning, 38*, 101–126.

Gardner, R. C., & Lambert, W. P. (1959). Motivation variables in second language acquisition. *Canadian Journal of Psychology, 13*, 266–272.

Gardner, R. C., & MacIntyre, P. D. (1993). A student's contribution to second-language learning. Part II: Affective variables. *Language Teaching, 26*, 1–11.

Garner, R. (1987). *Metacognition and reading comprehension*. Norwood, NJ: Heinemann.

Garza, T. (1987). Russians learning English: An analysis of foreign language instruction in Soviet specialized schools. Ann Arbor, MI: University Microfilms.

Gass, S. (1988). Integrating research areas: A framework for second language studies. *Applied Linguistics, 9*, 198–217.

Gaston, J. (1984). *Cultural awareness teaching techniques*. Brattleboro, VT: ProLingua Associates.

Geertz, C. (1983). *Local knowledge*. New York: Basic.

Genesee, F. (1978). Individual differences in second-language learning. *Canadian Modern Language Review, 34*(3), 490–504.

Gill, M. M., & Hartmann, P. (1993). *Get it? Got it!* Boston: Heinle & Heinle.

Gordon, C. (1987). *The effect of testing method on achievement in reading comprehension tests in English in English as a foreign language*. Unpublished master's thesis, Tel-Aviv University, Ramat-Aviv, Israel.

Grala, M., Oxford, R. L., & Schleppegrell, M. (1987). *Improving your language learning: Strategies for Peace Corps volunteers*. Washington, DC: Center for Applied Linguistics.

Green, J. M. (1991). *Language learning strategies of Puerto Rican university students*. Paper presented at the annual meeting of Puerto Rico Teachers of English to Speakers of Other Languages, San Juan, PR.

Green, J. M. (1992). *Additional analyses of Puerto Rican strategy data*. Unpublished manuscript, University of Puerto Rico at Mayaguez.

Green, J. M., & Oxford, R. L. (1993). *Learning strategies: Patterns of use by gender and proficiency*. Paper presented at the annual meeting of International Teachers of English to Speakers of Other Languages, Atlanta, GA.

Green, J., Oxford, R. L., & Green, C. (1995). *When students write their language learning histories.* Paper presented at the annual meeting of Teachers of English to Speakers of Other Languages, Long Beach, CA.

Griggs, S. A. (1991). *Learning styles counseling.* Ann Arbor: ERIC Counseling and Personnel Services Clearinghouse. ERIC Document Reproduction Service No. ED341890

Guiora, A. Z., Paluszny, M., Beit-Hallahmi, B., Catford, J. C., Foley, R. E., & Dull, C. Y. (1975). Language and person studies in language behavior. *Language Learning, 25*(1), 43–61.

Hajer, M. (1993). Onderwijs in schoolse taalvaardigheid. In C. Blankenstijn and A. Scheper (Eds.), *Taalvaardigheid: symposiumbundel.* Dordtrecht: ICG Publications.

Hajer, M., Meestringa, T., Oxford, R. L., & Park-Oh, Y. (1994). Language learning strategies (LLS): State of the art in an international perspective. *Dutch contributions to AILA (International Association of Applied Linguistics) selected in honor of Johan Matter* (pp. 80–95). Toegepaste Taalwetenschap in artikelen 46/47. Amsterdam: Nederlandse Vereniging voor Toegepaste Taalwetenschap (Netherlands Association for Applied Linguistics).

Hall, E. T., & Hall, M. R. (1990). *Understanding cultural differences.* Yarmouth, ME: Intercultural Press.

Hamp-Lyons, L. (1985). Two approaches to teaching reading: A classroom-based study. *Reading a Foreign Language, 3,* 363–373.

Hansen, J., & Stansfield, C. (1981). The relationship of field dependent-independent cognitive styles and foreign language achievement. *Language Learning, 3*(2), 349–367.

Hansen, J., & Stansfield, C. (1982). Student-teacher cognitive styles and foreign language achievement: A preliminary study. *Modern Language Journal, 66*(2), 263–273.

Hansen, L. (1984). Cultural differences in English language testing: Modality preference, test anxiety, and field sensitivity. *Language Learning and Communication: A Journal of Applied Linguistics in Chinese and English, 3,* 375–385.

Harris, K. R., & Graham, S. (1992). Self-regulated strategy development: A part of the writing process. In M. Pressley, K. R. Harris, & J. T. Guthrie (Eds.), *Promoting academic competence and literacy in schools* (pp. 277–309). New York: Academic Press.

Harshbarger, B., Ross, T., Tafoya, S., & Via, J. (1986, Apr.). *Dealing with multiple learning styles in the ESL classroom.* Symposium presented at the annual meeting of Teachers of English to Speakers of Other Languages, San Francisco, CA.

Hawkins, E. (1984). *Awareness of language: An introduction.* Cambridge: Cambridge University Press.

Helfeldt, J., & Henk, W. A. (1990, April). Reciprocal question-answer relationships: An instructional technique for at-risk readers. *Journal of Reading,* 509–514.

Hess, R. D., & Azuma, H. (1991). Cultural support for schooling: Contrasts between Japan and the United States. *Educational Researcher, 20*(9), 2–8.

Hofstede, G. (1986). Cultural differences in teaching and learning. *International Journal of Intercultural Relations, 10*, 301–320.

Holec, H. (1980). Learner instruction: Meeting the needs of self-directed learning. In H. B. Altman & C. V. James (Eds.), *Foreign language teaching: Meeting individual needs*. Oxford: Pergamon.

Holec, H. (1988). *Autonomy and self-directed learning: Present fields of application*. Strasbourg: Council of Europe.

Holm, S. (1979). A simple sequentially rejective multiple test procedure. *Scandinavian Journal of Statistics, 6*, 65–70.

Horiba, Y. (1990). Narrative comprehension processes: A study of native and nonnative readers of Japanese. *Modern Language Journal, 74*(2), 188–202.

Horwitz, E. K. (1988). The beliefs about language learning of beginning university foreign language students. *Modern Language Journal, 72*, 283–294.

Horwitz, E. K. (1990). Attending to the affective domain in the foreign language classroom. In S. S. Magnan (Ed.), *Shifting the instructional focus to the learner* (pp. 15–33). Middlebury, VT: Northeast Conference on the Teaching of Foreign Languages.

Horwitz, E. K., & Young, D. J. (1991). *Language anxiety: From theory and research to classroom practice*. Englewood Cliffs, NJ: Prentice-Hall.

Hosenfeld, C. (1976). Learning about learning: Discovering our students' strategies. *Foreign Language Annals, 9*, 117–129.

Hosenfeld, C. (1977). *A learning-teaching view of second-language instruction: The learning strategies of second language learners with reading-grammar tasks*. Unpublished doctoral dissertation, Ohio State University, Columbus, OH.

Hosenfeld, C. (1979). A learning-teaching view of second language instruction. *Foreign Language Annals, 12*(1), 51–57.

Hosenfeld, C. (1984). Case studies of ninth grade readers. In J. C. Alderson & A. H. Urquhart (Eds.), *Reading in a foreign language* (pp. 231–249). London: Longman.

Hosenfeld, C., Arnold, V., Kirchofer, J., Laciura, J., & Wilson, L. (1981). Second language reading: A curricular sequence for teaching reading strategies. *Foreign Language Annals, 14*, 415–422.

Howell-Richardson, C. (1989, Aug.). Using a diary. *EFL Gazette, 7*.

Huang, X-H. (1984). *An investigation of learning strategies in oral communication that Chinese EFL learners in China employ*. Unpublished master's thesis, Chinese University of Hong Kong.

Huang, X-H., & van Naerssen, M. (1987). Learning strategies for oral communication. *Applied Linguistics, 8*, 287–307.

Irwin, J. W. (1991). *Teaching reading comprehension processes*, 2nd Ed. Englewood Cliffs, N. J.: Prentice Hall.

James, G. (1993). *Passages: Exploring spoken English*. Boston: Heinle & Heinle.

Johnson, K. E. (1992). Learning to teach: Instructional actions and decisions of pre-service ESL teachers. *TESOL Quarterly, 26*, 507–536.

Jones, R. A. (1977). *Psychological, social and personal factors in second language acquisition*. Unpublished master's thesis, University of California at Los Angeles. Cited in Bailey, K. M. (1983). Competitiveness and anxiety in adult second language learning: Looking *at* and *through* the diary studies. In H. W. Seliger & M. H. Long (Eds.), *Classroom-oriented research on second language acquisition* (pp. 67–103). Rowley, MA: Newbury House. Now Boston: Heinle & Heinle.

Jones, B. F., & Idol, L. (Eds.) (1990). *Dimensions of thinking and cognitive instruction*. Hillsdale, NJ: Erlbaum.

Jones, B. F., Palinscar, A. M., Ogle, D. S., & Carr, E. G. (1987). Strategic thinking: A cognitive focus. In B. F. Jones, A. M. Palinscar, D. S. Ogle, & E. G. Carr (Eds.), *Strategic thinking and learning: Cognitive instruction in the content area*. Alexandria, VA: Association for Supervision and Curriculum Development.

Kachru, Y. (1988). Cognitive and cultural styles in second language acquisition. *Annual Review of Applied Linguistics, 9*, 149–163.

Kern, R. G. (1989). Second language reading strategy instruction: Its effects on comprehension and word inference ability. *Modern Language Journal, 73*(2), 136–149.

Kidd, R., & Marquardson, B. (1993). *A sourcebook for integrating ESL and content instruction using the Foresee Approach*. Winnipeg, Manitoba: Manitoba Education and Training.

Kidd, R., & Marquardson, B. (1994). *A sourcebook for integrating ESL and content instruction using the Foresee Approach*. (Rev. ed.) Winnipeg, Manitoba: Manitoba Education and Training.

Kim, J-D. (1990). *A comparison of learning strategies of college students enrolled in beginning and advanced English as a second language*. Unpublished doctoral dissertation, Loma Linda University, Loma Linda, CA.

Klassen, J. M. (1994). *The language learning strategies of freshman English students in Taiwan: A case study*. Paper presented at the Third International Symposium and Book Fair on English Teaching, Taipei, Taiwan.

Kolb, D. (1985). Learning Strategy Inventory. Boston: McBer.

Kramarae, C. (1981). *Women and men speaking*. Rowley, MA: Newbury House.

Krings, H. P. (1987). The use of introspective data in translation. In C. Faerch & G. Kasper (Eds.), *Introspection in second language research* (pp. 159–176). Clevedon, England: Multilingual Matters.

Krippendorf, K. (1980). *Content analysis: An introduction to its methodology*. Beverly Hills: Sage.

Kruidenier, B. G., & Clément, R. (1985). *The effect of context on the composition and role of orientations in second language acquisition*. Quebec: International Centre for Research on Bilingualism.

Lakoff, R. (1975). *Language and woman's place*. New York: Harper & Row.

Larsen-Freeman, D. (1991). Second language acquisition research: Staking out the territory. *TESOL Quarterly, 25*, 315–350.

Larsen-Freeman, D., & Long, M. (1991). *An introduction to second language acquisition research*. London: Longman.

Lave, J. (1988). *The culture of acquisition and the practice of understanding*. IRL Report 88–00087. Palo Alto: Institute for Research on Learning.

Lave, J., & Wenger, E. (1991). *Situated learning: Legitimate peripheral participation*. Cambridge: Cambridge University Press.

Lavine, R. Z., & Oxford, R. L. (1994). *Needs assessment for the Spanish language intelligent tutor*. Boulder, CO: Microanalysis and Design.

Leaver, B. L. (1988). *Report on differences in modes of strategy instruction*. Unpublished manuscript, Defense Language Institute, Monterey, CA.

Leaver, B. L. (1990). *Navigating the DSL Czech course: A guide for students*. Monterey, CA: The Defense Language Institute.

Leaver, B. L., & Flank, S. (1987). *American-Soviet differences in teacher perspectives and behavior among teachers of foreign languages*. Washington, DC: ERIC Clearinghouse for Languages and Linguistics. ERIC Document Reproduction Service No. ED281355

Leinhardt, G. (1983). Novice and expert knowledge of individual students' achievement. *Educational Psychologist, 18*, 165–179.

Lieberman, D. A. (1979). Behaviorism and the mind: A limited call for a return to introspection. *American Psychologist, 34*, 319–333.

Lijmbach, B., Hacquebord, H., & Galema, C. (1991). *Weet wat je leest*. Groningen: Jacob Dijkstra.

Littlewood, W. (1981). *Communicative language teaching: An introduction*. Cambridge: Cambridge University Press.

LoCastro, V. (1994). Learning strategies and learning environments. *TESOL Quarterly, 28*(2), 409–414.

Loew, H. Z. (1984). Developing strategic reading skills. *Foreign Language Annals, 17*(4), 301–303.

Long, D. R., & Macian, J. L. (1992). *¡A conocernos!* Boston: Heinle & Heinle.

Long, M. H. (1979). *Inside the "black box": Methodological issues in research on teaching*. Paper presented at the annual meeting of International Teachers of English to Speakers of Other Languages, Boston, MA.

Long, M. H. (1983). Inside the "black box": Methodological issues in research on teaching. In H. W. Seliger & M. H. Long (Eds.), *Classroom-oriented research on second language acquisition* (pp. 3–35). Rowley, MA: Newbury House. Now Boston: Heinle & Heinle.

Lott-Lage, M. H. (1993). *Metacognition in native and foreign language reading: A multiple-case study of Brazilian adult readers*. Unpublished doctoral dissertation, Georgetown University, Washington, DC.

Lowe, P. (1982). *Oral Proficiency Interview.* NY: ACTFL/ETS.

Luce, L. F., & Smith, E. C. (Eds.). (1987). *Toward internationalism: Readings in cross-cultural communication.* Cambridge, MA: Newbury House/Harper & Row.

Lund, R. J. (1991). A comparisons of second language listening and reading comprehension. *Modern Language Journal, 75,* 196–204.

Lyons, W. (1986). *The disappearance of introspection.* Cambridge: MIT Press.

MacLean, M., & d'Anglejan, A. (1986). Rational cloze and introspection: Insights into first and second language reading comprehension. *Canadian Modern Language Review, 42,* 814–826.

Maguire, J. (1989). Dialogue journals with learning disabled students: Some special considerations. *Dialogue, 6*(2), 25–26.

Mangubhai, F. (1991). *How do I learn a second language? Let me count the ways.* Paper presented at SEAMEO RELC 26th Annual Seminar.

Mann, S. J. (1982). Verbal reports as data: A focus on retrospection. In S. Dingwall & S. Mann (Eds.), *Methods and problems in doing applied linguistic research.* (pp. 87–104). Lancaster, UK: University of Lancaster.

Mansnerus, L. (1989, Aug. 6). SAT separates girls from boys. *New York Times, 4A,* 27–28.

Marshall, T. (1989). *The whole world guide to language learning.* Yarmouth, ME: Intercultural Press.

Matsumoto, K. (1994). Introspection, verbal reports, and second language learning strategy research. *Canadian Modern Language Review, 50,* 363–386.

McCombs, B. L. (1982, Apr.). *Enhancing student motivation through positive self-control strategies.* Paper presented at the annual meeting of the American Psychological Association. Washington, DC.

McCombs, B. L. (1988). Motivational skills training: Combining metacognitive, cognitive, and affective learning strategies. In C. Weinstein, E. T. Goetz, & P. A. Alexander (Eds.) *Learning and study strategies: Issues in assessment, instruction, and evaluation* (pp. 141–169). New York: Academic Press.

McGroarty, M. (1989). *The "good learner" of English in two settings.* ERIC Document Reproduction Service No. ED311733.

McKenna, M. C., & Kear, D. J. (1990, May). Measuring attitude toward reading: A new tool for teachers. *The Reading Teacher,* 626–639.

McLaughlin, B. (1987). *Theories of second language learning.* London: Edward Arnold.

McLaughlin, B. (1990). The relationship between first and second languages: Language proficiency and language aptitude. In B. Harley, J. Allen, J. Cummins & M. Swain (Eds.) *The development of second language proficiency* (pp. 158–174). Cambridge: Cambridge University Press.

Meath-Lang, B. (1990). The dialogue-journal: Reconceiving curriculum and teaching. In J. K. Peyton (Ed.), *Students and teachers writing together: Perspectives on journal writing* (pp. 3–17). Alexandria, VA: Teachers of English to Speakers of Other Languages.

Meestringa, T. (1993). Om te kunnen kiezen heb je een kader nodig. Een bespreking van Sijtstra 1991. *Spiegel, 11*, 1.

Met, M. (1988). Tomorrow's emphasis in foreign language: Proficiency. In R. S. Brandt (Ed.), *Content of the curriculum: 1988 ASCD handbook*. Alexandria, VA: Association for Supervision and Curriculum Development.

Moore, S. C., & Lemons, R. (1982, Oct.). Measuring reading attitudes: Three dimensions. *Reading World*, 48–57.

Mullins, P. (1992). *Successful English language learning strategies of students enrolled in the Faculty of Arts, Chulalongkorn University, Bangkok, Thailand*. Unpublished doctoral dissertation, United States International University, San Diego, CA.

Murphy, J. M. (1987). The listening strategies of English as a second language college students. *Research and teaching in developmental education, 4*, 27–46.

Naiman, N., Fröhlich, M., Stern, H., & Todesco, A. (1978). *The good language learner*. Research in Education Series No. 7. Toronto: Ontario Institute for Studies in Education.

Neubach, A., & Cohen, A. D. (1988). Processing strategies and problems encountered in the use of dictionaries. *Dictionaries: Journal of the Dictionary Society of North America, 10*, 1–19.

Nevo, N. (1989). Test-taking strategies on a multiple-choice test of reading comprehension. *Language Testing, 6*, 199–215.

Newcombe, P. J. (1982). *Communicating message and meaning*. Lexington, MA: Ginn.

Newell, A., & Simon, H. A. (1972). *Human problem solving*. Englewood Cliffs, NJ: Prentice-Hall.

Noblitt, J. S., Sola, D. F., & Pet, W. J. A. (1992). *Système-D: Writing assistant for French*. Boston: Heinle & Heinle.

Noguchi, T. (1991). *Review of language learning strategy research and its implications*. Unpublished bachelor's thesis, Tottori University, Tottori, Japan.

Nunan, D. (1992). *Research methods in language learning*. Cambridge: Cambridge University Press.

Nyikos, M. (1986). *Student-generated study techniques: A systems analysis*. Paper presented at the Southwest Conference on Language Teaching, Phoenix, AZ.

Nyikos, M. (1990a). *Factor analytic evidence for information processing*. Paper presented at the Second Conference on Second Language Acquisition and Foreign Language Learning, University of Illinois at Urbana-Champaign.

Nyikos, M. (1990b). Sex-related differences in adult language learning: Socialization and memory factors. *Modern Language Journal, 74*(3), 273–287.

Nyikos, M. (1991). Prioritizing student learning: A guide for teachers. In L. Strasheim (Ed.), *Focus on the foreign language learner: Priorities and strategies*. Lincolnwood, IL: National Textbook.

Nyikos, M. (1994). *Toward pedagogical knowledge: Belief systems of foreign language teacher-candidates.* Unpublished manuscript.

Nyikos, M., & Oxford, R. L. (1993). A factor analytic study of language learning strategy use: Interpretations from information-processing theory and social psychology. *Modern Language Journal, 7,* 11–22.

Oh, J. (1992). Learning strategies used by university EFL students in Korea. *Language Teaching* [Korea], *1,* 23–53.

Olijkan, E. (1993). *Lezen tot de tweede.* Groningen: Wolters Noordhoff.

Oller, J. R., Jr. (1981). Research on the measurement of affective variables: Some remaining questions. In R. W. Anderson (Ed.), *New dimensions in second language acquisition research* (pp. 14–27). Rowley, MA: Newbury House Publishers.

Olson, G. M., Duffy, S. A., & Mack, R. L. (1984). Thinking-out-loud as a method for studying real-time comprehension processes. In D. E. Kieras & M. A. Just (Eds.), *New methods in reading comprehension research* (pp. 253–286). Hillsdale, NJ: Erlbaum.

Omaggio, A. (1981). *Helping learners succeed: Activities for the foreign language classroom.* Washington, DC: Center for Applied Linguistics.

O'Malley, J. M. (1987). The effects of training in the use of learning strategies on acquiring English as a second language. In A. L. Wenden & J. Rubin (Eds.), *Learner strategies in language learning* (134–144). Englewood Cliffs, NJ: Prentice Hall.

O'Malley, J. M. (1992). *Learning strategies, learner effectiveness, and self-efficacy in foreign language instruction.* Paper presented at the American Educational Research Association annual meeting, San Francisco, CA.

O'Malley, J. M., & Chamot, A. U. (1987). The cognitive academic language learning approach: A bridge to the mainstream. *TESOL Quarterly, 21*(2), 227–249.

O'Malley, J. M., & Chamot, A. U. (1990). *Learning strategies in second language acquisition.* Cambridge: Cambridge University Press.

O'Malley, J. M., & Chamot, A. U. (1993). Learner characteristics in second language acquisition. In A. Omaggio Hadley (Ed.), *Research in language learning: Principles, processes, and prospects* (pp. 96–123). Lincolnwood, IL: National Textbook.

O'Malley, J. M., Chamot, A. U., & Küpper, L. (1989). Listening comprehension strategies in second language acquisition. *Applied Linguistics, 10,* 418–437.

O'Malley, J. M., Chamot, A. U., Stewner-Manzanares, G., Küpper, L., & Russo, R. P. (1985a). Learning strategies used by beginning and intermediate ESL students. *Language Learning, 35,* 21–46.

O'Malley, J. M., Chamot, A. U., Stewner-Manzanares, G., Russo, R. P., & Küpper, L. (1985b). Learning strategy applications with students of English as a second language. *TESOL Quarterly, 19,* 557–584.

Omori, M. (1992). *Learning strategies in the Japanese classroom.* Unpublished master's thesis, Georgetown University.

Oxford, R. L. (1986a). *Development and psychometric testing of the Strategy Inventory for Language Learning*. Alexandria, VA: U. S. Army Research Institute for the Behavioral and Social Sciences.

Oxford, R. L. (1986b). *Second language learning strategies: Current research and implications for practice*. Washington, DC: Center for Applied Linguistics, and Los Angeles: Center for Language Education and Research of the University of California at Los Angeles.

Oxford, R. L. (1989a). "The Best and the Worst": An exercise to tap perceptions of language-learning experiences and strategies. *Foreign Language Annals, 22*(5), 447–454.

Oxford, R. L. (1989b). The role of styles and strategies in second language learning. Washington, DC: ERIC Clearinghouse on Language and Linguistics. ERIC Document Reproduction Service No. ED317087.

Oxford, R. L. (1989c). Use of language learning strategies: A synthesis of studies with implications for strategy training. *System, 17*, 235–247.

Oxford, R. (1990a). Language learning strategies and beyond: A look at strategies in the context of styles. In S. S. Magnan (Ed.) *Shifting the instructional focus to the learner* (pp. 35–55). Middlebury, VT: Northeast Conference.

Oxford, R. L. (1990b). *Language learning strategies: What every teacher should know*. New York: Newbury House/Harper & Row. Now Boston: Heinle & Heinle.

Oxford, R. L. (1990c). *Strategy Inventory for Language Learning*. In *Language learning strategies: What every teacher should know*. Boston: Heinle & Heinle.

Oxford, R. L. (1992). The story of the *SILL*: Evolution, use, reliability, and validity of the *Strategy Inventory for Language Learning* around the world. Tuscaloosa, AL: University of Alabama.

Oxford, R. L. (1992/1993). Language learning strategies in a nutshell: Research update and ESL classroom implications. *TESOL Journal 1*(3), Cover & 18–22.

Oxford, R. L. (1993a). Instructional implications of gender differences in L2 learning styles and strategies. *Applied Language Learning, 4*(1–2), 65–94.

Oxford, R. L. (1993b). *La différence continue...*: Gender differences in second/foreign language learning styles and strategies. In J. Sutherland (Ed.), *Exploring gender* (pp. 140–147). Englewood Cliffs, NJ: Prentice-Hall.

Oxford, R. L. (1993c). Research on second language learning strategies. In W. Grabe (Ed.), *Annual Review of Applied linguistics* (pp. 175–187). Cambridge: Cambridge University Press.

Oxford, R. L. (1993d). Research update on L2 listening. *System, 21*(2), 205–211.

Oxford, R. L. (1993e). *Style Analysis Survey*. Tuscaloosa, AL: University of Alabama. Later published in: Reid, J. (3rd ed.) (1995). *Language learning styles in the ESL/EFL classroom*. Boston: Heinle & Heinle.

Oxford, R. L. (1994a, March). *Gender differences in language learning styles and strategies*. Paper presented at the AAAL/TESOL conferences, Baltimore, MD.

Oxford, R. L. (1994b). Individual differences among your ESL students: Why a single method can't work. *Journal of Intensive ESL Studies*, 27–42.

Oxford, R. L. (1995). *Patterns of cultural identity*. Boston: Heinle & Heinle.

Oxford, R. L., & Burry, J. A. (1993). *Evolution, norming, and psychometric testing of Oxford's Strategy Inventory for Language Learning*. Paper presented at the annual meeting of the National Council on Measurement in Education, Atlanta, GA.

Oxford, R. L., & Burry-Stock, J. A. (1995). Assessing the use of language learning strategies worldwide with the ESL/EFL version of the *Strategy Inventory for Language Learning*. *System, 23*(2), 153–175.

Oxford, R. L., & Cohen, A. D. (1992). Language learning strategies: Critical issues in concept and definition. *Applied Language Learning, 3*(1–2), 1–35.

Oxford, R. L., & Crookall, D. (1989). Research on language learning strategies: Methods, findings, and instructional issues. *Modern Language Journal, 73*, 404–419.

Oxford, R. L., Crookall, D., Cohen, A., Lavine, R., Nyikos, M., & Sutter, W. (1990). Strategy training for language learners: Six situational case studies and a training model. *Foreign Language Annals, 22*(3), 197–216.

Oxford, R. L., & Ehrman, M. E. (1993). Second language research on individual differences. *Annual Review of Applied Linguistics, 13*, 188–205.

Oxford, R. L., Ehrman, M. E., & Lavine, R. Z. (1991). Style wars: Teacher-student style conflicts in the language classroom. In S. S. Magnan (Ed.), *Challenges for the 1990s for college language programs* (pp. 1–25). Boston: Heinle & Heinle.

Oxford, R. L, Hollaway, M. E., & Horton-Murillo, D. (1992). Research and practical implications for teaching in the multicultural tertiary ESL/EFL classroom. *System, 20*(4), 439–456.

Oxford, R. L., & Lavine, R. Z. (1992). Teacher-student "style wars" in the language classroom: Research insights and suggestions. *ADFL Bulletin, 23*(3), 38–45.

Oxford, R. L., Lavine, R. Z., & Crookall, D. (1989). Language learning strategies, the communicative approach, and their instructional implications. *Foreign Language Annals, 22*, 29–39.

Oxford, R. L., & Nyikos, M. (1989). Variables affecting choice of language learning strategies by university students. *Modern Language Journal, 73*, 291–300.

Oxford, R. L., Nyikos, M., & Crookall, D. (1987). *Learning strategies of university foreign language students: A large-scale study*. Paper presented at the annual meeting of Teachers of English to Speakers of Other Languages, Miami, FL.

Oxford, R. L., Nyikos, M., & Ehrman, M. (1988). *Vive la différence?* Reflections on sex differences in use of language learning strategies. *Foreign Language Annals, 21*(4), 321–329.

Oxford, R. L., Nyikos, M., Nyikos, K., Lezhnev, V., Eyring, J., & Rossi-Le, L. (1989). *Learning strategies of adult ESL learners in the US: A collaborative study*. Unpublished manuscript, University of Alabama, Tuscaloosa, AL.

Oxford, R. L., & Shearin, J. (1994). Language learning motivation: Expanding the theoretical framework. *The Modern Language Journal, 78*(1), 12–28.

Oxford, R. L., Talbott, V., & Halleck, G. (1990). Language learning strategies, attitudes, motivation, and self-image of students in a university intensive ESL program. Paper presented at the 24th Annual TESOL Convention, San Francisco, CA.

Padron, Y. N., & Waxman, H. C. (1988). The effects of ESL students' perceptions of their cognitive strategies on reading achievement. *TESOL Quarterly, 22,* 146–150.

Palincsar, A. S., & Brown, A. L. (1984). Reciprocal teaching to promote independent learning from test. *The Reading Teacher, 39*(8), 771–777.

Palincsar, A. S., & Brown, A. L. (1986). Interactive teaching of comprehension-fostering and comprehension-monitoring activities. *Cognition and Instruction, 1,* 117–175.

Palincsar, A. S., & Klenk, L. (1992). Examining and influencing contexts for intentional literacy learning. In C. Collins & J. N. Mangieri (Eds.), *Teaching thinking: An agenda for the twenty-first century* (pp. 297–315). Hillsdale, NJ: Erlbaum.

Paris, S. G., & Winograd, P. (1990). How metacognition can promote academic learning and instruction. In B. F. Jones & L. Idol (Eds.), *Dimensions of thinking and cognitive instruction* (pp. 15–51). Hillsdale, NJ: Erlbaum.

Park-Oh, Y. Y. (1992a). *Strategy Inventory for Reading in ESL.* Tuscaloosa: University of Alabama.

Park-Oh, Y. Y. (1992b). *Attitudes Inventory for Reading in ESL.* Tuscaloosa: University of Alabama.

Park-Oh, Y. Y. (1994a). *Self-regulated strategy training in second-language reading: Its effects on reading comprehension, strategy use, reading attitudes, and learning styles of college ESL students.* Unpublished doctoral dissertation, University of Alabama, Tuscaloosa, AL.

Park-Oh, Y. Y. (1994b). *Validation of the Strategy Inventory for Reading in English as a Second Language (SIRESL).* Unpublished manuscript.

Pearson, E. (1988). Learner strategies and learner interviews. *ELT Journal, 42*(3), 173–178.

Penner, J. C. (1984). *Why many language teachers can no longer lecture: How to avoid communication breakdown in the classroom.* Springfield, IL: C. C. Thomas.

Perkins, D. N., & Solomon, G. (1987). Transfer and teaching thinking. In D. N. Perkins, J. Lochhead, & J. Bishop (Eds.), *Thinking: Second international conference.* Hillsdale, NJ: Erlbaum.

Perkins, D. N., & Solomon, G. (1988). Teaching for transfer. *Educational Leadership, 46,* 22–32.

Peyton, J. K. (Ed.). (1990). *Students and teachers writing together: Perspectives on journal writing.* Alexandria, VA: Teachers of English to Speakers of Other Languages.

Peyton, J. K., & Reed, L. (1990). *Dialogue journal writing with nonnative English speakers: A handbook for teachers.* Alexandria, VA: Teachers of English to Speakers of Other Languages.

Phillips, J. K. (1984). Practical implications of recent research in reading. *Foreign Language Annals, 17*(4), 285–296.

Phillips, V. (1990). *English as a second language learner strategies of adult Asian students using the Strategy Inventory for Language Learning*. Unpublished doctoral dissertation, University of San Francisco, San Francisco, CA.

Phillips, V. (1991, Nov.). A look at learner strategy use and ESL proficiency. *CATESOL Journal*, 57–67.

Pienemann, M. (1989). Is language teachable? Psycholinguistic experiments and hypotheses. *Applied Linguistics, 10*, 52–79.

Pierson, D. (1984, May). Toward a refinement in the use of the Kennedy-Halinski reading attitude inventory. *Reading World, 364–374*.

Politzer, R. L. (undated). *Motivation, language learning behavior, and achievement in an intensive ESL course*. Unpublished manuscript, Stanford University, Stanford, CA.

Politzer, R. (1965). *Foreign language learning: A linguistic introduction*, Englewood Cliffs, NJ: Prentice-Hall.

Politzer, R. L., & McGroarty, M. (1985). An exploratory study of learning behaviors and their relationship to gains in linguistic and communicative competence. *TESOL Quarterly, 19*, 103–123.

Porter, T. (1982). A developmental perspective on the acquisition of communication characteristics. In L. L. Barker (Ed.), *communication in the classroom: Original essays* (pp. 39–54). Englewood Cliffs, NJ: Prentice-Hall.

Porter, R., & Pellerin, C. (1989). *A la radio!* Toronto: Copp Clark Pitman.

Poulisse, N. (1989). *The use of compensatory strategies by Dutch learners of English*. Unpublished doctoral dissertation, University of Nijmegen, the Netherlands.

Poulisse, N., Bongaerts, T., & Kellerman, E. (1986). The use of retrospective verbal reports in the analysis of compensatory strategies. In C. Faerch & G. Kasper (Eds.), *Introspection in second language research* (pp. 213–229). Clevedon, England: Multilingual Matters.

Pressley, M., & Associates. (1990). *Cognitive strategy instruction that really improves children's academic performance*. Cambridge, MA: Brookline Books.

Pressley, M., & Afflerbach, P. (1995). *Verbal protocols of reading: The nature of constructively responsive reading*. Hillsdale, NJ: Lawrence Erlbaum.

Pressley, M., El-Dinary, P., & Brown, R. (1992). Skilled and not-so-skilled reading: Good and not-so-good information processing. In M. Pressley, K. R. Harris, & J. T. Guthrie (Eds.), *Promoting academic competence and literacy in school* (pp. 91–127). San Diego: Academic Press.

Pressley, M., & Harris, K. (1990). What we really know about strategy instruction. *Educational Leadership, 48*, 31–34.

Pressley, M., Levin, J. R., Nakamura, G. V., Hope, D. J., Bisbo, J. G., & Toye, A. R. (1980). The keyword of foreign language vocabulary learning: An investigation of its generalizability. *Journal of Applied Psychology, 65*, 635–642.

Prokop, M. (1989). *Learning strategies for second language users: An analytical appraisal with case studies*. Lewiston, NY: Edwin Mellen Press.

Putsch, M. D. (Ed.). (1986). *Multicultural education: A cross-cultural training approach*. Yarmouth, ME: Intercultural Press.

Radford, J. (1974). Reflections on introspection. *American Psychologist, 29*, 245–250.

Ramírez, A. G. (1986). Language learning strategies used by adolescents studying French in New York schools. *Foreign Language Annals, 19*, 131–141.

Red, D. L. (1989). *Reading academic texts in a foreign language: A case study in Nepal*. Unpublished doctoral dissertation, University of Texas, Austin, TX.

Rees-Miller, J. (1993). A critical appraisal of learner training: Theoretical bases and teaching implications. *TESOL Quarterly, 27*(4), 679–689.

Reid, J. M. (1987). The learning style preferences of ESL students. *TESOL Quarterly, 21*(1), 87–111.

Reid, J. M. (Ed.). (1995). *Learning styles in EFL/ESL classrooms*. Boston: Heinle & Heinle.

Reiss, M. A. (1983). Helping the unsuccessful language learner. *Canadian Modern Language Review, 39*(2), 256–266.

Richards, J. C. (1983). Listening comprehension: Approach, design, procedure. *TESOL Quarterly, 17*, 291–340.

Richards, J. C. (1990). *The language teaching matrix*. New York: Cambridge.

Rivers, W. M. (1979). Learning a sixth language: An adult learner's daily diary. *Canadian Modern Language Review, 36*(1), 67–82.

Rodgers, T. S. (1978). Towards a model of learner variation in autonomous foreign language learning. *Studies in Second Language Acquisition, 2*(1), 73–07.

Rogoff, B., & Lave, J. (Eds.). (1984). *Everyday cognition: Its development in social context*. Cambridge: Harvard University Press.

Rossi-Le, L. (1989). *Perceptual learning style preferences and their relationship to language learning strategies in adult students of English as a second language*. Unpublished doctoral dissertation, Drake University, Des Moines, IA.

Rost, M., & Ross, S. (1991). Learner use of strategies in interaction: Typology and teachability. *Language Learning, 41*(2), 235–273.

Rubin, J. (1975). What the "good language learner" can teach us. *TESOL Quarterly, 9*, 4151.

Rubin, J. (1981). Study of cognitive processes in second language learning. *Applied Linguistics, 11*(2), 118–131.

Rubin, J. (1987). Learner strategies: Assumptions, research history, and typology. In A. L. Wenden & J. Rubin (Eds.), *Learner strategies in language learning* (pp. 15–30). New York: Prentice Hall.

Rubin, J. (1989). The language learning disc. In W. F. Smith (Ed.), *Modern technology in foreign language education* (pp. 267–275). Lincolnwood, IL: National Textbook Company.

Rubin, J. (1990). Improving foreign language learning comprehension. In J. E. Alatis (Ed.), *Georgetown University Round Table on Languages and Linguistics*

1990: Linguistics, language teaching, and language acquisition — the interdependence of theory, practice, and research (pp. 309–316). Washington, DC: Georgetown University Press.

Rubin, J., & Henze, R. (1981). The foreign language requirement: A suggestion to enhance its educational role in teacher training. *TESOL Newsletter 17*, 19–24.

Rubin, J., Quinn, J., & Enos, J. (1988). *Improving foreign language listening comprehension*. Report submitted to the U. S. Department of Education, International Research and Studies Program, Washington, DC. Project No. 017AH70028.

Rubin, J., & Thompson, I. (1982). *How to be a more successful language learner*. Boston: Heinle & Heinle.

Rubin, J., & Thompson, I. (1994). *How to be a more successful language learner* (2nd ed.). Boston: Heinle & Heinle.

Russo, R., & Stewner-Manzanares, G. (1985a). *The training and use of learning strategies for English as a second language in a military context*. Paper presented at the annual meeting of the American Educational Research Association, Chicago, IL.

Russo, R., & Stewner-Manzanares, G. (1985b). *The training and use of learning strategies for English as a second language in a military context*. Rosslyn, VA: InterAmerica Research Associates.

SAS Institute. (1988). *SAS/STAT user's guide*. (Version 6.3). Cary, NC: Author.

Saville-Troike, M. (1987). *Private speech: Second language learning during the silent period*. Unpublished manuscript, ERIC Document Reproduction Service No. ED288373.

Scarcella, R. C. (1990). *Teaching language minority students in the multicultural classroom*. Englewood Cliffs, NJ: Prentice Hall.

Scarcella, R. C. (1993). *Power of the written word*. Boston: Heinle & Heinle.

Scarcella, R. C., & Oxford, R. L. (1992). *The tapestry of language learning: The individual in the communicative classroom*. Boston: Heinle & Heinle.

Schlebusch, J., Schijf, T., Taks, W., Liebrand, R., Kruiver, J., & Rijlaarsdam, G. (1990–1992). *Nieuw Nederlands*. Groningen: Wolters Noordhoff.

Schleppegrell, M., & Oxford, R. L.(1988). *Language learning strategies for Peace Corps volunteers*. Washington, DC: Center for Applied Linguistics.

Schmeck, R. R. (1980). Relationships between measures of learning style and reading comprehension. *Perceptual and Motor Skills, 50*, 461–462.

Schmeck, R. R. (1983). *Learning styles of college students*. New York: Academic Press.

Schmeck, R. R., Ribich, F. D., & Ramanaiah, N. (1977). Development of a self-report inventory for assessing individual differences in learning processes. *Applied Psychological Measurement, 1*, 413–431.

Schmidt, R. (1994). Deconstructing consciousness in search of useful definitions for applied linguistics. In J. Hulstijn & R. Schmidt (Eds.), *Consciousness and second language acquisition: Perspectives on form-focused instruction*. 1994 AILA Review. Amsterdam: AILA.

Schmidt, R., & Frota, S. N. (1986). Developing basic conversational ability in a second language: A case study of an adult learner of Portuguese. In R. Day, *Talking to learn: Conversation in second language acquisition* (pp. 237–326). Rowley, MA: Newbury House. Now Boston: Heinle & Heinle.

Schouten-van Parreren, C. (1985). *Woorden leren in het vreemde-talenonderwijs*. Apeldoorn: Van Walraven.

Schumann, J. H. (1975). Affective factors and the problem of age in second language acquisition. *Language Learning, 25*, 209–235.

Schumann, F. E., & Schumann, J. H. (1977). Diary of a language learner: An introspective study of second language learning. In H. D. Brown, R. H. Crymes, & C. A. Yorio (Eds.), *On TESOL '77* (pp. 241–249). Washington: Teachers of English to Speakers of Other Languages.

Scott, V. M., & Terry, R. M. (1992). *A teacher's guide: Système-D: Writing assistant for French*. Boston: Heinle & Heinle.

Scovel, T. (1991). *The role of culture in second language pedagogy*. Commissioned manuscript. Boston: Heinle & Heinle.

Seelye, H. N. (1987). *Teaching culture: Strategies for intercultural communication*. Lincolnwood, IL: National Textbook Co.

Seliger, H. W. (1983). The language learner as linguist: Of metaphors and realities. *Applied Linguistics, 4*, 1779–191.

Seliger, H. W., & Shohamy, E. (1989). *Second language research methods*. Oxford: Oxford University Press.

Selinker (1972). Interlanguage. *International Review of Applied Linguistics, 10*(3), 201–231.

Sharwood Smith, M. (1981). Consciousness raising and the second language learner. *Applied Linguistics, 2*(2), 159–168.

Shekhtmann, B. (1991). *How to improve your foreign language immediately*. Rockville, MD: Specialized Russian Instruction Center.

Shih Lo, S. C. (1990). *A causal model of factors affecting EFL reading comprehension of two-year college students in Taiwan*. Unpublished doctoral dissertation, University of Texas, Austin, TX.

Shuell, T. J. (1986). Cognitive conceptions of learning. *Review of Educational Research, 56*, 411–436.

Sijtstra, J. (1991). *Doel en inhoud van taalonderwijs. De ontwikkeling van een model voor domeinbeschrijvingen van taalonderwijs*. Arnhem: CITO.

Silver, E. A., & Marshall, S. P. (1990). Mathematical and scientific problem solving: Findings, issues, and instructional implications. In B. F. Jones & L. Idol (Eds.), *Dimensions of thinking and cognitive instruction* (pp. 265–290). Hillsdale, NJ: Erlbaum.

Skehan, P. (1989). *Individual differences in second-language learning*. London: Arnold.

Skehan, P. (1991). Individual differences in second language learning. *Studies in Second Language Acquisition, 13*(2), 275–298.

Slavin, R. (1988). Cooperative learning. *Review of Educational Research, 50*, 315–342.

Smagorinsky, P. (1989). The reliability and validity of protocol analysis. *Written Communication, 6*, 463–479.

Smith, M. C. (1990). The development and use of an instrument for assessing adults' attitudes toward reading. *Journal of Research and Development in Education, 23*(3), 156–161.

Snow, A., Met, M., & Genesee, F. (1989). A conceptual framework for the integration of language and content instruction. *TESOL Quarterly, 23*, 201–217.

Snyder, B., & Pressley, M. (1990). Introduction to cognitive strategy instruction. In M. Pressley & Associates (Eds.), *Cognitive strategy instruction that really improves children's academic performance* (pp. 7–26). Cambridge, MA: Brookline Books.

Sokolik, M. E. (1993). *Global views: Reading about world issues*. Boston: Heinle & Heinle.

Spack, R., & Sadow, C. (1983). Student-teacher working journals in ESL freshman composition. *TESOL Quarterly, 17*(4), 575–594.

Spolsky, B. (1989). *Conditions of second language learning*. New York: Oxford University Press.

SPSS Inc. (1989). *SPSS-X user's guide* (3rd ed.). Chicago: SPSS Inc.

Staton, J. (1980). Writing and counseling: Using a dialogue journal. *Language Arts, 57*(5), 514–518.

Staton, J. (1983). Dialogue journals: A new tool for teaching communication. *ERIC/CLL News Bulletin, 6*, 1–2, 6.

Staton, J. (1987). New research on dialogue journals. *Dialogue, 4*(1), 1–24.

Steffensen, M. S., & Lin, Z. (1989). Linguistics made easy with the dialogue journal. *Dialogue, 6*(2), 20–22.

Steinberg, E. R. (1986). Protocols, retrospective reports, and the stream of consciousness. *College English, 48*, 697–712.

Stemmer, B. (1991). *What's on a C-test taker's mind? Mental processes in C-test taking*. Bochum: Universitatsverlag Dr. N. Brockmeyer.

Stempel, G. H. III. (1989a). Content analysis. In G. H. Stempel III & B. H. Westley (Eds.), *Research methods in mass communication* (2nd ed.). (pp. 124–136). Englewood Cliffs, NJ: Prentice Hall.

Stempel, G. H. III. (1989b). Statistical designs for content analysis. In G. H. Stempel III & B. H. Westley (Eds.), *Research methods in mass communication*, 2nd Ed. (pp. 137–149). Englewood Cliffs, NJ: Prentice Hall.

Stern, H. H. (1975). What can we learn from the good language learner? *The Canadian Modern Language Review, 34*, 304–318.

Stevens, J. P. (1990). *Intermediate statistics: A modern approach*. Hillsdale, NJ: Erlbaum.

Stewner-Manzanares, G., Chamot, A. U., O'Malley, J. M., Küpper, L., & Russo, R. P. (1985). *Learning strategies in English as a second language instruction: A teacher's guide*. Washington, DC: National Clearinghouse for Bilingual Education. ERIC Document Reproduction Service No. ED338107.

Strichart, S. S., & Mangrum, C. T. (1992). *Teaching study strategies to students with learning disabilities*. Boston: Allyn & Bacon.

Suchman, L. (1987). *Plans and situated action*. New York: Cambridge University Press.

Sutter, W. (1987). *Learning styles in adult refugees in North Jutland*. Denmark: County of North Jutland. (in Danish)

Sutton, C. (1989, May). Helping the normative English speaker with reading. *The Reading Teacher*, 684–688.

Swaffar, J. K. (1988). Readers, texts, and second languages: The interactive processes. *Modern Language Journal, 72*(2), 123–145.

Sy, B. M. (1994). *Sex differences and language learning strategies*. Paper presented at the Eleventh National Conference on TESOL in the ROC, Taipei, Taiwan.

Syananondh, K. (1983). *An investigation of pronunciation and learning strategies: Factors in English listening comprehension of Thai-speaking graduate students in the United States*. Unpublished doctoral dissertation, Rutgers University, New Brunswick, NJ.

Tannen, D. (1986). *That's not what I meant!* New York: Morrow.

Tarone, E. (1983). Some thoughts on the notion of "communication strategy." In C. Faerch & G. Kasper (Eds.), *Strategies in interlanguage communication* (pp. 61–74). London: Longman.

Tarone, E., & Yule, G. (1989). *Focus on the language learner: Approaches to identifying and meeting the needs of second language learners*. Oxford: Oxford University Press.

Terrell, T., Andrade, M., Egasse, J., & Munoz, E. (1990). *Dos mundos*. New York: McGraw-Hill.

Thomas, J. R., & Nelson, J. K. (1990). *Research methods in physical activity*. Champaign, IL: Harmon Kinetics.

Thompson, I. (1987). Memory in language learning. In A. L. Wenden & J. Rubin (Eds.), *Learner strategies in language learning* (pp. 43–56). London: Prentice-Hall.

Thompson, I., & Rubin, J. (1993). Improving listening comprehension in Russian. Report submitted to the U. S. Department of Education, International Research and Studies Program, Washington, DC. Project No. P017A00032.

Thompson, I., & Rubin, J. (in press). Can strategy instruction improve listening comprehension? *Foreign Language Annals*.

Tichener, E. B. (1912). The schema of introspection. *American Journal of Psychology, 23*, 485–508.

Tinkham, T. (1989). Rote learning, attitudes, and abilities: A comparison of Japanese and American students. *TESOL Quarterly, 23*, 695–698.

Tomlinson, B. (1984). Talking about the composing process: The limitations of retrospective accounts. *Written Communication, 1*, 429–445.

Touba, N. (1992). *Language learning strategies of Egyptian student teachers of English.* Paper presented at the Twelfth National Symposium on English Teaching in Egypt, Nasr City, Cairo, Egypt.

Tran, T. V. (1988). Sex differences in English language acculturation and learning strategies among Vietnamese adults age 40 and over in the United States. *Sex Roles, 19,* 747–758.

Tyacke, M., & Mendelsohn, D. (1986). Student needs: Cognitive as well as communicative. *TESL Canada Journal, 1,* 171–183.

Ur, P. (1984). *Teaching listening comprehension.* Cambridge: Cambridge University Press.

van Ek, J. A., & Trim, J. L. M. (1991). *The threshold level 1990.* Strasbourg: Council of Europe.

van Loon, R. (1991). *Tekst en begrip.* Grou: De Kangeroe.

van Parreren, C. F. (1988). *Ontwikkelend onderwijs.* Leuven/Amersfoort: Acco.

Vandergrift, L. (1992). *The comprehension strategies of second language (French) learners.* Unpublished doctoral dissertation, University of Alberta, Edmonton, Alberta, Canada.

Vanett, L., & Jurich, D. (1990). A context for collaboration: Teachers and students writing together. In J. K. Peyton (Ed.), *Students and teachers writing together: Perspectives on journal writing* (pp. 49–62). Alexandria, VA: Teachers of English to Speakers of Other Languages.

Vann, R., & Abraham, R. (1990). Strategies of unsuccessful language learners. *TESOL Quarterly, 24*(2), 177–198.

Van Patten, W., Lee, J., Ballman, T., & Dvorak, T. (1992). *¿Sabías que...?* New York: McGraw-Hill.

Voogt, J. W., & Haelen, J. A. (1986/1987). *Aufzug.* Den Bosch: Malmberg.

Waern, Y. (1988). Thoughts on texts in context: Applying the think-aloud method in text processing. *Text, 8,* 327–350

Wang, L., Richardson, G., & Rhodes, N. (1988). *CLEAR Oral Proficiency Exam (COPE).* Washington, DC: Center for Applied Linguistics.

Wangsotorn, A., Sripaipan, T., Rattanaprucks, N., Jarunggidanan, T., Singkalwanij, P., & Vejaphurti, A. (1986). *Relationships between learning modes and the beginners' success in English.* Paper presented at the annual meeting of International Teachers of English to Speakers of Other Languages, Anaheim, CA.

Watanabe, Y. (1990). *External variables affecting language learning strategies of Japanese EFL learners: Effects of entrance examinations, years spent at college/university, and staying overseas.* Unpublished master's thesis, Lancaster University, Lancaster, UK.

Watanabe, Y. (1991). Classification of language learning strategies. *International Christian University Language Research Bulletin, 6*(1), 75–102.

Weeks, W. H., Pedersen, P. B., & Brislin, R. W. (Eds.) (1977). *A manual of structured experiences for cross-cultural learning.* Yarmouth, ME: Intercultural Press.

Weir, C. J. (1988). *communicative language testing with special reference to English as a second language.* Exeter: University of Exeter.

Weinstein, C. E., Goetz, E. T., & Alexander, P. A. (Eds.). (1988). *Learning and study strategies: Issues in assessment, instruction, and evaluation.* San Diego, CA: Academic Press.

Weinstein, C. E., & Mayer, R. E. (1986). The teaching of learning strategies. In M. C. Wittrock (Ed.), *Handbook of research on teaching* (pp. 315–327). 3rd Ed. New York: Macmillan.

Wen, Q., & Johnson, R. K. (1991). *Language learning approaches and outcomes: A study of tertiary English majors in China.* Paper presented at the Sixth Annual Conference of the Institute of Language in Education, Hong Kong University.

Wenden, A. L. (1983). Literature review: The process of intervention. *Language Learning, 33*(1), 102–121.

Wenden, A. L. (1985a). Facilitating learning competence: Perspectives on an expanded role for second language teachers. *Canadian Modern Language Review, 41*(16), 981–990.

Wenden, A. L. (1985b). Learner strategies. *TESOL Newsletter, 19*(5), 1–7.

Wenden, A. L. (1986a). Helping language learners think about learning. *English Language Teaching Journal, 40*(1), 3–12.

Wenden, A. L. (1986b). Incorporating learner training in the classroom. *System, 14,* 315–325.

Wenden, A. L. (1987a). Conceptual background and utility. In A. L. Wenden & J. Rubin (Eds.), *Learner strategies in language learning* (pp. 3–14). New York: Prentice Hall.

Wenden, A. L. (1987b). How to be a successful language learner: Insight and prescriptions from L2 learners. In A. L. Wenden & J. Rubin (Eds.), *Learner strategies in language learning* (pp. 103–117). New York: Prentice Hall.

Wenden, A. L. (1987c). Incorporating learner training in the classroom. In A. L. Wenden & J. Rubin (Eds.), *Learner strategies in language learning* (pp. 159–168). Englewood Cliffs, NJ: Prentice Hall.

Wenden, A. L. (1991). *Learner strategies for learner autonomy.* Englewood Cliffs: Prentice-Hall.

Wenden, A. L., & Rubin, J. (Eds.). (1987). *Learner strategies in language learning.* Englewood Cliffs, NJ: Prentice-Hall.

Westhoff, G. J. (1981). *Voorspellend lezen.* Groningen: Wolters Noordhoff.

Westhoff, G. J. (1989). Some common teaching practices and their effectiveness in foreign language instruction. *European Journal of Teacher Education, 12,* 121–130.

Willing, K. (1988). *Learning styles in adult migrant education.* Adelaide: National Curriculum Resource Centre.

Wipf, J. A. (1984). Strategies for teaching second language listening. W. Lafayette, IN: Purdue University.

Witte, T. (1992a, September). Vier nieuwe methoden voor basisvorming. Deel 2: Bespreking van Nieuw Nederlands, Klinker en Taalwijzer. *Levende Talen, 472,* 305–313.

Witte, T. (1992b, October). Vier nieuwe methoden vor basisvorming. Deel 3: Bespreking van Op niveau en nabeschouwing. *Levende Talen, 473,* 367–375.

Witkin, H. A., Moore, C. A., Goodenough, D. R., & Cox, P. W. (1977a). Field dependent and field independent cognitive styles and their educational implications. *Review of Educational Research, 47*(1), 1–64.

Witkin, H. A., Moore, C. A., Oltman, P. K., Goodenough, D. R., & Friedman, F. (1977b). Role of field dependent and field independent cognitive styles in academic evolution: A longitudinal study. *Journal of Educational Psychology, 69*(3), 197–211.

Yang, N-D. (1992a). *Preliminary statistical results of the beliefs and strategy use by students of an intensive English program in Taiwan.* Unpublished data. The University of Texas at Austin.

Yang, N-D. (1992b). *Second language learners' beliefs about language learning and their use of learning strategies: A study of college students of English in Taiwan.* (Doctoral dissertation, University of Texas, Austin, 1992). *Dissertation Abstracts International, 53,* 2722A.

Yang, N-D. (1993a). *Understanding Chinese students' language beliefs and learning strategy use.* Paper presented annual meeting of International Teachers of English to Speakers of Other Languages, Atlanta, GA. ERIC Document Reproduction Service No. ED371589.

Yang, N-D. (1993b). Beliefs about language learning and learning strategy use: A study of college students of English in Taiwan. *Papers from the Tenth Conference on English Teaching and Learning in the Republic of China.*

Young, D., & Oxford, R. L. (1993). Learner reactions to introductory Spanish textbooks. *Hispania, 76,* 593–605.

Young, D., & Wolf, D. F. (1990). *Esquemas.* New York: Holt, Rinehart, & Winston.

Zimmerman, B. J. (1990). Self-regulated learning and academic achievement: An overview. *Educational Psychologist, 25,* 3–17.

Zimmerman, B. J., & Pons, M. M. (1986). Development of a structured interview for assessing student use of self-regulated learning strategies. *American Educational Research Journal, 23,* 614–628.

Zion, J. S. (1985). *Prairie Dawn's purple book.* Open Sesame ESL Series, Level D. New York: Oxford University Press.

ABOUT THE AUTHORS AND HOW TO CONTACT THEM

THE EDITOR

Rebecca L. Oxford is Professor of Language Education in the College of Education and Associate Dean of the College of Education at the University of Alabama, where she earlier developed certification programs in ESL and Japanese language teacher education, directed the MA-TESOL Program, and headed the 1,800-student Area of Teacher Education. She produced books such as *Language Learning Strategies: What Every Teacher Should Know, Patterns of Cultural Identity, Language Learning Motivation: Pathways to the New Century,* and *The Tapestry of Language Learning: The Individual in the Communicative Classroom.* She has won teaching awards and has presented seminars throughout the world.

> Dr. Rebecca L. Oxford
> College of Education
> University of Alabama
> Tuscaloosa, AL 35487 USA
> Tel: 205–348–6051
> Fax: 205–348–6873
> E-mail: roxford@bamaed.ua.edu

THE AUTHORS

Neil J. Anderson is Assistant Professor in the Department of Linguistics at Ohio University, Athens, Ohio. His research interests include second language testing, second language reading, and learning styles and strategies. He holds a Ph.D. from the University of Texas at Austin. He has published articles in *Language Testing* and the *Modern Language Journal.* He is a leader in International TESOL and is chairing an upcoming annual convention.

> Dr. Neil J. Anderson
> Linguistics Department
> Gordy Hall
> Ohio University
> Athens, OH 45701 USA
> Tel: 614–593–4562
> Fax: 614–593–2967
> E-mail: anderson@ouvaxa.cats.ohiou.edu

Carol Ann Baily was awarded an Ed.D. in higher education administration by Vanderbilt University in 1992. She holds an M.A. in French from Vanderbilt and a B.A. in French and German from Eckerd College. She also completed a *Certificat d'études françaises* at the Université de Neuchatel in Switzerland. She is currently Director of the Adult Services Center at Middle Tennessee State University, Murfreesboro, Tennessee.

Dr. Carol Ann Baily
Adult Services Center
P.O. Box 646
Peck Hall 101-D
Middle Tennessee State University
Murfreesboro, TN 37132 USA
Tel: 615–898–5989
Fax: 615–898–5112

Sarah Barnhardt is Associate Director for language learning strategies studies and professional development activities at Georgetown University's Language Research Projects. Ms. Barnhardt, who holds a master's in Russian Linguistics from The George Washington University, has integrated and taught learning strategies in Russian foreign language and ESL classrooms. In addition, she has designed and written published materials incorporating learning strategies instruction and has developed and presented teacher workshops and scholarly papers at a number of language conferences.

Ms. Sarah Barnhardt
Language Research Projects
Georgetown University
1916 Wilson Blvd., Ste. 207
Arlington, VA 22204
Tel: 703–351–9500

David Bedell graduated from Swarthmore College with a degree in linguistics and then spent four years teaching English in China. He returned to the US and obtained his master's in TESOL at the University of Alabama, where he received top academic honors such as a Graduate Council Fellowship and (for his overseas thesis research in the PRC) a year-long Graduate Council Research Fellowship. He now teaches at the English Language Institute of the University of Bridgeport, Connecticut.

Mr. David Bedell
English Language Institute
University of Bridgeport
Bridgeport, CT 06602 USA
Tel: 203–576–4000
E-mail: bedell@cse.bridgeport.edu

Anna Uhl Chamot is Associate Professor in ESL teacher preparation in the Graduate School of Education at The George Washington University. As Associate Director of the National Foreign Language Resource Center (Georgetown University/Center for Applied Linguistics), she directed research on language learning strategy instruction and informal assessment in the Arlington, Virginia Public Schools. Dr. Chamot implemented the Cognitive Academic Language Learning Approach (CALLA), which she developed with J. Michael O'Malley.

Dr. Anna Uhl Chamot
Graduate School of Education
The George Washington University
Washington, DC 20052 USA
Tel: 202–363–3083
Fax: 202–686–6158
E-mail: auchamot@his.com

Andrew Cohen taught in the ESL section of the UCLA English Department, was Professor of Language Education at the Hebrew University of Jerusalem, and served as Fulbright Lecturer/Researcher in Brazil. He is now Professor of Applied Linguistics in the ESL Department and member of the Graduate Faculty in the Institute of Linguistics and Asian and Slavic Languages and Literatures, University of Minnesota. He has published numerous research articles, as well as books on bilingual education, language learning strategies (*Language Learning: Insights for Learners, Teachers, and Researchers*) and language testing (*Assessing Language Ability in the Classroom*).

Dr. Andrew Cohen
Institute of Linguistics and Asian and Slavic Languages and Literatures
196 Klaeber Court
320 16th Ave. SE
Minneapolis, MN 55455 USA
Tel: 612–624–3806 or 624–3331
Fax: 612–624–4579
E-mail: adcohen@maroon.tc.umn.edu

El Sayed Dadour graduated from the Department of English, Damietta College of Education, Mansoura University, Egypt. There he was awarded a Special Diploma in Curriculum and Instruction and Mental Hygiene, as well as a master's and a doctorate in Curriculum and Foreign Language Methodology. He was selected for a prestigious Channel Fellowship in the US by the Egyptian Cultural and Educational Bureau and studied for two years with Dr. Rebecca Oxford, who co-directed his dissertation with Dr. Awatef Shier of Mansoura University. Dr. Dadour now teaches at Mansoura University.

Dr. El Sayed Dadour
Department of Curriculum & Instruction
Damietta Faculty of Education
University of Mansoura
Damietta, Egypt
Fax: 2–05–733–787

Carisma Dreyer (Ph.D., Potchefstroom University for CHE) is Senior Lecturer at the Potchefstroom University in the Northwest Province of the Republic of South Africa. She is the graduate tutor and coordinator of the M.A. Programs in TESOL and Applied Language Study. Her interests include learning styles, language learning strategies, various other individual difference variables, and also classroom interaction. She works extensively with various language groups, including Afrikaans, Sotho, Setswana, and Zulu speakers.

Dr. Carisma Dreyer
English Language and Literature
Potchefstroom University for CHE
Private Bag X 6001 Potchefstroom 2520
South Africa
Tel: 27–148–299–1551 or 299–1552
Fax: 27–148–299–1562
E-mail: ENGALC@PUKNET.PUK.AC.ZA

Pamela Beard El-Dinary earned her Ph.D. in Educational Psychology at the University of Maryland. As Research Analyst for the National Foreign Language Resource Center at Georgetown University/Center for Applied Linguistics, Dr. El-Dinary designs and conducts qualitative and quantitative research studies on foreign language strategy instruction at all levels. She has also worked on developing models of strategy instruction, creating strategy instruction materials, and developing and providing professional support for teachers.

Dr. Pamela B. El-Dinary
Language Research Projects
Georgetown University
1916 Wilson Blvd., Ste. 207
Arlington, VA 22204
Tel: 703–351–9500

Gregory Felkins holds a master's degree in TESOL from the University of Alabama. During his undergraduate education, he studied overseas at the University of Extremadura in Spain, where he became fluent in Spanish and developed many ideas about foreign language learning strategies. He now teaches ESL in the English Language Institute of the University of Alabama. One of his hobbies is creative writing.

Mr. Gregory Felkins
English Language Institute
Comer Hall
University of Alabama
Tuscaloosa, AL 35487 USA
Tel: 205–348–7413

Carine Feyten holds a bachelor's and a master's degree in Germanic Philology from the University of Louvain, Belgium, her home country. She is fluent in five languages and received her Ph.D. in Interdisciplinary Education. She directs the Foreign Language Teacher Preparation Program at the University of South Florida in Tampa, coordinates all secondary teacher education programs, and is creating a new Ph.D. program in Second Language Acquisition and Instructional Technology. She directs the Suncoast Academic Alliance of Florida in Foreign Languages and Literatures, and was president of the Florida Foreign

Language Association. She has won several teaching awards and one research award, has presented nationally and internationally, and has published in such journals as *Modern Language Journal*, *Hispania*, *The Middle School Journal*, and *Language Quarterly*.

Dr. Carine Feyten
College of Education
University of South Florida
Tampa, Florida 33620 USA
Tel: 813–974–3533, 813–973–3691
Fax: 813–974–3826

Jeffra Flaitz received her bachelor's in Russian Language and Literature from the University of Minnesota, having studied at the Monterey Institute of International Studies and Leningrad State University. Her Ed.M. and Ph.D. are both in Foreign/Second Language Education from SUNY-Buffalo, where she was Visiting Assistant Professor for three years. She is currently Assistant Professor of Linguistics and Director of the English Language Institute at the University of South Florida in Tampa. She is the author of *The Ideology of English: French Attitudes toward English as a World Language* and articles published in *World Englishes*, *Hispania*, and *Contemporary French Civilization*. She is now competing Volume 2 of an EFL text (*We Speak*) designed for a Chinese audience. She has conducted workshops in Poland, the Czech Republic, Slovakia, Colombia, and China and has received an award for teaching excellence.

Dr. Jeffra Flaitz
English Language Institute
University of South Florida
Tampa, FL 33620 USA
Tel: 813–973–1646
Fax: 813–974–2769

Maaike Hajer studied Dutch Language and Applied Linguistics in Nijmegen, with bilingualism and Dutch as a second language as her specialization. She served as a curriculum developer for the National Institute for Curriculum Development (SLO) from 1982 to 1993 on the teaching of Dutch as a second language and migrant language teaching (especially Moluccan-Malay). Since then she has been training teachers in Dutch as a second language and is now preparing a dissertation on learning in a second language. She is affiliated with the Utrecht Institute for Higher Professional Education.

Dr. Maaike Hajer
Utrecht Institute for Higher Professional Education (HvU)
PO Box 14007
3508 SB Utrecht
The Netherlands
Tel: 31–30–254–7314
Fax: 31–30–254–3272
E-mail: Maaike.Hajer@FEO.HVU.NL

Mary Evelyn Hollaway holds a Ph.D. in English Education and ESL from the University of Alabama. Coming from a career in theological studies and administration, she altered her course and is now Chair, Department of English, Mountain Brook High School (one of the top secondary schools in Alabama). Her passions are poetry and other forms of literature. She has conducted workshops on language learning styles and strategies and has published poetry, as well as articles on cross-cultural perspectives on learning styles.

Dr. Mary Evelyn Hollaway
English Department
Mountain Brook High School
Mountain Brook, Alabama USA
Tel: 205–592–2434

Cora Kaylani received her doctorate in Foreign Language Education from the University of Pittsburgh in 1995. She has taught for over 15 years in ESL/EFL programs in the US and Saudi Arabia. She has coordinated several English for Specific Purposes projects in business and teacher training and has presented at local, national, and international conferences. She is currently a Visiting Assistant Professor in the Department of Foreign & Second Language Education at The Ohio State University.

Dr. Cora Kaylani
Department of Foreign & Second Language Education
249 Arps Hall
The Ohio State University
1945 North High Street
Columbus, OH 43210 USA
Tel: 614–292–8046
Tel/Fax: 614–459–7389
E-mail: ckaylani@magnus.acs.ohio-state.edu

Richard Kidd is Associate Professor in the Faculty of Education, University of Manitoba, Winnipeg, Manitoba, Canada, where he teaches graduate and undergraduate courses in TESL education. His research and scholarly interests include the teaching of ESL grammar and integrating language and content in ESL instruction. Since 1992 he has collaborated with Brenda Marquardson in developing the Foresee Approach and introducing it to teachers in Manitoba through university courses, publications, conference presentations, and local workshops.

Dr. Richard Kidd
Faculty of Education
University of Manitoba
Winnipeg, Manitoba R3T 2N2 Canada
Tel: 204–474–9092
Fax: 204–269–4261, 275–5962
E-mail: kidd@bldgeduc.lan1.umanitoba.ca

Roberta Z. Lavine is Associate Professor and Associate Chair of the Department of Spanish and Portuguese at the University of Maryland, College Park. She specializes in Spanish language pedagogy and second language acquisition and has worked in many areas of the field, including teaching and learning methodologies, language learning styles and strategies, curriculum design, instructional technology, and teacher training. Current research interests include learning disabilities, cross-cultural communication, and Spanish for business.

Dr. Roberta Z. Lavine
Department of Spanish and Portuguese
University of Maryland — College Park
College Park, MD 20742 USA
Fax: 301–314–9752
E-mail: rl10@umailsrv.umd.edu

Betty Lou Leaver is President, American Global Studies Institute. She served as Dean, School of Slavic Languages and School of Central European Languages, Defense Language Institute, and headed the Russian and Ukrainian programs at the Foreign Service Institute. She has instructed six languages in a variety of settings from preschool through university level, taught foreign language education methodology to hundreds of teachers in a number of countries, and published extensively on learning issues.

Ms. Betty Lou Leaver
American Global Studies Institute
747 St. Regis Way
Salinas, CA 93905 USA
Tel: 408–455–0403
Tel/Fax: 408–422–7445
E-mail: leaver@aol.com

Adina Levine holds a Ph.D. in linguistics from the Hebrew University, Jerusalem. She is Director of the EFL Program at Bar-Ilan University and author and co-author of a number of articles on various aspects of English reading comprehension. She is co-author of two books on reading comprehension for university students published by Collier-Macmillan.

Dr. Adina Levine
Department of English
English as a Foreign Language Division
Bar-Ilan University
Ramat-Gan 52900 Israel
Fax: 972–3–5347601
E-mail: F24047@VM.BIU.AC.IL

Brenda Marquardson is an ESL support teacher at Tyndall Park Community School in Winnipeg, Manitoba, Canada. From 1990 to 1992 she devised and experimented with a variety of original CALLA-based instructional procedures in her elementary classroom, and since then has collaborated with Richard Kidd in developing and revising the Foresee Approach. Since 1993 she has been actively involved in popularizing the approach through publications, conference presentations, school and division-wide in-services, and local teacher development projects.

Ms. Brenda Marquardson
Tyndall Park Community School
2221 King Edward Street
Winnipeg, Manitoba
Canada R2R 1M5

Theun Meestringa studied educational psychology in Groningen and has been working for the National Institute for Curriculum Development (SLO) in Enschede, the Netherlands, since 1979 as a curriculum developer. After working on syllabi and teaching materials for Frisian and migrant language teaching for elementary schools, he specialized in the field of Dutch as a second language in secondary education. Development of cognitive-academic language proficiency and the adjustment of the "language arts" curriculum to second language learners are now his main objectives.

Dr. Theun Meestringa
National Institute for Curriculum Development
Boulevard 1945 3
7511 AA Enschede
Postbus 2041
7500 CA Enschede
The Netherlands
Tel: 31–53–4840–646 or 4840–840
Fax: 31–53–4307–692

Martha Nyikos is Associate Professor and Director of Foreign Language Education at Indiana University, Bloomington. She teaches graduate and undergraduate teacher education courses for foreign languages and ESL. She serves on the editorial board of the *Modern Language Journal* and has lectured and taught in the People's Republic of China, Malaysia, Hungary, Australia, and Hong Kong. At

Purdue University, she led one of the largest learning strategy studies ever completed (with 1,200 students).

Dr. Martha Nyikos
Foreign Language Education
Wright Education Building
Indiana University
Bloomington, IN 47405–1006 USA
Tel: 812–856–8272
Fax: 812–856–8440

J. Michael O'Malley is Supervisor of Assessment and Evaluation in Prince William County Public Schools in Virginia. He was previously Director of the Evaluation Assistance Center (EAC) at Georgetown University. Dr. O'Malley has directed a number of studies of second language acquisition, including studies of learning strategies in English as a second language and foreign language instruction. Dr. O'Malley is co-developer of the Cognitive Academic Language Learning Approach (CALLA) and is also noted for his work on authentic assessment.

Dr. J. Michael O'Malley
Assessment and Evaluation
Prince William County Public Schools
Manassas, VA USA
Tel: 703–791–7277
Fax: 703–791–7412

Young Ye Park is Assistant Professor of English at Korea Advanced Institute of Science and Technology, where she teaches courses in English and coordinates intensive EFL programs for undergraduates and graduate students. Her research interests include the effects of strategy training, development of curriculum and teaching materials, and teacher training. She won the 1994 College of Education Dissertation of the Year Award at the University of Alabama for her study of reading strategies, attitudes, and performance.

Dr. Young Ye Park
School of Humanities
Division of English
Language Center
Korea Advanced Institute of Science and Technology
373–1 Kusung-dong, Yusung-gu
Taejon 305–701 Korea
Tel: 82–42–869–2114, 869–8731–3
Fax: 82–42–869–2110, 869–8730
E-mail: yypark@sorak.kaist.ac.kr

Thea Reves holds a Ph.D. from the Hebrew University, Jerusalem. She is Senior Teacher of EFL at Bar-Ilan University and Supervisor Emeritus of TEFL, Ministry of Education, Israel. Dr. Reves is the co-author of an oral proficiency test battery introduced as the national school-leaving exam. She is author and co-author of numerous articles on various aspects of language education.

Dr. Thea Reves
Department of English
English as a Foreign Language Division
Bar-Ilan University
Ramat-Gan 52900 Israel
Fax: 972–3–5347601
E-mail: F24047@VM.BIU.AC.IL

Jill Robbins has taught English as a second language in the US and Japan. She directed a research project at Georgetown University on language learning strategies instruction for US learners of Japanese. In Japan, she has conducted doctoral research on the strategies used by Japanese learners as they develop the pragmatic ability to make friends in English. She is also teaching future language teachers in Japan how to conduct learning strategies instruction.

Dr. Jill Robbins
Kyoto, Japan
Tel/Fax: 81–74–545–1732
E-mail: 74274.1755@compuserve.com

Joan Rubin (Ph.D., Yale) is a specialist in second language learning, listening comprehension, and language and technology. Renowned for her ground-breaking work on "Good Language Learners," Dr. Rubin has conducted research and given numerous workshops and seminars on facilitating learner autonomy. She is author/co-author of 13 books, including *How to Be a More Successful Language Learner* and *English Works!*, a video and workbook package with provides strategy instruction for listening.

Dr. Joan Rubin
Joan Rubin Associates
2011 Hermitage Ave.
Wheaton, MD 20902 USA
Tel: 301–933–6931
Fax: 301–949–0651

Amany Saleh, a Ph.D. candidate in Teacher Education at the University of Alabama, received a bachelor's degree in geology from Cairo University in Egypt and an MA-TESOL degree from the University of Alabama. She has taught EFL/ESL classes at the elementary, secondary, and college levels. She currently works as a supervisor of student interns in foreign languages at the secondary level. Her dissertation is on the nexus of learning styles, learning strategies, gender, aptitude, and other individual difference factors in language learning.

Ms. Amany Saleh
204 Graves Hall
College of Education
University of Alabama
Tuscaloosa, AL 35487 USA
Tel: 205–348–6070
Fax: 205–348–9863
E-mail: AMANYSALEH@aol.com

Kimberly Scott teaches Japanese in the Minneapolis Public School District. She recently received her Master's of Education in Second Languages and Cultures from the University of Minnesota. She has worked as a research assistant for Andrew Cohen on the Language Learning Strategies Project of the Center for Advanced Research on Language Acquisition (CARLA), and she is currently participating in the joint CARLA-Minneapolis Public Schools Critical Languages Project.

Ms. Kimberly Scott
Folwell Middle School
3611 20th Ave. South
Minneapolis, MN 55407 USA
Tel: 612–627–2604
Fax: 612–627–2612

Laurens (Larry) Vandergrift (Ph.D., University of Alberta) is Assistant Professor in the Faculty of Education of the University of Ottawa, Ontario, Canada. He works in French as a Second Language Teacher Education in the B.Ed., B.A., and M.Ed. programs in Second Language Teaching. He is currently the coordinator of the interdisciplinary B.A. in Second Language Teaching. His research interests include listening comprehension, learning strategies, and effective delivery of Core French programs.

Dr. Laurens Vandergrift
Faculty of Education
University of Ottawa
145, rue Jean-Jacques-Lussier C.P. 450, Succ. A
Ottawa, Ontario K1N 6N5 Canada
Tel: 613–562–5800, x 4331
Fax: 613–562–5146

Nae-Dong Yang (Ph.D., University of Texas at Austin), is Associate Professor in the Department of Foreign Languages and Literatures at National Taiwan University, Taipei, Taiwan, Republic of China. Her major interests include second language acquisition, psycholinguistics, ESL reading and composition, and teacher education. Her current research centers on second language learners' beliefs about language learning, language learning strategies, and learner strategy training.

Dr. Nae-Dong Yang
Department of Foreign Languages & Literatures
National Taiwan University
Taipei 10764 Taiwan, Republic of China
Fax: 886–2–927–5772
E-mail: naedong@cc.ntu.edu.tw

SLTCC

TECHNICAL REPORTS

*The Technical Reports of the Second Language Teaching and Curriculum Center
at the University of Hawai'i (SLTCC) report on ongoing curriculum projects,
provide the results of research related to second language learning and teaching,
and also include extensive related bibliographies. SLTCC Technical Reports are available
through University of Hawai'i Press.*

**RESEARCH
METHODS
IN
INTERLANGUAGE
PRAGMATICS**

GABRIELE KASPER
MERETE DAHL

This technical report reviews the methods of data collection employed in 39 studies of interlanguage pragmatics, defined narrowly as the investigation of nonnative speakers' comprehension and production of speech acts, and the acquisition of L2-related speech act knowledge. Data collection instruments are distinguished according to the degree to which they constrain informants' responses, and whether they tap speech act perception/comprehension or production. A main focus of discussion is the validity of different types of data, in particular their adequacy to approximate authentic performance of linguistic action. 51 pp.

(SLTCC Technical Report #1)   ISBN 0–8248–1419–3 $10.

**A FRAMEWORK
FOR
TESTING
CROSS-
CULTURAL
PRAGMATICS**

THOM HUDSON
EMILY DETMER
J. D. BROWN

This technical report presents a framework for developing methods that assess cross-cultural pragmatic ability. Although the framework has been designed for Japanese and American cross-cultural contrasts, it can serve as a generic approach that can be applied to other language contrasts. The focus is on the variables of social distance, relative power, and the degree of imposition within the speech acts of requests, refusals, and apologies. Evaluation of performance is based on recognition of the speech act, amount of speech, forms or formulæ used, directness, formality, and politeness. 51 pp.

(SLTCC Technical Report #2)   ISBN 0–8248–1463–0 $10.

PRAGMATICS OF JAPANESE AS NATIVE AND TARGET LANGUAGE

GABRIELE KASPER
(Editor)

This technical report includes three contributions to the study of the pragmatics of Japanese:

- A bibliography on speech act performance, discourse management, and other pragmatic and sociolinguistic features of Japanese;
- A study on introspective methods in examining Japanese learners' performance of refusals;
- A longitudinal investigation of the acquisition of the particle *ne* by nonnative speakers of Japanese.

125 pp.

(SLTCC Technical Report #3) ISBN 0–8248–1462–2 $10.

A BIBLIOGRAPHY OF PEDAGOGY & RESEARCH IN INTERPRETATION & TRANSLATION

ETILVIA ARJONA

This technical report includes four types of bibliographic information on translation and interpretation studies:

- Research efforts across disciplinary boundaries: cognitive psychology, neurolinguistics, psycholinguistics, sociolinguistics, computational linguistics, measurement, aptitude testing, language policy, decision-making, theses, dissertations;
- Training information covering: program design, curriculum studies, instruction, school administration;
- Instruction information detailing: course syllabi, methodology, models, available textbooks;
- Testing information about aptitude, selection, diagnostic tests.

115 pp.

(SLTCC Technical Report #4) ISBN 0–8248–1572–6 $10.

PRAGMATICS OF CHINESE AS NATIVE AND TARGET LANGUAGE

GABRIELE KASPER
(Editor)

This technical report includes six contributions to the study of the pragmatics of Mandarin Chinese:

- A report of an interview study conducted with nonnative speakers of Chinese;
- Five data-based studies on the performance of different speech acts by native speakers of Mandarin: requesting, refusing, complaining, giving bad news, disagreeing, and complimenting.

312 pp.

(SLTCC Technical Report #5) ISBN 0–8248–1733–8 $15.

THE ROLE OF PHONOLOGICAL CODING IN READING *KANJI*

SACHIKO MATSUNAGA

In this technical report the author reports the results of a study that she conducted on phonological coding in reading *kanji* using an eye-movement monitor and draws some pedagogical implications. In addition, she reviews current literature on the different schools of thought regarding instruction in reading *kanji* and its role in the teaching of non-alphabetic written languages like Japanese. 64 pp.

(SLTCC Technical Report #6) ISBN 0–8248–1734–6 $10.

DEVELOPING PROTOTYPIC MEASURES OF CROSS-CULTURAL PRAGMATICS

THOM HUDSON
EMILY DETMER
J. D. BROWN

Although the study of cross-cultural pragmatics has gained importance in applied linguistics, there are no standard forms of assessment that might make research comparable across studies and languages. The present volume describes the process through which six forms of cross-cultural assessment were developed for second language learners of English. The models may be used for second language learners of other languages. The six forms of assessment involve two forms each of indirect discourse completion tests, oral language production, and self assessment. The procedures involve the assessment of requests, apologies, and refusals.

(SLTCC Technical Report #7) ISBN 0–8248–1763–X $15.

VIRTUAL CONNECTIONS: ONLINE ACTIVITIES & PROJECTS FOR NETWORKING LANGUAGE LEARNERS

MARK WARSCHAUER
(*Editor*)

Computer networking has created dramatic new possibilities for connecting language learners in a single classroom or across the globe. This collection of activities and projects makes use of e-mail, the World Wide Web, computer conferencing, and other forms of computer-mediated communication for the foreign and second language classroom at any level of instruction. Teachers from around the world submitted the activities compiled in this volume — activities that they have used successfully in their own classrooms.

(SLTCC Technical Report #8) ISBN 0–8248–1793–1 $30.

ATTENTION & AWARENESS IN FOREIGN LANGUAGE LEARNING

RICHARD SCHMIDT
(*Editor*)

Issues related to the role of attention and awareness in learning lie at the heart of many theoretical and practical controversies in the foreign language field. This collection of papers presents research into the learning of Spanish, Japanese, Finnish, Hawaiian, and English as a second language (with additional comments and examples from French, German, and miniature artificial languages) that bear on these crucial questions for foreign language pedagogy.

(SLTCC Technical Report #9) ISBN 0–8248–1794–X $20.

LINGUISTICS AND LANGUAGE TEACHING: PROCEEDINGS OF THE SIXTH JOINT LSH-HATESL CONFERENCE

C. REVES,
C. STEELE,
C. S. P. WONG
(*Editors*)

Technical Report #10 contains 18 articles revolving around the following three topics:

- Linguistic issues: These six papers discuss various linguistics issues: ideophones, syllabic nasals, linguistic areas, computation, tonal melody classification, and *wh*-words.
- Sociolinguistics: Sociolinguistic phenomena in Swahili, signing, Hawaiian, and Japanese are discussed in four of the papers.
- Language teaching and learning: These eight papers cover prosodic modification, note taking, planning in oral production, oral testing, language policy, L2 essay organization, access to dative alternation rules, and child noun phrase structure development.

(SLTCC Technical Report #10) ISBN 0–8248–1851–2 $20.

LANGUAGE LEARNING MOTIVATION: PATHWAYS TO THE NEW CENTURY

REBECCA L. OXFORD
(*Editor*)

This volume chronicles a revolution in our thinking about what makes students want to learn languages and what causes them to persist in that difficult and rewarding adventure. Topics in this book include the internal structures of and external connections with foreign language motivation; exploring adult language learning motivation, self-efficacy, and anxiety; comparing the motivations and learning strategies of students of Japanese and Spanish; and enhancing the theory of language learning motivation from many psychological and social perspectives.

(SLTCC Technical Report #11) ISBN 0–8248–1849–0 $20.

TELECOLLABORATION IN FOREIGN LANGUAGE LEARNING: PROCEEDINGS OF THE HAWAI'I SYMPOSIUM

MARK WARSCHAUER
(*Editor*)

The Symposium on Local & Global Electronic Networking in Foreign Language Learning & Research, part of the National Foreign Language Resource Center's *1995 Summer Institute on Technology & the Human Factor in Foreign Language Education* included presentations of papers and hands-on workshops conducted by Symposium participants to facilitate the sharing of resources, ideas, and information about all aspects of electronic networking for foreign language teaching and research, including electronic discussion and conferencing, international cultural exchanges, real-time communication and simulations, research and resource retrieval via the Internet, and research using networks. This collection presents a sampling of those presentations.

(SLTCC Technical Report #12) ISBN 0–8248–1867–9 $20.

**LANGUAGE
LEARNING
STRATEGIES
AROUND
THE WORLD:
CROSS-
CULTURAL
PERSPECTIVES**

Language learning strategies are the specific steps students take to improve their progress in learning a second or foreign language. Optimizing learning strategies improves language performance. This ground-breaking book presents new information about cultural influences on the use of language learning strategies. It also shows innovative ways to assess students' strategy use and remarkable techniques for helping students improve their choice of strategies, with the goal of peak language learning.

REBECCA L. OXFORD
(*Editor*)

(SLTCC Technical Report #13) ISBN 0–8248–1910–1 $20.